WAR CRIMES IN

BOSNIA-HERCEGOVINA

VOLUME II

Helsinki Watch

A Division of Human Rights Watch

New York • Washington • Los Angeles • London

Copyright © April 1993 by Human Rights Watch.
All rights reserved.
Printed in the United States of America.

Library of Congress Catalogue Card Number: 92-73777.
ISBN: 1-56432-097-9.

Cover design by Robert Kimzey.

Helsinki Watch was formed in 1978 to monitor and promote observance of domestic and international compliance with the human rights provisions of the 1975 Helsinki Accords. The Chair is Jonathan Fanton; Vice Chair, Alice H. Henkin; Executive Director, Jeri Laber; Deputy Director, Lois Whitman; Staff Counsel, Holly Cartner; Research Associates, Erika Dailey, Rachel Denber and Ivana Nizich; Associates, Pamela Cox, Christina Derry and Alexander Petrov.

Helsinki Watch is affiliated with the International Helsinki Federation for Human Rights, which is based in Vienna.

TABLE OF CONTENTS

Acknowledgments ix

Frequently Used Abbreviations x

Introduction 1
    Methodology 4

Patterns of Abuse 7
    Introduction 7
    Abuses by Croatian and Muslim Forces 7
    Abuses by Serbian Forces 8
    Forced Displacement 10
    Attacks Against Civilian Targets, the Use of
        Siege Warfare and the Indiscriminate and
        Disproportionate Use of Force 13
    Pillage and Destruction of Villages and
        Cultural Objects 14
    Summary Executions 15
    Abuse in Detention 17
    Rape 20
    Mutilation 23
    Hostage-Holding 24
    Obstruction of Humanitarian Aid and
        Attacks on Relief Personnel 25

Abuses in Northwestern Bosnia 30
    Abuses by Serbian Forces 34
        Summary Executions 34
            Vlašić 34
        Forced Displacement 42
            Prijedor 42
            Banja Luka 49
            Blagaj 49
            Hambarine 53
            Trnopolje 56
            Kevljani 59
            Kozarac 61
            Prnovo 74
            Brdjani 75

    Gornja Sanica 77
    Rizvanovići 80
    Čarakovo 81
    Bišćani 82
    Ključ 83
  Abuses in Detention 84
    Omarska Detention Camp 87
    Keraterm Detention Camp 121
    Manjača Detention Camp 133
    Trnopolje Detention Camp 139
    Bosanski Novi 155
    Ključ 159
    Kotor Varoš 160
    Banja Luka Hospital 161
  Rape 163
    Omarska 163
    Keraterm 165
    Čarakovo 168
    Rakovčani 171
    Municipality of Ključ 172
    Vojići 178
    Trnopolje 181
  Reported Castration 186
  Obstruction of Humanitarian Relief 187
    Bosanska Krupa 187
  Indiscriminate Use of Force 188
    Jajce 188

Abuses in Northeastern Bosnia 189
  Abuses by Serbian Forces 191
    Abuses in Detention 191
      Brčko 191
      Luka 197
      Batković 211
    Rape 214
      Obudovac 214
      Doboj 215
    Forced Displacement 220
      Brezovo Polje 220
      Zvornik, Cerska and
        Konjević Polje 222
    Other Abuses 223

Incident at Bridge in Doboj Involving Forced Displacement, Killings, Use of Human Shields and Other Abuses 223
Abuses by Croatian Forces 228
   Abuses in Detention 228
      Orašje 228
   Rape 228
      Posavska Mahala 229
      Bosanski Brod 233
Abuses by Unknown Forces 235
   Attacks on Aid Convoys 235
      Tuzla 235

Abuses in Southeastern Bosnia 236
   Abuses by Serbian Forces 237
      Abuses in Detention 237
         Foča 237
      Rape 242
      Mutilation 253
      Summary Executions 256
         Skelani 256
         Rudo 257
      Forced Displacement 258
         Foča 258
         Šukovac 260
         Godijevno 261
         Jelec 263
         Zagradje 265
         Velika Daljegošta 266
         Skelani 267
         Mioća 268
   The Use of Siege Warfare in Sarajevo 268
   Abuses by Muslim Forces 271
      Summary Executions of Disarmed Combatants and Civilians 272
         Near Bratunac 272
         Kamenica 272
      Attacks on Civilian Targets 273
         Goražde 273
   Abuses by All Parties 275

Obstruction of Humanitarian Aid and
Attacks on Relief Personnel 275
 Attacks on Sarajevo Airport and
 Relief Flights 277
 Attacks on, and Obstruction of,
 Aid Convoys 282
  Goražde 282
  Sarajevo 284
  Srebrenica 286
  Žepa 288
  Cerska 290
 Attacks on Medical Personnel
 and Hospitals 291
  Sarajevo 291

Abuses in Southwestern and Central Bosnia 293
 Abuses by Croatian Forces 197
  Abuses in Detention 303
   Abuses by HVO Forces 304
    Mostar 304
    Livno Police Station 315
    Livno School 320
    Livno HVO Headquarters 327
    Tomislavgrad School 328
   Abuses by HOS Forces 331
    Mostar 331
    Dretelj 335
  Rape 344
   Mostar 344
  Hostage-Holding 346
   Raščani 346
   Donje Selo 349
  Assassination 352
  Unlawful Searches and Seizures and
  Arbitrary Dismissal from Employment 353
 Abuses by Muslim Forces 354
  Abuses in Detention 354
   Čelebići 355
   Konjic Sports Hall 366
   Bradina School 368
   Zenica 371

  Abuses by Croatian and Muslim Forces 372
    Forced Displacement 372
      Bradina 372
    Pillaging and Destruction of Villages and
      Cultural Objects 374
      Čapljina 374
      Livno and Tomislavgrad 375
      Bradina 376
      Mostar 377
      Livno 378
    Fighting Between Croatian and Muslim
      Forces in Central Bosnia 379
    Attacks on Aid Convoys 381
      Vitez 381
  Abuses by Serbian Forces 382
    Forced Displacement 382
      Trebinje 382
    Summary Executions 390
      Trebinje 390
    Indiscriminate and Disproportionate
      Use of Force 391
      Mostar 391

Appendix A: Memorandum of Law: Elements of the
  International Crime of "Crimes Against Humanity"
  Applied in the Former Yugoslavia 394
Appendix B: Human Rights Watch/Helsinki Watch Letter to
  President George Bush, August 7, 1992 398
Appendix C: Human Rights Watch/Helsinki Watch Letter to
  Honorable Boutros-Ghali, August 11, 1993 401
Appendix D: Human Rights Watch/Helsinki Watch Letter to
  Honorable Boutros-Ghali, January 14, 1993 403
Appendix E: Human Rights Watch/Helsinki Watch Letter to
  Cyrus Vance, February 2, 1992 406
Appendix F: A Chronology of the Siege of Sarajevo 410
Appendix G: Relevant International Law as it Applies
  to Siege Warfare and Its Aim in the
  Current Conflict 420

ACKNOWLEDGMENTS

This report is based on missions conducted by Dinah PoKempner, Counsel to Human Rights Watch, and Ivana Nizich, Research Associate of Helsinki Watch, between September 26 and November 2, 1992; by Jeri Laber, Executive Director of Helsinki Watch, and Regan Ralph, Counsel to the Women's Rights Project of Human Rights Watch, between January 11-22, 1993; and by Aryeh Neier, Executive Director of Human Rights Watch, between January 2-6, 1993, and February 9-11, 1993. Interviews also were conducted by local Helsinki Watch representatives in the former Yugoslavia between August 1992 and March 1993. Displaced persons, refugees, medical and relief personnel were interviewed during each of the missions. Journalists, lawyers, combatants and civilian representatives of the parties to the conflict also were interviewed.

This report was written by Ivana Nizich, Research Associate of Helsinki Watch. Aryeh Neier, Executive Director of Human Rights Watch; Ken Anderson, Director of the Arms Project of Human Rights Watch; Regan Ralph, Counsel to the Women's Rights Project of Human Rights Watch; and Pamela Cox, Associate of Helsinki Watch, contributed to sections of this report. Jeri Laber, Executive Director of Helsinki Watch, edited the report.

Helsinki Watch thanks Christina Derry, Associate of Helsinki Watch, and Suzanne Guthrie, Publications Manager of Human Rights Watch, for preparing the maps contained in this report, Pamela Cox, Associate of Helsinki Watch, for her invaluable administrative and production assistance, and Barbara Grenquist for her assistance with copyediting.

Helsinki Watch expresses its appreciation to the Open Society Fund for its support of our work in the former Yugoslav republics. Helsinki Watch also expresses its gratitude to human rights activists in Bosnia-Hercegovina, Croatia and Yugoslavia for their assistance. Above all, Helsinki Watch thanks the many Muslims, Croats, Serbs and others who provided testimony to representatives of Helsinki Watch and Human Rights Watch and its Women's Rights Project. Helsinki Watch regrets that, for their protection, the human rights activists and the witnesses cannot be identified.

FREQUENTLY USED ABBREVIATIONS

EC	European Community
HDZ	Croatian Democratic Union (Hrvatska Demokratska Zajednica)
HOS	Croatian Defense Forces (Hrvatske Obrambene Snage)
HV	Croatian Army (Hrvatska Vojska)
HVO	Croatian Defense Council (Hrvatsko Vijeće Obrane)
ICRC	International Committee of the Red Cross
JNA	Yugoslav People's Army (Jugoslavenska Narodna Armija)
NATO	North Atlantic Treaty Organization
SDA	Party of Democratic Action (Stranka Demokratske Akcije)
SDS	Serbian Democratic Party (Srpska Demokratska Stranka)
TO	Territorial Defense (Teritorijalna Odbrana)
UN	United Nations
UNHCR	United Nations High Commissioner for Refugees
UNPROFOR	United Nations Protection Force

INTRODUCTION

The enormity of the war crimes in Bosnia-Hercegovina is matched only by the international community's lack of political will to intercede effectively to stop these crimes against humanity. Some of the atrocities are being carried out in full view of the world as they are taking place; details of the siege of Sarajevo, for example, including the privations suffered by its residents, and the relentless shelling and sniping that are gunning them down, have been reported and broadcast more promptly and more fully than in any other place or at any other time in history. Although this is going on in the center of Europe, the governments of powerful European countries and of the United States, and such intergovernmental bodies as the European Community (E.C.), North Atlantic Treaty Organization (NATO) and the United Nations (U.N.) have been unable or unwilling to do no more than intermittently and, in many cases, inadequately deliver humanitarian assistance; adopt resolutions; and conduct seemingly endless and fruitless negotiations. Meanwhile, "ethnic cleansing" — which includes abuses such as deportations, confinement of civilians in detention camps, torture, rape, murder and indiscriminate bombardment of civilian communities — is apparently being completed.

Helsinki Watch has been monitoring abuses in the wars in the former Yugoslavia since they began, in Slovenia and Croatia, in the summer of 1991. We have monitored abuses connected with the war in Bosnia-Hercegovina since its start, in April 1992. In August 1992 we published Volume One of *War Crimes in Bosnia-Hercegovina*. In issuing that report, we called on the United Nations to take appropriate steps to prevent and suppress genocide and to establish an international war crimes tribunal to try and punish those responsible for crimes against humanity in the former Yugoslavia. Although all sides have committed serious abuses, Helsinki Watch's findings indicate that the most severe and overwhelming number of crimes have been committed by Serbian forces.

Now, eight months after our previous report, we are issuing Volume Two of *War Crimes in Bosnia-Hercegovina*. The proposal for a war crimes tribunal has gained some momentum, most notably in the United Nations Security Council's Resolution No. 808 of February 22, 1993, deciding that an international tribunal should be established and calling for a report by the Secretary General within sixty days on all aspects of this matter. International efforts have focused mainly on the need to deliver humanitarian aid to besieged villages, towns and cities. Little or nothing has been done to end the intense bombardment of the areas under siege or to stop the systematic process of "ethnic cleansing." No effective measures have been taken to date to prevent or suppress genocide. Despite the weighty evidence contained in this report and other evidence that has been presented to the United Nations, extreme abuses continue in Bosnia-Hercegovina without respite. A year has passed since the conflict in Bosnia-Hercegovian began, with no effective actions by the international community to end the suffering.

What is taking place in Bosnia-Hercegovina is attempted genocide — the extermination of a people in whole or in part because of their race, religion or ethnicity.[1] This is the gravest crime known to humankind. The nations of the world have entered into a treaty that pledges them to "prevent and suppress" genocide. The parties to the Genocide Convention and the United Nations as its sponsor have failed in meeting their treaty obligation to take appropriate measures to stop genocide. The abuses occurring in Bosnia-Hercegovina also constitute crimes against humanity as that term was defined at the Nuremberg trial and within the meaning of customary international law.[2]

In the eight months that have passed since the publication of Volume One of *War Crimes in Bosnia-Hercegovina*, Human Rights Watch and its Helsinki Watch division have, among other things, called upon the President of the United States and the Secretary General of the United Nations to seek and take "action that is appropriate for the prevention and suppression of acts of genocide as provided in Article VIII of the 1951 Convention on the Prevention and Punishment of the Crime of Genocide." We called upon the President of the United States to urge the Security Council of the United Nations to establish an international tribunal to investigate, prosecute and punish war crimes, or "grave

---

[1] For a discussion of the 1951 Genocide Convention on the Prevention and Punishment of the Crime of Genocide and its relation to the abuses taking place in the former Yugoslavia, see Helsinki Watch, *War Crimes in Bosnia-Hercegovina*, August 1992, pp. 1-2.

[2] See Appendix A for a discussion of the law governing crimes against humanity.

breaches" of the 1949 Geneva Conventions and the 1977 Protocol.[3] We have called upon the Secretary General of the United Nations to expand the mandate of the United Nations Protection Forces (UNPROFOR) in Bosnia-Hercegovina to include military protection of the delivery of humanitarian assistance to noncombatants of all ethnic and religious groups whose lives are at risk due to sieges and other practices associated with "ethnic cleansing."[4] We have called upon the U.N. peace negotiators to call a halt to the peace negotiations until a neutral body certifies that the abuses associated with "ethnic cleansing" have ceased and the delivery of humanitarian aid to civilians in besieged communities has been facilitated.[5] We also expressed our concern that individuals who may ultimately stand trial for war crimes "do not appear to derive undeserved legitimacy" from their appearance at the negotiating table.[6]

Helsinki Watch has made and will continue to make available information on which our reports are based to the Commission of Experts established by the United Nations Security Council and to the office of prosecutor for a U.N. war crimes tribunal, as soon as one is established.

In presenting our latest report, Human Rights Watch and its Helsinki Watch division call on the United Nations Security Council, the United States, and other governments and intergovernmental bodies to take the following steps:

---

[3] See, in Appendix B, Human Rights Watch/Helsinki Watch letter to President George Bush, August 7, 1992 and Appendix C, Human Rights Watch/Helsinki Watch letter to Honorable Boutros-Ghali, August 11, 1993.

[4] See, in Appendix D, Human Rights Watch/Helsinki Watch letter to Honorable Boutros Boutros-Ghali, January 14, 1993.

[5] See, in Appendix E, Human Rights Watch/Helsinki Watch letter to Cyrus Vance, February 2, 1993.

[6] In a meeting with Cyrus Vance, the then U.N. mediator assured Helsinki Watch that he would oppose any effort, as part of the peace settlement, to provide for an amnesty for individuals responsible for international war crimes.

1. Commit themselves to take measures immediately to prevent and suppress genocide in Bosnia-Hercegovina, and implement those measures;
2. Proceed as quickly as possible with the actual establishment of a war crimes tribunal and the office of a prosecutor for the tribunal.
3. Use such military force as is required to protect the delivery of humanitarian assistance to those civilians who are now threatened with starvation utilized as a weapon and directed against them in violation of the laws of war; and
4. Deploy United Nations human rights monitors right away, without waiting for a cease-fire or peace agreement — as was done in El Salvador six months before a cease-fire — in all parts of Bosnia-Hercegovina to report publicly on "ethnic cleansing" and other human rights abuses.

Helsinki Watch understands and sympathizes with the difficult task faced by diplomats and negotiators who are striving to bring an end to the misery that has befallen the peoples of the former Yugoslavia. However, the U.N. Secretary General, members of the U.N. Security Council and U.N. and E.C. negotiators often appear to be neglecting the human rights of the people of Bosnia-Hercegovina in the interest of signing a peace accord. Serbian forces have delayed the process of negotiating that accord as they attempt to complete the "ethnic cleansing" of non-Serbs in territory they control or continue to besiege. Helsinki Watch fears that peace in Bosnia-Hercegovina — and, indeed, throughout the former Yugoslavia — will warrant the description by Tacitus in *The Agricola* of how the ancient Romans in Britain "created a desolation and called it peace."

METHODOLOGY

This report focuses on violations of the rules of war by all parties to the conflict in Bosnia-Hercegovina. The information in this report supplements the Helsinki Watch report of August 1992 and is based on numerous missions to and investigations conducted by Helsinki Watch and Human Rights Watch representatives between September 1992 and March 1993.

The vast majority of those interviewed by Helsinki Watch have asked that their names be kept confidential and, in some cases, that the place of the interview remain secret because it might help identify them. Many people fear for the lives of friends and relatives who remain in the war zone or that their enemies might find them in refugee camps and other placement centers, even when these areas are far removed from the arena of warfare. In deference to their concerns, Helsinki Watch has adopted a policy of using pseudonyms or initials for all witnesses and avoiding specifics as to the places where the witnesses were interviewed. The names, dates, and places of such interviews and other supplemental information are kept in secure files outside the Helsinki Watch office and, under appropriate safeguards, will be made available, in a fashion consistent with our agreements with witnesses, to the prosecution for the U.N. War Crimes Tribunal.

Human Rights Watch and its Helsinki Watch division base their reports on direct testimony from victims or witnesses to abuses taken at sites where those abuses have taken place or at sites to which the victims have been displaced. It is not our practice to deal with the parties to a conflict, or groups allied with them, in locating those from whom we wish to take statements. Our general practice is to seek out witnesses ourselves, preferably those who have not had advance warning that we will talk to them. We prefer to take testimony when it is fresh and from witnesses who have not become practiced in giving statements to interviewers. We attempt to interview outside the presence of friends, family or other witnesses; and the interviewers are generally members of our staff or of our committees who speak the language of those from whom we take testimony. When we need to use translators, we make every effort to provide our own. We conduct interviews in depth and seek corroboration through independent testimony and through other evidence.

In a number of cases in this report, circumstances required us to diverge from the policies that we ordinarily follow in collecting information. Some of the information we use about Croatian and Bosnian Muslim abuses against Serbs, for example, was obtained from testimony from witnesses located for us by the Yugoslav State Commission on War Crimes and Genocide in Belgrade. Also, in a few cases, we were not able to interview witnesses confidentially but had to do so in front of groups. We publish such testimony here because we judged it to be credible and it provided information that we were not otherwise able to gather. Because we did not conform to our usual methodology in gathering the information, we have taken care in every case to specify when a party to the conflict or a group allied to a party to the conflict helped us locate witnesses or when we interviewed witnesses in a group setting. If we subsequently obtain information suggesting that such testimony, or any other testimony set forth in this report, is in fact not reliable, we will publish that information at once.

This report also contains sketches of maps of some detention camps in Bosnia. The maps were compiled by Helsinki Watch representatives on the basis of testimony taken from witnesses and their sketches of the detention facilities in which they were held. The maps of the camps do not include every detail of the grounds, but Helsinki Watch includes the rough sketches as a guide to various detention facilities discussed in this report.

PATTERNS OF ABUSE

INTRODUCTION

All parties to the conflict in Bosnia-Hercegovina[1] are guilty of human rights abuses, although to varying degrees. Helsinki Watch adheres strictly to impartial standards in investigating these abuses. Because we discuss abuses in this report on a regional basis, the main perpetrators of the abuses may vary from section to section depending on which forces are in control in the region discussed. On the whole, however, the chief offenders have been the Serbian military and paramilitary forces. As the aggressors, they are in a position to inflict great damage and their policy of "ethnic cleansing" provides the pretext for their actions.

ABUSES BY CROATIAN AND MUSLIM FORCES[2]

Most of the abuses attributable to Bosnian Croatian and Muslim[3] forces are perpetrated by individuals and do not appear to be part of a pre-meditated plan of the Bosnian government or the authorities of the self-proclaimed "Community of Herceg-Bosna." Nevertheless, Bosnian Croatian and Muslim forces are guilty of serious abuses of human rights

---

[1] Hereinafter referred to as Bosnia.

[2] The government of the Republic of Croatia has provided military and other aid to Croatian and, to a lesser extent, Muslim forces in Bosnia. The Yugoslav government, including Montenegro and Serbia, has provided similar assistance to Serbian forces in Bosnia. Given the participation of agents of the Federal Republic of Yugoslavia and the Republic of Croatia in the Bosnian war, both governments are considered parties to the conflict in Bosnia-Hercegovina. (For further descriptions of Yugoslavia's and Croatia's involvement in the Bosnian war and the relevant application of international humanitarian law, see Helsinki Watch, *War Crimes in Bosnia-Hercegovina*, August 1992, pp. 32-49 and 199-202.)

[3] Although Serbs and Croats are members of the armed forces loyal to the Bosnian government, Muslims comprise the majority of those troops. For the purposes of this report, Bosnian government forces will be identified as Muslim forces. If Serbian or Croatian members of the Bosnian armed forces are mentioned, their ethnicity will be noted.

and humanitarian law. Moreover, the destruction of Serbian property and the holding of hostages in many cases appear to be known to local or regional officials who have done little, if anything, to prevent such abuses. Commanders of at least two detention facilities appear to have known of, or participated in, the commission of abuses in the facilities under their control. Croatian officials have taken disciplinary measures against some members of their armed forces or paramilitary groups. Muslim forces have improved treatment in detention centers but it is not known if Muslim soldiers have been held accountable for any abuses they may have perpetrated.

ABUSES BY SERBIAN FORCES[4]

Many of the abuses attributed to Serbian forces have long followed a recognizable pattern that has come to be known as "ethnic cleansing," first used during the war in Croatia and, more recently, in Bosnia-Hercegovina. The primary aim of Serbian forces is to capture or consolidate control over territory by forcibly displacing or killing non-Serbs in the area. In most Serbian-held areas of Bosnia, abuses against non-Serbs are the result of a pre-meditated plan by local and regional civilian, military and/or police authorities. In some instances, such abuses are perpetrated by individual soldiers or single military, paramilitary and police units. The public nature of the abuses, and the frequency with which they take place indicates that individual soldiers and military units do not anticipate disciplinary action by their superiors. The

---

[4] When fighting broke out in early April 1992, the Yugoslav People's Army (Jugoslavenska Narodna Armija – JNA) and paramilitary groups based in Serbia proper fought openly on behalf of indigenous Serbian forces in Bosnia-Hercegovina. On May 19, 1992, the JNA announced its withdrawal, although those Bosnian Serbs who were JNA officers and soldiers were permitted to remain behind and fight on behalf of Serbian forces in Bosnia. The JNA also passed on most of its weaponry to Bosnian Serb forces, which now call themselves the "Army of the Serbian Republic" (Vojska Republike Srpske – VRS) and are commanded by a JNA general, Ratko Mladić. Despite claims by the Yugoslav government that citizens of Serbia and Montenegro do not participate in hostilities in Bosnia, Serbian and Montenegrin members of paramilitary groups and the JNA continue to fight on behalf of, or provide military and other aid to, Serbian forces in Bosnia. (See Helsinki Watch, *War Crimes in Bosnia-Hercegovina*, August 1992, pp. 32-49 and 199-202.)

lack of punishment of Serbian soldiers for their abuses implies complicity on the part of the civilian, military and police authorities of the self-proclaimed "Serbian Republic" (Republika Srpska)[5] in Bosnia-Hercegovina. Helsinki Watch is not aware of any case in which Serbian forces guilty of abuses have been punished by their superiors for their crimes.

The main objective of "ethnic cleansing" is the forced displacement of civilians. Forced displacement is itself a violation of international humanitarian law (the laws of war). Serbian forces, in pursuit of this objective, have been responsible for many other violations of human rights and humanitarian law that have occurred, each of which is described separately in this section, although the abuses often occur together in various combinations: attacks against civilian targets, the use of siege warfare and the indiscriminate and disproportionate use of force; pillage and the destruction of civilian homes and cultural objects; summary executions; abuse in detention; rape; mutilation; hostage-holding; and the obstruction of humanitarian aid and attacks on relief personnel. As mentioned before, Croatian and Bosnian forces are also guilty of many of these abuses, as is indicated in the sections that follow.

---

[5] The self-proclaimed Bosnian Serb state will be referred to as the "Serbian Republic" in this report. References to the Yugoslav republic of Serbia is distinguished from its self-proclaimed Bosnian counterpart where relevant.

Forced Displacement[6]

Throughout Serbian-occupied areas of Bosnia-Hercegovina, the forced displacement, or "ethnic cleansing," pattern is similar, if not identical. In almost all cases, a city, town or village which Serbian forces seek to capture is attacked by heavy and light artillery for several days, weeks or months. Many civilians flee the area during the siege.

Prior to the attack, Serbian civilian, military and/or police officials sometimes call on the population of a given village or city to relinquish their weapons. The call is usually broadcast over the radio. In areas in which Serbian forces already have a strong presence, the local

---

[6] Article 49 of the Geneva Convention Relative to the Protection of Civilian Persons in Time of War of August 12, 1949, [hereinafter Fourth Geneva Convention] states:

> Individual or mass forcible transfers, as well as deportations of protected persons from occupied territory to the territory of the occupying power or to that of any other country, occupied or not, are prohibited, regardless of motive.

There are only two exceptions to the prohibition on displacement, for war-related reasons, of civilians: for their security or for imperative military reasons. "Imperative military reasons" require "the most meticulous assessment of the circumstances" because such reasons are so capable of abuse. One authority has stated:

> Clearly, the imperative military reasons cannot be justified by political motives. For example, it would be prohibited to move a population in order to exercise more effective control over a dissident group.

(See International Committee of the Red Cross, *Commentary on the Additional Protocols of 8 June 1977 to the Geneva Conventions of 12 August 1949*, (Geneva: Martinus Nijhoff Publishers, 1987) at 1472 [hereinafter *1977 ICRC Commentary*].

Mass relocation or capture of civilians for the purpose of changing the ethnic composition of territory, in order to later justify annexation is a political, not a military, move and does not qualify as an "imperative military reason." Destruction of civilian homes as a means to force those civilians to move is as illegal as a direct order to move.

non-Serbian population usually complies with the demand and relinquishes any weapons in their possession. The arms are usually collected at the local town or city council or a similar public building. On some occasions, non-Serbian men are called in for questioning after the weapons are collected.

In other areas, Serbian forces conduct an over-night "coup," during which they assume control of the local government and disarm the non-Serbian members of the local police force. Several days thereafter, mortar attacks begin on a given village, forcing many to flee into the forests or to Muslim- or Croatian-controlled areas.

The attacks initially involve light and heavy artillery, which often is used indiscriminately and disproportionately in order to terrorize the local population and force it to flee from the besieged area. Even in cases where there is no armed resistance to Serbian attacks, the area is besieged solely for the purpose of displacing or terrorizing the population. In cases where armed resistance to Serbian attacks does take place, the disproportionate use of force by Serbian troops is aimed at weakening the area's defenses and forcing the flight of its residents. After several hours, days or weeks of mortar attacks, the defenses of the besieged village, town or city are weakened and Serbian infantry units enter the besieged area. Those who remain in the vicinity either are summarily executed or taken to detention facilities. Some are allowed to flee but often are shot at while retreating.

Serbian forces, particularly in eastern Bosnia, often have shelled various Muslim-held enclaves in order to induce the population to flee to one central enclave, upon which the Serbian forces then concentrate their attack. Muslims who have fled from a recently captured enclave arrive in another Muslim-held area with tales of atrocities, which induce the residents of the second enclave to flee before the fall of their respective town or village. The flight of the residents and the increasing attacks demoralize and militarily weaken those defending the besieged area.

Non-Serbs residing in areas heavily controlled by Serbian authorities and therefore not under siege, often are victimized by arbitrary arrest, interrogation and physical violence which causes them to flee. Non-Serbs have also been confined to their villages or taken to other areas, where they are held hostage until they are exchanged for persons held by Muslim and Croatian forces.

After Serbian troops occupy an area, the residents are taken from their homes, separated by sex and age and taken to places of detention.

In the northwestern and northeastern parts of Bosnia, civilians were frequently interned in camps, where they were registered, interrogated, physically abused and, in some cases, summarily executed. Many of these camps have since been closed. Former detainees, however, frequently allege that prisoners were transferred to camps which remain unknown to the international community and the International Committee of the Red Cross (ICRC). Helsinki Watch has not been able to verify these allegations.

After a period in detention, detainees are commonly placed on buses, trains or cattle cars and are taken to the front lines, where they are exchanged or allowed to cross over to Muslim- or Croatian-controlled territory. Serbian soldiers who escort the convoys of expelled persons frequently demand that the detainees relinquish any valuables or money on their persons. Some have been taken from the vehicles in which they were being moved and summarily executed or "disappeared."

Prior to their expulsion from Serbian-controlled areas of Bosnia, some non-Serbs are forced to sign statements that they are voluntarily leaving the area. In other cases, civilian authorities draft and issue statements in which the signatory relinquishes all claims to his or her property to the local Serbian-controlled agencies, usually to the municipal [*opština*] authorities or to the town council [*mesna zajednica*]. Helsinki Watch also has received reports that non-Serbs have had to sign loyalty oaths to the regional Serbian authorities. In almost all cases, the aforementioned documents have been prepared, issued, signed and stamped by high- or mid-ranking civilian or military authorities in the region.

The fact that the civilian authorities of the so-called "Serbian Republic" in Bosnia-Hercegovina are involved in the displacement of non-Serbs and, in some cases, the interrogation and registration of detainees attests to the fact that the practices associated with "ethnic cleansing" are part of a coordinated effort by Serbian military and civilian leaders — at least on a municipal level — to rid Serbian-controlled areas of non-Serbs and, also, of those Serbs who disagree with their policies.

Bosnian Muslim and Croatian troops have forced the displacement of Serbs in southwestern and central Bosnia where they are in control. After an area is captured by Muslim troops, Serbian men between the ages of eighteen and sixty frequently are taken to detention facilities and women, children and elderly persons are asked to which area they want to be evacuated. They are then placed on buses or trains and taken to the destination of their choice. While some are allowed to stay in their place of residence, most are taken to Serbian-controlled territory or are brought to other villages in Muslim- and Croatian-controlled areas of Bosnia, where they may be held as hostages. In areas controlled by Muslims and Croats, Serbs most frequently flee because of fear after their property has been destroyed or as a result of increasing paramilitary violence against Serbs in the region. Serbs living in Croatian- and Muslim-controlled areas of Bosnia have been required to sign loyalty oaths to the respective Bosnian or Croatian authorities.

ATTACKS AGAINST CIVILIAN TARGETS, THE USE OF SIEGE WARFARE AND THE INDISCRIMINATE AND DISPROPORTIONATE USE OF FORCE[7]

Serbian forces have consistently used force to achieve non-military objectives. Attacks against civilian targets, the use of siege warfare as a means through which to forcibly displace the civilian population and the indiscriminate and disproportionate use of force are war crimes, i.e., "grave breaches" of the Geneva Conventions of 1949 and the Additional Protocol I of 1977.

The purpose of the siege of Sarajevo and other Bosnian towns is aimed at furthering the goal of "ethnic cleansing" by driving out civilian populations or by killing those who refuse to leave. Coupled with their obstruction of humanitarian aid to an area under attack, Serbian forces

---

[7] An elaborate legal regime governs the use of force affecting non-combatants in times of war. For a more detailed explanation of the relevant laws, refer to Helsinki Watch, *War Crimes in Bosnia-Hercegovina*, August 1992, pp. 203-19. Customary international law and the Geneva Conventions and their Protocols expressly recognize that civilians and civilian objects may not be the direct object of attack, notwithstanding that damage may occur among civilians and civilian objects collateral to a legitimate attack against military targets. (See *Respect for Human Rights in Armed Conflicts*, General Assembly Resolution 2444, 23 U.N. GAOR Supp. (No. 18), p. 164; U.N. Doc. A/7433 (1968); and Articles 48, 50, 51(2), 52, and 53 of the 1977 Protocol Additional to the Geneva Conventions of 12 August 1949, and Relating to the Protection of Victims of International Armed Conflicts [hereinafter Protocol I], which prohibit attacks against civilians or cultural property and define the principle of proportionality, which places a duty on combatants to choose means of attack that avoid or minimize damage to civilians.) Appendix G of this report further explicates provisions of international law as they relate to siege warfare.

also have utilized siege warfare as a means through which to starve the civilian population and thereby force it to leave the besieged region.

The siege of villages, towns or cities involves both the indiscriminate use of force and deliberate attacks against civilians and civilian objects. Sniper and mortar attacks against civilians are a common occurrence in Sarajevo and other besieged towns and cities in Bosnia. Further, Serbian troops have used disproportionate amounts of firepower to attack Muslim and Croatian military targets.

Generally, the use of force by Muslim and Croatian forces against Serbian targets has not been disproportionate. Because Croatian and, particularly, Muslim troops have less firepower than Serbian forces, their attacks have been aimed primarily at Serbian military targets. However, Croatian forces appear to have used force disproportionately and indiscriminately against Muslim civilian and military targets during battles between the Croatian Defense Council (Hrvatsko Vijeće Obrane — HVO) forces and Bosnian government troops in west–central Bosnia. Muslim commando units have ambushed Serbian civilians traveling along roads in eastern Bosnia.

PILLAGE AND DESTRUCTION OF VILLAGES AND CULTURAL OBJECTS[8]

Serbian, Croatian and Bosnian military, paramilitary and police forces are destroying and looting each other's villages, cultural monuments and places of worship. Moreover, civilians have harassed and destroyed property belonging to members of other ethnic groups. Scores of villages, homes and other property have been burned or otherwise destroyed after hostilities have ceased. Such crimes have been committed with impunity throughout Bosnia-Hercegovina.

The destruction of Serbian villages, homes or property by Croatian and/or Muslim troops is, in most cases, neither condoned nor prevented by their superiors. In some cases, civilian, military or police officials in Croatian- and Muslim- controlled areas have arrested soldiers or civilians accused of destroying Serbian property outside the arena of warfare, but few, if any, of those arrested are prosecuted and punished.

---

[8] According to Article 147 of the Fourth Geneva Convention, "extensive destruction and appropriation of property, not justified by military necessity and carried out unlawfully and wantonly" is considered a "grave breach" of the Geneva Conventions of 1949.

In Serbian-controlled areas of Bosnia, the destruction of Muslim and Croatian homes and cultural and religious objects is pervasive. Mosques and, to a lesser extent, Catholic churches have been bulldozed in city centers during daylight hours. Such public displays of destruction suggest that local and regional Serbian authorities issued orders, organized or condoned efforts to destroy such non-Serbian buildings. Helsinki Watch knows of no cases in which Serbian authorities have made even a half-hearted effort to arrest those guilty of such destruction.

SUMMARY EXECUTIONS[9]

Serbian, Muslim and Croatian forces have summarily executed civilians and persons *hors de combat* in areas under their control. Croatian HVO forces are implicated in the assassination of members of their Croatian political rival, the Croatian Party of Rights (Hrvatska Stranka Prava — HSP) and its paramilitary wing, known as the Croatian Defense Forces (Hrvatske Obrambene Snage — HOS).

Many summary executions of non-Serbs by Serbian forces in northwestern and eastern Bosnia take place immediately or soon after a

---

[9] The summary execution of civilians and persons *hors de combat* is prohibited under Article 75 of Protocol I and, moreover, under Article 85(3)(e) of Protocol I and Article 147 of the Fourth Geneva Convention is considered a "grave breach." (Refer to footnote number 11 of this chapter for an explication of these provisions of international law.) Moreover, Article 13 of the Geneva Convention Relative to the Treatment of Prisoners of War of August 12, 1949, [hereinafter Third Geneva Convention] states:

> Prisoners of war must at all times be humanely treated. Any unlawful omission by the Detaining Power causing death or seriously endangering the health of a prisoner of war in its custody is prohibited, and will be regarded as a serious breach of the present Convention.

Prisoners are to be treated humanely "from the time they fall into the power of the enemy and until their final release and repatriation" (Article 5, Third Geneva Convention); i.e., after the combatants are rendered unable to bear arms as a consequence of surrender, wounds, illness or otherwise, the person no longer constitutes a legitimate military threat and, therefore, cannot be the subject of attack and is to be treated humanely and cannot be summarily executed.

village has fallen to Serbian forces. Serbian infantry units enter a village and summarily and randomly execute civilians in their path. Others are pulled from columns of persons being evacuated from the area, taken aside — usually to a nearby house — and summarily executed. Paramilitary groups based in Serbia proper[10] have participated in such executions in eastern Bosnia, particularly in the Bijeljina and Brčko municipalities.

When prisoners were released from Serbian detention camps in northwestern Bosnia, they were taken to Muslim- or Croatian-controlled territory, but some were summarily executed en route by Serbian soldiers. "Disappearances" of persons released from Serbian-operated detention facilities also have occurred.

Muslim forces have summarily executed civilians and disarmed combatants in eastern Bosnia. In some cases, the summary executions may have been the work of commando units skilled in hit-and-run attacks against Serbian positions. In other cases, the victims appear to have been killed while in the custody of, or living in areas controlled by, Bosnian government forces.

Serbian, Muslim and Croatian forces have summarily executed persons detained in their custodies.

---

[10] The forces may have been local "chapters" of the Yugoslav-based paramilitary group but some appear to have been from Serbia proper, as well. The proliferation of Serbian paramilitary groups is pervasive, and victims, as well as members of such groups, often cannot identify the units correctly. (For a further description of Serbian paramilitary groups operating in Bosnia, see Helsinki Watch, *War Crimes in Bosnia-Hercegovina*, August 1992, pp. 32-39.)

ABUSE IN DETENTION[11]

---

[11] Article 75 (2) of Protocol I states:

> The following acts are and shall remain prohibited at any time and in any place whatsoever, whether committed by civilian or by military agents:
> (a) violence to life, health, or physical or mental well-being of persons, in particular:
>   (i) murder;
>   (ii) torture of all kinds, whether physical or mental;
>   (iii) corporal punishments; and
>   (iv) mutilation;
> (b) outrages upon personal dignity, in particular humiliating and degrading treatment, enforced prostitution and any form of indecent assault;
> (c) the taking of hostages;
> (d) collective punishments; and
> (e) threats to commit any of the foregoing acts.

Also, Article 147 of the Fourth Geneva Convention states:

> Grave breaches ... shall be those involving any of the following acts, if committed against persons or property protected by the present Convention [i.e., civilian persons]: wilful killing, torture or inhuman treatment, including biological experiments, wilfully causing great suffering or serious injury to body or health, unlawful deportation or transfer or unlawful confinement of a protected person, compelling a protected person to serve in the forces of a hostile Power, or wilfully depriving a protected person of the rights of fair and regular trial prescribed in the present Convention, taking of hostages and extensive destruction and appropriation of property, not justified by military necessity and carried out unlawfully and wantonly.

"Protected persons" are defined by Article 4 of the Fourth Geneva Convention as:

> .. those who, at a given moment and in any manner whatsoever, find themselves, in case of a conflict or occupation, in the hands of a Party to the conflict or Occupying Power of which they are not nationals.

All parties to the conflict have mistreated persons held in detention facilities under their control. Prisoners have been summarily executed, beaten (sometimes to death), raped, starved, sexually humiliated and otherwise mistreated in detention in Bosnia-Hercegovina.

Military and police forces of the self-proclaimed "Serbian Republic" of Bosnia-Hercegovina detained prisoners in four detention camps in northwestern Bosnia which were subsequently closed as a result of international condemnation. In two of the camps — Omarska and Keraterm — detained persons, primarily men, were regularly beaten to death, starved and terrorized. Members of the intelligentsia were detained in the camps, many of whom remain "disappeared" or are known to have been killed. Some men were summarily executed. The abuses perpetrated in these two camps were systematic and intentional. Abuses also took place in the other two camps in the region — Manjača and Trnopolje. Women were raped in the Omarska and Trnopolje camps. The fact that the four largest detention camps in Bosnia were situated so close to Banja Luka — a center of power for the self-proclaimed "Serbian Republic" — makes it virtually impossible for Serbian civilian and military officials in the region to claim that they did not know of the camps' existence or of the abuses perpetrated within their confines.

Serbian forces also have mistreated prisoners in northeastern and southeastern areas of Bosnia, particularly in the municipality of Brčko. The abuses perpetrated by Serbian forces in eastern Bosnia mirror those committed against prisoners in the western half of the country.

Between April and September, many abuses took place in Bosnian Muslim- and Croatian-operated detention facilities. Prisoners were commonly beaten by guards and, occasionally, during interrogation. A paramilitary group known as the Croatian Defense Forces (HOS) severely mistreated prisoners in a HOS-operated detention facility in the Čapljina municipality, which has since been closed. Muslim forces are guilty of bestial abuses in a detention facility that they control in the village of Čelebići in the municipality of Konjic. In each case, the commanders either knew or participated in the abuse of prisoners and should be held accountable for their role in these abuses.

Conditions for prisoners held both in Bosnian Muslim and Croatian detention centers have improved since the ICRC visited the facilities, during the latter part of the summer of 1992. In August, the Croatian Defense Council (HVO) — which is loyal to the authorities of the self-proclaimed "Community of Herceg-Bosna" — took control of or closed detention facilities operated by the Croatian paramilitary group,

HOS. Since the assumption of HVO control and the ICRC's frequent visits to such facilities, the treatment of prisoners held by Bosnian Croat forces in southwestern Bosnia has improved. However, the treatment of prisoners in the Croatian–controlled town of Orašje in northern Bosnia remains unsatisfactory.

RAPE[12]

---

[12] Rape and sexual abuse constitute violations of international human rights standards and humanitarian law. Article 147 of the Fourth Geneva Convention specifies that "torture or inhuman treatment" and "wilfully causing great suffering or serious injury to body or health" are "grave breaches" and hence judicially actionable war crimes. The *1977 ICRC Commentary* explains that "'inhuman treatment' ... does not mean only physical injury or injury to health. Certain measures ... which caused grave injury to [a person's] human dignity, could conceivably be considered as inhuman treatment." The *1977 ICRC Commentary* also notes that the scope of the phrase "wilfully causing great suffering" can encompass "punishment, in revenge or for some other motive, perhaps out of pure sadism ... [that] can quite legitimately be held to cover moral suffering also." (*1977 ICRC Commentary* at 598–99.) Since in the view of the ICRC "moral suffering" is covered by "inhuman treatment," it is axiomatic that rape is covered also. Moreover, Article 27 of the Fourth Geneva Convention calls for the protection of women "against any attack of their honour, in particular against rape, enforced prostitution, or any form of indecent assault." Further, Article 76 (1) of Protocol I states that women "shall be protected in particular against rape, forced prostitution and any other form of indecent assault." This language makes it clear that rape constitutes both a grave breach of the Convention and a violation of several explicit prohibitions.

In addition, under Article 85 (4)(c) of Protocol I, "inhuman and degrading practices involving outrages upon personal dignity, based on racial discrimination" — a provision that almost certainly applies in many particular instances, given the ethnic character of this conflict — are also "grave breaches" and hence judicially actionable war crimes. Article 86 (2) of Protocol I makes commanders who had information about such crimes punishable themselves "if they did not take all feasible measures within their power to prevent or suppress" a grave breach.

Finally, rape — like murder, extermination, deportation and other equally serious crimes — can be a constituent crime against humanity, as that term was defined in the Nuremberg trial and in Article 6(c) of the Nuremberg Charter, provided that it is part of a mass pattern of such crimes and other definitional elements are met. See Appendix 5 of Middle East Watch/Physicians for Human Rights, *The Anfal Campaign in Iragi Kurdistan: The Destruction of Koreme*, January 1993, for the opinion of Human Rights Watch as to the definitional elements of crimes against humanity. Rape was specifically enumerated in the second set of Nuremberg war criminal trials, conducted under the authority of Control Council Law No. 10, which named with greater specificity the constituent crimes falling with crimes against humanity. See generally Diane Orentlicher, "Setting Accounts: The Duty to Prosecute Human Rights Violations of a Prior

Each of the parties to the conflict in Bosnia–Hercegovina, have used rape as a weapon of war. Soldiers attacking villages have raped women and girls in their homes, in front of family members and in the village square. Women have been arrested and raped during interrogation. In some villages and towns, women and girls have been gathered together and taken to holding centers — often schools or community sports halls — where they are raped, gang-raped and abused repeatedly, sometimes for days or even weeks at a time. Other women have been taken seemingly at random from their communities or out of a group of refugees with which they are traveling and raped by soldiers.

Whether a woman is raped by soldiers in her home or is held in a house with other women and raped over and over again, she is raped with a political purpose — to intimidate, humiliate and degrade her and others affected by her suffering. The effect of rape is often to ensure that women and their families will flee and never return.

Women interviewed by Helsinki Watch and the Women's Rights Project described how they were gang raped, taunted with ethnic slurs and cursed by rapists who stated their intention forcibly to impregnate women as a haunting reminder of the rape and an intensification of the trauma it inflicts.[13] In our view, the forcible impregnation of women,

---

Regime," 100 *Yale L.J.* 2537 (1991).

Rape can also be one of the crimes used as a means of carrying out genocide, although rape does not by itself constitute genocide, even when committed on a mass basis.

The status of rape as a war crime in international humanitarian law and the ability to prosecute it is accordingly not at issue.

[13] It is at present unclear how many women are being forced to bear children consequent to rape. Dr. Veseljko Grizelj, the director of the Petrova Hospital in Zagreb, knows (as of January 13, 1993) of five women pregnant consequent to rape who have been treated at his hospital. One woman had her baby, two received abortions, and two sought abortions more than ten weeks after conception and thus were required by Croatian law to carry their pregnancies to term. Dr. Miomir Krstić, the director of the family planning and childbirth division of the GAK Clinical Center in Belgrade, stated in late 1992 that, since September 1992, he knows of four women pregnant consequent to rape in Bosnia and, earlier, in Croatia. One woman gave birth to a girl and two received abortions. Because she arrived at the clinic in the latter stages of her pregnancy, the fourth woman was carrying the pregnancy to term. (Dr. Kristić made these

or the intention to so impregnate them, constitutes an abuse separate from the rape itself and should be denounced and investigated as such. Moreover, the rape of women in an organized fashion — whether in buildings where they are kept for the purpose of being raped or by soldiers extracting women from camps where they are detained with family members — establishes that local commanders must know that their soldiers are raping women and are doing nothing to stop these abuses. The failure to punish rapists appears to be as consistent and widespread as the act of rape itself.

Although we have not found hard evidence showing a policy of deploying rape as a means of tactical warfare, we also found no evidence that any soldier or member of a paramilitary group has been punished or held to account for raping women and girls. To the contrary, soldiers often rape without regard for witnesses, and, on occasion, identify themselves to their victims. These are not the actions of men who fear retribution.

More documentary work must to be done to determine the extent of sexual abuse committed against women in Bosnia by all parties to the

---

statements for a program entitled "Trampled Honor" (*Pogažena Cast,*) for Radio Television Serbia. The program was taped in 1992, but the exact date of the interviews are not given. It appears that they were taken in late 1992.) Helsinki Watch and the Women's Project of Human Rights Watch do not possess similar medical statistics about the number of raped women treated in hospitals in Bosnia-Hercegovina.

A team of experts visited six major medical centers in Zagreb, Sarajevo, Zenica and Belgrade in the former Yugoslavia in January 1993 on behalf of the U.N. Human Rights Commission. The team identified 119 pregnancies as a result of rape in 1992 at these centers. The team concluded that "it is not possible to know precisely the actual number of rapes or the number of pregnancies due to rape that have occurred." Nevertheless, the team believed "that the incidence of rape in the conflict . . . has been widespread." (See "Report of the Team of Experts on Their Mission to Investigate Allegations of Rape in the Territory of the Former Yugoslavia from January 12-23, 1991 [sic] [stated correctly in the report as 1993], Annex II, *The Situation of Human Rights in the Territory of the Former Yugoslavia: Note by the Secretary-General, United Nations General Assembly and Security Council*, S/25341, February 26, 1993. See also Jeri Laber, "Bosnia: Questions of Rape," *The New York Review of Books*, March 25, 1993, pp. 1-4.

conflict.[14] The various estimates that have emerged thus far of the number of women raped in the conflict have done little to advance efforts to document rape in Bosnia and, unfortunately, may contribute to an eventual backlash which could undercut the seriousness of the abuse if the high numbers cannot be substantiated.

MUTILATION[15]

Prisoners held by Serbian, Muslim and Croatian forces have been sexually humiliated and some have been sexually mutilated by Serbian forces. Helsinki Watch has taken several testimonies indicating that Serbian forces either castrated or attempted to castrate at least one Muslim youth in the Omarska detention camp in mid-July.

---

[14] Documenting the sexual abuse, including rape, of women and, to a lesser extent, men presents a distinct set of problems. Women typically do not report rape, nor in many cases do they seek medical attention after being raped unless they fear that they are pregnant as a consequence of rape. The reluctance to report rape is attributable to the dual obstacles of fear and shame, a disabling combination that contributes to rape's strategic function as a weapon of war: the victim is terrorized and will not identify her tormentor. As the testimonies in this report demonstrate, rapists threaten their victims with future harm to them and their family members in order to ensure women's silence. Aggressors presume that their victims will not report rape, and, very often, they are correct. Rape victims also harbor great shame associated with the nature of the abuse they have suffered; they thus are reluctant to reveal what has happened to them. This reluctance is exacerbated by the fact that when women do come forward to report rape in times of peace as well as of war, they are confronted with unresponsive officials and inadequate support services. The human rights community, too, has been remiss in overlooking rape as a human rights abuse in the past. (For a Human Rights Watch report on rape in situations of conflict, see *Untold Terror: Violence Against Women in Peru's Armed Conflict*, Americas Watch and the Women's Rights Project, 1993.)

[15] Article 75 of Protocol I expressly forbids mutilation. (Refer to footnote 8 for an explication of these provisions of international law.) Also, Article 11 (1) and (2) of Protocol I states that "physical mutilations" shall not be carried out on "persons who are in the power of the adverse Party and who are interned, detained or otherwise deprived of liberty" as a result of an international armed conflict.

Helsinki Watch also documented a case in which a woman was given the choice of having her face carved with a knife or her body tattooed by a Serbian combatant. The name of the woman's captor was tattooed on the woman's arms and legs. The abuse appears to have been a unilateral act of brutality and Helsinki Watch has found no evidence of other such practices by Serbian or other forces party to the war in Bosnia.

Hostage-Holding[16]

Serbian, Croatian and Bosnian forces frequently detain civilians, who are then exchanged for civilians and combatants held by the opposing side(s). In international humanitarian law, the detention of civilians against their will amounts to hostage-taking.

The taking of civilian hostages is a more pronounced practice among Muslim and Croatian forces than among Serbian troops. Croatian and Muslim forces readily admit that they detain Serbian civilians living in areas under their control with the intention of exchanging them for combatants held by the Serbian side. For example, the holding of hostages by Croatian military and civilian authorities in Tomislavgrad is known to the leaders of the self-proclaimed "Community of Herceg-Bosna" but little pressure is exerted on local leaders in Tomislavgrad to release the hostages.

To a lesser extent, Serbian forces also retain non-Serbian civilians, usually in urban areas under their control. Although in most cases, Serbian forces have tried to expel non-Serbs, in several instances, persons have been denied papers allowing them to exit Serbian-held

---

[16] Article 75 of Protocol I and Article 147 of the Fourth Geneva Convention expressly forbid the taking of hostages. (Refer to footnote 11 for an explication of these provisions of international law.) "Hostages" are defined by the *1977 ICRC Commentary* [at 874] as follows:

> Hostages are persons who find themselves, willingly or unwillingly, in the power of the enemy and who answer with their life or their freedom for compliance with the orders of the latter and for upholding the security of its armed forces.

Civilians captured and held for exchange purposes are hostages, since they answer with their freedom for compliance with the orders of their captors.

territory. This problem is most acute in the city and suburbs of Banja Luka in northwestern Bosnia.

All parties to the conflict detain civilians without legal basis in detention facilities under their control. In such cases, the only criteria for detention is affiliation with another ethnic or religious group.

OBSTRUCTION OF HUMANITARIAN AID AND ATTACKS ON RELIEF PERSONNEL[17]

---

[17] Attacks against, and harassment of, humanitarian and medical actions and personnel are prohibited under international law. With regard to relief actions and personnel, Articles 70 and 71 of Protocol I state, in part:

> 1. If the civilian population of any territory under the control of a Party to the conflict, other than occupied territory, is not adequately provided with the ... [basic needs of existence], relief actions which are humanitarian and impartial in character and conducted without any adverse distinction shall be undertaken, subject to the agreement of the Parties concerned in such relief actions. Offers of such relief shall not be regarded as interference in the armed conflict or as unfriendly acts. ...
>
> 2. The Parties to the conflict and each High Contracting Party shall allow and facilitate rapid and unimpeded passage of all relief consignments, equipment and personnel provided in accordance with this Section, even if such assistance is destined for the civilian population of the adverse Party.
>
> 3. The Parties to the conflict and each High Contracting Party which allow the passage of relief consignments, equipment and personnel in accordance with paragraph 2:
>
>> (a) shall have the right to prescribe the technical arrangements, including search, under which such passage is permitted;
>> (b) may take such permission conditional on the distribution of this assistance being made under the local supervision of a Protecting Power;
>> (c) shall, in no way whatsoever, divert relief consignments from the purpose for which they are intended nor delay their forwarding, except in cases of urgent necessity in the interest of the civilian population concerned.

4. The Parties to the conflict shall protect relief consignments and facilitate their rapid distribution.

. . .

1. Where necessary, relief personnel may form part of the assistance provided in any relief action, in particular for the transportation and distribution of relief consignments; the participation of such personnel shall be subject to the approval of the Party in whose territory they will carry out their duties.

2. Such personnel shall be respected and protected.

With regard to medical actions and personnel, Articles 12 and 13 of Protocol I state, in part:

1. Medical units shall be respected and protected at all times and shall not be the object of attack.

. . .

4. Under no circumstances shall medical units be used in an attempt to shield military objectives from attack.

. . .

1. The protection to which civilian medical units are entitled shall not cease unless they are used to commit, outside their humanitarian function, acts harmful to the enemy. ...

2. The following shall not be considered acts harmful to the enemy:

> (a) that the personnel of the unit are equipped with light individual weapons for their own defence or for that of the wounded and sick in their charge;
> (b) that the unit is guarded by a picket or by sentries or by an escort;
> (c) that small arms and ammunition taken from the wounded and sick, and not yet handed to the proper service, are found in the units;

Disrespect for the Red Cross emblem and relief personnel has been pervasive throughout Bosnia-Hercegovina. Armed forces have attacked or otherwise harassed domestic and international medical and relief personnel and a number of people engaged in humanitarian aid have been killed or wounded. Relief convoys have been targeted for attack, primarily by sniper and mortar fire. Hijackings of relief convoys also have occurred. Bosnian Muslim and Croatian forces have targeted U.N. relief convoys for attack in order to express their impatience with what they view as the United Nations' timidity toward Serbian forces and its general ineptitude in the former Yugoslavia.

Serbian forces have stolen food, medicine and other humanitarian aid intended for civilians in besieged areas. Vehicles transporting humanitarian aid also have been confiscated by Serbian forces.[18] Serbian troops persistently have prevented convoys of the United Nations High Commissioner for Refugees (UNHCR) from delivering aid to besieged Muslim areas. In many cases, Serbian troops have launched attacks against the area for which humanitarian aid is destined, thereby preventing convoys from delivering supplies to the besieged region. In addition, water pumping stations and electrical transmission towers have repeatedly been the targets of shelling, leaving Bosnian towns and cities without water or the electricity to pump it for weeks at a time.

Ambulances and other medical vehicles and relief personnel have repeatedly come under fire during the conflict. In December 1992, the ICRC expressed its concern that its workers in Bosnia-Hercegovina continued to be attacked. According to Philippe Gauthier, an ICRC relief coordinator:

> Blatant disrespect for the Red Cross emblem makes ICRC relief assistance extremely dangerous because we never really know if the different parties to the conflict

---

(d) that members of the armed forces or other combatants are in the unit for medical reasons.

[18] The U.S. State Department issued a report in January 1993 concluding that Serbian forces in Bosnia have been skimming nearly 23 percent of all relief supplies sent into the area, contributing to the general failure of the relief effort. (See Michael R. Gorgon, "U.S. Finds Serbs Skimming 23% of Bosnian Aid," *The New York Times*, January 13, 1993.)

will let our trucks pass through the areas under their control. The short winter days, bad roads and mountainous terrain render our task even more difficult.[19]

Other medical facilities such as hospitals also are targets of shelling and gunfire, especially in Sarajevo. In addition, the lack of water, electricity and heat has severely affected the ability of those doctors able to report to work to perform properly. Patients have died due to lack of medicines, antiseptics and antibiotics. The cold has claimed hundreds, possibly thousands, of lives, and deaths have resulted from necessarily primitive surgical methods and unsanitary conditions.

International governments have hesitated to provide the personnel, troops, supplies and vehicles needed to provide humanitarian relief effectively. Despite diplomatic assurances that "all measures" would be taken to ensure the delivery of humanitarian aid in Bosnia, by mid-October UNHCR relief workers were pleading with international governments to provide the necessary supplies, troops and vehicles to move relief supplies into Bosnia before the onset of the Balkan winter.

In early August, the U.N. Security Council met to discuss the use of force to deliver humanitarian aid. A resolution[20] authorized U.N. escorts, who formerly could only fire in self-defense, to "use all necessary means to ensure that humanitarian relief" gets to its destination.[21] On September 14, the Security Council of the U.N. voted to send up to 6,000

---

[19] See statement of Philippe Gauthier in *ICRC Bulletin: Special Edition — Bosnia-Herzegovina*, December 1992.

[20] The resolution was initiated by the United States and co-sponsored by Britain, France, Belgium and Russia. Japan, Austria, Ecuador, Morocco, Venezuela, Hungary, and Cape Verde voted in favor and the resolution was passed on August 13, 1992. (See Michael Gorgon, "NATO Seeks Options to Big Troop Deployment for Insuring Delivery of Aid to Bosnia," *The New York Times*, August 14, 1992, and Trevor Rowe, "U.N. Approves Use of Force to Deliver Bosnia Aid, Requests War Crime Data," *The Washington Post*, August 14, 1992.)

[21] Gary Lee and Edward Wash, "U.N. Accord on Bosnia Aid Near," *The Washington Post*, August 10, 1992.

more troops, in addition to the 1,500 already in place, to protect humanitarian efforts in Bosnia-Hercegovina.[22]

Despite its mandate to use force to ensure the delivery of humanitarian aid, U.N. forces in the field have sought to appease the warring factions — particularly Serbian troops — rather than enforce the will of the international community and international law. U.N. officials and relief workers, though their escorts have been given authority to use force to defend supply shipments, often give in to the demands of Serbian forces, allowing them to decide what aid is provided and who will receive it.[23]

---

[22] Patrick Moore, "U.N. to Increase Role in Bosnia-Hercegovina," Radio Free Europe/Radio Liberty *Daily Report*, No. 177, September 15, 1992.

[23] Michael R. Gorgon, "U.S. Finds Serbs Skimming 23% of Bosnian Aid," *The New York Times*, January 13, 1993.

ABUSES IN NORTHWESTERN BOSNIA

Northwestern Bosnia is almost exclusively controlled by Serbian forces. Bosnian Muslim forces maintain control over two municipalities in the area, Velika Kladuša and Čazin and the municipalities of Bosanska Krupa and Bihać are controlled partially by Serbian troops and partially by Muslim forces. The following municipalities are under the control of Serbian forces: Bosanski Novi, Bosanska Dubica, Bosanska Gradiška, Srbac, Prnjavor, Laktaši, Prijedor, Sanski Most, Banja Luka, Čelinac, Kotor Varoš, Skender Vakuf, Jajce, Donji Vakuf, Mrkonjić Grad, Glamoč, Bosansko Grahovo, Titov Drvar, Bosanski Petrovac, Ključ and Šipovo.

"Ethnic cleansing" by Serbian forces has been highly organized and widespread in the northwestern part of the country, particularly in the municipalities of Prijedor[1] and Banja Luka.[2] Helsinki Watch has interviewed scores of former residents of the northwestern regions of Bosnia; almost all have recounted the same pattern of abuse involving sieges of their villages, arrests, detentions, deportations and, in some cases, executions.[3] Most of the former residents interviewed by Helsinki Watch had been interned in detention camps. From mid- to late September 1992, many Muslim villages were destroyed by Serbian forces going "from house to house lobbing grenades, shooting — killing dozens."[4] International relief officials say that Serbian troops are now

---

[1] Prior to the war, the population of Prijedor was 112,470, of which 44 percent were Muslims, 42.5 percent Serbs, and 5.6 percent Croats.

[2] Prior to the war, the population of the municipality of Banja Luka was 195,139, of which 54.8 percent were Serbs, 14.9 percent Muslims, and 14.6 percent Muslims. Twelve percent of Banja Luka's population identified themselves as "Yugoslavs" in the 1991 census.

[3] The pattern of forcible displacement of non-Serbs in Bosnia is set forth in the Patterns of Abuse section of this report.

[4] Radio Free Europe/Radio Liberty, "Weekly Review," *Research Report*, Vol. 1, No. 40, October 9, 1992. See also Mary Battiata, "Muslims Fleeing New Serb Purges," *The Washington Post*, September 29, 1992.

ABUSES IN NORTHWESTERN BOSNIA

BOSNIA-HERCEGOVINA

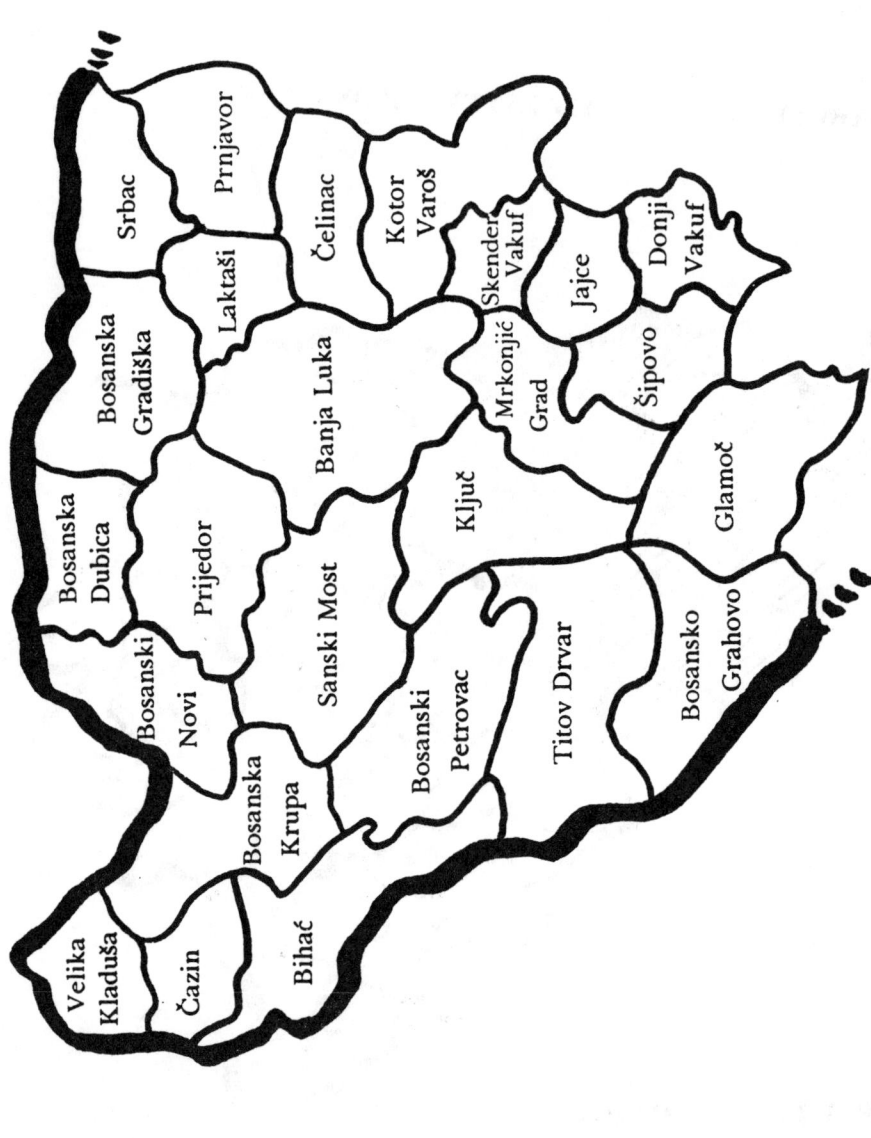

NORTHWESTERN BOSNIA

engaged in a systematic purge of the remaining 200,000 Muslim residents in the region, especially from Banja Luka.[5]

In recent months, the siege and overt destruction of Muslim villages in northwestern Bosnia appears to have subsided. Nevertheless, non-Serbs who remain in villages under Serbian control are often beaten, threatened with death and otherwise terrorized if they do not leave the area. In one case documented by Helsinki Watch, a Muslim woman from the municipality of Ključ was raped because her husband refused to leave the area and to sign over their property rights to the local Serbian authorities.[6] Non-Serbs in urban centers in northwestern Bosnia — such as in Banja Luka and Prijedor — often are harassed and threatened by Serbian paramilitary forces in the area. Muslims and Croats have been dismissed from their jobs, and many are afraid to leave their homes. Some are arbitrarily arrested and detained by local officials.

Serbian military and civilian authorities continue to deport non-Serbs from urban, suburban and rural areas. U.N. officials reported that as many as 25,000 refugees left through January 1993.[7] Some who leave this area of Bosnia are reportedly required "voluntarily" to sign over their homes and other possessions to Serbian authorities and must pay for documents attesting that they have no unpaid debts. Finally, they are charged $200 for bus transportation to Croatia.[8]

In late February, U.N. officials reported that Bosnian Serb forces expelled a mixed group of 360 Muslim and Croatian civilians[9] and forced them to make a dangerous four-mile trip between Turbe and

---

[5] Mary Battiata, "Muslims Fleeing New Serb Purges," *The Washington Post*, September 29, 1992.

[6] See the following section concerning rape.

[7] Jonathan C. Randal, "Serbs Turn Focus on West Bosnia," *The Washington Post*, March 6, 1993. See also Amnesty International Urgent Action Appeal "Bosnia-Hercegovina: Non-Serbs in the Serbian-Controlled Town of Banja Luka," March 1993.

[8] Jonathan C. Randal, "Serbs Turn Focus on West Bosnia," *The Washington Post*, March 6, 1993.

[9] The article does not state which town the refugees were fleeing.

Travnik through gunfire. A week later, a group of 1,036 civilians was also forced to make the perilous journey to Travnik. In early March, a bridge on the border between Croatia and Bosnia-Hercegovina in the city of Bosanska Gradiška was reopened and now provides a less hazardous route through which about 1,500 Muslims and Croats have been displaced.[10] Croatian police statistics show that more than 40,000 Bosnian refugees have crossed the Bosanska Gradiška bridge into Croatia; an estimated 80 percent were Muslims.

U.N. officials also have reported that in Glamoć, Serbian gunmen killed six Muslims and burned down their homes. A wounded woman who witnessed the shooting fled to Banja Luka and was being tracked down by Serbian military police, according to U.N. officials.[11] In a similar incident on February 25, U.N. officials reported that Serbian gunmen shot and killed five Muslims and two Croats on a crowded main street in the village of Bosanska Kostajnica, near the Croatian border.[12]

Cooperation among Serbian civilian authorities, police, military and paramilitary forces is commonplace in northwestern Bosnia. The involvement of local governmental and political figures indicates that a civilian infrastructure exists to facilitate military and paramilitary efforts to displace non-Serbs from the region.

In northwestern Bosnia, civilian officials have been involved in the interrogating and registering of some prisoners, including judges and prominent members of the Serbian Democratic Party (Srpska Demokratska Stranka — SDS). The Serbian authorities in northwestern Bosnia also are responsible for issuing the prepared statements that Muslims and Croats must sign before leaving.

The Serbian military and, possibly, paramilitary forces are the best organized in this region and appear to be operating under a well-organized chain of command. Second only to Pale (south of Sarajevo), Banja Luka is a center of power for the civilian and military authorities of the self-proclaimed "Serbian Republic of Bosnia-Hercegovina," now referred to as the "Serbian Republic"

---

[10] Jonathan C. Randal, "Serbs Turn Focus on West Bosnia," *The Washington Post*, March 6, 1993.

[11] *Ibid.*

[12] *Ibid.*

(Republika Srpska).[13] Even before the war in Bosnia-Hercegovina, Serbian paramilitary forces and the Yugoslav Army (JNA) used Banja Luka as a base from which to attack military and civilian targets during the war in Croatia.[14]

Banja Luka has been under the *de facto* control of Serbian authorities since late March 1992, when Serbian paramilitary groups assumed positions within and outside the city.[15]

The municipality of Prijedor was the site of four detention camps[16] discovered by the press in the summer of 1992: Omarska, Keraterm, Manjača and Trnopolje. Of the four, Omarska and Keraterm appear to have been the most brutal. The camps were established sometime in late May or June 1992. Each camp appears to have had a commander, and, in the case of Omarska, a high-level member of the government of the self-proclaimed "Serbian Republic" visited the camp on at least one occasion. Trnopolje was initially a camp in which women, children and elderly persons were detained. After the discovery of the four camps, Trnopolje was transformed into a holding center for non-Serbs administered by local Serbian authorities.

It was only after international exposure and condemnation that Serbian authorities took steps to close the camps. Omarska and Keraterm were closed in late August 1992; Trnopolje and Manjača were shut down in November and December 1992, respectively. Although the

---

[13] The self-proclaimed Bosnian Serb state will be referred to as the "Serbian Republic" in this report. References to the Yugoslav republic of Serbia is distinguished from its self-proclaimed Bosnian counterpart where relevant.

[14] Helsinki Watch representatives traveling from Belgrade to Knin were prevented from entering Banja Luka in late March 1992. When permission to proceed was finally granted, the Helsinki Watch representatives witnessed open Serbian paramilitary activity throughout the city. (See Helsinki Watch, *War Crimes in Bosnia-Hercegovina*, August 1992, p. 149.)

[15] During Helsinki Watch's visits to the region in July, August and December 1991 and January 1992, a strong Yugoslav Army (JNA) presence was evident in Banja Luka and throughout northern Bosnia.

[16] A detailed description of each of these camps and of other detention facilities, and of the abuses that occurred at each site, is contained in this section of the report.

Serbian authorities released those detained in the camps, many former detainees of these camps remain unaccounted for and others have been moved to other Serbian-operated detention facilities, such as Batković (northeast Bosnia) Kotor Varoš (northeast Bosnia or Serbian-controlled areas in the municipality of Sarajevo.[17] Many former detainees interviewed by Helsinki Watch representatives identified areas where they believe prisoners have been transferred and are being held clandestinely.[18]

As mentioned above, Bosnian forces control territory in the extreme northwestern pocket of Bosnia, including the Čazin, Velika Kladuša and parts of the Bihać and Bosanska Krupa municipalities. Helsinki Watch has not yet conducted an investigation there.

ABUSES BY SERBIAN FORCES

Summary Executions

Vlašić

In August 1992, thousands of non-Serbs were released from detention camps in northwestern Bosnia. Many were then loaded on buses, expelled from the area and taken toward the Muslim- and Croatian-controlled town of Travnik in Bosnia. On August 21, a convoy of non-Serbs released from the Trnopolje camp was sent toward Travnik. En route, approximately 150 to 200 men were taken from two buses and

---

[17] On February 18, 1993, the ICRC visited the Serbian run Kula Butmir prison in Sarajevo, where ICRC delegates registered and interviewed ninety-five Muslims and Croats. Prior to the ICRC's visit on February 18, thirty-four detainees at the prison had been transferred from the Manjača camp to the prison; they were released near the town of Jablanica (in southwest Bosnia) on February 8, 1993.

[18] Former prisoners have identified areas in which they believe Serbian authorities operate "secret camps." Although Helsinki Watch retains the names of several such locations is secure files outside its offices, Helsinki Watch has not been able to confirm or refute the existence of such camps.

summarily executed in a mountainous area known as Vlašić.[19] Serbian police officers are alleged to have executed the men.

Esad, a thirty-year-old Muslim resident of the village of Trnopolje,[20] described the August 21 evacuation from the Trnopolje camp to Helsinki Watch representatives:

> While we were in the Trnopolje camp, our neighbors in the village started to persecute us. They would tell people that they could go home to get food or clothes and then return to the camp. These people never returned. People started to disappear. So I decided to join the convoy and leave. They organized our exodus. They didn't pick the people who would go. They just brought four buses to the camp at about 11:00 a.m. on August 21. Those who got on the bus were lucky.

Helsinki Watch interviewed B.J.,[21] a Muslim resident of the village of Kevljani in the municipality of Prijedor, who survived the Vlašić massacre. According to B.J., on August 21, a convoy of twelve or thirteen buses and trucks first evacuated women and children from Trnopolje. Four buses then evacuated a group of men:

> After the women and children were taken away, about 250 men remained.[22] We [men] were [then] taken in

---

[19] According to Western press reports, at least 188 men were taken from the convoy and executed by Serbian police. (Mary Battiata, "Muslims Flee Renewed Drive by Serb Forces," *The Washington Post*, October 11, 1992.) For an account of the massacre, see also Mary Battiata, "Bosnian Serb Police Unit Is Accused of Massacre of Muslim Prisoners," *The Washington Post*, September 22, 1993 and Mary Battiata, "Slayings in Bosnia Confirmed," *The Washington Post*, September 28, 1992.

[20] The witness was interviewed on October 17, 1992, in a refugee camp in Croatia but chose to withhold his name. The name used here is a pseudonym. The village of Trnopolje is in the municipality of Prijedor.

[21] Interviewed on October 17, 1992, in a refugee camp in Croatia.

[22] It is unclear whether 250 men remained in the entire camp or in the area of the camp where the witness was detained.

the direction of Travnik in four buses. When we got to Kozarac, we waited for another convoy to come from Prijedor. [While we waited,] they robbed us — they took our gold [and our] German marks. Serbian soldiers, a driver and an escort[23] were on each bus.

We then went toward Banja Luka to Skender Vakuf and stopped en route to get some water. After we passed Skender Vakuf, we drove toward Travnik, but we got off the main road and onto a side road. We stopped again for about fifteen minutes and got some water from a river. We got on the buses again and turned to leave. Then our escort got on the bus and said, "Whoever I call is to get off the bus." Then he started pointing at people, saying "You, you and you — get out." We were made to line up along the bus. About 200 to 250 men had been taken from the buses.[24]

Esad was on another bus in the convoy and corroborated B.J.'s account:

We headed toward Travnik, and when we reached Kozarac — at about 12:00 p.m. — another convoy hooked up with our buses. The people on this second convoy were primarily residents of Sanski Most. We headed toward Banja Luka, but the buses kept stopping along the way. We stopped twice. We stopped the first time in order to go to the bathroom and to get water. When we stopped the second time, I saw many men dressed in blue uniforms that belonged to the special units of the police. That is when I saw Dragan Mrdja — he had a radio in his hand and said something like "in a half hour."

---

[23] The escort appears to have been a member of the Serbian armed forces who was assigned responsibility for the prisoners in the bus.

[24] The witness was among the men called off the bus.

> We got back on the buses, and they passed out plastic bags and told us to deposit all our belongings and possessions. We stopped another three times. A man got on the bus and told all the men to get off the bus. He pointed to people and said, "You, you and you, get off." They left most of the minors alone but seventeen- and eighteen-year-old youths were also told to get off the bus. The elderly men stayed on the bus. When we got off the bus, we were told to keep our heads down.

Two buses of women and children arrived, and the passengers were told to get off the buses. The men then got onto the two buses that the women and children had left. The convoy then proceeded, with the two busloads of men following in the rear. According to B.J., only the two busloads of men had military escorts; the remaining buses in the convoy had only a driver. B.J. said that the escort on his bus was named Igor Čurguz and the commander in charge of the troops was Dragan Mrdja, whom Esad also indentified. According to Esad, who was on the second bus:

> We got onto an empty bus and we went in through the front door of the bus. I was the first in the line, so I ended up sitting at the back of the bus, by the back door. Again, they asked us for all our money. Over one hundred people were on the bus, and we were crowded in and hit with rifle butts so that they could pack the bus still further. We then drove for about ten minutes. The other buses in the convoy had passed us.

Ten or fifteen minutes thereafter, the two busloads of men stopped at a cliffside area known as Korčanske Stijene, on the Vlašić plateau. According to B.J., this site is between Skender Vakuf and Travnik but closer to Skender Vakuf. The rest of the convoy proceeded in the direction of Travnik. The men were told to get off the bus and line up along the side of a ravine,[25] and most were summarily executed thereafter.[26] According to B.J.:

> We had to keep looking at the floor, and I couldn't see how many soldiers were present. They told us to line up along the wall of the cliff. They made us perform military movements [i.e., salutes, marches, etc.] and told us to go to the other side of the road — to the edge of the ravine — where they told us to kneel and bow our heads.
>
> I heard shots and saw people falling off the side of the cliff, so I jumped into the ravine. I fell about twenty meters and, as I rolled down, I saw the periphery of a forest so I ran into the trees. I walked downward, toward a creek, before I looked up to see what was going on.[27] Some of the men didn't jump into the ravine but waited for a bullet to be shot into them.

As the men from the first bus were being executed, those on the second bus were also being taken from that vehicle, but in groups of three. According to B.J., who watched from below:

> The men from the second bus were made to stand on the edge of the road, where they were shot, and their bodies fell into the ravine.

---

[25] In Bosnia-Hercegovina circuitous roads are narrow and dangerous. Usually, the side of a cliff rises to one side of the road and there is a steep ravine along the other side. The width of the road is approximately that of two cars.

[26] Press accounts have identified the scene of the massacre as "a narrow mountain track at a place known as Varjanta, near the confluence of the Ugar and Ilomska Rivers about fifteen miles north of Travnik." (See Mary Battiata, "Bosnian Serb Police Unit Is Accused of Massacre of Muslim Prisoners," *The Washington Post*, September 22, 1992.)

[27] The witness claims to have been 100 meters away from the site of the executions.

Esad, who was on the second bus, recounted his experience:

After ten minutes, the bus stopped. The soldier on the bus said, "Now you'll be placed under UNPROFOR's [United Nations Protection Forces] control. Life for the living and for the dead. . . well, you know." They told us to get off the bus and line up in pairs, in a column. I was the last one in the column. We walked about fifty meters toward the back of the bus. I saw another bus in front of us, but I didn't know that people were inside.

They took us to the edge of the ravine. There were over one hundred meters between the edge of the ravine and Korčanske Stijene. They told us to march [to the edge of the road] and to kneel. Then we heard gunfire. I was the last to have emerged from the bus and the first one facing the ravine. The hill wasn't too steep, so someone pushed me and I fell — rather rolled — into the canyon. There were dead people falling over us. People may have just been wounded, and then they may have thrown them into the ravine — I don't know. Some were wounded after they were pushed into the ravine, and others were still alive but the soldiers started shooting down into the canyon from above. More then ten but fewer than fifteen police officers did this [i.e., committed the massacre].

I hid and ran. I saw my colleague and we wandered around on Vlašić for three days. We wanted to get to Travnik.

According to B.J.:

I waited in my [hiding] spot until nightfall. Then I climbed up to see the dead. [In addition to those that had been executed that same day,] there were old corpses there as well. They were swollen, many were black and the bodies were rotting and the smell was bad.[28] There were many corpses, but probably fewer than two hundred.

At least seven men are known to have survived the massacre. Five of the survivors — including Esad and B.J. — were later recaptured by Serbian forces.[29] According to B.J.:

> I found another man who had survived and we walked about one kilometer away [from the site of the massacre] and waited until morning, when we headed for Travnik. We walked up to the road and started walking toward the radio transmitter. We traveled for two days. On the evening of the second day, we were captured by the Serbian army. They took us to their commander in Vlašić, near Galica. We hadn't eaten in two days, and they gave us some food. Then they took us to the post office in Skender Vakuf, which was used as their main headquarters. They took us to the basement, and we found three more men who had survived the massacre but they were in a sorry state. They appeared to have

---

[28] In June 1992, Helsinki Watch representatives gathered evidence that strongly points to the summary execution of at least fifteen disarmed Croatian combatants on the Vlašić plateau. Thirteen of the bodies were recovered and brought to the Travnik hospital, where autopsies were conducted. The executions took place on or about May 15, 1992, and appear to have been perpetrated by members of the military police of the Yugoslav Army (JNA). For an account of the abuse, see Helsinki Watch, *War Crimes in Bosnia-Hercegovina*, August 1992, pp. 56-59.

[29] In addition to the five identified by the two witnesses interviewed by Helsinki Watch, foreign journalists interviewed another survivor of the massacre. The man, whose nickname is Cerni ["Black"], claims that he and another man survived the massacre but, unlike the other five men, were not recaptured by Serbian forces. Cerni reportedly arrived in Jajce, controlled by Muslim and Croatian forces at the time, but the other survivor died along the way. Cerni arrived in Travnik on August 29, where he was interviewed by reporters. See Mary Battiata, "Bosnian Serb Police Unit Is Accused of Massacre of Muslim Prisoners," *The Washington Post*, September 22, 1992.

been badly bruised from falling into the ravine. We were taken to see a commander with the rank of major, to whom we gave our statement. We told them what happened, and he said that the army didn't do that [i.e., commit the massacre] — that it was the police and that they would be punished.[30]

Esad wandered around, too, only to be recaptured.

One night, it rained and we asked a peasant to help us. He refused, but he gave us some bread and cheese. He reported us to the [Serbian] army and we were eventually arrested at Galica, near the front lines. The soldiers wore olive uniforms, which originally belonged to the Yugoslav Army but now were being worn by the [Bosnian] Serb Army. They threatened us, and one of the soldiers said to his colleagues, "Give me a knife so that I can slaughter them." We told them our entire ordeal, including the [massacre of the men from the] convoy. They knew nothing about the convoy.

We got to a command center, ate some dinner and then we were taken to Skender Vakuf. We found three other men who had been arrested as well. We spent the night in Skender Vakuf, and in the morning we were interrogated by a colonel or a lieutenant colonel and then the military police questioned us.

Five of the seven survivors were taken to the Banja Luka hospital, where they were mistreated.[31]

For more than one month, the regional Serbian militia commander, Colonel Boško Peulić, failed to respond to requests for an

---

[30] The witness claims that this is probably true. As far as he remembers, the organizers of the convoy with whom he had contact in Trnopolje were police officers from Prijedor.

[31] For an account of the witnesses' mistreatment, see the relevant section below.

explanation of the fate of men who "disappeared" in Vlašić. Requests by the Bosnian government for an independent, third-party inspection of the site of the massacre were refused.[32] On September 27, 1992, Stojan Župljanin, chief of security services in Banja Luka, confirmed the killing of the Muslim prisoners.[33] Župljanin reportedly commands a 6,000-square-mile area that includes the site of the massacre.[34] He claimed that an investigation was proceeding and that those responsible for the crime would be brought to justice.[35] Helsinki Watch has not received any information concerning the status of the investigation or of the arrest, prosecution or imprisonment of any suspects.

Forced Displacement

Serbian civilian and military authorities have discriminated against, terrorized and attacked Muslims and Croats in northwestern Bosnia, intending to force them from Serbian-controlled territory. This section describes the methods used to displace non-Serbs forcibly in northwestern Bosnia.

Prijedor[36]

On April 30, Serbian authorities assumed control of Prijedor in an overnight coup. Hundreds of Muslim and Croatian police officers were relieved of their weapons and sent home. Muslim employees in hospitals, schools and factories reportedly were dismissed. Serbian-manned roadblocks were put in place and snipers were

---

[32] Mary Battiata, "Bosnian Serb Police Unit Is Accused of Massacre of Muslim Prisoners," *The Washington Post*, September 22, 1992.

[33] Mary Battiata, "Slayings in Bosnia Confirmed," *The Washington Post*, September 28, 1992.

[34] *Ibid*.

[35] *Ibid*.

[36] According to a witness, the prewar population of the city of Prijedor was approximately 50 percent Muslim, 44 percent Serbian and 6 percent Croatian.

positioned on rooftops.[37] On May 30, fighting broke out in the town and Prijedor's elected Muslim mayor and police chief were arrested and jailed soon afterwards.

According to K.B.,[38] a forty-nine-year-old Muslim schoolteacher for mentally retarded persons in Prijedor, tensions between the various ethnic groups and discrimination against non-Serbs surfaced in Prijedor before fighting broke out in late May:

> Tension could be felt long before the war started. There was a large sign in Prijedor that read, "There is no flour for Muslims or Croats." In front of the "Žitopromet" silo there were two lines for flour; one for Serbs, the other for the rest — but there was never any flour left for "the rest."
>
> On May 23, my colleague, a Serbian elementary-school teacher named M.R. from Kozarac, told me to get off the local bus and said, "Muslims are not allowed."

J.,[39] a thirty-nine-year-old Croatian woman from the town of Prijedor, recounted the transformation of Prijedor's local government and police and military forces. According to J.:

> The Serbian Democratic Party [Srpska Demokratska Stranka – SDS] took control of all institutions in Prijedor with the help of the JNA. The takeover occurred without bloodshed because the Muslims and Croats did not resist with weapons at first. The JNA staged a show of force in the streets, and the Serbian flag was put on the city council building and on the Hotel Prijedor, which was

---

[37] Mary Battiata, "A Town's Bloody 'Cleansing,'" *The Washington Post*, November 2, 1992.

[38] Interviewed by Helsinki Watch representatives in December 1992, in Zagreb, Croatia.

[39] Interviewed by Helsinki Watch representatives on October 15, 1992, in Zagreb, Croatia. The witness chose to withhold her name.

being used by the SDS as its headquarters. People claimed that Arkan's paramilitary forces[40] also had their headquarters in the hotel, but I cannot confirm that allegation. However, I can confirm that paramilitary units were roaming the streets in Prijedor. The insignia on their hats was that of the Serbian eagle and, therefore, they were commonly referred to as the "White Eagles." As part of the takeover, all the Croatian and Muslim police officers were told to go home and the Serbs took over the police force. The Serbian police officers replaced the Yugoslav red star on their hats with a Serbian cross. A curfew was then imposed. We could move about freely between 6:00 a.m. and 10:00 p.m. but not between 10:00 p.m. and 6:00 a.m.

In mid-May, non-Serbs in Prijedor were arbitrarily arrested by Serbian authorities, and attacks on surrounding villages started. According to J.:

> Silvije Šarić, the president of the local chapter of the Croatian Democratic Union [Hrvatska Demokratska Zajednica – HDZ], was among the first to be arrested. All prominent leaders or persons in Prijedor were the first to be arrested.

> Then, in mid-May, the first military attack staged by the Serbs in the area took place in the village of Kamičani, near the town of Kozarac. Kamičani is a very small village, and the Serbs attacked it because they claimed that the Muslims had first attacked them. However, we heard huge detonations for about four days; only the Serbs and the JNA have weapons that are capable of making such noise. Then we heard that the town of Kozarac also had become engulfed in the fighting.

---

[40] One of the Serbian paramilitary groups that is a party to the conflict is referred to as the "Tigers." The group is based in Serbia proper and is headed by Željko Ražnjatović, whose *nom de guerre* is "Arkan."

After the attack on Kozarac [from May 24 to 26], the "cleansing" started. The camp in Trnopolje was established, and we heard that it was a refugee camp. The Serbs then said that an attack on the villages of Čarakovo and Hambarine was being planned, i.e., that the Muslims were planning to attack the Serbs in those villages. But, in fact, after the attack on Kozarac, the "cleansing" of Hambarine commenced. Two Serbian soldiers were killed, and that was used to justify the destruction of the village and its inhabitants. The attack on Hambarine was primarily one involving the use of tanks. I should add that for about five months, a unit of tanks had been stationed in the village of Tomašića, which is just outside Prijedor. These tanks were brought from Banja Luka and taken directly to Tomašića. They bypassed Prijedor and only a few tanks roamed the streets in Prijedor at first. I assume that they didn't want the entire unit roaming around the town right away, but every day one more tank was seen on the streets of Prijedor. Eventually, fighting broke out in Prijedor as well.

When asked where she was during the attack on Prijedor, she replied:

I was in my apartment. It was 4:30 a.m. on May 30. I heard shooting on the outskirts of the city. At about 5:40 a.m., the battle had reached the city center. I heard detonations, and when I looked out the window I saw two soldiers from the Patriotic League[41] who were trying to reach the Hotel Prijedor. Paramilitaries were shooting from the windows, and I assume they wanted to shoot back. The battle lasted for about thirteen and a half hours, and I stayed in the house the entire time. At about 6:45 p.m., the shooting stopped, but I continued to hear

---

[41] The woman explained that the Patriotic League was a group of Croats and Muslims who served as a local militia. She claimed that they wore camouflage and the Bosnian coat of arms on their uniforms.

huge detonations. Suljanović Street was totally destroyed, and there were some destroyed tanks littering the streets. At about 7:30 p.m., the mosque was burned. I saw this from my window. Two soldiers dressed in JNA uniforms with JNA hats on their heads carried something that resembled a tent canvas. They walked into the mosque and then walked out. About ten minutes later, flames started to spew from the mosque.

The woman claimed that the regular JNA troops were active participants in the battle and that they fought openly on behalf of the Serbian forces. According to J., the military barracks in Prijedor were closed in the mid-1970s, but in 1992 a military base was again established by Serbian forces. She claims that the commander of the JNA during the battle in the Prijedor area was a man named Arsić and that he was not from Bosnia. She believed that he was either from Serbia or Montenegro. J. continued:

During the battles, a Serb named Zoran Karlica was wounded. He was taken to the military hospital in Belgrade, where he was said to have died from his wounds. His death was used as an excuse to form yet another paramilitary group, whose members called themselves "Karlica's soldiers" [*Karličini vojnici*]. This group sought to take revenge for Karlica's death and embarked on a huge "ethnic cleansing" campaign. The "cleansing" of the villages of Trnopolje and Kozarac lasted all of June, and there were constant attacks on the villages.

J. was arrested at home on June 14, at approximately 7:30 p.m. She was interrogated at the local police station. According to J.:

I was arrested because they claimed that they "found me at my military position," when in fact I was cleaning my carpet with a brush at the time. (We didn't have electricity, so I couldn't use the vacuum cleaner. Because it was being rationed, we only received electricity once a week.) Two Serbian soldiers came to my door and told me that I had to go for an "evaluation" and for an "informative discussion", i.e., an interrogation. I asked where they would interrogate me and I assumed it would be in the Prijedor police station, but the soldiers said they thought that I was to be taken to Omarska. The soldiers were very polite when they came to get me.

First we went to the Prijedor police station in a car. I was put in a flea hole [i.e., a cell] with steel doors. [The cell] contained a bed with dirty sheets. The room's walls were sprayed with fresh blood. Another man was in the room with me.[42] Two hours later, another man was brought into the cell, but I do not know his name. Two hours thereafter, three more people were brought into the cell. One was a man whom I did not know. The other two were women whom I knew.[43] In total, there were six of us in the cell, and two hours later we were asked if we wanted something for lunch.

J. was then taken to the camp at the Omarska mine.[44]

In September 1992, Radio Prijedor reportedly announced that Serbs were now a majority in the area and that they were willing to hold any referendums required.[45]

According to Selima,[46] a Muslim woman in her forties, when fighting broke out in Prijedor on May 30, Serbian soldiers came to her

---

[42] The witness identified the man by name.

[43] The witness identified the two women by name.

[44] See section below for the witness' account of her treatment at the Omarska detention camp.

[45] Mary Battiata, "A Town's Bloody 'Cleansing,'" *The Washington Post*, November 2, 1992.

[46] Interviewed by Helsinki Watch representatives on February 22, 1993, in Zagreb, Croatia. The woman provided her name to Helsinki Watch representatives but asked that it remain confidential. The name used here is a pseudonym, and other identifying features have been deleted to protect the confidentiality of the witness.

home and arrested her, members of her family and others in her neighborhood. Selima testified that the men who arrested the people were local Serbs who wore a *kokarda*[47] on their hats. She said that many had formerly been employed at the Omarska mine. Selima was detained for four days in a former local government buiding and then released. According to Selima:

> [During the fighting in Prijedor on May 30,] we could hear shooting and screams everywhere. They [i.e., Serbian soldiers] were forcing people to come out of their homes. Women, small children and elderly persons — they were all forced to come out of their apartments. They separated the men from the women and children. . . . They put all of us — we were all from the same neighborhood — into buses. Before we left, soldiers entered the bus and said, "If there are any Serbs on this bus, feel free to step off. Muslims and Croats must stay." It was terrible, the way they said that. Then, all my Serbian neighbors got off the bus and we stayed on. We were taken to Orlovača but, at that point, we didn't know where we were being taken.

Selima claims that Orlovača was the site of a bulding that had formerly been used by the local government. The building had been transformed into a detention facility for women and children. Selima was interned in Orlovača for four days and was then sent home. She claims that she and others were not physically mistreated in Orlovača but that they were frequently threatened. According to Selima:

> I stayed there [i.e., in Orlovača] for four days and during that time I was not beaten or tortured. They [i.e., the guards] were cursing and insulting us all the time but, as far as I know, there was no physical violence. On the fifth day, I was taken back home. They told us that we

---

[47] The *kokarda* (*kokarde* in the plural) is a Serbian nationalist symbol using a double-headed eagle. During World War II, it was often equated with Serbian Četnik forces loyal to the Serbian king in exile. Serbian paramilitary forces in the current conflict have incorporated the insignia into their uniforms.

were kept in Orlovača because they wanted to protect us from Muslim extremists. It was a lie. When I came back to Prijedor, I saw that my house had been robbed and all my valuables were missing.

Selima remained in her home until June 11, when she again was arrested and subsequently taken to the Keraterm, Omarska and Trnopolje camps.[48]

Banja Luka

During a visit to Banja Luka in August 1992, Helsinki Watch representatives spoke to Muslims who said that a succession of five draft notices had been issued to men in the Banja Luka area since the beginning of the war in April 1992. Mobilization calls were reportedly broadcast on the radio. Those who responded were given mobilization slips, which allowed them to go to work. Those who refused to join the [Bosnian] Serb Army — mostly Muslims and Croats — were not given the necessary papers that allowed them to enter their places of employment. Because they were not able to go to work, many were fired from their jobs. Those interviewed said that until recently, they have "lived like rats," not daring to leave their homes. The Muslims reported that businesses owned by Muslims had been destroyed and that the frequent and random shooting of weapons into the air was meant to intimidate the non-Serbian population in the area, heightening their fear of attack and hastening their departure from the region.

During its visit, Helsinki Watch received reports that notices had been posted at the Banja Luka bus station stating that, unless Croats and Muslims presented documents from the local military stating that they had agreed to leave the area permanently, bus tickets would not be sold to non-Serbs.

Blagaj

Blagaj, located between Bosanski Novi and Prijedor, is and was almost exclusively Muslim. Enes, a young Muslim man from the village

---

[48] For an account of the witness's experience in the camps, refer to the relevant section below.

of Blagaj[49] believes Serbian forces staged an attack, implicating Muslims in an assault on Serbian police officers. Enes believed that the staged attack was used to justify a counterattack by Serbian forces on Blagaj.[50] According to Enes:

> On May 9, the village was surrounded by Serbian artillery from all sides. Serbian police fabricated a Muslim attack on their police force. I saw a Serbian military patrol car approach Blagaj from Bosanski Novi and then switch off its lights. Then I saw the police throw a grenade at the car, and in response, other police officers started the shooting. At that point the artillery attack began on the village, as though in response to some provocation.

Helsinki Watch has not been able to confirm whether the oncoming car posed a significant military threat to the Serbian police or whether it actually belonged to Serbian forces. It remains unclear whether Serbian forces encircled the village with weaponry or roadblocks. Nevertheless, the increased military presence prior to the siege indicates that Serbian forces had anticipated an attack. In response to a car that may or may not have posed a threat, Serbian forces attacked the entire village of Blagaj, thereby using excessive and disproportionate force to respond to the posed threat.

Enes continued:

---

[49] Interviewed by Helsinki Watch representatives in October 1992 in Varaždin, Croatia. The witness chose to withhold his name, and the name used here is a pseudonym.

[50] Claims that each party to the conflict intentionally attack and destroy their own forces and civilians are widespread throughout the former Yugoslavia. Such allegations are rarely proven to be correct. However, the *staging* of attacks appears to have been practiced by Serbian forces in Croatia. During a visit to the Vukovar area in January 1992, JNA soldiers and others to which Helsinki Watch spoke claimed that Serbian paramilitary groups often staged attacks and blamed them on the non-Serbian population, thereby providing the justification for the forcible displacement of non-Serbs in Serbian-occupied areas of eastern Croatia.

The next day, sixteen mortars fell during the artillery attack. I heard the radio broadcast that "a military patrol was attacked by people from Blagaj." It called upon the people of Blagaj to surrender their weapons, but we couldn't comply with the demand because none of us had any weapons.

The next day we were given a deadline. If we didn't produce our weapons by 2:00 p.m., another attack would be launched. Everyone ran into the woods outside of the village, and we spent all night in the forest. At 5:00 a.m., the rain began. Many young children, men and women were huddled together.

When the next attack stopped, the Serb[ian forces] called people into their houses because they wanted to search them. The infantry entered the village and began the searches. They destroyed the mosque and blew up several houses owned by men they suspected of having done something. They then occupied the village and raised their flag.

Several days after Blagaj was occupied, fighting in Prijedor erupted and Serbian soldiers were killed during the latter battle. Enes claims that, in response to the deaths of Serbian soldiers in Prijedor, Muslims were killed in Blagaj. Blagaj's residents sought protection at the local police station. The officers claimed that they were not a police station but rather a checkpoint and therefore unable to protect Blagaj's residents. Eventually, the police left the area. Enes claimed that whenever Serbian soldiers died at the front, there would be a wave of revenge killings against Muslims.

According to Enes, his village became a refugee center for as many as 7,000 Muslims from villages in the Japra valley who had fled to Blagaj. However, Serbian attacks on the village did not stop. According to Enes:

It was fine during the day, but at night they would try to terrify people. Artillery attacks would begin, and soldiers would go through the streets shooting. Food shortages began. The way out was blocked from all sides. There was no explanation for the blockade. We tried to telephone the Bosanski Novi police station, but no help came.

In mid-June, soldiers from the self-proclaimed "Serbian Republic" arrived in the village with a list of approximately 250 Muslims who were designated for deportation to a predominantly Serbian village nearby called Svodna. Enes and his family were among those deported.[51]

Enes's sister, Melida,[52] said that the family stayed in Svodna for one day and then returned to Blagaj in the evening. She told Helsinki Watch representatives that, when they returned to the village, they saw about four or five corpses on their way to Blagaj. She testified that Serbian soldiers arrived with bulldozers the next day, to bury the bodies.

According to Enes and his sister, the people who remained in Blagaj were allowed to bring food to men detained at the stadium in Bosanski Novi for two days only. When they were in Blagaj, youths claim, they were used as an unpaid work force by the Serbs. According to Melida:

> We did things such as gather hay for them. Serbs would come and take everything they could. We had to have special permission to go to Bosanski Novi. We could see the convoy of men from the stadium leaving but we couldn't go with them. Some people from the city got in

---

[51] Enes claims that, after the 250 people were taken to Svodna, the remaining inhabitants of Blagaj were divided according to age and sex and taken to Doboj in cattle cars. The men were then taken back to a detention facility in a stadium in Bosanski Novi, and the women and children were allowed to flee to Travnik. Enes also claims that Serbian forces summarily executed residents of, and burned homes in, Blagaj as they were deporting people from the village. Helsinki Watch has confirmed that non-Serbian residents of northwest Bosnia were deported to Doboj and that prisoners were detained in a stadium in Bosanski Novi. Helsinki Watch has not been able to identify residents of Blagaj who were deported to Doboj or detained in Bosanski Novi.

[52] Interviewed by Helsinki Watch representatives in October 1992 in Varaždin, Croatia. The witness chose to withhold her name, and the name used here is a pseudonym.

touch with the UNPROFOR on the Croatian side [of the River Una] by swimming across the river. In the end, we joined a convoy and spent seven days in Dvor [a Serbian–occupied town in Croatia], but we were attacked and had to leave.

Hambarine

Hambarine is a village on the outskirts of Prijedor. It is considered by some to be a suburb of the city. According to Haris,[53] a fifty-six-year-old Muslim house painter from the village of Hambarine, one of a chain of six predominantly Muslim villages with approximately eight hundred households each. Hambarine is on a road that connects Prijedor with the Ljubija mine, giving it some strategic importance. According to witnesses interviewed by Helsinki Watch representatives, Hambarine was the first village in the area to be attacked.

On the evening of May 22, a radio broadcast warned that the village would be attacked the following day at 12:15 p.m. unless it surrendered. According to Haris:

> The attack took place at the exact day and time as had been announced. They attacked the village with tanks, cannons, mortars and howitzers. The attack lasted until the evening, when infantry units entered with [vehicles.][54] Then they divided Hambarine into two sections; the part which they claimed for themselves was the section that led to the [Ljubija] mine. They looted and burned the houses and killed a lot of people in that zone. The attacks later progressed to the other part [of

---

[53] Interviewed by Helsinki Watch representatives in October 1992 in a refugee camp in Croatia. The witness chose to withhold his name, and the name used here is a pseudonym.

[54] The witness used the word *transport*. In Serbian/Croatian, the word *transporteri* refers to armored personnel carriers (APCs). Presumably, the witness was describing an APC, but his pronunciation of the word was somewhat unclear.

Hambarine] and to other villages, such as Rakovčani, Rizvanovići and Bišćani.[55]

According to Haris, Serbian troops looted all the houses in Hambarine. He said that the soldiers were accompanied by women and children, all of whom quarreled among themselves over who would get which articles. Haris did not recognize anyone, and he surmised that they were probably from outside the area. He reported that the soldiers had covered their faces. Haris believes that the soldiers belonged to the [Bosnian] Serb Army. However, he added that the soldiers wore a variety of insignia, making it difficult for him to distinguish to which military or paramilitary force they belonged.

According to Haris, the Muslims stayed in the villages until July 19, during which time Serbian soldiers continued to rob the villagers of their property.

On July 20, Serbian forces surrounded Hambarine and neighboring villages in the morning and then entered the villages and started beating people, both women and men. Haris reported that many people were killed during the attack on July 20 and that those who survived were taken to detention camps.

A.H., a thirty-eight-year-old[56] resident of Hambarine,[57] said that he was in his home with his family when he was arrested by Serbian soldiers on July 20, 1992:

> The Serbian army arrested us in the morning. They were either dressed in camouflage uniforms or civilian clothing. Others were dressed in the old Yugoslav Army

---

[55] Helsinki Watch has interviewed former residents of these three villages who have confirmed that their respective villages had been attacked. See sections below. (The accounts regarding the forcible displacement of Rizvanovići and Bišćani follow. The attack on Rakovčani is described by a woman who was raped in the village. For her account, see the section of this report on rape.)

[56] Interviewed by Helsinki Watch representatives on October 17, 1992, in a refugee camp in Croatia.

[57] The witness claims that approximately 5,000 people lived in the village, which is about four kilometers from the city of Prijedor.

[JNA] uniforms, but they either had the Serbian flag or a *kokarda* on their hats. I saw one armored personnel carrier. They told us to put our hands up, and they hit my brother in the head with the butt of a gun. We walked one hundred meters and, as we walked, we heard shooting. They cursed at us while we walked and, after we got one hundred meters from my house, they started to divide people [into two categories]: those who would stay in the village and those who would be taken to a camp. A man said that he had a Serbian friend, and ten of the soldiers started to kick him.

According to Haris:

I would estimate that about 50 percent of our people were killed at this time. I had to walk on corpses and through gore and I counted bodies in the hundreds. There were bodies everywhere, lying on the roads, in the fields, in gardens. Thousands of people were rounded up and sent to camps.

On that day — July 20 — they separated men from women and took the men to Keraterm. We were rounded up at gathering points where we waited with our hands over our heads.

The group of people of which A.H. was part were taken to the mosque in the village of Rakovčani via bus. According to A.H.:

They told us to put our heads between our legs, and we saw nothing. An unarmed soldier in his fifties walked up and down the aisle in the bus. There were other soldiers in the bus but I don't know how many. They started to beat us. We went over the bridge to Prijedor. Someone [from outside] asked, "What are you driving?" and the driver responded, "We're driving fresh meat." We got to the factory in Keraterm, which is about two kilometers from Prijedor.

Haris also was taken to the Keraterm camp, where he remained until August 5. Both men were transferred to the Trnopolje camp and eventually left Bosnia on October 1.[58]

Trnopolje

Ismet, a forty-year-old Muslim resident of Trnopolje,[59] located in the municipality of Prijedor, said that the residents of his village were forcibly displaced by soldiers of the self-proclaimed "Army of the Serbian Republic," some of whom were dressed in camouflage and others who wore a JNA uniform. He reported that the village's residents were expelled from their homes incrementally, from May 26 throughout June and possibly later. The Trnopolje camp had been established in late May and people expelled from their homes were interned in the camp, which was very close to some of the detainees' homes. He said that women and children were first interned in the Trnopolje camp. According to Ismet:

> On June 9, my wife and I were picked up. I was sent to the school [the camp grounds] and my wife [was sent to Travnik] on a train. We were in the camp for ten days. They arrested people from about twenty or thirty houses and took them to the camp. They looted the houses for about ten days, but they didn't burn them down. [The soldiers] left the camp once, to bring back the stolen goods, and then they returned for a second round of looting. I wasn't there while they were looting but I saw them returning with the stolen materials while I was in the camp. Most of the men doing the looting were local Serbs, who wore olive-colored army pants; sometimes they wore civilian clothing, and they were armed with guns and automatic weapons. A Major Kuruzović, who

---

[58] For an account of the witnesses' treatment in Keraterm and Trnopolje, see relevant sections below.

[59] Interviewed by Helsinki Watch representatives on October 17, 1992, in a refugee camp in Croatia. The witness chose to withhold his name, and the name used here is a pseudonym.

was an officer at the camp, worked with the looters. The camp was about 800 meters from my home.[60]

S.S. is a forty-year-old Muslim woman from Trnopolje who worked in a factory before the war. She has one daughter and three sons, one of whom was two months old at the time of her interview with Helsinki Watch and the Women's Rights Project.[61] Her husband had been detained in Keraterm and Trnopolje but was eventually resettled in a third country. S.S. had not been reunited with her husband at the time of the interview.

S.S. reported that she was forced from her home in Trnopolje after it was burned and then was interned in the village camp. According to S.S.:

> We were forced to abandon our home on June 28 when our house was burned. There was "ethnic cleansing" and my husband was taken to a detention camp. We left our house but not the village. We moved all the time because of the shelling, looking for shelter with our neighbors and children. We would hide in cellars.
>
> [My house was burned at] about 4:00 a.m., before dawn. We weren't in our house; we were staying together in groups because we were afraid of the infantry. The house in which I was staying was only one hundred meters from our home. We weren't sleeping; we were all dressed because of the shelling — you had to be ready to go to the woods. My daughter asked for water and, when I went to get it, a man said that our house was burning. We left the house in which we were staying when the shooting ended and went to the woods. All night soldiers were walking through the village burning houses.

---

[60] See relevant section below for the witness's account of his treatment in the Trnopolje camp.

[61] Interviewed on January 16, 1993, in a refugee camp in Croatia.

S.S. claims that men were summarily executed in the village.

> The army came to the village to take the men to detention centers. There was a lot of blood on the streets. They killed and tortured them. I saw it happen; they put the men together and called out names. Those called by name were taken to a barn, and all we could hear were gunshots. I didn't know where my husband was for eight days, then I heard that he was in Keraterm.

> In my village, about 180 men were killed. The army put all men in the center of the village. After the killing, the women took care of the bodies and identified them. The older men buried the bodies.

S.S. identified some of the men from her village who were killed: Adham Elez, Halil Elez, Amir Elez, Rifat Elez, Salih Elez, Edin Elez, Fikrat Hodžić, Munib Hodžić and Nermin Hodžić.

S.S. testified that, after the men were executed or taken to detention camps, Serbian soldiers pillaged the area. According to S.S.:

> After the men were taken away, soldiers came to the village to steal from us — our jewelry, money, fuel, bicycles. We had to give them everything. They would come to our houses asking for car keys and would take what they wanted. They asked my neighbor for 2,000 German marks. They threatened to kill my son if she [the neighbor] didn't give them the money. They knew us and knew that this woman had money. People who were rich were killed on the spot, not taken to detention centers. I didn't see anyone raped, but I saw two women killed in front of their house.[62]

The women were eventually taken to the camp in their village. According to S.S.:

---

[62] The witness identified the two women who had been killed as Mevla and Senija Redžić, who were mother and daughter-in-law.

> One day, a soldier came and told us to go away because we had no right to be there. He said there would be no Muslims in the area and that we should be ready to go by 10:00 a.m. or else the Red Berets and White Eagles[63] would come and kill us. Soldiers of the "Serbian Republic" told us to leave. They all were our neighbors. They just put on uniforms and acted as if they didn't know us. At the end, we were all gathered together and taken to [the] Trnopolje [camp].

Kevljani

According to Sulejman,[64] a young Muslim farm worker from Kevljani, in the municipality of Prijedor:

> Kevljani is a Muslim village that was lumped together with Omarska so it [Omarska] could benefit from municipal services, such as [a better] school system. The towns are "enemies," however, and, since the elections in 1990, Serbs from Omarska terrorized Kevljani. In particular, a taxi driver nicknamed "Cigo" ["Gypsy"] formed his own squad of Serbian extremists and they took charge of my village.

B.J.,[65] a former resident of Kevljani, reported that about 150 families lived in the predominantly Muslim village. On May 26, at approximately 2:00 p.m., Serbian forces took control of the village. B.J.

---

[63] Members of Arkan's paramilitary group are often called "Red Berets" because they wear red berets. The "White Eagles" [*Beli Orlovi*] are another paramilitary group whose purported leader is Vojislav Šešelj, a member of parliament in Serbia proper.

[64] Interviewed by Helsinki Watch representatives in October 1992, in a refugee camp in Croatia. The witness chose to withhold his name, and the name used here is a pseudonym.

[65] Interviewed by Helsinki Watch representatives on October 17, 1992, in a refugee camp in Croatia.

claims that many of Kevljani's inhabitants were taken to Trnopolje. From Trnopolje, they were deported from the area. According to B.J.:

> They entered the village and took all the inhabitants to Trnopolje. I don't know how many soldiers there were. They belonged to the Serbian Army and were armed with automatic weapons. Three tanks were also brought into the village. They surrounded the village, set up buses and took all the people to Trnopolje, which is about ten kilometers from our village.
>
> When we approached the train station, they divided the men from the women and children. We had been all together, and convoys of people left the area. They "cleansed" each village in the area — one by one.

According to Sulejman, Kevljani was attacked on May 23, the same day as Kozarac.

> Everyone spent two days in shelters. We wanted to go to Kozarac to hide, but the way was blocked. On Tuesday morning, we were told to go to Prijedor for two days; the Serbian forces claimed that they needed to inspect the village for weapons.

The Serbian forces reportedly assured the villagers that they could return to Kevljani after it had been searched. However, the inhabitants were interned in camps in the area. Sulejman continued:

> We were put on a bus and driven to Prijedor. Six buses were filled with men, women and children, but there was still not enough transportation, so people used their own cars and trucks. We spent the night sleeping in a sports hall. The next day the women and children were separated [from the men], and the men were put back on the bus and taken to Omarska.[66]

---

[66] For an account of the treatment of prisoners in the Omarska camp, refer to the relevant section below.

Kozarac

The approximately 25,000 residents of the town of Kozarac, in the municipality of Prijedor, were predominantly Muslim, although a small Croatian and Serbian population lived in the town as well. Kozarac officials claim that, on May 9, Serbian authorities in the city of Prijedor gave the leaders of Kozarac seven days to sign a loyalty oath to the self-proclaimed "Serbian Republic" or they would be considered a paramilitary threat.[67] In late May, Serbian forces increased their military presence near Kozarac, severed the town's telephone links and threatened its residents with attack. Despite the residents' efforts to negotiate with Serbian authorities in Prijedor, Serbian forces attacked Kozarac and interned its population between May 26 and 28. The residents of Kozarac at first tried to resist the Serbian offensive but eventually were forced to surrender. Kozarac's intellectuals and prominent citizens were interned in the Omarska or Keratarm camps and others were taken to Trnopolje. Some were summarily executed immediately after the town fell to Serbian forces. Kozarac has since been looted and burned and remains "off limits" to journalists and others who travel to the region.[68]

---

[67] Mary Battiata, "A Town's Bloody 'Cleansing,'" *The Washington Post*, November 2, 1992.

[68] Despite restrictions on travel to Kozarac, several foreign journalists have visited Kozarac or its immediate environs without Serbian authorization. According to a correspondent for *The Washington Post* who visited the town after its pillage:

> The destruction of the town is clearly visible from the highway — mile after mile of scorched buildings, collapsed red-tile roofs and houses reduced to shoulder-high piles of rubble.
>
> But six months after the attack, the ruins of Kozarac are still sealed, guarded by heavily armed and hostile Serb soldiers. Militant Serb authorities in Prijedor do not allow interviews, visitors or photographs.

(See Mary Battiata, "A Town's Bloody 'Cleansing,'" *The Washington Post*, November 2, 1992. See also the British Channel Four television documentary segment "Dispatches," by Ed Harris titled *Bosnia: A Town Called Kozarac*, produced by Goldhawk Productions, 1992.)

Before the siege of Kozarac, Serbian authorities began consolidating control over the town. Prior to the May 26 attack on Kozarac, Serbian forces increased their military presence in the area and cut off the town's communication with neighboring villages. According to K.D., a Muslim resident of Kozarac:[69]

> Two months before the siege, there had been movements of weapons and military reorganization, so one could see that trouble was brewing, but we all thought it could be settled peacefully. On May 23 or 24,[70] the Serbs cut all phone lines, although the Muslims were still able to communicate directly with the Bosnian government through the radio at the Kozarac police station. Ten days before the attack, we talked by phone to someone in the [Bosnian] Interior Ministry to ask for help, but no one thought the threat was serious.

H.H., a twenty-seven-year-old Muslim, confirmed that tensions were felt before the outbreak of fighting:[71]

> Kozarac was the biggest Muslim town in the area, and there were several provocations before the war. On May 22, they [i.e., Serbian forces] brought two tanks and two cannons into the village, and they disconnected the electricity. The telephones were disconnected a couple of days earlier.

---

[69] Interviewed by Helsinki Watch representatives in October 1992 in a refugee camp in Croatia.

[70] It is unclear exactly on which day the phone lines were cut. Although this witness claims that the lines were severed on May 23 or 24, another witness claims that they were disconnected earlier. Foreign press reports claim that telephone service was cut off on May 14. (See Mary Battiata, "A Town's Bloody 'Cleansing,'" *The Washington Post*, November 2, 1992.)

[71] H.H. was interviewed by Helsinki Watch representatives in December 1992 in Zagreb, Croatia.

> Draft-age Muslim men were not allowed to leave Kozarac. The police demanded that we surrender any guns, while we said that we only wanted to defend Kozarac and we would not advance [against their forces].
>
> About a month before the war started, Serbs took over the police station in Prijedor and other municipal offices. In the bars in Kozarac, they used to sing Serbian and Četnik songs and they drove around in cars that had "Wolves of Vukovar" [*Vukovi Vukovara*][72] written on them.

K.D. had been a member of the civilian defense council of Kozarac, a community board charged with organizing shelters and alerts in times of crisis. It was responsible for negotiating with the Serbian authorities in Prijedor. According to K.D., the siege of Kozarac followed what he referred to as "the military coup in Prijedor." According to K.D.:

> Serbian forces took over the police station and asked each Croat and Muslim to sign a loyalty declaration. These soldiers from Prijedor asked the Kozarac police to wear their party's [Srpska Demokratska Stranka – SDS] insignia. Naturally, the Muslims and Croats[73] wanted no part of this party-affiliated police force. Every other day, we were given ultimatums that we had to sign declarations of loyalty or else Kozarac would be attacked. In the meantime, the civilian defense council was trying to negotiate a peaceful solution.

---

[72] Vukovar is a city in eastern Croatia that fell to Serbian forces in November 1992. When Serbian and Yugoslav forces destroyed the city, hundreds of residents were summarily executed after the fighting and thousands remain missing.

[73] The witness claims that the population of Kozarac included about 25,000 Muslims and five hundred Croats. He did not specify the number of Serbian residents in Kozarac.

K.D. testified that officers of the JNA were involved in the attack on Kozarac. He identified Major Arsić as the highest-ranking member of the "Serbian Army" and the man responsible for planning the attack of Kozarac.[74] K.D. also claimed that a Serbian commander named Zeljaje, the commander of JNA reservists from twelve municipalities in the area, also was involved in the siege. According to K.D.:

> Major Arsić, a JNA officer and ex-commander of the federal barracks in Prijedor, took all the weapons from the territorial defense unit [*teritorijalna odbrana*] and gave them to the Serbian Army. . . . Everything became Serbian — radio, health services, etc. Kozarac was surrounded; you couldn't leave.[75]

Helsinki Watch representatives interviewed R.K., an eighteen-year-old Muslim woman, a student from Kozarac.[76] R.K. said that several days before the attack on Kozarac, Serbian forces announced a planned offensive over the radio. According to R.K.:

---

[74] It is unclear whether the witness referred to Arsić as the commander of JNA forces in Kozarac or the self-proclaimed Bosnian Serb Army. An earlier witness identified Arsićas a commander of the JNA during battles in the Prijedor area. (See the section on forced displacement of residents of Prijedor.)

[75] It remains unclear whether Serbian forces had surrounded the town with weapons or whether the residents of Kozarac were afraid to leave the town because they were "surrounded" by Serbian-controlled territory.

[76] Interviewed in Posušje, Bosnia-Hercegovina, on October 26, 1992. At the time of the interview, two of R.K.'s brothers were being detained at the Bosanska Gradiška prison, and another brother was detained in the Manjača camp. Her father had recently been released from the Trnopolje detention area. She claims that her father and one of her brothers were survivors of the massacre at Vlašić. Helsinki Watch representatives interviewed two survivors. It is believed that at least seven more men survived the massacre, one of whom died after the escape and four of whom reportedly have been resettled in Western Europe. R.K.'s father resettled in Western Europe and may have been among the known or unknown survivors. Her brother was recaptured and remained interned in a Serbian prison at the time of Helsinki Watch's interview. (See preceeding section for an account of the massacre at Vlašić.)

On Sunday, May 24, there was an announcement on Radio Prijedor that the Serbs were going to shell the area until May 27.

On May 26, while a delegation from the Kozarac civilian defense council was negotiating with Serbian authorities in Prijedor, Serbian forces attacked Kozarac, and the siege of the town began — at approximately 2:00 p.m.[77] H.H. stated that over three thousand shells were fired into the village and that the attacks were launched from Prijedor and eight surrounding Serbian villages (i.e., Jakupovići, Janjići, Balte, Božići, Orlovci, Žuti Put, Benkovac and Jarug.)

When the attacks on Kozarac increased in strength, many fled to the forest, where they were found by Serbian forces. K.B., a forty-nine-year-old Muslim schoolteacher for mentally retarded persons,[78] described her flight from Kozarac during the attack:

> Kozarac was surrounded. People panicked and fled to Kozara [a mountain north of Kozarac]. There were many old people and children who could not walk. My schizophrenic brother, my seventy-nine-year-old mother and I also left.
>
> My brother was killed. He got angry and ran out of hiding and was shot. Due to the constant shelling, we decided to surrender. Draft-age men were immediately

---

[77] K.D. was not present during the negotiations but claims to have met three members of the delegation from Kozarac during their subsequent internment in Trnopolje. According to K.D., the three delegation members claimed that they were sitting in a room with a Serbian commander named Željaja, who was part of the JNA and allegedly commanded JNA reservists in twelve municipalities in the region. Željaja allegedly gave the delegation an ultimatum: either it signed a loyalty pledge to the Serbian authorities or Kozarac would be attacked. The delegation asked for two days to consult with the villagers. In response, the members of the delegation were placed in a cellar and Kozarac was attacked.

[78] Interviewed by Helsinki Watch representatives in December 1992 in Zagreb, Croatia.

separated from us, while we [women, children and the elderly] were forced to go in the direction of Prijedor.

R.K. described the attack on Kozarac:

> When the shelling started, we were drinking coffee in the garden, and then we went to the basement. We spent a good part of the next two days in the basement, especially at night. Two or three pieces of shrapnel flew in. I, my mother, my two sisters-in-law, my fifteen-year-old brother and five children — the oldest of whom was four years old — were in the basement. My father and the other men in my family were at their military positions.

A doctor who was on duty in Kozarac at the time of its siege reported that, after two days of shelling in Kozarac, the town's clinic was moved to a sheltered house in a valley. The house had a large cellar, which the doctors believed would afford some safety from the attacks and the necessary medical equipment, and patients were transferred to the house. According to the doctor:

> The attack [on Kozarac] took place on Sunday morning. That morning, two women delivered babies. The next job was amputating the finger of a boy who had shot himself with a hunting rifle, which many of the boys had. When the shelling started, many wounded people started coming to the clinic — even one of the wounded Serbian soldiers came. Because the clinic was coming under fire, we moved to a motel but then moved back [to the house] again. There was no special mark on the health clinic, but everyone knew it was a medical institution and there were ambulances parked out front. A lot of wounded women and children came. People lost their legs after a shell hit them as they were leaving the shelter and running toward the forest. The soldiers were shooting at every moving thing, with no discrimination among targets. I spent twenty-four hours in this clinic. We had some defense in Kozarac, but it was a very small number

of people who couldn't withstand cannons and heavy artillery.

According to R.K.:

> On the third day of fighting, my brother came back to the house and told us to flee to the forest. I went with my mother, father and the little girl [her brother's newborn daughter]. We hid for an entire day and night until about 3:00 a.m. or 4:00 a.m., when a messenger came to us and said that we had to leave the forest and that the men had to stay. I didn't know this messenger. He said that the village would only be "cleansed" for two days and that we could return thereafter. He said, "You should descend into the village and they will put you in a hall in Prijedor, and then you can return in two days."

Although some were captured in the forest, others surrendered and gathered on the main road, where men were separated from women, children and the elderly. Most of the town's residents were taken to detention camps; others were summarily executed in the village. According to H.H.:

> They demanded that we give up our weapons and that all the civilians surrender. Beginning on the morning of May 26, large groups of civilians holding white flags started returning to the intersection on the road that led to Banja Luka and Prijedor.

> We were met by the Četniks, who were separating women and children from the men. Many of the men were killed on the spot — mostly over old, private disputes. The rest of us were put on buses and they started to beat us. The people who were beating us were Čedo, a military policeman from Orlovac; Goran Borovnica from Kozarac; Vaso Majkić; Nedjo Kos; and Goran Jesić — all [of whom were] from Prijedor.

> There were many buses, and they were all owned by the Autotransport–Prijedor [company]. We were the very

first prisoners taken to Keraterm. We were beaten terribly. After two days, they put us on buses and transferred us to Omarska.[79]

According to Jasmina, a Muslim woman from Kozarac:[80]

People were killed when the villagers were first rounded up and while we were traveling in the convoy. Soldiers pointed a gun at one of our babies and told us to give up all we had.

My own grandmother — who was 107 years old — was killed during the initial evacuation from Kozarac. She said she was just too old to go on any convoy. The soldiers injured her first and then they burned her in her house. All the others who tried to stay in their houses were killed.

According to R.K., a Major Kuruzović was the leader of the attack on Kozarac:[81]

Kuruzović told us that his forces would not attack us and that they would allow us to leave. We picked up our things, got on tractors and went toward Prijedor. There

---

[79] In October 1992, Helsinki Watch representatives interviewed a Muslim family from Kozarac that had fled to Posušje, Bosnia-Hercegovina. According to the family, people spent three days and nights during the attack either in shelters or in the forest. When they received the order to surrender, they joined a convoy and were taken to Trnopolje for two days. They were then placed in cattle cars bound for Doboj (in northeastern Bosnia), where they were exchanged for Serbian forces. The family had brothers who were or had been detained in the Omarska and Manjača camps.

[80] Interviewed by Helsinki Watch representatives in October 1992 in Livno, Bosnia-Hercegovina. The witness chose to withhold her name, and the name used here is a pseudonym.

[81] An earlier witness claims that Major Arsić was reponsible for planning the attack of Kozarac.

were many buses, full of women and children. We were in our own vehicle. When we were about halfway between Kozarac and Prijedor, we stopped for about an hour and the [Serbian forces] divided the men aged sixteen and older. One took out two knives and started sharpening one against the other. He asked, "Do you want to be killed and tortured?" They told us to get off the tractor with our belongings because they wanted to search our things. Then the women and children were loaded onto a truck and the men traveled behind us.

K.D. confirmed R.K.'s account of the exodus of Kozarac's residents:

All civilians in Kozarac had to leave. Twenty-four thousand people got on the road toward Prijedor, forming a four- to five-kilometer-long line along the road. Halfway to Prijedor, we were met by the Serbian police, who started to set houses on fire. They promised not to touch anyone with "clean hands." The Serb[ian forces] started dividing the men from the women and children. Serbian neighbors began to point fingers at some people, and those persons were killed immediately.

According to K.D., as the procession of people went along the road, men in various uniforms watched from the balconies of houses on both sides. K.D. claims that the uniformed men wore various insignia that belonged to the "White Eagles of Knin." However, K.P. was not able to verify whether these were actual paramilitary forces because "all these insignia had become very trendy and many people have started to wear them." According to K.D., approximately three hundred soldiers remained on the road. Of the three hundred, K.D. recognized approximately 250 soldiers as locals but he claims not to have known the remaining fifty.

Mehmet, a Muslim from Kozarac in his late fifties,[82] testified that the town's defenders surrendered machine guns, rifles, pistols and some antitank weapons. The Serbian forces pulled aside disarmed

---

[82] Interviewed by Helsinki Watch representatives in October 1992 in Posušje, Bosnia-Hercegovina.

combatants and wealthy residents suspected of having acquired the weapons. Mehmet reported that these persons were taken to two adjoining houses on the side of the road and executed in the houses. Among those killed were Fadil Mujkanović, an acquaintance of Mehmet, and a man named Blažević, who owned a shop called "Mazalica." According to Mehmet:

> They were taking people out of the convoy who had dirty clothes [and so looked as if they had been fighting]. My son-in-law's father was killed. They took my new Mercedes. One of my neighbors was taken into the house but a Serbian friend spoke up, so he was released.

According to R.K., when the villagers reached the village of Susići, some men were summarily executed and people were separated and placed on buses. The women and children were taken to Trnopolje, and the men followed thereafter.[83] According to R.K.:

> While we were in Susići during that hour, the men were taken into a house. I saw a neighbor named Meho taken from the line and beaten as he was being taken into the house. Then I heard gunfire. I never saw Meho again. They would take men into the house and then kill them. I remember twenty or twenty-five such cases but we couldn't look at the house; I only managed to steal a quick glance every now and then.

According to Jasmina:

> There was a six-kilometer-long convoy of people from Kozarac on the road, where they separated women and children from the men. Kozarac is a very big place and everything was destroyed. In the middle of that road, there was a house in which people were being beaten to death and people were being cut with bottles. We heard noise at that point. They were going through lists and

---

[83] The witness was unclear about whether or not the division took place in Kozarac, in Susići or somewhere in between.

picking out people from the convoy to kill. "Šarac," "Mumin" and Bećir Medunjanin — who was the leader of the SDA[84] in Kozarac — were killed during the convoy['s exodus].

The attack appears to have been led by Serbian paramilitary forces and forces of the newly-formed "Army of the Serbian Republic." According to Edin,[85] a Muslim repairman from Kozarac, the forces responsible for the siege of, and subsequent abuses in, his village wore Yugoslav Army uniforms and most were neighbors:

> The Serbs carrying out this operation wore the five-pointed [JNA] star on their caps and no other insignias. This particular major's unit was specially marked with a badge or emblem that said "Karlica Zoran 72" or, in other words, the seventy-two-man unit under this major. The full name of the unit is the "'Karlica Zoran 72' reconnaissance platoon." There were no rank insignia visible on the shoulders or chest. This unit wore

---

[84] The Muslim-based Party for Democratic Action (Stranka Demokratske Akcije — SDA) won a majority eighty-six seats in parliament, the Serbian Democratic party (Srpska Demokratska Stranka — SDS) received seventy-two; the Croatian Democratic Party (Hrvatska Demokratska Zajednica — HDZ) received forty-four; and other parties received thirty-three. Candidates from the three aforementioned parties were elected to seats in the republic's collective presidency. (See National Republican Institute for International Affairs, *The 1990 Elections in the Republics of Yugoslavia*, pp. 35-47; "Democratic Action Party Wins Majority," Tanjug Yugoslav News Agency report of December 12, 1990, as reported in Foreign Broadcast Information Service *Daily Report* [hereafter FBIS], December 13, 1990, p. 47; "Further on Election Results," Tanjug Yugoslav News Agency report of December 12, 1990, as reported in FBIS on December 13, 1990, pp. 47-48.)

[85] Interviewed by Helsinki Watch representatives in October 1992 in Posušje, Bosnia-Hercegovina. The witness chose to withhold his name, and the name used here is a pseudonym.

different camouflage uniforms. I heard that Zoran Karlica was killed later.[86]

The medical staff was among the last to leave Kozarac. According to the doctor interviewed by Helsinki Watch representatives:

> Eventually, three soldiers arrived at the clinic. I knew one of them, but the other two were probably Serbs from Serbia, judging from their accents. One of the soldiers wanted to kill us, but the soldier I knew didn't let them. The soldiers were dressed in camouflage, with yellow ribbons tied around their arms, but I don't recall any emblems or insignia. They searched the doctors. The three soldiers began breaking down the doors, destroying everything and, again, the local Serb had to stop them from doing this. A young woman of Serbian nationality worked with us as a medical assistant, so we were not badly treated.
>
> They brought a truck, loaded the equipment and medicines onto it and drove away. Then some other soldiers came and they started walking around. Houses started burning. There was no shooting. Soldiers were coming out of houses, looting, trying to take cars or push them from garages.

A car came to transport the doctors and, as they were leaving the area, the doctor could see houses burning. Although they were told that they were being taken to Prijedor, the doctors were eventually taken to the Trnopolje camp.[87]

---

[86] Helsinki Watch interviewed J., a woman from Prijedor who also identified the Karlica paramilitary unit. She, too, claimed that the leader of the group, Zoran Karlica, was killed. See preceding section concerning the forced displacement of residents of Prijedor.

[87] According to foreign press reports, a sixty-three-year-old Muslim construction worker from Kozarac named Hasan alleged that in mid-June, he was one of forty men selected for a prison work gang that was sent back into

A *Washington Post* journalist who made an unauthorized trip to Kozarac in late October or early November reported that every house in the town,

> no matter its condition, is marked with the same color-coded symbol: an "X" inside a circle. Yellow means "to be inhabited," a soldier explained. Blue means "rebuild." And red means "destroy."[88]

Kozarac to pick up bodies. The men kept count of how many corpses they collected, and Hasan said they reached a total of 610. (See Mary Battiata, "A Town's Bloody 'Cleansing,'" *The Washington Post*, November 2, 1992.) Helsinki Watch has not been able to confirm the report.

The same press account claims that prominent Muslims in Kozarac were identified "for arrest, detention and eventual elimination." Those identified included members of Bosnia's parliament, judges, police officers, restaraunt owners, entrepeneurs, factory managers and local sports heroes. Some were shot on the spot, while others were pulled aside and killed. The aforementioned testimonies gathered by Helsinki Watch representatives confirm much of the journalists' observations. In addition, Helsinki Watch believes that prominent members of Kozarac's community were interned, "disappeared" or killed while in the Omarska or Keraterm camps. (See following sections for accounts of abuses in Omarska and Keraterm.)

[88] These color-coded instructions on houses in Kozarac are similar to the color-coded stripes used by Serbian authorities after the fall of the Croatian city of Vukovar in November 1991. During repeated visits to the city after its fall, Helsinki Watch representatives saw yellow, red and green stripes on each house. The number of stripes ranged from one to three. A JNA soldier on duty in Vukovar in January 1992 told Helsinki Watch representatives that the various colors and stripes served as codes to construction workers who either were supposed to rebuild or destroy the houses. The destruction of the house appeared to be based on its physical condition, not the identity of the original owner. As in the case of Kozarac, the "labeling" of houses appears to have been ordered by a local or regional military or civilian authority.

Prnovo

S.H. is a twenty-five-year-old Muslim woman with two children from the village of Prnovo in the municipality of Ključ.[89] According to S.H., Serbian forces entered her village on May 30 and ordered the village's men to surrender their weapons. The women and children were made to form a line and the men were beaten. According to S.H., the soldiers were shooting as the women and children remained in the line, and several children were killed; others lost both their parents. The soldiers destroyed furniture and burned a house. The next day, the soldiers returned to the village. According to S.H.:

> On [May] 31, they came back. We knew the people coming into the village. On June 1, Monday, there was shelling all around and shooting until the afternoon. We saw smoke coming from Plamenice, a nearby Muslim village.[90] We couldn't leave because they were shelling the forest. The army came to the village that day. They took us from our houses. The men were beaten. The army came in on trucks and started shooting at the men and killing them. The women and children lined up. They insisted that the men come from the forest, but no one was there. We didn't resist. They killed sixty

---

[89] Interviewed by Helsinki Watch and the Women's Rights Project on January 15, 1993, in Zagreb, Croatia.

[90] The witness asserts that twenty-five persons were taken from the village to the Manjača detention camp. The witness claims that ten of the twenty-five later returned to the village and told her that the remaining fifteen had been killed along the way. The witness listed those killed as: Ekrem Hadžić, Suad Haždić, Senad Hadžić, Ilfad Brković, Nedžad Jusić, Camil Medanović, Suad Medanović, Vahid Medanović, Enes Medanović, Ahmo Medanović, Isak Mešić, Ismet Mešić, Tehlid Osmanović, Mehmed Dedić and Zijad Hadžić. The witness's husband was among those reportedly killed.

people.[91] We went by those bodies nine days later. We went to bury the bodies. My husband and my relatives were killed. Twenty members of my family were killed. We were chased out of the village that day. We all fled to the forest.

The soldiers had red and white ribbons around their arms. Our neighbors, too, are responsible for all those murders.

Brdjani

Rasim,[92] a Muslim man, reported that his village was one of several villages in which the residents had been forcibly displaced at approximately the same time in late May 1992. He identified the villages as Brdjani, Kamićani, Jakupovići, Hadžići and Sovtići.[93] According to Rasim:

> Women and children from all [of the aforementioned] villages gathered around the house of a Serb named

---

[91] According to the witness, the following persons and family members were among the sixty killed in her village on June 1:

- The Mesanović family: Hasan, Halil, Mujo, Enesa, Hasiba, Farida, Hava, Hadžira, Indira, Fatima, Teufik, Sefik, Midheta, Arif and Sulejman
- The Jusić family: Zamina, Emira, Samira, Latif, Hirmo, Enisa and Ramiza
- From the Hadžić family: Hajro, Rubija, Amel, Amela, Hasim and Izet
- Rasema and Hisveta Brković
- Isma and Gana Mešić

[92] Interviewed by Helsinki Watch representatives in October 1992 in a refugee camp in Croatia. The witness chose to withhold his name, and the name used here is a pseudonym.

[93] Helsinki Watch has interviewed people forcibly displaced from Kamićani, Jakupovići and Hadžići.

Milan in Brdjani. [A large number of people][94] gathered as soon as the shooting began. This man [Milan] — whom people considered a neighbor and someone who could protect them — told us that we had ten minutes to leave and head toward Kozarac.[95]

The villagers then got onto tractors and trucks in which they had come to Brdjani and headed toward Kozarac. About five hundred meters on the road to Kozarac, the displaced villagers saw a tank that Rasim claims destroyed two or three houses before it moved off the road to allow the convoy of displaced persons to pass. At this point, soldiers surrounded the convoy and acted as a military escort for the remainder of the trip to Kozarac.

When they reached Kozarac, Rasim saw four persons with their arms spread, standing against a wall. One was his brother-in-law, and the others were relatives of his wife. Rasim heard a spray of gunfire. He was afraid to watch what he believed were executions and he looked away. He is convinced that the four persons were killed. Rasim identified the men as: Ismet Karabašić, Ekrem Karabašić (Ismet's brother), Sejdo Karabašić (a cousin) and Redžep Forić (a neighbor). Rasim claims that the men's executioner was dressed in a uniform belonging to the self-proclaimed "Serbian Republic."[96]

After a brief stop in Kozarac, the convoy proceeded toward Prijedor. Acording to Rasim:

> The convoy passed through Kozarac toward Prijedor. We were stopped at the Zikina Gostiona restaurant in Kozaruša, which is where we had to empty our pockets for the soldiers. At that point, the soldiers divided the men from the women and children. The latter were put

---

[94] The witness claims that "several thousand" people flocked to this man's house, but he was not able to explain how he arrived at such an estimate.

[95] The witness suspected the neighbor of having collaborated with the Serbian militia but provided no proof to support his allegations.

[96] The witness did not indicate whether the uniform belonged to the police or army units of the self-proclaimed "Serbian Republic."

on buses and were driven away. They then began to register the men. I think about four thousand men were gathered there. They divided us into groups.

As soon as they wrote down the men's names, they were put onto the bus. Some men were registered and then left. At the end, about five or six buses were filled with unregistered men. The unregistered were sent to Trnopolje. Others were sent to Keraterm, Omarska and Trnopolje.

Gornja Sanica

According to Amina,[97] a thirty-two-year-old Muslim mother of three daughters from the village of Gornja Sanica in the municipality of Ključ, both Serbs and Muslims lived in her village. The witness reported that, on June 1, Muslims were forcibly evicted from the villages of Gornja Sanica, Gornji Buldelj, Donji Buldelj and Biljani. According to Amina:

On June 1, we were in the fields, and we came to the house to eat something. Our neighbor came and started to collect the people. Five or six Serbs went from house to house until they assembled a large group of people, which was then broken up into individual groups of five or six persons. The Serbs were dressed in JNA uniforms with a *kokarda* [on their hats], and others wore camouflage. There was one Muslim who was on their side and all the rest were Serbs, although some were not from our locality.

Amina said that the men in her village were taken away on June 1 and the women were allowed to remain temporarily. According to Amina:

---

[97] Interviewed by Helsinki Watch representatives on October 26, 1992, in Posušje, Bosnia-Hercegovina. The witness chose to withhold her name, and the name used here is a pseudonym.

> I was in my house when they were taking the men away.[98] Five or six Serbs searched my house and left. They were looking for weapons and we said we didn't have any. Then they only said, "He will be questioned," and they took my brother and said that he'd be back, but we never saw him again.[99]

Women, children and elderly persons remained in the village until Serbian paramilitary groups forced them to flee. According to Amina:

> I went to the store in my neighborhood, which was operated by the [local] Red Cross. A man in uniform was in front of the supermarket with an AK-47 and he said "You can't come in here. There is nothing here for Muslims and Croats."
>
> Fifteen days later — sometime between June 15 and 20 — another army came through the village. They had white cloths tied to their lapels. These soldiers rounded up the people. There was also a third army, which was dressed in camouflage and they wore stockings over their heads

---

[98] The witness claims that women were raped while the men were being arrested. According to the witness:

> While they were taking away the men, they were raping the women. I know that one woman named K.O., who lived near me, had been raped. The men came up to her door and started banging on it. I went to my neighbor's to see what all the noise was about. Then this woman came to the neighbor's and said that her daughter was still in the house. Ten younger women were raped. Some of the girls later reported this to the military police. The police came around for three days, but they couldn't find those Serbs [i.e., the rapists.]

As of this writing, Helsinki Watch has no other evidence to support the allegation that women were raped in Gornja Sanica.

[99] According to the witness, the ICRC later learned that his brother was being detained in the Manjača camp.

and red scarves. These soldiers killed people and burned houses. In Sanica, three of the soldiers entered my house and looked through my drawers but didn't touch me. I didn't recognize any of them. They wore beards and were from Djelasenovac and Petrovac, which are near Bihać. There was no government in the town, and they did what they wanted. They told me to leave. My neighbor — a Serb and a good man — said that Sanica would be like Vukovar.[100] He said when five of their men [Serbs] were killed, they killed five of our people [Muslims] from Sanica.

Amina named five persons who had been killed two days before her flight from the village.[101] Sanica's inhabitants were then taken to the village of Biljane and then to Ključ, where Amina spent fifteen days with a relative. Non-Serbs were then relocated from Ključ by bus to the Croatian-controlled village of Turbe near Travnik. En route, the passengers were robbed near Vlašić. According to Amina:

When we got to Vlašić, they told us to get off the bus. Četniks were waiting, and they demanded money and gold from my mother and they threatened to kill her. My mother started to cry. Men with stockings on their heads took a girl into the forest, and I never saw her again. We were taken twenty-seven kilometers across a field to [the village of] Turbe at approximately 6:00 p.m.

Amina sought refuge in central and western Bosnia. Her husband and brothers were detained in the Manjača camp at the time of Helsinki Watch's interview.

---

[100] Vukovar is a Croatian city that was besieged and destroyed by Serbian and Yugoslav forces. After the city fell in mid-November 1991, Serbian troops summarily executed at least 180 disarmed combatants and civilians.

[101] The witness named the deceased as Dedo Kucković, approximately thirty-eight years old; an old man named Avdaga and his daughter-in-law; "Fiko" Karadžić, a Muslim born in 1960; and Camka and Ibrahim Huskić, a married couple.

Rizvanovići

Meliha is a thirty-four-year-old Muslim woman from the village of Rizvanovići, near Prijedor, the mother of two children, ages nine and twelve.[102] According to Meliha, violence broke out on April 29 and continued until late July. On July 20, Serbian forces entered her village. According to Meliha:

> On Monday, July 20, the Četniks, came to our village and started killing. There were very many. They came in trucks, tanks and cars. I knew some of them; they were from Tukovi, a mixed [multi-ethnic] village. My village was only Muslim [and] there were 350 houses in the village. We were at home [but] they chased us out, told us to leave. They went inside, started beating my husband and brother. They took them away, then brought them back, had coffee and took them to the camp at Keraterm.

Meliha claims that Serbian forces executed many of the men in her village. According to Meliha:

> The army took most of the men and killed them. There were bodies everywhere. Somebody recognized my husband's brother and saved all four, took them out [of the group that was to be killed]. Now they are gone; Keraterm is empty, but our people are gone.
>
> Some of the soldiers [who came to our village] were from Montenegro. They wore all kinds of uniforms, such as [those belonging to the paramilitary group known as the]

---

[102] Interviewed by Helsinki Watch and the Women's Rights Project on January 16, 1993, in a refugee camp in Croatia. The witness chose to withold her identity, and the name used here is a pseudonym.

White Eagles. One tiny man had "Serbian SAO Krajina"[103] on his shoulder.

The women were outside, too. They did what they wanted in the house. We stayed there Monday night. They came every half-hour. On Tuesday, they said we should go.

Fikreta, a twenty-five-year-old mother of an eighteen-month-old child, also recounted the abuses in Rizvanovići:[104]

> Everything happened on July 20 — killing, burning. I was not hurt. Quite a few women were killed. They were harassed and shot. We left; we did not know where to go; there were dead people lying along the road.

Čarakovo

F.S., a thirty-two-year-old Muslim mother of two young children,[105] lived in the village of Hambarine. During the attack on her village, F.S. and her family fled to the village of Čarakovo, where they spent two months, from late May to late July. After Čarakovo fell to Serbian forces in late July, F.S. reported that the village's inhabitants were arrested, raped, summarily executed and terrrorized. According to F.S.:

> We spent two months . . . in Čarakovo. Then the fighting started in Čarakovo. The soldiers came and took people

---

[103] "SAO Krajina" was initially the name used by Serbs to identify Serbian-occupied areas of Croatia. The region is now called the Serbian Republic of Krajina.

[104] Interviewed by Helsinki Watch representatives on January 16, 1993, in a refugee camp in Croatia. The witness chose to withhold her name, and the name used here is a pseudonym.

[105] Interviewed by Helsinki Watch and the Women's Rights Project on January 14, 1993, at the Resnik refugee camp in Croatia.

to detention camps, and rapes[106] occurred. Čarakovo surrendered. Each house had to have a white flag. The soldiers could come and go as they pleased. They came every day and would take cars, tractors, fuel. We were not allowed to stand in front of our houses and talk. Our men had to hide. My husband was with us, but hiding.

I saw my uncle being beaten on July 25 when there was a kind of massacre. The Serbs were searching for arms. Three hundred men were killed that day. Later we tried to make a list of all the people that died that day — my father helped with this. The bodies were lying in the streets. We were not allowed to collect the bodies. I know many of the people who were killed that day: Mirzan Mujdžić, Mirzan Mušić, Feriz Mušić, Hasim Siječić, Ragib Siječić, Nazif Mušić, Adem Mušić, Jasmin Kljajić, Hazim Rekić.

Bišćani

Zilhada, a Muslim housewife in her early thirties, is from the village of Bišćani, near Prijedor. She testified that, during the shelling of her village, she was in a shelter with three other families. She described to Helsinki Watch representatives the forced displacement of her village's inhabitants:[107]

> They were shelling our village [while] I was in a shelter. Some men got away. Those who were in their homes were beaten, tortured and killed by the Četniks.

Zilhada claims that she was not harmed but that others were beaten and executed.

---

[106] See relevant section below for the witness's account of rape in the village of Čarakovo.

[107] Interviewed on January 14, 1993, in the Resnik refugee camp in Croatia. The witness chose to withold her name, and the name used here is a pseudonym.

> They didn't do anything to us [those in the shelter where she had taken refuge]. There were more children than adults in the shelter. If we didn't have the children, they would have killed us.
>
> Four Četniks came [to the shelter]. They lined us up [and] they were looking for soldiers. Then they left us, telling us we should leave.

When Zilhada emerged from the shelter, she saw men being beaten.

> We came out of the shelter. They were looking for men. They got them all together. We saw them beating the men. We heard the sounds of the shooting. One man survived the executions.[108] They killed his brother and father. Afterwards the women buried the men.

Zilhada and other women and children then walked toward Prijedor and were interned in Trnopolje. According to Zilhada:

> We went to Prijedor. We walked. We had to walk by dead people. Their heads were smashed. We could see their brains. It was three miles to Prijedor. In the village of Tukovi, buses were waiting. Serbian Četnik soldiers were running the buses. They forced us to get in them. We spent fifteen days in Trnopolje, in a school.

Ključ

According to Western press reports, in early October, 4,000 Muslims in Ključ were given twenty-four-hours' notice by Serbian authorities to leave the area.[109]

---

[108] The witness gave the present location of the survivor.

[109] Mary Battiata, "Muslims Flee Renewed Drive by Serb Forces," *The Washington Post*, October 11, 1992.

Abuses in Detention

Helsinki Watch has interviewed scores of men and women who had been in detention camps in northwestern Bosnia. Almost all those interviewed reported that they had been victims of or eyewitnesses to gross abuses while detained in various camps or detention facilities. Those detained in the Omarska and Keraterm camps, in the municipality of Prijedor, for example, reported systematic beatings, which often resulted in death. The civilian and police authorities of Prijedor administered the most brutal of the detention camps in the village of Omarska. The Manjača camp was administered by the self-proclaimed "Army of the Serbian Republic." In almost all cases, the name, residence and date of birth of the detainees were recorded by Serbian authorities prior to or during their detention, and they were classified according to the "severity of their crimes."

During a visit to Banja Luka in August 1992, Helsinki Watch spoke to Muslim residents and Serbian military and civilian authorities in the area. Muslims claimed that, on August 6, 1992, a large convoy of between fifteen and eighteen trucks and buses drove through the city. The convoy was carrying prisoners, who had had their heads shaved, and was coming from the direction of the Omarska camp, headed in the direction of the Manjača camp.

Serbian military officials to whom Helsinki Watch representatives spoke confirmed this allegation. These officials explained that they had categorized the prisoners and detainees. Leaders of the predominantly Muslim Party of Democratic Action (Stranka Demokratske Akcija — SDA) and those who organized the "rebellion against the Serbs" were placed in the first category of prisoners. Muslim combatants comprised the second category of prisoners; the officials said that these prisoners were first taken to Omarska, where they were interrogated, and then transferred to the Manjača camp, thereby supporting the Muslims' suspicions about the August 6 convoy.

According to the Serbian officials, the third category of prisoners consisted of "those that we could not prove were guilty." These prisoners were sent to the Trnopolje camp, where they were interned with other non-Serbs who had sought refuge from actual or potential Serbian attacks on their villages.

In mid-July, *New York Newsday* was the first known Western newspaper to publish stories about the camps in northwestern Bosnia.[110] After *Newsday* reporter Roy Gutman and free-lance photographer Andrew Kaiser visited the Manjača and Omarska detention camps, international pressure led to the "opening" of the camps to the ICRC and the foreign press corps. The ICRC visited the camps soon thereafter.[111] Broadcast and print-media coverage of the deplorable condition and treatment of prisoners in the camps led to their eventual closure. The Omarska and Keraterm camps were closed in August, and most of the prisoners were transferred to the Trnopolje and Manjača camps, which were emptied of prisoners in November and December, respectively. Remaining prisoners that the Serbian authorities did not release were taken to other camps in Serbian-controlled areas of Bosnia, and some have been "disappeared."

After an ITN television crew filmed the Omarska camp, the Serbian military in August began taking journalists and others on arranged tours of the camps. They drove the journalists from Banja Luka to Trnopolje and three other camps in the area: Omarska, Keraterm and Manjača. Helsinki Watch visited the four camps in August 1992, and saw that they had been recently cleaned or painted. Most of the detainees were terrified and refused to speak to foreigners, although some sneaked bits of information under their breath. According to one detainee:

> Don't believe what you see. They have made this place into a tourist attraction.

---

[110] See the following articles by Roy Gutman in *New York Newsday*: "Hidden Horror," July 19, 1992; "Witness Tells of Serbian Death Camp," July 19, 1992; "For Muslims, Misery," July 21, 1992; "'Like Auschwitz,'" July 21, 1992; and "Students Beat [sic] by Serbs," July 29, 1992. See also Roy Gutman, "The Savagery," *New York Newsday*, October 18, 1992, and Nina Burstein, "Holocaust Parallel to Bosnia Horrors," *New York Newsday*, October 22, 1992.

[111] The ICRC first visited the Manjača camp on July 14, 1992, Trnopolje on August 10 and Omarska in mid-August. The ICRC never visited the Keraterm camp.

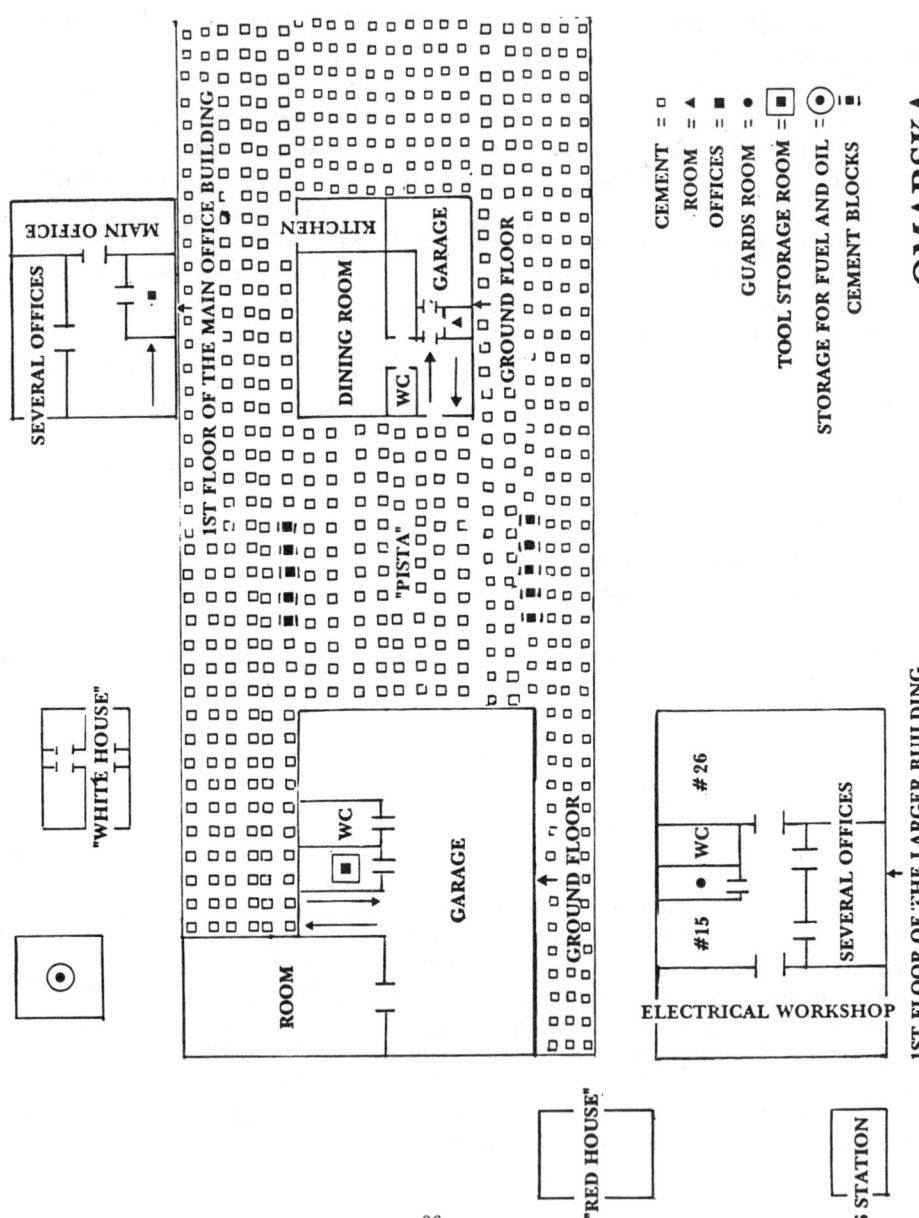

Omarska Detention Camp

Omarska was a predominantly Serbian village in the Prijedor region in which an open ore mine operated. The mine was converted into a detention camp by the Serbian civilian and military authorities, probably in late May or early June 1992. Before the camp was discovered by the foreign press in the summer of 1992, Omarska detained approximately two thousand Muslim and, to a lesser extent, Croatian men. Between thirty-three and thirty-eight women[112] were held in the Omarska camp. The men were kept in two warehouse-type buildings. During the day, the women were detained in a restaurant on the ground floor of a building, and, in the evenings, they returned to the offices on the floor above the restaurant where they slept.

The camp authorities maintained their headquarters in offices on the floor where the women were held. The offices of these authorities were used for interrogating and beating prisoners. Two one-story houses — one white and the other red — on the camp grounds also were alleged to have been areas where prisoners were beaten and tortured, sometimes to death.

The female prisoners had no contact with the male detainees, except during meals, when the women distributed food to the men. The restaurant in which the women spent their days had a glass wall, through which the women could witness the activity on the camp grounds. One witness claims that a high-ranking member of the self-proclaimed "Serbian Republic," whose surname was Brdjanin, visited the camp on at least one occasion.[113]

---

[112] Helsinki Watch representatives interviewed three women, two Croatian and one Muslim, who had been held in the Omarska camp. One estimated that thirty-three women were detained in the camp and another claimed that thirty-seven or thirty-eight women were interned in Omarska. The women identified many of their former female inmates; most were Muslims, at least two were Croats and one was presumed to have been an Albanian.

[113] Another witness claims that the local Serbs in the village of Omarska quarreled with the Serbian authorities in Prijedor about the location of the camp. According to the witness, the Serbs in Omarska did not want the prisoners in their village, and some appeared bothered by the presence of the camp. According to the witness:

After the camp was discovered by the foreign press in late July 1992, international condemnation forced its closure. At the time of the Helsinki Watch visit to the Omarska camp in August 1992, most of the prisoners had been or were being transferred to other camps in Serbian-controlled areas of Bosnia. During Helsinki Watch's visit, approximately 180 men were known to be detained; they were in a building that resembled a warehouse. The prisoners had bunk beds and blankets, but they had been given them only three days before. Prior to the distribution of the blankets and beds, the prisoners had slept on the floor.

The Serbian authorities who were in charge at the time of the Helsinki Watch visit claimed that approximately 3,500 people had entered and left the camp. The authorities referred to the camp as "an interrogation center." The camp authorities claimed that, although the "center" was guarded by soldiers of the "Army of the Serbian Republic," prisoners were interrogated by the local police.[114] Helsinki Watch representatives were told that forty-two interrogators were responsible for questioning the prisoners at Omarska. The camp was guarded by dozens of guards wearing both army and police uniforms. They were armed with AK-47s, other automatic weapons and rubber truncheons.

During Helsinki Watch's visit, the guards demonstrated how "well treated" the prisoners were by taking fifteen prisoners to a cafeteria, where they were fed beans, a portion of meat and a quarter loaf of bread. In the presence of many guards, the prisoners claimed that they had been at Omarska for only a few days and that they received the same food

---

> Serbian women brought food to Omarska; they didn't want to make it an Auschwitz.

Nevertheless, the Serbs in Omarska allowed the mine to be used as a camp. According to the witness, in exchange, the village of Omarska was given the status of a separate municipality and Muslim villages were annexed to the new municipality. Helsinki Watch interviewed one other witness who claimed that Muslim areas had been annexed to Omarska. Helsinki Watch has not been able to confirm the allegations.

[114] In order for Helsinki Watch representatives to gain access to the camp, permission had to be granted by police, not military, officials.

every day.[115] Food was carried to those who were unable to leave their beds.

Out of the presence of the guards, a prisoner told a Helsinki Watch representative:

> There are no sick people here. When someone gets sick, he is shot immediately.

Another said:

> Until August 6, there were over two thousand of us here. Five hundred have been killed in this camp. They were beating us with sticks, rifle butts and knives. We received food only once a day and were beaten while we were eating. It is a lot better now than it was a few days ago.

He and other prisoners begged for help and expressed fear for their future once the press stopped visiting the camp and international attention turned elsewhere.

Omarska appears to have been the most brutal of the four Serbian-operated camps that were discovered by the press during the summer of 1992.[116] Almost all former Omarska detainees interviewed by Helsinki Watch claimed that they had been bestially beaten, that scores had died from the beatings and that some were executed.

J., a thirty-nine-year-old Croatian woman from the town of Prijedor,[117] was arrested at her home in Prijedor and held in the local

---

[115] Helsinki Watch representatives were not permitted to interview the prisoners individually during their visit to the Omarska camp.

[116] i.e., Omarska, Keraterm, Manjača and Trnopolje

[117] Interviewed by Helsinki Watch representatives on October 15, 1992, in Zagreb, Croatia. Helsinki Watch interviewed two other women who had been held in Omarska. One of the witnesses asked that her testimony not be made public. Her testimony is kept in a secure place outside our office. Both women corroborated J.'s description of the camp and the abuses perpetrated therein.

police station with several other prisoners for several hours before being brought to the Omarska camp.[118] According to J.:

> At 4:30 [a.m.], they took all of us to the courtyard, and we were put in a paddy wagon and the door was locked behind us. We drove through the village of Marička, where someone stopped the car and yelled that the door should be opened and that we should all be killed. The police officers then shot in the air, and we moved on until we got to Omarska. Army soldiers opened the door and told us to get out of the car. They had Serbian crosses, and some had the Yugoslav red star on their hats. They were all dressed in camouflage uniforms, and there also were several police officers present.

When the prisoners arrived at Omarska, the men were separated from the women. According to J.:

> They divided the men from the women, and we three women were brought before a building made of brick. They told us to turn around and put our hands against the wall, and they pointed their guns at us. They told us to empty our pockets, and I became so nervous that I started to laugh. I know it sounds stupid but I couldn't stop laughing — it was a nervous reaction. They then divided us and took us to a building which had a restaurant with glass walls on the first floor. There was a garage behind the restaurant and, the next day, we saw that about four hundred men were detained in this area. In the hall there were about six hundred men. We were kept in offices on the second floor. We were taken to office number 102, which was across the hall from the office used by police officers.

> Between 7:00 a.m. and 7:00 p.m., prisoners were interrogated in the offices on that floor and, during that

---

[118] See section above concerning the forced displacement of Prijedor's non-Serbian residents.

time, we women were moved downstairs to the restaurant. Because two of the restaurant's walls were made of glass, we could see everything that happened outside. A small white building, commonly referred to as the "white palace,"[119] was about fifteen meters from the restaurant. They kept 150 to 200 men on the ground floor of this white house; these were allegedly the "extremists," according to the Serbs. Across from this building was a large hangar which housed about 1,600 people. In the evenings, we women were taken from the restaurant and back to the offices, which is where we slept. On June 14, there was a total of nine women in the office[120] but more came later. That day, the police on duty shared their food — roasted lamb — with us and gave us cots and blankets.

Most of the non-Serbian intelligentsia, political activists and local government officials from northwestern Bosnia were interned in the Omarska camp. J. claims that the guards explained to her and the other women which prisoners were brought to Omarska. According to J.:

In Omarska they held three categories of prisoners. First, the so-called extremists, the leaders of the various national communities, were to be executed. The second category consisted primarily of political activists for whom they did not have "proof" of "extremism." Persons held without charge or without reason were part of the third group of prisoners. However, no differentiation was

---

[119] With the exception of this witness, all former Omarska detainees interviewed by Helsinki Watch representatives referred to the building as "the white house."

[120] The witness identified the women by name and, in cases that she could remember, their political affiliation, profession and place of residence. Of the nine women in the room, six were Muslim, two were Croatian and one appeared to have been an Albanian according to the witness. The female prisoners were primarily political activists or had a background in law. A small number of women were laborers and farmers.

made between these groups when it came time for the torture — they were all beaten, and only those in the third category had any hopes of remaining alive.

J. claimed that some of the prisoners in the Omarska camp had been drafted by the Yugoslav Army (JNA) to fight in the war in Croatia in 1991. They were relieved of their duties only to be arrested by Serbian forces several months later. She also claimed that a member of the Croatian Army who had fought in the war in Croatia in 1991 had been interned in the Omarska camp. According to J.:

> Forty-six of the men in Omarska had participated in the war in Pakrac [Croatia], usually after they had been mobilized into the Yugoslav Army [JNA]. There was one Croatian Army soldier who was being held in Omarska. He had fought on the Croatian side during the battles for Kostajnica during the war in Croatia. He was a member of [what was then called] the Croatian National Guard [Zbor Narodne Garde — ZNG].

The woman said that the Croatian soldier's clothing was in tatters but that the "ZNG" insignia could still be seen on his uniform. She reported that this soldier had initially hidden in the village of Kozarac and that he was then brought to Omarska.[121]

J. described the facilities in which the female prisoners were detained in Omarska:

---

[121] The battle for the Croatian village of Kostajnica took place in July and August of 1991 and the village eventually fell to Serbian forces in late August 1991. From the witness's account, it appears that the soldier had taken refuge in Kozarac during the battle for, or after the fall of, Kostajnica. (The village is on the Croatian side of the Una River in northwestern Bosnia.) The presence of Serbian paramilitary forces and the Yugoslav Army (JNA) was evident during the summer of 1991 in northwestern Bosnia. Perhaps out of fear of being arrested by Serbian or Yugoslav forces, the Croatian soldier may have been hidden by the locals and later found and brought to Omarska.

On June 16, three more women were brought to the office,[122] and during my detention a total of thirty-three women were held in Omarska, as far as I know.[123] They ranged in age from twenty-two to fifty. The thirty-three women were kept in two offices in the building that housed the restaurant. One of the offices was numbered 102, but I cannot remember the number of the adjoining office where the rest of the women were held.[124] Seventeen women were kept in one office, and sixteen were kept in the other.[125]

Sulejman, a young Muslim farm worker from Kevljani,[126] arrived in Omarska via bus with scores of other men who had been arrested after the village fell to Serbian forces in late May. He and other former prisoners claimed that prisoners were beaten when they arrived at the camp. According to Sulejman:

> I was taken to a warehouse where trucks were repaired. There were about twenty guards receiving [men emerging from] the buses. When men left the bus, guards would beat them. Four men who observed this tried to escape. Three of them were killed with rifles. One was wounded in the leg and managed to escape but, one month later, he was caught and brought back to the

---

[122] The witness identified the women by name.

[123] Another woman who had been detained in Omarska claimed that thirty-seven or thirty-eight women were interned in the camp.

[124] Helsinki Watch interviewed another woman who had been detained in the Omarska camp and who identified the adjoining office as number 103.

[125] J. was raped during her internment in Omarska. For a description of her account, see the section below on rape.

[126] Interviewed by Helsinki Watch representatives in October 1992 in a refugee camp in Croatia. The witness chose to withhold his name, and the name used here is a pseudonym.

camp. The bodies of the three who were killed were not removed — they lay on the ground for seven days. It was hot, and the bodies putrefied. One of men who had been killed while trying to escape was Huse Tadžić.

Sulejman complained of the overcrowded conditions in the camp.

There were so many people that there was no place to put them. One hundred and fifty people were put into a garage, where they could barely stand. Three men there suffocated to death, and their bodies were just put near the other three corpses.

At first, there were about three thousand people there. Then they brought more prisoners from other camps such as Trnopolje until, finally, they had to keep some people outdoors.

H.H., a twenty-seven-year-old Muslim detained at the Omarska mine, reported:[127]

They put us in room number 15. Muslim policemen and local businessmen were taken out and killed that same night. The rest of us were registered in the morning.

For the first sixty hours, we were given no food or water and we had to relieve ourselves in the same room. Later, they started giving us an eighth of a loaf of bread each per day, although it often happened that we would go for forty-eight hours without any food.

We got very little to eat. Five hundred forty people ate within twenty minutes, in groups of thirty. We had three minutes in which to make a group, run to the kitchen, eat and return to our rooms. Five or six of them [the guards] were always standing in front of the kitchen

---

[127] Interviewed by Helsinki Watch representatives in Zagreb in December 1992.

armed with sticks. They enjoyed pouring water on the tiled floor, and whoever fell would be beaten to death. Many people decided not to eat to avoid the beatings. After all, we received only a little stew and a slice of bread.

We could not wash. They only took us once out to the field and hosed us with freezing water. We were beaten going to the toilet and were given one minute in the bathroom. They used to put so much chlorine in the toilet that you could not breathe inside. Sometimes they would say that we were not allowed to go to the bathroom at all. Eventually, they gave the whole group of us only one hour, so some people did not get to the toilet at all and had to use a corner of the room. Many people died of dysentery.

According to F.M., a Muslim metal worker from Kozarac:[128]

They kept 180 of us in a small garage [which was] four by five [meters in size; it was] the smaller of two buildings. The first five days we were not given any water. It was so humid in there that the plaster was peeling off the walls. We had to relieve ourselves in the room. They started filling our shoes with water and letting us drink out of our shoes. They sometimes urinated in the water we were given to drink.

Mirsad,[129] a Muslim resident of Kozarac, was taken from his village with approximately 200 to 250 people to the Keraterm camp on May 26. He was registered and beaten in Keraterm and, at approximately 11:00 p.m., he and about 30 other men were driven to Omarska on buses belonging to the Autotransport–Prijedor company. According to Mirsad:

---

[128] Interviewed by Helsinki Watch representatives in December 1992 in Zagreb.

[129] Interviewed by Helsinki Watch representatives in October 1992 in a refugee camp in Croatia.

> I was taken to room number 26. They threw us on the floor and said that they would shoot anyone who moved. They robbed us. There were too many of us, so they could not search us properly. They would come into the room and order us to put our watches or shoes in a pile. We heard them shouting "Anyone need a size forty-three?" or "Who wants a watch?" Whatever they didn't like, they would throw back into the room.
>
> They would sometimes tell a prisoner that his life would be spared if he gave them one hundred German marks. They would then collect the money among us, until we eventually had no money at all. They made us sing Četnik songs, which was not really bad, in comparison to other things they did to us.

According to Amir, a Muslim man who had been interned in Omarska:[130]

> There were four hundred men in my cell [which was approximately] one hundred square meters. We had to crouch. The guards used to sell water; one hundred German marks for a liter of clear clean water. Without the water, people would begin to hallucinate. We normally had one meal per day but sometimes there would be no food for over sixty hours. The meal was one-eighth of a loaf of bread and soup or beans, not enough to sustain anyone.

R.J. is a twenty-two-year-old Croatian welder from the village of Briševo, near Prijedor.[131] After Prijedor fell to Serbian forces on June

---

[130] Interviewed by Helsinki Watch representatives in October 1992 in a refugee camp in Croatia. The witness chose to withhold his name, and the name used here is a pseudonym.

[131] Interviewed by Helsinki Watch representatives February 10, 1993, in a refugee camp in Croatia. The witness claims that he worked in Prijedor during the latter part of 1991. In September 1991, he was asked to show his identity card

30, R.J. and approximately twenty other men were arrested and taken to the local police station and then to the Omarska camp. According to R.J.:

> We were taken into a yard where there was oil on the ground. We were forced to lie in the oil. A friend and I were beaten with the butt of a rifle. A guard asked if anyone had a match. Then buses arrived; some men were already in them — about seventy to a bus. No one touched us on the way to Omarska.
>
> [When we got to Omarska,] we were put into a large hall with about two thousand prisoners. We did not get any food for three days. On the fourth day, we each got about an eighth of a loaf of bread. Later, we got more. We were fed once every twenty-four hours. Interrogations started five or six days [after my arrival]. We were asked who had organized an attack on Prijedor and who had smuggled arms?

Prisoners were beaten not only upon their arrival but also throughout their detention. Many were beaten to death in the Omarska camp. Helsinki Watch representatives spoke with Fikret, an eighteen-year-old youth from the village of Kozarac who spent eighty

---

near the Bosnian border with Serbian-controlled territory in Croatia. He claims that police officers told him to follow them to the police station in Dvor na Uni, a town controlled by Serbian insurgents in Croatia. The witness said that he was beaten and then taken to the station's basement, where he was forced to "swim" on his stomach and back in fifteen to twenty centimeters of water. According to the witness, he was kept in the basement for two or three hours. He then claims to have been taken upstairs and held for fourteen days in the police station, during which he was beaten repeatedly. He said that two ribs were "half broken" and that he only learned of this after he caught a severe cold and his lungs were x-rayed. The witness claims that one of the men who beat him in Dvor was a police officer named Pero Nišević. Another man, a reserve police officer, protected him from abuse when possible. The witness claims that the commander of the police station was Dragan Vranišević, who told him he was supposed to be killed. After his release, the witness went to Montenegro, where he worked for two weeks before returning to Prijedor.

days in Omarska.[132] The youth claims to have been the victim of, and an eyewitness to, severe beatings in Omarska. According to Fikret:

> I was badly beaten. I was kneeling with my hands against a wall and they were hitting me from behind for two hours. After that first day, I was beaten at random. People were dying of internal injuries they had received from the beatings. I carried out the bodies. Then trucks came and took them away.

The youth was held on the upper floor in one of the buildings in the Omarska mine, from where he saw corpses being piled up. According to Fikret:

> From upstairs, I could see a couple of bodies every day in the field, but I'm not sure this was the only place where they threw away the bodies. It is horrible to say, but we were happy when new prisoners were brought in because then they did not beat us, but them.

Suad, a forty-five-year-old locksmith from the municipality of Prijedor, spent seventy-six days in Omarska.

> One night, at about 1:15 a.m., men came into the hall in which we were detained. They were cocking their guns and demanding that we hand over any money we had [on our persons]. We did so but were then beaten mercilessly. The bestial beatings were a typical, daily occurrence.

Sulejman confirmed Suad's claim that prisoners were beaten that evening. According to Sulejman:

---

[132] Interviewed by Helsinki Watch in August 1992 in the Trnopolje detention camp.

> The night the men were castrated,[133] another three or four men were killed outside — we heard shots. The bodies were put on a little truck and driven away. Almost every night, between midnight to 2:00 a.m., drunken guards would take away approximately five men who never came back.

> Prisoners were beaten every day, especially at night. The soldiers would pick out ten people, take them out [of the warehouse] and beat them. The wealthier or more educated persons [were usually the victims of such beatings].

Sulejman testified that the following men were killed in Omarska: Alen Jakupović, Senad Sivac, Medo Hadžić and Sakib Permanić.

In addition to the beatings, Suad said that the prisoners were mistreated in other ways.

> When we had to make the dash to eat, sometimes they would put oil on the floor to make us slip and fall, thereby making it easier for them to beat us. We would get about two finger-widths of bread a day.

> Not one evening passed where four or five youths, between the ages of eighteen and twenty-five, weren't taken out and killed. There were also times when we had to lie down with our faces pressed against the courtyard floor and, if we were not lying closely enough, ten men would jump on us. They also used a hose to spray us with ice-cold water. They made us stand on one foot and those who couldn't were pulled out and beaten.

Several prisoners interviewed by Helsinki Watch claim that the Serbian soldiers beat detainees with clubs atop of which a circular structure was attached. According to Suad:

---

[133] Refer to section on reported castration below.

Soldiers would also take knives and twirl them around in prisoners' mouths. This was done mostly to men in their early twenties. During the time I was in Omarska, [prisoners] died of starvation.

M.K. also described the mistreatment in Omarska:

They kept 730 of us in a large garage. It had a cement floor, and it was coated in engine oil. They repeatedly poured cold water over the floor, and we were forced to lie in it. Sometimes a guard would yell at us to "Sit down!" Whoever did not sit down quickly enough was shot. They killed the directors [of firms], private businessmen, intellectuals and all who had money. They would remove people at night and they would never be seen again.

During the fifty-six days that I spent there, my body weight decreased by twenty-five kilograms. They did not let us wash but they hosed us down once with very cold water. [The pressure] was very strong, and a lot of people fell down and were hurt. On my fifty-seventh day at Omarska, they put some of us on a bus and took us to Trnopolje, without any explanation.

H.H. described further the beatings and other forms of mistreatment in the camp.:

Khoja[134] Husein Granol, from Mujkanovići, was forced to eat ham, and they made him say that it was very good. Faruk's — I forget his last name — head was cracked open with a rifle butt. Dr. Esad Sadiković[135] tied Faruk's hair in a knot so his skull would not open. Another

---

[134] A *khoja* is an Islamic scholar or teacher.

[135] Dr. Sadiković was a prominent doctor who was "diappeared" after the Omarska camp was closed. Many persons to whom Helsinki Watch representatives spoke presume that he was executed.

prisoner picked maggots out of his wound. He survived Omarska, but he is now blind in one eye. Most of us, myself included, had maggot-infested wounds. One man was clubbed on the head with a rifle butt until his scalp was ripped off. They would let him heal for a few days and then do it again.

Another large group of prisoners was kept on the open cement lot between the two main buildings. They had to lie facedown so as not to see what was going on around them. A few of them were killed on the lot; most were taken to the "slaughterhouse" or to the field in the back to be killed. I could see from the window upstairs that bodies were pulled into the field by the "white house" almost every morning.

F.M. described the severity of the beatings and general conditions in Omarska.:

Human life was worth less than two German marks — the price of a bullet. We prayed to God that we would be killed by a bullet, yet they were beating us with sticks and clubs. It would have been better if they had burned us alive.

Mirsad also described the apparatuses used to beat prisoners in Omarska:

They beat us with clubs, bats, hoses, rifle butts. Their favorite was a thick rubber hose with metal on both ends.[136] They also smashed people's heads with hammers. Still, I think most of the prisoners died of dysentery.

---

[136] The hose appeared to have been taken off the engine of a heavy truck that was used at a mining site.

J. and other female prisoners who were detained in the restaurant during the day witnessed men being mistreated through the restaurant's glass wall. According to J.:

> Most of the prisoners brought to Omarska were men, ranging in age from fifteen to about fifty-five. They most frequently arrived in a paddy wagon, although some arrived in buses. All were beaten as soon as they emerged from the vehicle. They were then beaten against the wall and thrown into various buildings on the camp grounds. After lunch, they were made to sit on the concrete courtyard regardless of whether or not it was raining or sunny. If new arrivals came in a bus or paddy wagon, the prisoners on the runway had to lie face down on the tarmac. Men were stripped naked and hosed down. The water was full of chlorine. When the new prisoners arrived, there usually were fifteen guards present. Two workers from the local Red Cross who worked in the kitchen also were present — one was named Dr. Ivić, and the other man had an amputated hand and was called Mico. The new prisoners were usually brought to Omarska from the Trnopolje or Keraterm camps or from villages that were being "cleansed." The Serbs regarded Omarska as a military interrogation center for prisoners of war. But none of the prisoners arrived in uniforms.[137]
>
> During the day, we could see what was going on outside from the restaurant. The prisoners would pass by frequently, usually en route to interrogation. Corpses also were thrown by the hedges; some had been wrapped in blankets. Other prisoners carried the corpses. We saw the men being tortured. They were beaten with braided cable wires. Pipes filled with lead were also used to beat the men.

---

[137] The woman gave a rough estimate of approximately 12,000 prisoners who were detained in Omarska during her detention but she could not explain how she arrived at such a figure.

On June 17, I was washing the dishes and [another female prisoner] V. had to get the water that we had boiled to wash the dishes. A police officer pushed her toward me, and the boiling water spilled and scalded my left arm. A military doctor put gauze on my arm for two hours.

J. claims that bodies were deposited in one area, from where they were eventually taken from the camp grounds. According to J.:

The most traumatic experience for me was to see all the corpses. We saw corpses piled one on top of another, and some of the bodies had been there for forty-eight hours — we saw them in the day and the following morning. The office in which we slept had a window, and we saw bodies being thrown onto the pile at night as well. The bodies eventually were gathered with a forklift and put onto trucks — usually two large trucks and a third, smaller truck. The trucks first would unload containers of food, and then the bodies would be loaded onto the trucks and taken to an unknown destination. This happened almost every day — sometimes there was a lesser number of bodies — twenty or thirty — but usually there were more. I saw this take place during much of the duration of my captivity [i.e., from June 14 to August 3]. Most of the deaths occurred as a result of beatings. First, the bodies were lined up against the gray fence, and then they were taken to the grass.

On or about June 14, Selima, a Muslim woman in her forties,[138] was transferred from the Keraterm camp to Omarska. Before the woman was taken to Omarska, she had spent two nights

---

[138] Interviewed by Helsinki Watch representatives on February 22, 1993, in Zagreb, Croatia. The woman provided her name to Helsinki Watch representatives but asked that it remain confidential. The name used here is a pseudonym, and other identifying features have been deleted to protect the confidentiality of the witness.

locked in a van in Keraterm, where she previously had been raped.[139] Selima and one other woman were taken to Omarska with other male prisoners from Keraterm. During the ride to Omarska, Selima claims that a Serbian soldier named Dragan Mrdja beat the male prisoners. Selima spent fifty days at Omarska. She described her experience at the camp:

> It was the most horrible place you can imagine. I watched my children being beaten, and I couldn't cry.[140] They were killing and torturing all the time. We women stayed in this restaurant, which had a glass wall. We were ordered to sit and watch how they beat and tortured our men all morning. We slept in offices above this restaurant and, during the day, they [the offices] were used for so-called interrogations, that is, for torture. Through this [glass] wall, I could see them moving dead bodies from one part of the camp to another [section].

R.J. was held in Omarska for two and a half months. He confirmed that women were held in the interrogation room. R.J. said that although he did not see any woman being abused, he did hear screams, shouts and crying. R.J. claims that, although prisoners were tortured in the "white house," he was only kicked in the stomach once and hit several times. At one point, he was sent to sleep outdoors on the concrete. He slept on concrete for eight days but was taken into the kitchen when it rained.

J. testified that she had been threatened with death and brought before a firing squad twice:

> I had been designated as the person in charge of the room [sobna starešina] and the camp commander told me that I would be responsible for whatever happened in the room. For four days in July, beginning, I believe, on July 17 or 18 at 1:15 p.m., I was twice taken outside before a

---

[139] For an account of the woman's rape, see relevant section below.

[140] The witness's two sons — both in their twenties — were interned in the Omarska camp at the same time as their mother.

firing squad. They threatened to execute me the first time because I slipped a piece of bread to a fifteen-year-old prisoner. On the second occasion, they saw me speaking with another prisoner,[141] and a guard accused me of plotting a rebellion. The guard was pulling and shaking my head for about ten minutes. Then the commanding officer on duty said that I should be executed before a firing squad but then he relented, saying there was no point in wasting bullets on me.

Although most of the deaths that occurred at the camp were a result of bestial beatings, some prisoners appear to have been summarily executed or shot by firing squads in Omarska. According to Selima:

One day, I saw how Serbian soldiers shot a group of men. They were lined up in front of a hedge and, all of a sudden, they started to shoot all over them. I never believed that one human being could do these kinds of things to another human being.

Dževad, a Muslim man detained in Omarska for seventy-three days, said that he witnessed the execution of a prisoner at Omarksa. According to Dževad:[142]

I saw one former policeman taken out and shot on May 24 at 2:00 a.m. in the detention center. The [victim] was a colleague of the two Željkos [Željko Kvocka, the former commander of the camp, and Željko Mejakić, the camp commander for much of the prisoner's detention] from the police department. As soon as [the guards] spotted him, they took him and killed him.

---

[141] The witness identified the prisoner by name.

[142] Interviewed by Helsinki Watch representatives in October 1992 in a refugee camp in Croatia. The witness chose to withhold his name, and the name used here is a pseudonym.

R.J. testified that his uncle, Jozo Buzuk, was killed in Omarska. He claimed that his uncle was called out for interrogation and then his throat was slit. R.J. said that he saw his uncle's body after he had been executed. He stated that the brothers Paspalj were the worst of the guards; he said that the brothers did not kill his uncle, but that two men who worked their shift did.

R.J. said that just prior to his release from Omarska, a television crew visited the camp. However, he and other prisoners were taken to another room during the journalists' visit.

Prisoners also were beaten when they were taken to eat in the restaurant. The food was delivered from outside the camp, and the women detained in Omarska were charged with distributing the food to the male prisoners, under the guard of Serbian soldiers. The guards often beat the detainees as they ate, and they were given only a short period of time in which to finish their meal. Many suffered from malnutrition, and almost all former Omarska detainees claimed to have lost at least ten pounds during their detention. According to J.:

> On June 15, we women were given kitchen duty. Lunch frequently was served between the hours of 8:00 a.m. and 3:00 p.m. to the prisoners. The hours may seem strange for lunch but, because there were so many prisoners, it took hours to feed everyone. On that day, we women were told to sit on the radiators, and tables were put in front of us. First, we were given something to eat, and then we were told to distribute the food to the prisoners. The food was not prepared in the restaurant; it was brought from elsewhere, and we had to distribute it. The meal consisted of half a loaf of bread and a scoop of some dirty, waterlike substance. Groups of thirty men would come into the restaurant. They smelled bad and half of them bore visible signs of torture, usually severely beaten.

J. reported that during the distribution of the food every day, some of the women and prisoners whispered to one another and conveyed information, usually about who had died in detention. J. said that she knew many of the prisoners.[143] She claims that most of the men spoke of severe beatings and shootings in detention but that she could not confirm things she did not see. According to J.:

> They had three minutes for lunch, and the food was distributed in a cafeteria-like system. They then had to go to their table, stand with their food in their hands and wait until the other prisoners were standing in position at their designated tables. Four men were assigned to each table, although at one table, only two men were assigned. They were then ordered to sit down simultaneously and start eating. We [women] ate the same food as the men. The guards walked among the men while they were eating and beat them. On June 15, 2,776 men passed through the cafeteria — I made little lines on a piece of paper while we were giving out the food. Among the prisoners I saw the president of the Prijedor chapter of the Croatian Democratic Union, [Silvije Šarić].[144] He did not appear to have been beaten at that point, but he was very skinny. He had been kept in the military jail and then had been transferred to Omarska. I also saw the vice-president of the Croatian Democratic Union, Jozo Maračić. He had been severely beaten and his face was badly disfigured from the abuse. I was washing dishes when I saw Jozo and he looked at me and said, "Help me." The guard then yelled and told everyone to get out. There were men who had been so badly beaten that they could not walk. They remained outside and the food was brought to them. There were about fifty such men.

---

[143] During the course of her testimony, the witness identified several prisoners whom she knew. She identified these men by their name, profession, place of residence and political affiliation. The prisoners she identified were political activists, judges, doctors and economists.

[144] She claimed that Šarić was born in 1942.

Several prisoners spoke about the feeding methods at the camp. The prisoners were fed once a day. According to Sulejman:

> We left the room [in which we were detained] only once a day, for a meal. When we were taken to eat, we had to run with our hands behind our heads and we were not allowed to look right or left. The food consisted of a kilogram of bread every eight days per man[145] and a bit of soup, which was mostly water. We were given one minute to gulp down the food. They sent groups of thirty people to eat at a time, and the shift for feeding them was so short that the thirtieth person never had time to eat his food.[146] My cousin died of malnutrition. There were no doctors in the camp.

According to Mirsad:

> We had three minutes to form a group of thirty, eat and get back to our room. Whoever didn't make it would get beaten or killed. The soldiers, armed with sticks, stood in front of the canteen, ready to beat us. The stew we were given was boiling hot — they laughed as we struggled to drink it — so we all had "inside burns." The inside of my mouth was peeling.

In addition to beatings upon arrival, at mealtime and throughout their detention, prisoners were bestially beaten during interrogation. The prisoners were questioned in offices where the female prisoners slept and in adjoining offices. The testimonies of men who had been the victims of such beatings and the women who had witnessed such abuses corroborated each other in almost every case. According to J.:

---

[145] The prisoners were given a small piece of bread with their daily meal. Their weekly intake of bread equaled roughly one loaf or one kilogram of bread.

[146] This does not appear to correspond with the prior witness's claim that the men were told to sit down and eat their meals simultaneously. It is possible that the guards' practices varied day to day or from shift to shift.

In the morning of June 15, I saw the interrogators. Some were from Banja Luka and one was called "Duck" [*patak*]. There was also a female interrogator who was supposedly a lawyer from Pakrac [Croatia]. I recognized three of the interrogators: Dragan Radaković, a teacher; Ratko Milosavljević, who had an education in art; and Professor Zorić, from the electrical school. There also was a film director among them who had worked for Jadran Films for ten years but had gone to Switzerland to earn his master's degree, then returned to Banja Luka.

We saw people being taken to the offices, where they were interrogated. The prisoners walked into the offices able-bodied but some had to be carried out after their interrogation. On June 15, at about 7:00 p.m., we had to wash the floors of the offices where the interrogations had taken place. The police gave us buckets and rags, and we had to wash the blood from the floors, mattresses and furniture. We then were put back in the offices where we otherwise slept.

According to Amir, a Muslim man who had been interned in Omarska:[147]

> Everyone was interrogated. They asked questions such as, "Who had weapons?" "Where were you when the shooting started?" "Who were the organizers of resistance?" "Admit you're a Muslim extremist!" "Admit you've organized a rebellion!"
>
> Regular procedure involved that the person being questioned was beaten during interrogation. I was asked about my whereabouts during the attack. I told them that I had hidden by a creek to escape the mortars, and that's where I was arrested. They joked, "What did you expect, the Sixth Fleet to come to help!"

---

[147] Interviewed by Helsinki Watch representatives in October 1992 in a refugee camp in Croatia.

According to Sulejman:

> My two brothers and I voluntarily went to be questioned. We hoped that we would be released and able to join our family in Trnopolje. On June 6, I was interrogated. The interrogator asked, "Where were you during the attack [on your village]?" "Have you ever had weapons?" etc. One of the men who interrogated me had been my math teacher. He recognized me and kicked me in the chest. I was hit fifteen or twenty times and then one of the interrogators asked, "What should we do with him?" and another answered, "Take him away and shoot him." They did this just to terrorize me.

J. and H.H. described the killing of Silvije Šarić, the president of the Croatian Democratic Union (Hrvatska Demokratska Zajednica – HDZ) in Prijedor, who died as a result of the beatings that were inflicted during his interrogation. According to J.:

> [On or about June 15] at 9:30 p.m., I heard a guard yell that the following people were to be brought to him: Jozo Maračić, Professor Puškar and Silvije Šarić. Only the latter two were brought to him. Hellish yelling ensued and someone said "Leave Jozo alone tonight. He was worked over the previous day."
>
> When the two men were brought to them, I heard beating and yelling. The guards yelling at the two men demanded that they admit to being Ustašas. There were pauses between the beatings. At times it sounded as if wood was being shattered, but those were bones that were being broken.
>
> They took me out of the office at 4:30 a.m. When they opened the door to our office, they started yelling at us. "Ustaša slut, see what we do to them!" They were, of course, referring to Puškar and Šarić. I was taken out of the office and saw two piles of blood and flesh in the corner. The two men were so horribly beaten that they no longer had the form of human beings. The guards

then told me to wash the floor. One of them hit me in the hip with the butt of his rifle, and they started to beat my back until I fell unconscious. When I regained consciousness, they told me that I should not say anything. The men who beat the two men [Šarić and Puškar], were called Vuk, Zdravko, Rajko and Krle/Krkan,[148] the latter of whom was the commander of the shift.

I was dragged back into the office at about 6:20 a.m., but the guards did not touch the other women then. In the morning, I had to go back down to the restaurant, but I could barely walk and I was vomiting blood. I realized that my ribs had been broken and that I had been bleeding. I was sick throughout my internment and I had my period for fifty-six days. The local Red Cross gave us women cotton, which we used as hygienic napkins.

J. said that she did not see Silvije Šarić for ten days after the beating. On June 26, another prisoner[149] told her that Šarić had died. This prisoner asserted that Šarić never regained consciousness after his beating and that he died ten days later in the "white house" in the Omarska camp.[150]

H.H. confirmed that Šarić had died as a result of his injuries.:

Silvije Šarić, the president of the HDZ in Prijedor, died after nine days. His sternum had been broken, and the area around his kidneys was blackened by bruises.

---

[148] It is unclear if the woman referred to a guard nicknamed Krle or a man whose surname is Krkan, a commander of one shift of guards at Omarska.

[149] The witness identified the prisoner by name.

[150] It is unclear whether Šarić died in the "white house" or if he was returned to the other prisoners, where he died.

On June 19, J. was formally charged with an offense by the Serbian officials in the camp. She was indicted for having been an official in the Prijedor city government.[151]

> On June 19, I was interrogated again. I was questioned and then I saw that two other women had been brought to Omarska.[152] It was becoming clear that anyone who was not a Serb and had a diploma was being brought to Omarska. All the intellectuals were brought to Omarska.

After Omarska was discovered by foreign journalists in the summer of 1992, many of the camp's prisoners were transferred to the Manjača camp and some were taken to the Trnopolje camp.

J. reported that sometime in late July, the number of killings decreased and the maltreatment lessened, probably because the camps had been discovered by then. She also said that the women were told to clean the camp, probably to eradicate any evidence of mistreatment before international monitors visited the area. Indeed, many former inmates to whom Helsinki Watch representatives spoke said that many former Omarska prisoners were "disappeared" before the camp was emptied of detainees. Most believe that the surviving members of the intelligentsia and those who bore visible signs of torture were taken from the camp and executed. According to J.:

> At 7:30 a.m. on August 3, we were told to clean the rooms and the guard told us that the U.N. was coming. The male prisoners also were washing the walls of the central building, which was made of brick. This is where men's heads were beaten against the walls. Brains and blood were splattered all over the place. We used to watch as the new prisoners were unloaded and lined up

---

[151] The woman elaborated on the specific charges contained in the indictment. Because this information would disclose her identity, Helsinki Watch will not make the information public in deference to the woman's wishes that her identity remain confidential.

[152] She identified the two women by name and profession.

against this wall. We would ask to go to the bathroom so that we could look out of the window, from where we could see this maltreatment; we wanted to see if one of our family members was among those being abused. Their heads were beaten so hard against the wall — you could actually hear the pounding.

J. reported that most of the female prisoners were evacuated from the camp before the ICRC and foreign journalists were allowed to inspect the camp. According to J.:

We women were moved to Trnopolje before the U.N. came. In fact, other prisoners in Omarska began to be moved to Trnopolje and elsewhere on August 3. I know that twenty-nine of the thirty-three or thirty-four women[153] left Omarska alive. Four, possibly five, women[154] remained behind. They instructed twenty-nine of us to go to the hall and told us that we were going home. Then a bus arrived and we were taken to Trnopolje.

According to Mirsad, several hundred men were taken to Trnopolje on August 6. Most of those remaining were transferred to Manjača, while approximately 180 prisoners remained in Omarska, including Mirsad. Helsinki Watch visited the camp after most of the prisoners had been moved elsewhere. According to Mirsad:

---

[153] Another female prisoner who was detained in Omarska claims that thirty-seven or thirty-eight women were detained in Omarska.

[154] The witness identified four of the women by name. Helsinki Watch representatives interviewed one of the four women named by J. in October 1992 but she asked that her testimony not be made public. The other remaining four or five women were released from Omarska on August 23, 1992, and two of them were taken to Trnopolje. Helsinki Watch has not been able to determine the fate of the other women.

Five women stayed in the camp with us [after the men had been evacuated] — they worked in the kitchen — but I don't know what happened to them later. All men were put in one room; we were given beds and covers and were instructed to tell the ICRC and any journalists who came to visit that we had only been there for two weeks. We were kept there for show until August 21. Then we were taken to Manjača.

The ICRC visited the Omarska camp on August 23, at which time many of the inmates already had been removed or "disappeared." According to Amir, a Muslim man who had been interned in Omarska:[155]

The day before the detention camp was cleared out, I saw a line of men who had been so heavily beaten they could hardly stand; they were being taken away in an unknown direction. I think that the guards were trying to get rid of any evidence of torture, such as persons with ugly scars. There were about fifty men in the line, but I didn't know them. Everyone who had scars was taken out and removed.

They had lists and used to come to the rooms and read out the names. About twenty buses left Omarska for Manjača.[156] Another eight hundred were sent to Trnopolje. There was no reason anyone could figure why some were selected for Trnopolje and some for Manjača. The departure was August 6.

---

[155] Interviewed by Helsinki Watch representatives in October 1992 in a refugee camp in Croatia. The witness chose to withhold his name, and the name used here is a pseudonym.

[156] The witness claims that approximately 1,400 men were taken to Manjača and that approximately twelve were killed en route, but he provided no evidence to support this claim.

On August 7, R.J. was transfered by bus to Manjača in a convoy of fifteen buses which left Omarska at 3:00 p.m. R.J. reported that one of the men on his bus was killed. According to R.J.:

> A soldier hit the man in the chest with his rifle. The man cried out, [and] the soldier stabbed him in the mouth with his bayonet. Then the body was thrown out of the bus. I don't know the victim's name.

The prisoners finally arrived at the Manjača camp between 10:00 to 10:30 p.m. However, they were kept in the buses all night with no water and survived by licking the condensation off the buses' windows. They were not allowed off the bus to urinate nor were they allowed to open the windows. According to R.J.:

> "Spaga" had been in charge. He supervised a roll call in the morning outside Manjača. More buses had come, bringing a total of about three thousand to Manjača. Before we arrived, there had been fewer than two thousand in Manjača. When Manjača was filled with the new arrivals, the remainder were sent back to Omarska. I believe they disappeared.

Many former Omarska detainees to whom Helsinki Watch spoke identified guards and soldiers responsible for the abuses in the camp.[157] The original commander of the camp appears to have been a man named Miroslav Kvočka. He was later replaced by Željko Mejakić, whom most of the former detainees blamed for the atrocities.

According to the former detainees, most of the guards at Omarska were local Serbs who wore uniforms belonging to the self-proclaimed "Army of the Serbian Republic." Others were dressed in civilian attire, and some reportedly wore uniforms belonging to the

---

[157] Some of former camp detainees interviewed by Helsinki Watch representatives also identified Serbian soldiers or guards who were kind to the detainees and treated the prisoners appropriately, in Omarska and in the other camps. Helsinki Watch will not make public the name of those guards for fear that it might endanger them. Their names are in a secure area outside Helsinki Watch's offices.

Bosnian territorial defense[158] and police. Many of the camp interrogators were said to have been teachers from the area. According to J:

> The commander of the camp, Željko Mejakić, was about twenty-eight years old and he had attended the Zagreb training school for police officers. His first deputy was Miroslav Kvočka . . . The second deputy was named Drago Prcač. He was between forty and fifty years old and he was horrible; he was the worst and most brutal of all the soldiers.

---

[158] The armed forces of the Bosnian government, formally called the Army of the Republic of Bosnia and Hercegovina, were formed from the republic's territorial defense (*teritorijalna obrana* – TO) units, which comprise local defense forces separate from the federal Yugoslav Army. After World War II and during Tito's reign, the official Yugoslav position maintained that Yugoslavia, as a nonaligned state, was surrounded by external enemies, such as the North Atlantic Treaty Organization (NATO) to the west and the Warsaw Pact to the east. In light of these "threats," Yugoslavia had to be prepared to defend its "territorial integrity, unity and independence." In preparation for possible attacks from "outside enemies," weapons for the general population were stored at the local level throughout the country. The weapons were purchased from workers' revenues at local enterprises and kept in various storage areas throughout each locality. Each of Yugoslavia's six constituent republics maintained a territorial defense structure, which included a civilian security force (*civilna zaštita*) and a local reserve militia. All former soldiers who served in the federal army could be called up to serve as reserve police officers for the republican police force or members of the local territorial defense unit. The TO's weapons could be distributed by the republican government, in consultation with the federal army and the federal government. Most of the weapons stored in territorial defense arsenals in Croatia were confiscated by the Yugoslav Army (JNA) prior to the outbreak of war in that republic. The TO arsenals in Serbian-controlled areas of Bosnia-Hercegovina also have been confiscated by Serbian paramilitaries and the Yugoslav Army. With the escalation of armed conflict throughout Bosnia-Hercegovina, the Bosnian Presidency announced a general mobilization of the territorial defense units on April 4, 1992. The current Bosnian Army units fighting on behalf of the Bosnian government are armed, in part, with weaponry taken from local TO weapons caches.

The head of the local Red Cross had been a founding member of the Serbian Democratic Party (SDS) in the area, and his name was Srdjo Srdić. He was a dentist and a member of the Parliament of the "Serbian Republic" [in Bosnia-Hercegovina]. Simo Drljača was the president of the crisis center [*krizni štab*] in Prijedor.

All of these men in the camp were Serbs from Omarska; none of them had come from elsewhere, although I did see one Serb from Banja Luka. The guards would speak to us, and they told us where they were from and how the prisoners were grouped.

The largest numbers of prisoners were killed in June because they were planning to further "cleanse" the surrounding villages and they needed room for the new prisoners at the time.

The camp guards worked in shifts, and some of the former detainees interviewed by Helsinki Watch representatives claimed that the commanders of the different shifts varied in the degree of brutality they showed toward the prisoners. J. claims that when the women were confined to their rooms, approximately thirty guards were on duty in the vicinity or in the building. She claimed that about fifteen guards lingered outdoors, and about fifteen remained on the same floor of the building where they were housed. She reported that the guards changed shifts three times per day. According to H.H.:

> There were three sets of guards but only two twelve-hour shifts between 7:00 a.m. and 7:00 p.m. so that, each day, one shift was free. There were several layers of guards around the camp, and if there were guards missing, they would call in backups from Banja Luka.

Sulejman reported that the following Serbian soldiers were primarily responsible for torturing prisoners at Omarska: Željko Topić,

Zoran Kvočka[159] and Slavko Mihajlović. Another prisoner said that local paramilitary groups also abused prisoners at Omarska. According to Amir:

> Milan Andjić had his own private army. The particularly abusive officer, [nicknamed] Cigo [Gypsy], was a commander in Milan Andjić's militia.

According to Selima, many guards from Keraterm also came to the Omarska camp. She said that most of the guards were local Serbs and, because she had worked in the area before the war, she knew many of the soldiers at both camps. In addition to Željko Mejakić and Miroslav Kvočka, she identified them as: Zoran Žigić, Dušan Duca, Predrag Banović, Dragan Laić, Saša Topić, Dragan Mrdja, Djole Macura,[160] Goran Mrkan, Nikola Družić, Dragan Prcač, Mladjo Krkan and a man whose nickname was "Krle."[161]

J. testified that a high-ranking member of the government of the self-proclaimed "Serbian Republic" visited the Omarska camp. According to J.:

> In mid-July, the prime minister of the "Serbian Republic" — a man called Brdjanin — came to Omarska, and the prisoners were paraded before him. Before his visit, the prisoners were made to sing "*Od Topole pa do Ravne Gore.*"[162] They had to do the three-finger Serbian salute and to sing Serbian national songs.

---

[159] It is unclear if this is the same man as Miroslav Kvočka mentioned above.

[160] These guards appear to have been on duty in the Keraterm camp, but the witness did not explicitly indicate this. She spoke of them in the context of her detention at Keraterm and claimed that they traveled between the Keraterm and Omarska camps.

[161] The witness stated explicitly that these guards were on duty in Omarska. "Krle" may also be the nickname used by Mladjo Krkan.

[162] The song is a Serbian national song that was sung by Serbian forces loyal to the king during World War II.

Brdjanin came in a luxury car which was followed by helicopters. We were not shown to him, and I do not know if he knew that women were being held in the camps.

According to *Politika* and *Borba*, two Belgrade-based daily newspapers, the Assembly of the "Serbian Republic" elected a prime minister and cabinet at its January 20, 1993, session in Pale, Bosnia-Herecgovina. Although the newspaper accounts are incomplete, Radoslav Brdjanin was identified as the newly appointed minister for urban affairs of the "Serbian Republic."

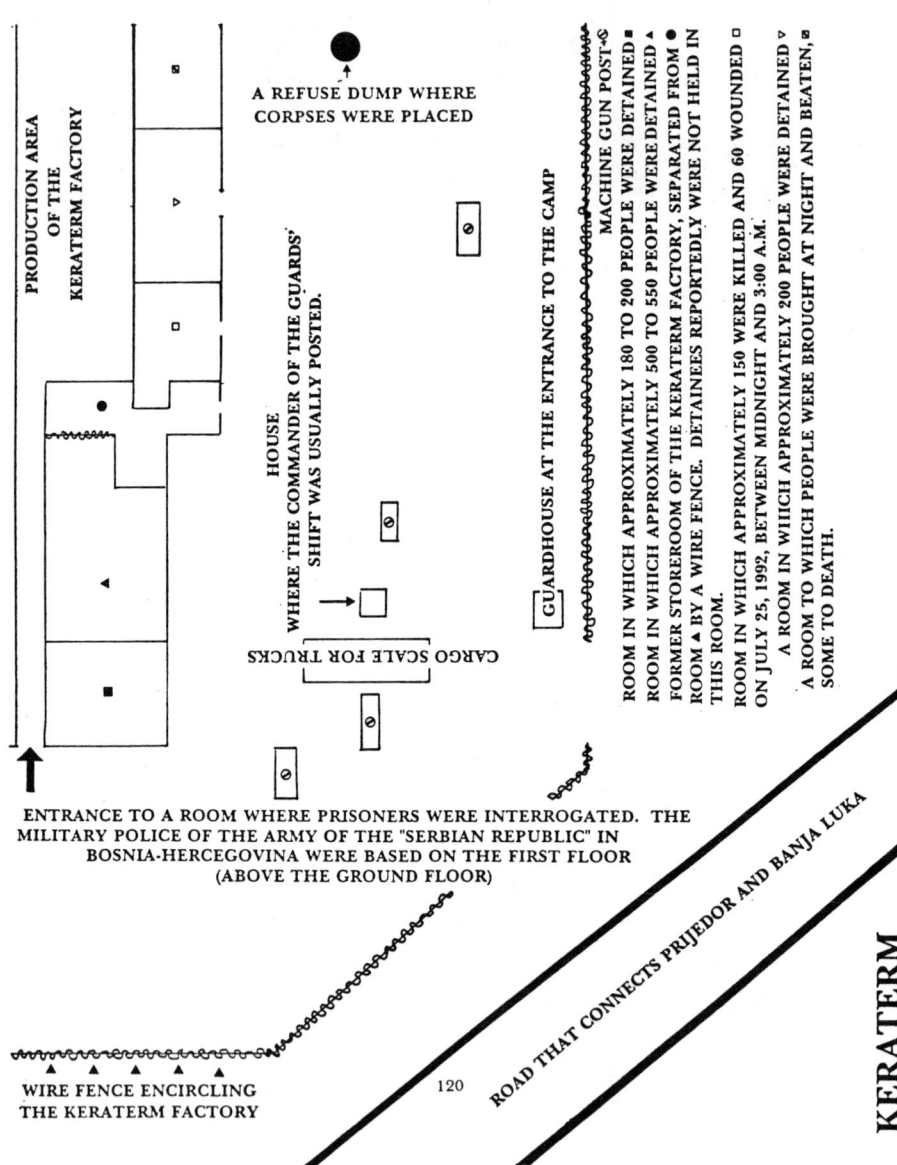

Keraterm Detention Camp

The Keraterm camp was on the site of a ceramics factory, just outside the city of Prijedor. When Helsinki Watch representatives visited the camp in August 1992, Serbian military authorities showed them one part of the factory which was empty. The area had been cleaned, and the walls were freshly painted. There was a large ceramic baking kiln in the hall. Helsinki Watch representatives have interviewed former Keraterm detainees, none of whom claimed to have remembered a kiln in their place of detention. This would indicate that Helsinki Watch representatives were not shown all or any of the areas of Keraterm in which prisoners were kept.

Haris, a fifty-six-year-old house painter from the village of Hambarine,[163] was taken to Keraterm on July 20. According to Haris:

> I was placed in room number 3, where the mass murders took place. The room was ten by ten square meters in size, with about four hundred men from the whole area piled into it. People were standing on top of each other; there was no air to breathe and it was very hot. We were given some type of polluted water to drink. We were not fed for the first five or six days.

Thereafter, Haris reported that the prisoners in his area of detention were fed a meal once a day, usually outdoors. However, he said that, on occasion, food was withheld as a punitive measure. According to Haris:

> Sometimes, we were not fed. We were being specially punished. The men in the other rooms were fed but we were not.

---

[163] Interviewed by Helsinki Watch representatives in October 1992 in a refugee camp in Croatia. The witness chose to withhold his name, and the name used here is a pseudonym. For an account of the forcible displacement and summary execution of Hambarine's residents, see relevant section above.

Haris believes that the men in his area of detention were being singled out for punishment because they all came from exclusively Muslim villages. When asked if the men with him had offered armed resistance to the Serbian forces, thereby incurring particularly harsh treatment, Haris said that the Muslims in his room were not combatants. He claims that some of the Muslims had possessed weapons before the attacks, but the self-proclaimed "Serbian Army" in Bosnia issued an ultimatum and the Muslims surrendered their weapons before the attacks on their villages commenced.

According to Haris, prisoners were continuously being brought to the room in which he was detained. He believes that prisoners from the Omarska camp frequently were transferred to Keraterm. Haris claims to know of the existence of four rooms in which prisoners were held. He believes that approximately four hundred prisoners were held in each room and a total of about 1,700 men were detained at Keraterm.

Idriz, a twenty-six-year-old salesman from Kozarac,[164] claims that "Serbian Army" soldiers dressed in Yugoslav Army (JNA) uniforms interned him at the Keraterm camp. Idriz claims that between 1,000 or 1,200 men were detained in Keraterm and that people were transferred to Omarska periodically.

A.H., a thirty-eight-year-old resident of Hambarine, was arrested by Serbian soldiers on July 20, 1992, and taken to Keraterm via bus. According to A.H.:

> All the men in the bus got out, and we had to put our hands up in the air. One by one, we went to the porter. They took all our belongings, and we were taken to a larger room, which already housed prisoners. There were about 300 of us in there. More buses kept arriving. We were able to see through the windows, which had bars on them. Pallets were on the floor, and a thin metal sheet of corrugated steel was on the walls. The room appeared to have been some type of a warehouse. We already were crowding against the walls, but they kept putting more men inside. By the afternoon, an additional one hundred

---

[164] Interviewed by Helsinki Watch representatives in October 1992 in a refugee camp in Croatia. The witness chose to withhold his name, and the name used here is a pseudonym.

men came. We were given no food or water. Eventually, four hundred men crowded into a room of about one hundred square meters.

Idriz appears to have been held in a second room, which was not the same as the area in which Haris and A.H. were detained. According to Idriz:

> There were 550 men in the room, so you couldn't lie down to sleep. Only the oldest and sickest had beds. The others took turns standing so some could lie or sit. My room was the largest, about fifteen by eight meters. There were three such rooms at the beginning, and later a fourth [room] was used [to house prisoners].

Haris continued to describe the conditions in Keraterm:

> [In total,] we were denied food for fifteen days. At 6:00 a.m., we were allowed to remain outdoors for about an hour, during which time we could clean ourselves. If you had to use the bathroom at another time, you had to relieve yourself in the room.

Haris said that prisoners were beaten in the camp:

> Every night, guards would read ten or fifteen names from a list. They read out the person's first name, his surname and his date of birth. These men were then taken from the room and returned later in awful condition. They were bloody, their bones were broken and they were falling down, vomiting blood and fainting. By morning, some would be dead. Actually, very few survived [the beatings].

Haris also was beaten, and he sustained head and chest wounds. According to Haris:

> They beat us with one- or one-and-a-half-meter-long iron bars. When they opened up the room in the morning, we would report to the guards the number of corpses — ten,

forty, whatever — that needed to be removed [from the room].

My rib was snapped by a guard for no special reason. From time to time, we were forced to line up and to lie on the ground with our faces in the blood and dirt. The soldiers would then walk between us with sticks and bars, beating people. I had lost a lot of weight in Keraterm, and my ribs were protruding through my skin. One soldier pulled me up by the hair, reached over, grabbed my rib and snapped it.

A.H. also confirmed that men were bestially beaten in Keraterm:

Every evening, a truck of drunken soldiers pulled up, and these drunken guys were responsible for beating us. They called out people by name, and they obviously knew them. That [first] night about thirty or forty people were taken out of the room. Some [of those who had been beaten] walked in later and others were carried in. In the morning, we found dead [bodies] amongst us again, and a truck arrived to take out the dead and wounded.

In the evening of July 20, the door was shut and we heard screaming. We didn't sleep that night. They were taking people out of the room and beating them. The door stayed closed, and we were not fed the next day. In the evening of July 21, they started to take us out again and beat us. This lasted until July 24. We were beaten with pipes, feet, etc. I was not taken out and beaten, but most of the men were. People died from their beatings. For four days we received no food or water.

Haris identified the guards at Keraterm as "Serbian Army soldiers." Idriz confirmed both Haris's and A.H.'s allegations of beatings:

Every night guards would come [into the room] with about five soldiers. They used metal pipes and beat people to death. They used to line up fifty prisoners and force them to fight each other with their bare hands. Soldiers would stand nearby with metal bars topped with a sort of ball and if anyone fell down, they would strike him on the head. If someone survived this ordeal, they would finish him off another time. I witnessed this myself.

Idriz testified that he was detained in Keraterm for fifty-five days (i.e., from June 14 to August 5) and that he can recall only five days when beatings did not occur. According to Idriz:

They used to beat us when we went to lunch. We had to pass through a narrow door with bars. There would be guards waiting inside with baseball bats to beat us. If you fell down, you were finished. Sometimes, we had to crawl the last fifteen meters to where lunch was distributed. Every day the guards would invent new games. We had to shovel our food into our mouths quickly. We received about one or one and a half decaliters of soup and two small pieces of bread. This was the only meal of the day, and usually half the soup wound up on the floor. About fifty to one hundred men were left without food each day.

Four days after their arrival — on July 24 — both Haris and A.H. described a massacre that took place in Keraterm during the early morning hours on July 25. According to Haris:

It was a very hot evening, and all the windows and doors were shut. We only had the dirty water [to drink], and people started to faint. We started yelling for the guards to help. The guards arrived, cursed at us from outside the door and then shot through the corrogated metal doors.[165] One hundred and fifty men were killed,[166] and forty were wounded.

A.H. confirmed Haris's account:

> On the fourth day, July 24 — a Friday — we were taken to a larger room and given some water. At about 8:00 p.m., while we were drinking the water, they took out about twenty or thirty people. The worst beatings took place then. People came back with broken heads and ribs. People cried and screamed. Some in the room tried to save them and cried for water. Some were already hallucinating from the heat, and a ruckus ensued. The guards started screaming that they would shoot us. A general panic gripped the room. The door was large and made of thin aluminum sheet. Then they started shooting from the other side of the door with machine guns and automatic weapons. People started to fall to the floor. The shots were fired at random and they pierced the door. I lost consciousness then.

Haris reported that the door to the room was narrow, about one and a half meters wide and about three meters long, and was made of corrugated steel. However, he claims that when the guards shot into the room, the bullets penetrated not only the door but also came in through the windows, which lined the room. Haris continued:

> There was blood all over the place. I tried to shield myself with a corpse. When the shooting stopped,

---

[165] When Helsinki Watch representatives visited the camp in August 1992, they observed that the outside wall in front of a room (number 11 on the drawing) had been reparied. Most of the shots appear to have been fired into the back of the room, from the direction of room 17 on the drawing.

[166] Idriz, who appears to have been held in another room, claims that the following men were among the victims of the shooting: Taib Brkić, Safet Brkić, Jusa Brkić, Emsud Bahonjić, Dževad Brkić and Fikret Avdić.

everything was full of holes. Then the soldiers threw something inside the room, and the prisoners couldn't breathe — some suffocated on the gas. Everyone tried to hide their faces with their clothing.

In the morning, the guards opened the door, part of which had been destroyed, with a piece of metal waving about. The prisoners were told to push the dead through the broken door. Ten prisoners were taken from the room to help carry the bodies. The prisoners had to crawl through the broken part of the door. They then had to pull out the bodies and line them up in rows. According to Haris, the ten prisoners who helped remove the corpses never returned to the room. Soldiers standing outside the door took the corpses from the prisoners, and they were taken elsewhere. According to Haris:

> Through the holes we could see into the corridor. The soldiers then said, "Now give us the wounded, and we'll take them to the hospital." However, the wounded were put on the same truck as the corpses. I started to crawl through the door, thinking that I could go to the hospital because I had a broken rib. But when I saw the wounded being loaded onto the truck with the corpses, I said, "No, it was a mistake. I was just looking for my shoe." The room was half empty after [the massacre].[167]

A.H. was wounded during the shooting and showed his wounds to a Helsinki Watch representative. According to A.H.:

> In the morning, I awoke and saw dead bodies on the concrete floor. There were so many bodies that you had to walk over them. A few stayed alive but most of them were killed or wounded. People were moaning and the guards broke down the door. They said they were looking for the leaders of the riot and that those people had to be thrown out of the room. Unfortunately, some of the prisoners panicked and grabbed the first man that

---

[167] The witness claims that his brother was killed that evening, but he did not describe the circumstances of his death.

was standing next to them. About twenty men were taken out, and the door was opened.[168]

I heard shots and screams. I also heard trucks pulling up outside. They asked for any other organizers of the rebellion and asked for two volunteers to carry out the dead and to load them onto the truck. I didn't see the bodies being loaded onto the truck, and no one had counted how many there were dead among us but I would guess that there were about 140 dead and about forty or fifty wounded. The wounded and the dead were taken out together, and I presume that they went out in the same truck.

Then those of us who remained in the room were taken outside. We had to keep our hands up in the air. Some were made to stand on the concrete outside and others on the grass. We stayed there until the "Serbian Army" and police officers came and started to beat us, one by one with the butts of their guns. I couldn't look up, and I don't know how many soldiers and police officers were there, but I heard gunshots occasionally.

They asked, "Which one of you are the Cerić brothers?" There were three of them, and then we heard screams, beatings and three gunshots. During this time the temperature was increasing outside. We were on the concrete all day and some asked for water. They then plugged in a fireman's hose and hosed us down for about thirty minutes. Since then I have had problems with my hearing.

This mistreatment lasted several hours, until about 4:00 p.m. or 5:00 p.m.. Then we heard trucks pulling up again. They probably took away those that had been killed. We figured that about thirty or forty had been

---

[168] It is unclear whether the door remained open during the executions or if it was shut immediately after the twenty men were removed.

killed on the concrete. The took us back to the same room, but they had taken out the wooden pallets. They [probably] took them out to wash the blood off and when we got there we had no pallets. I think they gave us water and some bread then but I can't really remember.

A.H. reported that in the evening, more prisoners were brought to the camp. He said that the new prisoners were all Muslims from the villages of Čarakovo, Hambarine, Zecovi, Rakovčani, Rizvanovići and Bišćani. A.H. could not recall the number of the new arrivals.

The following day, at approximately 6:00 a.m., the guards opened the door and removed about forty men who were nearest the door. Haris claims that the prisoners who remained in the room looked through the holes in the door and saw the prisoners lined up with their backs to the door. According to Haris, the men were lined up against a wall outside the door and shot at point blank range.[169]

Haris and A.H. both described "disappearances" in the camp. According to Haris:

> Anyone who was called for work — for example, the ten men who had to remove the first massacre victims from the room — never came back. Those who helped to load the trucks never came back. Soldiers also came to collect prisoners for work duty. These men never came back either.[170]

According to A.H.:

---

[169] Helsinki Watch has received further testimonies from former Keraterm detainees in January 1993 that confirm the accounts stated here.

[170] Helsinki Watch representatives interviewed former residents of northwestern Bosnia who surmised that these men had been taken to another "secret" camp in the region. Witnesses allege that the "camp" functions as a "plantation," where detainees are forced to labor in the fields. Helsinki Watch retains the name of the allegedly secret camp in a secure area outside Helsinki Watch's offices, but has not been able to confirm allegations of its existence.

They sought ten to fifteen people for some type of work and they left, but no one knows what happened to them thereafter. While I was in Keraterm, over one hundred people were taken out for work duty but they never came back. On July 26, my brother was taken away for work duty, and he never reappeared. Throughout this ordeal, men were taken out of the room and beaten every night.

A.H. testified that Serbian military officials visited or administered the camp. According to A.H.:

A Major Slobodan Kuruzović came to us and gave a lecture. He said that it would be good for us here [in Keraterm] and that the mistreatment that had taken place would not repeat itself. However, he also said that if anything happened to any of their soldiers, we would all be killed.

A Helsinki Watch representative asked A.H. who was responsible for the mistreatment in Keraterm. A.H. replied:

While we were in Keraterm, there were three to five Muslims who beat us. They had been given weapons and threatened us but, in general, all were Serbs.

A.H. identified guards or soldiers whom he recognized in Keraterm during his detention. When asked how he knew the names of these men, A.H. said that he knew them from the area or heard them call one another while he was in detention, especially those who were called by their nicknames. According to A.H., most of the guards and soldiers in the camp were from Prijedor or its environs. He said that various prisoners recognized them.[171]

---

[171] It is not clear whether A.H. had recognized the soldiers himself or whether he was told their names from other prisoners. For this reason, Helsinki Watch will not make public the names of the men identified by A.H. The names are kept in a secure area outside Helsinki Watch's office.

Both A.H. and Idriz reported that the commander of the camp was surnamed Sikirica. Selima, a woman who was interned in the Keraterm camp for one evening, claims that she was raped by a man named Zoran Sikirica, whom she identified as the camp commander.[172]

On August 5, Haris and Idriz were transferred to Trnopolje. A.H. followed shortly thereafter. According to A.H.:

> On either the first or second of August, they started calling people out by name and loading them onto buses. Two busloads were filled with men, who supposedly were taken to Manjača and Omarska. We never saw those people again. The rest of us, myself included, were taken to Trnopolje. We were beaten as we were taken from the room.

---

[172] Interviewed by Helsinki Watch representatives in February 1993 in Zagreb, Croatia. For an account of the woman's sexual mistreatment in the Keraterm camp, see following section on rape.

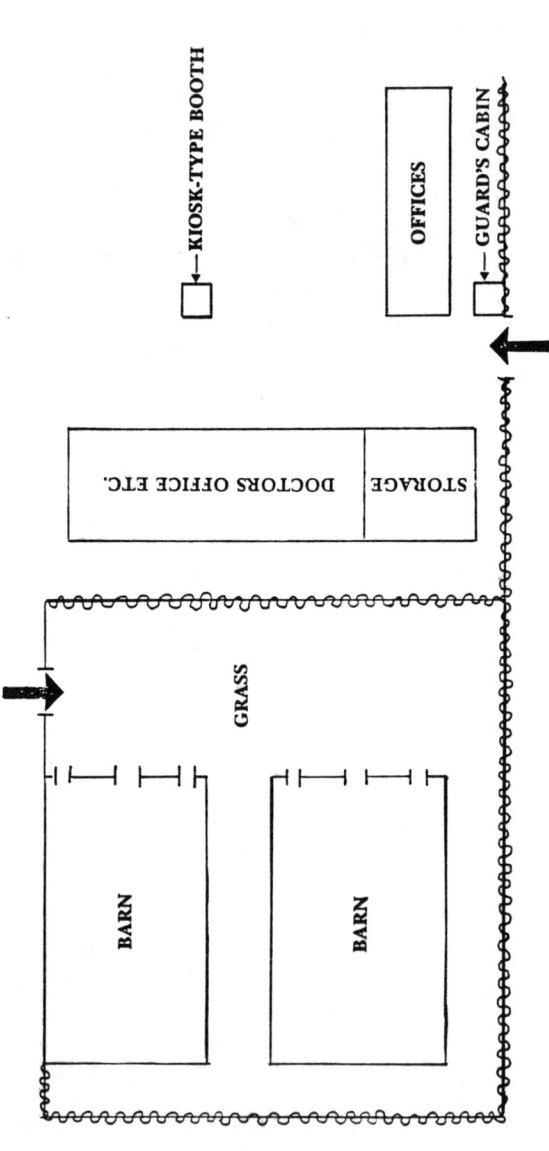

MANJAČA

⌇⌇⌇ = WIRE FENCE

Manjača Detention Camp

Manjača was a Yugoslav Army camp before the current war. The camp was located on top of Manjača Mountain, south of Banja Luka, and consisted of several barracks and about half a dozen large barns. The prisoners were kept in the barns, without heat or bedding. After Omarska was closed in late August 1992, many of its detainees were transferred to Manjača. When Helsinki Watch representatives visited the camp in mid-December 1992, the prisoners complained that they were freezing despite the blankets provided by the ICRC. Manjača was emptied of prisoners between December 14 and December 19.[173]

On September 15, sixty-eight detainees were resettled in Western Europe. On November 14, 755 detainees were released and taked to Croatia. Approximately 529 were transferred to the Batković camp in northeastern Bosnia and approximately 129 had been transferred to the Serbains controlled Kula Butmir prison in Sarajevo. On December 14, 1,009 detainees were taken to Croatia. On December 16, 1,001 prisoners were released and the remaining 426 were released on December 18. According to the number released, at least 3,917 prisoners had been detained in the Manjača camp.

On December 13, Helsinki Watch witnessed 500 men (319 Muslims, 180 Croats and one German)[174] being taken away from Manjača on buses marked "VRS" (Vojska Republike Srbije — Army of the Serbian Republic). They allegedly were being taken to a point where they would be exchanged for prisoners held by Bosnian and Croatian forces. For several days, the whereabouts of these prisoners remained unknown. The ICRC announced the following week that they had found the missing

---

[173] After its initial visit to the Manjača camp in mid-July 1992, ICRC delegates visited the camp weekly and facilitated the release of most of the camp's detainees.

[174] Serbian authorities administering the camp stated the ethnicity of the five hundred men. The commander of the camp during Helsinki Watch's visit was Božidar Popović.

prisoners at a camp in Batković, near the northeastern town of Bijeljina.[175]

Asim,[176] a youth who had been interned in Manjača, later described the detention facilities to Helsinki Watch representatives:

> Barbed wires and mines effectively divided the camp into two sections. Each barn was divided into three separate areas, where cattle had been kept. I was in one section with 186 people; they had been accused of possessing arms, but fifty of us didn't have our documents so we were put in with this group. Most of the people [in my area of detention] were from Sanski Most.

Aziz, a Muslim man who had been detained at the Omarska camp before being brought to Manjača, described conditions at the camp during his detention from August 6 to September 1.[177] The ICRC had visited the camp in mid-July and conditions at the camp improved thereafter but beatings continued. According to Aziz:

> We were kept in stables, just like cattle, with nothing to sleep on but concrete floor and mown grass. There were two [sections of the] camp, divided by a wire fence and a mine field. One [section of the] camp was filled with men from Ključ, Sanski Most and Prijedor who came before the attack [on their villages]. In the part of the camp in which I was held, there were three stables. In one [of the

---

[175] According to the ICRC, "during a visit to a camp in Batković, in north-eastern Bosnia, delegates found some of the 529 detainees who had been tranferred from Manjača on 13 December without the ICRC's knowledge." (International Committee of the Red Cross, "Bosnia-Hercegovina: Manjača Camp Closed Down," Communication to the Press, No. 92/37, December 18, 1992.) For a description of the Batković camp, refer to the section on abuses in northeastern Bosnia.

[176] Interviewed in a refugee camp in Croatia on October 17, 1992. The witness chose to withhold his name, and the name used here is a pseudonym.

[177] Interviewed by Helsinki Watch representatives in October 1992 in a refugee camp in Croatia.

stables], there were men from Sana [i.e., Sanski Most] and in the other [stable], men from the Kozarac and Prijedor areas [were detained].

In the morning, we would get a thin slice of bread and plain tea. Lunch [consisted of] another slice of bread and a small amount of cooked food, usually soup or gruel. We would get 3,000 liters of water for 2,000 men, so it worked out to about a liter and a half for each man each day. We used some of the water for ordinary cleaning. They also had organized a bath every fifteen days — you would have about sixty seconds to wash. We were allowed to wash our laundry every Sunday if there was water. Men were allowed to walk out of their stable only with permission of the guard. It wasn't so hard to get permission to visit another stable.

H.P., a forty-three-year-old resident of Prijedor, said that between 110 and 120 persons were transferred from a detention facility in a sports hall in the town of Ključ[178] to the Manjača camp on June 27.[179] According to H.P.:

[When we arrived at Manjača,] we were stripped naked and our belongings were taken from us. We didn't have time to get dressed again before they started to beat us; they beat us for five hours. My right rib was broken, and not one man was spared. Usually, at any given time, about ten guards were present during the beatings. We were beaten in front of the barn in Manjača. We were terrified.

---

[178] Refer to the section on Ključ for an account of the witness's treatment in the town's sports hall.

[179] H.P. spent fifty-five days in the Manjača camp and was then transferred to Trnopolje.

H.P. claims that the Serbian military police responsible for the region were not present when he arrived at the Manjača camp.[180] According to H.P.:

> We were then taken to the barn, and we slept on the floor for fifteen days. On August 27, 1992, I was beaten and my two left ribs were hurt. My kidneys are ruined. On August 28, the president of the Party for Democratic Action [Stranka Demokratike Akcije — SDA] in Prijedor, Omer Filipović, and two other men were killed. I saw this from the barn. One of the two men died five hours after he had been beaten. They were taken outside and thrown back into the barn after they had been beaten. They beat us in an area that was used for the solitary confinement of prisoners; it was about one hundred meters from the barn.

H.H., a former resident of Kozarac,[181] testified that he and his brother were taken from the Omarska camp to Manjača on August 6. According to H.H.:

> We were brought to Manjača by bus, and we had to spend our first day sitting on the bus, with our heads down and without water.

Both H.H. and H.P. claim that conditions for the prisoners improved after the ICRC visited the camp. However, H.H. claims that the guards in the camp confiscated the aid brought by the ICRC. He also said that prisoners were assigned work.

---

[180] H.P. claims that the military police officers were attending a six-month military-training program in the Serbian-occcupied town of Knin in Croatia but he provided no proof to support his allegation. Helsinki Watch representatives have spoken to several Western and Serbian journalists who claim that Serbian forces from Knin have participated in hostilities in Bosnia, particularly in the Doboj municipality in northeastern Bosnia.

[181] Interviewed by Helsinki Watch representatives in December 1992 in Zagreb.

At first one loaf of bread had to be divided between twenty-four people, but about a month later, the ICRC started feeding us. We even got vitamin tablets. But the guards stole much of our food. They called us "the pets of Europe" and took away our fruits and vegetables. They stole our shoes. We were forced to work, chop wood and repair roads. We built an Orthodox church on the grounds of the camp.[182] We repaired their vehicles and cared for the livestock.

H.P. confirmed that conditions at Manjača improved and mistreatment diminished after the ICRC's visit:

We were beaten [soon] after the ICRC came [to the camp], but they didn't touch us after that. Then some journalists came, and the mistreatment decreased. We were only hit five or six times with truncheons. Otherwise, we were usually beaten with cables or kicked. They had some kind of metal on their shoes, which made the blows particularly painful.

Although prisoners were beaten in Manjača, H.H. claims that the frequency of beatings was less in Manjača than in Omarska. Although this may be attributable to better camp administrators, it should also be remembered that the Manjača camp had been visited by foreign journalists and relief workers, which may account for an improvement in treatment. H.H. claims that after the prisoners left Omarska and arrived at Manjača, "Our hell became better." According to H.H.:

Those who volunteered for work would get extra food. They sometimes beat prisoners in Manjača, but much less so than in Omarska. They only beat you if you were guilty of not keeping your hands behind your back, for example. We showered once in four months and it was freezing cold at night. Conditions improved, and they stopped beating us once the international public discovered we were there.

---

[182] Helsinki Watch has not been able to confirm this allegation.

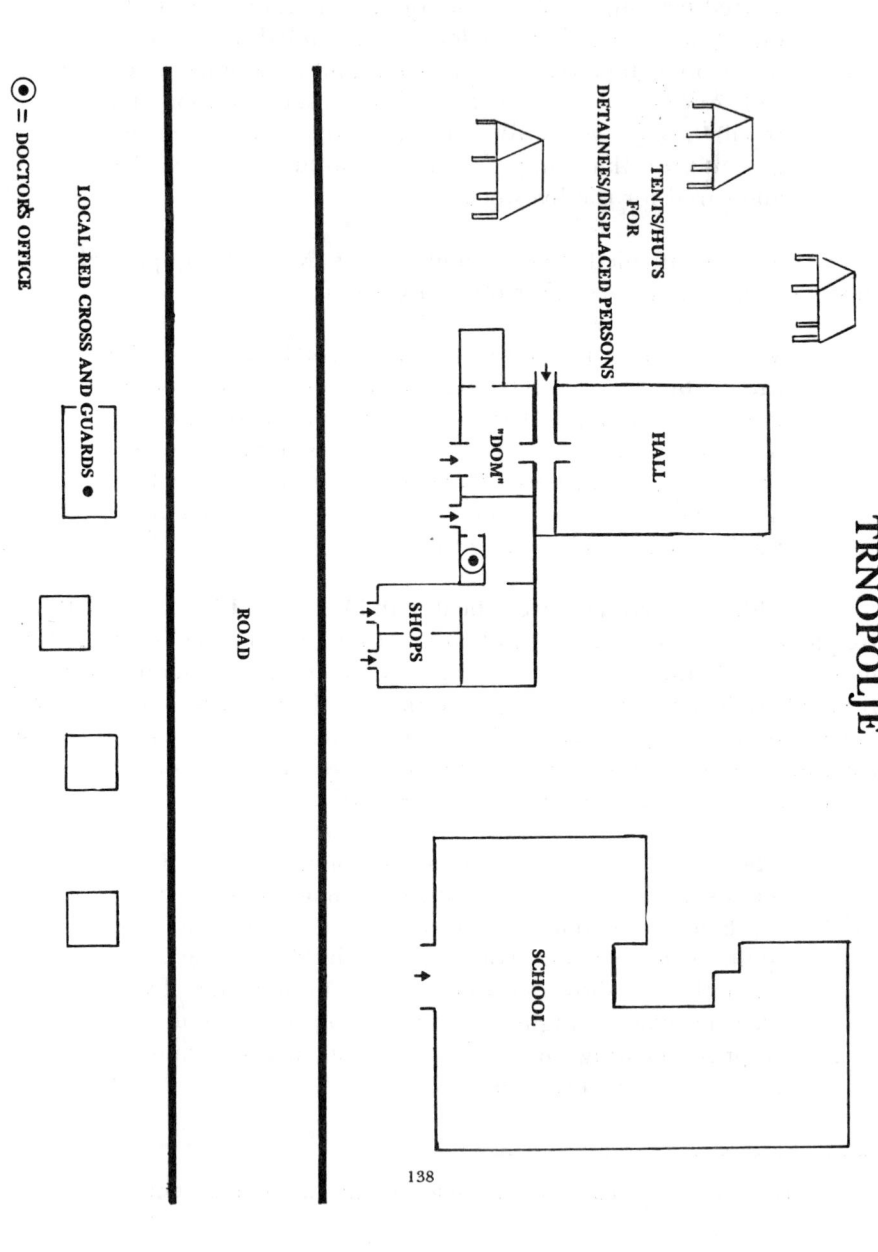

Trnopolje Detention Camp

In late May, part of the predominantly Muslim village of Trnopolje, in the municipality of Prijedor, was transformed into a detention camp, primarily for non-Serbian women, children and elderly persons. The Serbian authorities who administered the Trnopolje camp referred to it as a "refugee reception center" or "an open camp" for Muslims who were "hiding from Muslim extremists." Between May and August, Trnopolje was a detention camp, similar to, but less brutal than, the Keraterm, Omarska and Manjača camps. After Trnopolje was discovered by the Western press in late July 1992 and the barbed wire that surrounded it was removed, the Trnopolje camp became, *de facto*, a "ghetto" or holding center for non-Serbs in the area. Most of those detained in the Trnopolje camp lived in tents, the school or other buildings within the camp's perimeter.

On the basis of interviews with former Trnopolje detainees, at least three categories of persons interned in the Trnopolje camp can be identified. The first category included those who were kept at the Trnopolje camp after Serbian forces attacked and forcibly displaced the non-Serbian population in the area. Women, children and elderly persons comprised the majority of such forcibly interned persons. The men who had been forcibly displaced from their villages were most frequently detained in the Omarska, Keraterm or Manjača camps.

Another category of detainees included those persons, mostly men, who were transferred to Trnopolje after the Omarska and Keraterm camps were closed. At first, these former camp inmates were separated from the rest of the detainees in Trnopolje and were frequently interned in the school, where some were beaten.

A third category of detainees included Muslims and Croats who voluntarily abandoned their villages in Serbian-occupied regions of northwestern Bosnia and came to Trnopolje, thinking it was safer for them to remain in the camp than in their homes. These people believed that they would be registered by the ICRC at Trnopolje and resettled in another country. When the camp became overcrowded, Serbian authorities deported the Trnopolje detainees from the area, at first in cattle cars and then in buses. Those taken from the ghetto were sent to Muslim- and Croatian-controlled areas of Bosnia.

Although abuses in the Trnopolje camp were more random and not as bestial as in Omarska, Keraterm and Manjača, gross abuses did occur. Men were taken from the camp by guards and were subsequently "disappeared." In a few cases, detainees were shot at random by guards. Trnopolje inmates were forced to bury the bodies under orders of the Serbian authorities that administered the camp.

Helsinki Watch representatives who visited Trnopolje in August 1992 asked to see persons detained in a room near the ghetto's health clinic but were refused by the Serbian authorities. Helsinki Watch had received reports that persons were being mistreated in that room.

Evidence gathered by Helsinki Watch indicates that women were taken from the camp and possibly raped in neighboring houses by guards, police officers and military personnel; some of the women were returned to the camp and others were "disappeared."[183]

R.K., an eighteen-year-old Muslim student from Kozarac, and members of her family were taken to the Trnopolje camp after the fall of their village on May 27, 1992. She claims that other villages also were attacked in late May and that their inhabitants were forcibly interned at the Trnopolje camp. According to R.K.:[184]

> About 5,000 to 6,000 people were brought in on May 27. All the villages in the area were "cleansed." They were given an ultimatum similar to ours: We had to give up or be bombed by planes. Banja Luka is only forty kilometers from us, and they had the capabilities to do something like that, so we all took the threat seriously.
>
> They took us to Trnopolje by bus. Then the buses turned around and came back with the men. When we got to Trnopolje, we went to the fields. We saw the buses arriving and we started to look for our men. They wanted to lock up the men in a separate room but someone fired a shot and then the men scattered into the

---

[183] See following section concerning rape.

[184] Interviewed by Helsinki Watch representatives on October 26, 1992, in Posušje, Bosnia-Hercegovina. At the time of Helsinki Watch's interview with R.K., she did not know of the whereabouts of two of her brothers. She claimed that one of them had been wounded in the fighting and was taken to the prison in Bosanska Gradiška as a "war criminal." Her other brother was taken to Keraterm and then to the Omarska camp.

crowd with the women. Then they started to shoot in the air. They were shooting near the building to scare us.

She claims that the people from the following towns and villages were brought to Trnopolje in late May: Sanski Most, Jakupovići, Kamčani, Softići, Kozaruša, Mahmuljini, Susići, Kozarac, Civci, Suhi Brod, Kevljani, Hadžići, Besići and Brdjani. R.K. described the conditions at Trnopolje:

> We were first held in a school auditorium. During the first several days, we were not given any food, but we did manage to get some water. On the fifth day, I fainted because I had not eaten. A man handed my mother some bread and a soldier gave us some juice. We slept on a bench. When they saw that women and children were begining to faint, those who had family in the area were allowed to go to Trnopolje.

K.B. worked as a schoolteacher for mentally retarded children in Prijedor. The forty-nine-year-old woman lived in Kozarac[185] and was interned at the Trnopolje camp after the fall of her village. K.B. described her arrival at Trnopolje:

> We reached the Trnopolje camp by a back road I never knew existed. It was raining, and they staged an attack as if it were the "Green Berets."[186] For the next two hours, we had to lie in the mud, our heads down, while they were yelling at us, "Lie down, cattle! These are your own shooting at you!"

---

[185] Interviewed by Helsinki Watch representatives in December 1992 in a refugee camp in Zagreb, Croatia.

[186] The "Green Berets" were a paramilitary group that surfaced in Sarajevo when violence broke out in the city in late March and early April 1992. Most of the group's members are closely linked to the regular Army of Bosnia-Hercegovina. Serbian forces continue to refer to Bosnian Muslim forces as the "Green Berets."

K.B. was later moved into the overcrowded classrooms of the old school building. She spent twenty-five nights in the same room, without blankets or additional clothes.

Helsinki Watch also interviewed a Muslim doctor who treated the sick and wounded at the Trnopolje camp.[187] According to the doctor:

> During the "ethnic cleansing" [of the village of Trnopolje and surrounding villages], they brought families to the camp and transported the women and children from the area. Guards would beat and kick apart families that didn't want to be separated.

Trnopolje's detainees were allowed to leave the ghetto and scavenge for food in surrounding areas. The food was brought back to the camp, where it was prepared on makeshift cooking facilities. However, many feared attacks once they left the ghetto and preferred to stay within its confines. The doctor further described the conditions at the camp to Helsinki Watch representatives:

> Nothing was organized at Trnopolje; there was no food, even the water pipes didn't function. Whatever we had to do to survive, we did for ourselves. We got a communal kitchen working and some among us would act as butchers and catch cows, slaughter and cook them. Some of the people who had been expelled from their homes had brought stoves and wood. Later the ICRC came with supplies.

> The town was controlled through checkpoints around it, and wires were placed around the central public buildings. People were coming in from all over, sleeping in their cars, farm machinery, up to nine or ten thousand [people came]. Muslim families in the area were the only source of food. Some of those who came by themselves brought food.

---

[187] Interviewed by Helsinki Watch representatives in October 1992 in a refugee camp in Croatia.

In order to obtain food, the detainees pooled any money they possessed. The money then was given to the local Serbian Red Cross which sold, rather than distributed, bread to the ghetto's inhabitants. Some detainees who had no money went hungry, although other detainees frequently shared food with them. Muslim families that still lived outside the camp brought food, as well. In some cases, Serbs living in the area would sneak food to the Muslims and Croats detained in the camp.

R.K. and her family left Trnopolje but eventually returned to the ghetto. According to R.K.:

> My sister-in-law's father came and took us to the village of Muranovići, which is two kilometers from Prijedor. We were there for one month. But there were only about ten Muslim houses in Muranovići and the rest were Serbian homes. They made us sign loyalty oaths but we were scared to go out and get shot. My fifteen-year-old brother was released from Trnopolje ten days after we were, and he came to us in the village. There were seven of us in that house.
>
> Then, after one month, my sister-in-law's mother told us to leave. She didn't like us. She was afraid that we would be targeted. Then my mother, my little sister, my brother, my sister-in-law and her two children and I went back to the Trnopolje camp again. When we got there, they searched all of us. Again, we had nothing to eat but the local Red Cross eventually sold us some bread. You had to pay a day in advance and then, the next day, you would get the bread. They also gave us half a cup of milk for the children.
>
> They let people from Kamičani go home, so my sister-in-law went to her mother's and then she would bring us some food. But my family didn't want me to leave the ghetto because we were afraid of being raped, so we didn't leave the area.

Hygiene in the camp was abysmal. When Helsinki Watch representatives visited the Trnopolje camp in August 1992, the area smelled from the open toilets that had been dug in an adjoining field. The camp was plagued by flies during the summer. With the onset of winter, many of those who lived in tents were at risk from the cold.

Adequate medical care was virtually nonexistent in Trnopolje. During their visit to Trnopolje, Helsinki Watch representatives visited a tiny health clinic, which was about four square meters in size. Two people who earlier had been brought from the Omarska camp lay on the tile floor. Both were covered with flies. One had an open wound on one leg, which had toilet paper wrapped around it. The other person's face was completely swollen and covered with dried blood. Both were conscious but appeared to be in shock. Two Muslim doctors were also being detained in Trnopolje and they attended to the ghetto's sick and beaten. The doctors appeared to have no medicine, antibiotics or anesthetics.

Mehmet, a man in his fifties,[188] said that the camp's residents were poorly fed and that many people got dysentery. He claims that two or three people died of diseases. Mehmet asserts that conditions worsened on a daily basis during his internment but that the situation improved after a visit by the ICRC. According to Mehmet:

> When the women and children arrived [at the camp], we tried to give them our place because there were heavy rains in June. Nevertheless, some still had to live outside in the mud and rain. When the ICRC arrived, things got better.

According to R.K., Serbian authorities interrogated the camp's inhabitants.

> In Trnopolje, they were always shooting and cursing at us. They took out men who disappeared and they beat us. One night, they came to the room where we women and children slept. They told the younger women to get out. They said, "You in the blue sweat suit, get out. Then they got to me and told me to get out. I got halfway down the hall and then they said, "Not you — go back,"

---

[188] Interviewed by Helsinki Watch representatives in October 1992 in Posušje, Bosnia-Hercegovina. The witness chose to withhold his name, and the name used here is a pseudonym.

and they got my friend instead. She returned later and said she had been questioned.

The next day, they came back and told those of us who had not gotten out last night to get out of the room. I walked into a room but they didn't want to turn on the light. There was a man on the couch and one candle was burning. He told me to answer his questions or you know what will happen. He asked, "Who was your father?" "Did you vote?" "Why did you vote?" "What is a *jihad*?" He said, "Show me how you pray to God." I didn't want to get on the floor and pray because I was afraid. He asked me if I went to the mosque and about my father's whereabouts. I was crying throughout the interrogation. He suggested that we go into a house, where there were soldiers. I said no. I said I wanted to go back with the rest of the people and he told me to go. Then he asked, "How about if you and I take a walk?" Again I said no. Then he said, "You and I will see one another tomorrow." I was able to go back to my family then. During our interrogation, men in camouflage uniforms were walking around.

The doctor said that guards had chosen a room in which they interrogated and beat detainees:

There was a little room in the community center [*dom*] — a lab — that was emptied to serve as a room for interrogation and torture. Several people were beaten to death there and their bodies were taken out in blankets. A relatively small number died.

Women were sometimes interrogated at night about their husbands but the women were not heavily abused; they were just slapped several times. I would watch through the windows and could see who was being taken for an interrogation. Only one woman was killed. She was standing in front of the school while a quarrel broke out among some soldiers over whether to kill a young man. One of the soldiers fired a round indiscriminately and she was hit. Her name was Branka Topola.[189]

Mehmet had been taken to the Trnopolje camp after the fall of Kozarac. He testified that Major Kuruzović was in charge of the camp and that, during his first evening in the camp, detainees were killed, beaten and harassed by Serbian soldiers. According to Mehmet:

> When we entered Trnopolje, the Četniks started filming with a camera and shooting off guns, making it look as though they were protecting us from attack. They told us — for the camera — "We're protecting you from your own fighters." But actually, everything was perfectly quiet and locked up, except for the Četniks shooting off their guns.
>
> They took us to an old movie hall that had no chairs and bare walls. The soldiers — mostly neighbors — would walk through the crowd and if you looked them in the eye, they would beat you. That first night, we were beaten. Two or three more buses with younger men arrived. My son was among them and he was beaten with rifle butts. Mostly the well-to-do were killed.[190]

Mehmet remained in the community hall for the duration of his fifty-day stay in the ghetto. Mehmet believes that approximately two hundred people disappeared during his fifty days in the camp:

---

[189] The doctor also claimed that women were raped while they were in Trnopolje. See the section concerning alleged rape below.

[190] The witness claims that women were raped in the Trnopolje camp. See the section concerning alleged rape below. He also claims that not many people were murdered on the first evening. The witness claims not to have known the names of all those killed, although he alleged that a man named Klipić (the father of a policeman), six members of the Forič family and a wealthy man named "Čupa" Mujkanović were killed in the camp. It remains unclear whether Mehmet witnessed the killings or was told of the deaths by others.

> There was a big yard behind the community hall. The yard was full of the vehicles in which people had driven to get to the camp. A warehouse and a school also were [within the confines of the camp]. The [wire fence] enclosure was a sort of circle surrounded by machine-gun nests — you could move a little but not far, not much. Sometimes it was difficult [to move] because 6,000 people were in the enclosure. They were bringing in people all the time, and the population fluctuated between 2,000 and 6,000. Every day they went through lists and pulled people out for beating or killing. I didn't see people being killed; I only saw corpses. No one tried to look or listen too much.

When asked which people were called from the lists and taken from the ghetto, Mehmet replied:

> They were looking for people who had arms; people who had quarreled with their neighbors and were fingered by them; teachers, professionals, rich men. Only the working class lived. People who knew how to read and write were taken away every day. No teachers survived.

Mehmet reported that the soldiers who stood guard over the detainees were responsible for "disappearing" those called from the aforementioned list. Mehmet reasoned that these soldiers were local Serbs because soldiers from outside the area would not have been able to identify the detainees.

Rasim,[191] a former resident of the village of Brdjani,[192] was brought to Trnopolje on May 26. One month after his arrival, Rasim was one of at least eight men chosen to dig the graves for those who had been killed in the ghetto. According to Rasim:

---

[191] Interviewed by Helsinki Watch representatives in October 1992 in a refugee camp in Croatia. The witness chose to withhold his name, and the name used here is a pseudonym.

[192] For an account of the forced displacement of Brdjani's population, refer to the relevant section above.

My brother, six others and I were taken by some men to a place where there were corpses on the floor. When we were digging the graves, some soldiers or guards from the camp watched us and then three police officers replaced them. There were three bodies [to be buried] and I knew two of the [victims]. One was a man named Ante, who worked in the school in Kozarac, and the other was his son, Zoran. The day before, these men [those whom they were burying] had come from Omarska. Both had the back halves of their heads missing and one had been shot through the eye. We found the third corpse in a burned-down house, near a group of burned houses. This was an old corpse; it was falling apart and the head had been bashed beyond recognition.

Rasim said that he buried Meho Krajina and Tofa Furić, both of whom had had their throats slit. He also buried a third man whom he recognized but whose name he did not know; this corpse had a bullet wound in its head. All three men were buried on the same day and all had been interned in the Trnopolje ghetto. Rasim also said he buried a man named Aziz Talić, whose throat had been slit. He claims that Hase Softić, Braco Pidić and Vaskan Fazlić also were buried.

Rasim reported that the men he buried had been killed in one of the following scenarios: leaving the Trnopolje ghetto to scavenge for food, after being "disappeared" from the ghetto, or in the ghetto itself and during the "ethnic cleansing" of villages in the area.

Rasim eventually was given other work, at which point he no longer buried the corpses and could not identify any further victims. He stated that he could not be sure who or how many were buried because he feared reprisals if he spoke to the other grave diggers. According to Rasim:

> Grave diggers were supposed to be quiet and deny that they had seen anything. Otherwise they would be killed.

Edin, a repairman from Kozarac,[193] worked as a cook for about thirty-five days in the camp and claims to have gotten to know the camp authorities well. He reported that a special unit acted as "escorts" for those being evacuated from the camp or as "security" guards. According to Edin:

> They wore camouflage uniforms and "White Eagles" [Beli Orlovi] insignia. They also were called "cleaners" because they would shoot or kill you if you did not hand over your money or gold or if you tried to get out of line. They escorted me and others to Vlašić.[194] Mišo Radulović, a former teacher, was a first class captain with the unit.
>
> We were allowed to leave the camp grounds to scavenge for food. When I went out, I saw six or seven bodies that the cats and dogs were eating. Half of the population of the area was gone. It was not easy to "clean" out 24,000 people, so they went over the area, village by village.

Ismet, a forty-year-old resident of the village of Trnopolje,[195] told Helsinki Watch representatives:

> [The Trnopolje ghetto] is not a refugee reception area — only after the ICRC came, did they [i.e., the Serbian authorities] begin calling it [that]. We were first kept in the elementary school and the camp eventually spread around the school, which became its central locus point.

---

[193] Interviewed by Helsinki Watch representatives in October 1992 in Posušje, Bosnia-Hercegovina.

[194] Vlašić is the point at which many former detainees were released and allowed to cross over to Croatian- and Bosnian-controlled territory.

[195] Interviewed on October 17, 1992, in a refugee camp in Croatia. The witness chose to withhold his name, and the name used here is a pseudonym.

The camp was about three hundred square meters[196] and about 4,000 people were detained there [at the time of my detention]. There were guards walking about — usually fifty during a given shift. The guards would walk among us in the camp and take people away from time to time, including women.

Four men beat me that day — one was an interrogator and there were three others present. They beat me for half an hour. They kept asking me, "Where's the gun — who had a *pumparica*?" I don't even know what that is; later I was told that it's some type of U.S.-made gun that resembles a hunting rifle. They kept beating me.

According to Ismet, a man wearing a black hat with the letters SDS[197] affixed, interrogated and beat him:

He handcuffed me and took me to be interrogated in a small room, where I was beaten. Then he asked me who had arms legally and I told him. I said I didn't have a gun and then he beat me on the head. He beat me with steel rods, table legs and truncheons. He even hit me over the head with a rocket-propelled grenade launcher. He stabbed me with a knife and cut a nerve in my left leg.

Ismet showed a small knife wound, located near his kneecap, to Helsinki Watch representatives. Ismet continued:

I went to a doctor after the beating. [The man who beat me] sat in the room with me [while I was being attended to by the doctor]. Another man without a hand who had worked as a doctor in Prijedor [also accompanied the

---

[196] The camp was much larger than the witness recalls.

[197] SDS is the acronym for the Serbian Democratic Party [Srpska Demokratska Stranka], the political party that initiated the Serbian rebellion in Bosnia and, earlier, in Croatia.

interrogator]. Both took me to see the doctor in Prijedor. They told me to lie in the back seat while I was handcuffed. He told the doctor to stitch my wounds. No anesthesia was used.

The three men stopped in Keraterm before they returned to Trnopolje. When they returned to the camp, Ismet witnessed other people being beaten.

> I asked if they were going to kill me. The other guy said they would not. I was put in a room for forty-eight hours, and I saw people being beaten. They took people from the camp and brought them to the room in which I was interned. There were eight of us in the room and a ninth person also was brought in later. A total of twelve people were eventually held in the room, and some were women, but they were later separated from us. They took two girls from the building in which I was being held and brought them back two days later. They didn't beat people in public, on the camp grounds. They would summon them to this room and then beat them.
>
> They would let us go to our homes to get clothes, food and other things. Although they let us go to our house, someone always waited for us at the house; so, effectively, we were under constant watch. They took people from the tent area. The bodies of six Muslims and two Croats were later found.
>
> One or two days later, they let us out of the camp. I left Trnopolje on October 1. I spent four months in the camp, primarily in the school, which is where I slept. We who were arrested on June 26 — approximately 1,600 to 2,000 people — were put in the school. They allowed us to go outside, but only if we paid them in German marks.

K.B. identified some of the guards in the ghetto:

Two of the guards in Trnopolje, Čedo Dragojević and Rajko Damjanović, were both in their early twenties and had been students at the special school [for the mentally disabled]. They were placed in the class for maladjusted children. Čedo Dragojević was aggressive. He would beat several detainees every day.

K.B. was eventually allowed to leave the ghetto and stay with friends and relatives in the area. However, she was eventually brought back to Trnopolje and deported from the area.

In late August, former inmates from the Keraterm and Omarska camps were transferred to Trnopolje. According to the doctor:

> When people from other camps such as Omarska and Keraterm came to Trnopolje, they were thrilled — it was like a vacation in Switzerland for them! I saw some people who had lost forty kilograms [in the other camps].

Because the Trnopolje camp had been discovered, the guards became more lenient with the prisoners but abuses continued, particularly in the evenings. At first the Keraterm and Omarska prisoners were kept segregated from the Trnopolje detainees. However, after the press discovered Trnopolje, the restrictions in the camp were loosened. The local Serbian Red Cross gave detainees identity cards and they were allowed to work outside the camp. However, many feared attack once they left the ghetto and preferred to remain within its confines. According to the doctor:

> Although we were allowed to work, that became very risky because you could be killed, so many people came back to Trnopolje. For example, five men wanted to go to Prijedor but there were no cars. They were interrogated, beaten, kicked and taken away by the military police.

A.H., a thirty-eight-year-old former resident of Hambarine,[198] was transferred from the Keraterm camp to Trnopolje in early August. He identified a man whose surname is Žigić as one of the more brutal soldiers in Trnopolje. A.H. claims that Žigić had been a taxi driver in Prijedor.

> The first day I was there [i.e., in Trnopolje], this Žigić guy came and found a man named Hasan. Žigić started to hit Hasan and he [i.e., Hasan] was covered with blood. Then the guard on duty came and stopped Žigić from beating him further.
>
> In Trnopolje, we were encircled by wire, and there were many prisoners who had been there before we arrived. We were separated from the others by this wire, and we couldn't have any contact with them. Most of them were women and children from Kozarac.
>
> While I was in Trnopolje, they took people away and beat them. Some people disappeared. We were allowed to go the village [of Trnopolje] to get food. The village was deserted, but we could gather potatoes and other crops.

According to Edin:

> At the end of July, a French woman journalist driving a car with Belgrade plates came to the [Trnopolje] camp. Then more prisoners arrived. Seventy buses from Keraterm arrived. Prisoners from Omarska also arrived. Then the wire encircling the camp was dismantled on August 3. After the wire came down, we were allowed to walk out of the camp if we left our identification papers

---

[198] Interviewed by Helsinki Watch representatives on October 17, 1992, in a refugee camp in Croatia. The witness had been interned in the Keraterm camp prior to his arrival at Trnopolje. See relevant sections above for accounts of the witness's treatment in detention at Keraterm and the forced displacement of his village's inhabitants.

> [with the guards]. The guards would ask when you would be back and you could say by 9:00, and all would be fine, but they'd tell you that if you were late you'd be butchered.

According to Edin, a bribe of one hundred German marks would buy a release form, which is the way Edin secured his release from Trnopolje on August 21.

Sulejman, a young farm worker from Kevljani,[199] spent seventy-five days in the Omarska camp before he was transferred to the Trnopolje ghetto. According to Sulejman:

> In Trnopolje, we could eat by stealing from gardens, finding potatoes, and so forth. We went to destroyed houses and took food from those gardens. Guards would follow us and shoot at us; it was pure luck if you managed to get away. We were provided the same amount of food as at Omarska, but we were allowed to walk about. This period lasted only fifteen days. Thereafter, they provided no food — only water — until the ICRC came. The people were sustained by scavenging, if someone could go into the village.

Edin had been detained in Omarska before he was interned in Trnopolje. One day, the Serbian soldiers issued release forms to Trnopolje's residents who were otherwise from Prijedor. Edin took the opportunity to ask for his release and for the release of former Omarska prisoners. According to Edin:

> On June 4, I asked Major Slobodan Kurozović, the commander of the camp, whether we [i.e., the former Omarska detainees who were now interned in Trnopolje] also could leave, but he said that we were a special case. I remained in Trnopolje for sixty-three days. They moved out women, and only the men had to remain.

---

[199] Interviewed by Helsinki Watch representatives in October 1992 in a refugee camp in Croatia. The witness chose to withhold his name, and the name used here is a pseudonym.

They were not interrogating people, just beating them. Occasionally, they sent men to Omarska. People from Čela, Puharska and Ljubija were sent to Keraterm.

According to the doctor, the "official policy" at Trnopolje was that women, children, the sick and boys under sixteen and men over sixty-five could leave Trnopolje on organized convoys. According to the doctor:

> In the beginning, the convoys consisted of suffocating cattle cars bound for Doboj [in northeastern Bosnia]. When it was no longer possible to use the train, they [deported the ghetto's inhabitants in] large trucks bound for Travnik.

Bosanski Novi

In early July, field officers affiliated with the civilian and political affairs section of the United Nations Protection Forces (UNPROFOR) in the former Yugoslavia[200] identified a Serbian-operated detention facility in a stadium in Bosanski Novi.[201] According to witnesses, former prisoners and relief workers interviewed by Helsinki Watch representatives, men also were detained in the hotel in Bosanski Novi and at the local fire station.

Jasmin, a young man from Bosanski Novi,[202] claims that, on June 1, 1992, Serbian military police officers began arresting men from Muslim villages in the municipality of Bosanski Novi. According to Jasmin:

---

[200] The UNPROFOR in the fromer Yugoslavia retains a section for civilian and political affairs (CIVPOL) headed by Cedric Thornberry.

[201] See Helsinki Watch, War Crimes in Bosnia-Hercegovina, August 1992, pp. 168-69 and 228-29 (Appendix B).

[202] Interviewed by Helsinki Watch representatives in October 1992 in Varaždin, Croatia. The witness chose to withhold his name, and the name used here is a pseudonym.

All the men aged fifteen and older — regardless of their military status — had to go with the police officers. The roundup took place over a fifteen-day period and involved inhabitants of [the village of] Blagaj and [the town of] Bosanski Novi. I and thirty other men were taken away by ordinary civilian police.

First, we were taken to the police station, where I was interrogated. They asked questions such as, "Why do you hate Serbs?" I was not beaten. Eventually, I was told to leave.

The men were then taken to the sports stadium in Bosanski Novi. According to Jasmin, men were sleeping in dressing rooms, on the floor, in corridors, on blankets and some huddled together without blankets. Jasmin described the treatment in the stadium:

We received food twice a day, usually a seventh of a kilo of bread and gruel with beans and peas; but only the luckiest got that, most of the others got just the watery soup. The men guarding us were reservists of the "Army of the Serbian Republic." The guards changed every seven days. When a captain of the "Serbian Army" was killed on the front, they reduced our meals to only one a day. It was hot, conditions were bad and older men began to collapse. So we complained to the commander, and he reinstated the second meal.

According to Jasmin, some of the prisoners had to sign documents according to which they relinquished their property to the Bosanski Novi town council. According to Jasmin:

The military police came [to the stadium] with a list of names and asked each person [on the list] to sign a paper giving all their property to the city. I glimpsed one of the documents the men were supposed to sign, and in a corner of that paper I read the words "because of security reasons." Of those who had to sign the documents, two were members of the Party of Democratic Action (SDA), four or five were rather rich, but I really have no idea why they were singled out beyond that.

Jasmin claims that fifteen men, including himself, were on a special list. These men were separated from the other prisoners and taken to the basement of the hotel in Bosanski Novi. Some of the detainees were beaten. According to Jasmin:

> The guards made jokes when they read out the fifteen names. They picked one guy who was simpleminded and gave him an empty revolver. Then they beat him in front of everybody. Another seventeen-year-old from Blagaj was taken to a separate room and kicked and struck a few times and then he returned.
>
> Of the fifteen, four were handcuffed; one man's hand was handcuffed to another's. Then we had to proceed in a line to the hotel. They gave us oars to hold so that we looked like a kayaking club or something. We walked to the hotel. We were not allowed to look to the right or left and we were surrounded by soldiers. Nevertheless, some people recognized us as we walked through the streets. When we reached the hotel, we had to wait until someone found the key to the cellar.

According to Jasmin, the prisoners were placed in a storeroom in the hotel cellar. The room was dark, without furniture, about four by three square meters in size, and four men were already being held in the room when they arrived. Jasmin described the conditions in the cellar:

> There was some cardboard and blankets in the room, but no light or windows — a totally dark room. There were pipes near the ceiling, dripping water, and the place was very humid. We had a little piece of candle but there wasn't enough air to sustain the flame; it was hard to breathe. There was a little pipe in the corner with a sink. We used the pipe for drinking water, and the sink was used as a toilet. We had to defecate into a nylon bag and put it in the corner. No one would take it out.

> For three days and nights, we had nothing to eat except the water [from the pipe] and a little salt which we had brought with us from the stadium.

The four men who were being detained in the cellar at the time of Jasmin's arrival were all Muslims. According to Jasmin, one was a soldier, and another had been accused of trading in arms on the black market. The third and fourth detainees had been in the cellar for ten days before the others arrived. Jasmin said that the soldier had had his jaw broken, and his face was swollen.

According to Jasmin, the day after they were brought to the hotel — on July 23 — a convoy evacuated the men held in the stadium. On the seventh day of their detention, the men were moved from the cellar. Jasmin claims that the military police were ordered to vacate the hotel and occupy the local fire brigade's office instead. According to Jasmin:

> Things were much better there [i.e., at the fire brigade's office]. We had to work; for example, we had to cut grass by hand. We also began to get food twice a day. We received the same food as the military police, although they were fed three times a day. Nineteen of us prisoners stayed in a room six by four meters in size. We had pallets of board and cardboard. We didn't have blankets but it was still warm.

According to Jasmin, prisoners were interrogated, some were charged with a crime and others were beaten:

> The other prisoners were beaten from time to time, but I knew some of the police officers — they had been my friends — so I was not beaten. Others were interrogated for five hours at a time and beaten. When they returned, they were bruised, in pain and unable to lie down.
>
> I was accused of selling two hand grenades. They had no evidence; a neighbor accused me. During the interrogation, I had to sign some sort of plea, and I was

> allowed to sign a statement expressing my innocence.[203]

Jasmin remained in detention until August 10, when he received release papers. After he was released, he had to report to the local police station three times a day. According to Jasmin:

> [When I was released,] I went to live at my uncle's place. He and his wife had left the area in an earlier convoy. But a Serbian woman occupied their house and she had some type of document from the authorities stating that the house now belonged to her.

Ključ

Helsinki Watch representatives interviewed H.P.,[204] a forty-three-year-old resident of Prijedor who had fled the city out of fear. He traveled to his place of birth in the municipality of Ključ, where he was arrested and detained. According to H.P.:

> I ran to my mother's in [the municipality of] Ključ. If I had stayed in Prijedor, I would have been a dead man. I was at my mother's in [the village of] Pudin when the attack on that village took place on June 2. We fled to Vukovska Brda which is another village with only fifteen houses. I was hiding there for about twenty-six days and they arrested me on June 26, while I was having coffee. The men who arrested me were either the Serbian police or army. They wore camouflage or olive uniforms and there were also civilians with beards among them. I don't know how many there were — I only remember that many of them surrounded the entire village.

---

[203] Jasmin claims that two other prisoners, however, had to sign statements in which they admitted to organizing some type of rebellion, but Jasmin did not specify his source of information.

[204] Interviewed by Helsinki Watch representatives on October 17, 1992, in a refugee camp in Croatia.

Fifteen men, including H.P., were taken from Vukovska Brda to a detention facility in a sports hall in the town of Ključ, where they were beaten. According to H.P.:

> We fifteen men were taken two and a half kilometers through the forest. Of those arrested, about five were minors and three were elderly men. Three times they said that they would shoot me in the forest. We were taken to the sports hall in Ključ, and throughout the night we were interrogated and beaten. Three men whose names I do not know were beaten and later died. They died at my feet; they were between twenty-three and forty-five years old.

H.P. spent one day in the Ključ sports hall and then was transferred to the Manjača camp. Between 110 and 120 other detainees who had been taken from four villages in the area also were taken to Manjača with H.P.[205]

Kotor Varoš

In mid-October, 6,500 Muslim civilians from Kotor Varoš were gathered behind barbed wire in an open field in bad weather conditions, awaiting evacuation by international agencies. Sixteen busloads of women and children left the detention center for the town of Travnik. Sixty men on the buses were taken away by armed Serbian guards to an unknown destination.[206]

According to foreign relief workers and press reports, Serbian Red Cross officials administer the camp in Kotor Varoš as a detention facility. Serbian authorities claim that the camp is an "open reception center" and that the inhabitants come of their own free will and want an "easy route" to Western Europe. When questioned by journalists about why they had left their homes in and around Prijedor, many of the

---

[205] See relevant section above for an account of H.P.'s treatment in the Manjača camp.

[206] Chuck Sudetic, "Bloody and Unshod, Refugees Flee Serbs," *The New York Times*, October 20, 1992.

inhabitants of the camp said that their villages had been burned down and made gestures indicating guns pointed at their heads and knives at their throats.[207]

Banja Luka Hospital

Five of eight survivors of the Vlašić massacre,[208] were recaptured by Serbian forces and briefly detained in Skender Vakuf. They then were taken to the Banja Luka hospital, where they were detained and mistreated by patients and soldiers for twenty-five days with the apparent acquiescence of the hospital staff and the Serbian armed forces. According to B.J.:[209]

> Detectives[210] from Banja Luka arrived in Skender Vakuf and took us to Banja Luka with them. We were taken to the hospital in Banja Luka, and we gave a statement to the police. I spent twenty-five days in the Banja Luka hospital. That was real hell. They beat me more in that hospital than they had in the camp [Trnopolje]. The army, the police and Serbian patients in the hospital beat us. No one bothered to stop them or to prevent their entrance into our room. They would freely enter the room. There was a guard outside our room, but he let anyone come in, even if they carried truncheons and cable wire.

---

[207] Mary Battiata, "Muslims Flee Renewed Drive by Serb Forces," *The Washington Post*, October 11, 1992.

[208] For an account of the massacre, see relevant section above.

[209] Interviewed by Helsinki Watch representatives on October 17, 1992, in a refugee camp in Croatia.

[210] The witness referred to them as "the criminal division" (*kriminalna služba*), presumably of the Banja Luka police.

B.J.'s account was corroborated by Esad, another survivor of the Vlašić massacre:[211]

> We spent twenty-three or twenty-four days in Banja Luka. The patients in the hospital beat us. We had a guard outside our door — they were police officers. One police officer was on duty during each shift [and] there were three shifts per day. The names of the three guards that changed shifts every day were Saša, Milenko and Zoran. These guards let anyone enter our room. There were six of us [i.e., survivors of the Vlašić massacre] plus five other [prisoners]. Another prisoner arrived later.
>
> Soldiers and patients beat us, especially those patients who arrived in the hospital ten days after our arrival. A Croat named Milan Rozanković was brought into the room, and then the number of guards per day increased to four.[212] Milan was a member of the Croatian Army [HV] from Croatia proper. He was born in Sisak and had a wife and two children in Gorica. He was beaten especially badly at the hospital and he eventually died from the beatings.
>
> The ICRC visited us after our twenty-third day in the hospital. They registered us, but the second time they came, they didn't let them come into the room, probably because Rozanković was in such bad shape.

---

[211] The witness was interviewed by Helsinki Watch representatives on October 17, 1992, in a refugee camp in Croatia. He chose to withhold his name, and the name used here is a pseudonym.

[212] The witness was not clear as to the number of guards on duty and the number of shifts per day. It appears that four, as opposed to three, shifts guarded the detainees after the Croatian prisoner arrived. However, it is possible that the number of guards per shift increased from one to four and that the shifts remained at three per day.

After the twenty-fifth day in the hospital, the survivors were taken to the local court, where B.J. and Esad gave a statement to a magistrate. According to Esad:

> We were taken to Banja Luka to the police station [*Kriminalna služba*]. None of the men wore uniforms, but they were armed. They told us to get into a truck and asked us if we had relatives in Banja Luka. They took us to the court, and we gave our statements about what happened — it was the same testimony we had to give in Skender Vakuf.

The prisoners were then handed over to workers of the Muslim relief agency, Merhamet, in Banja Luka, where they stayed for fifteen days. Six of the survivors were then evacuated from Bosnia.

Rape

Omarska

J.,[213] a thirty-nine-year-old Croatian woman from the town of Prijedor, was raped by a reserve captain of the self-proclaimed "Serbian Republic:"

> The commanding officer told me to make coffee for him and two other men present. One was a man named Babić who was the manager of the mine in Omarska, and he was serving his military duty and was in uniform. A second man was named Nedeljko Grabovac, and he was a reserve captain in the "Serbian Army." He said that the Muslims were raping Serbian women. Grabovac told me to get out of the room but then he grabbed me and took

---

[213] Interviewed by Helsinki Watch representatives on October 15, 1992, in Zagreb, Croatia. Helsinki Watch interviewed two other women who had been held in Omarska, and they confirmed that women had been raped in the camp. For an account of mistreatment in the Omarska camp, see the relevant section above.

me into another office. He threw me on the floor, and someone else came into the room. During that period, the electricity would go on and off at intervals. When I was assaulted, there was no electricity in the building, and I could not identify the second man who had entered the room. Both Grabovac and this other man started to beat me. They said I was an Ustaša and that I needed to give birth to a Serb — that I would then be different. I was raped only by Grabovac; the other man had left the room. After he raped me, I was ordered to go back to my room with the other women.

The next evening, Grabovac came to my door and told me to get out and I did so. He said that I must have gotten a cold the night before, and he gave me some tea — but I didn't want to drink it. He then hit me in the head with the butt of his revolver. He grabbed my chest and dragged me to the bathroom, where he beat me. The commanding officer was present during this entire abuse. I should add that all the women were beaten at various points during our detention, but none of us was ever beaten in the face; they only beat our bodies.

On the third evening, Grabovac took me out again and started to excuse himself for his actions the previous evening, explaining that "our nationalities are at war." Then he started to show me what he called "instruments of torture used by the Muslims against Serbs." He showed me a fishhook that he claimed was used to cut the veins of Serbian men and a ball-and-chain contraption which he claimed was used to strangle Serbs. But these instruments were covered with blood, and they must have been used very recently. It would have been virtually impossible for a Muslim to have done this to a Serb in Omarska and I thought to myself that those weapons had probably been used against the prisoners, not the Serbs but I said nothing. He then started to beat me again because I did not respond to his statements.

On the fourth night, the reservist [Grabovac] came back again. He alleged that I was the lover of [another prisoner][214] and that, because of this, I was shunning his advances. Then he beat me with a wire and hit me in the chest with his revolver. The guard who frequently gave us food came into the room. This guard was not a reservist but an active member of the "Serbian Army" and he kicked Grabovac out of the room. The commanding officer on duty then came into the room and asked me who had raped and beaten me. I replied that no one had touched me. The commanding officer told me that he would punish the perpetrator if I identified him. Again I answered that no one had touched me because I was afraid of retribution later.

Keraterm

Selima,[215] a Muslim woman in her forties, was arrested in her home in Prijedor on May 30 and detained in a former local government building for four days. She was allowed to go home and was rearrested on June 11 and detained subsequently in the Keraterm, Omarska and Trnopolje camps. While in Keraterm, Selima was raped by an unknown assailant and by Zoran Sikirica, whom she claimed was the commander of the camp. Other former Keraterm detainees interviewed by Helsinki Watch representatives also identified Sikirica a soldier at the Keraterm detention facility.[216] Selima described her arrest and internment at the Keraterm camp to Helsinki Watch representatives:

---

[214] Grabovac named a prisoner with whom the witness spoke when he came for his food in the restaurant.

[215] Interviewed by Helsinki Watch representatives on Februray 22, 1993, in Zagreb, Croatia. The woman provided her name to Helsinki Watch representatives but asked that it remain confidential. The name used here is a pseudonym, and other identifying features have been deleted to protect the confidentiality of the witness.

[216] For an account of the treatment in the Keraterm camp, see relevant section above.

That day [i.e., August 11], two Serbian policemen came [to my door.] It was 9:30 p.m. I knew both of them — they worked in our [local] police station. They told me that I had to go to the police station with them to give a statement and that I'd go home immediately after I finished [giving a statement]. I was not very scared because I knew I was not guilty of anything. I was not politically active, I was not a member of any political party and I believed them when they said that I would only have to make a statement and then go home. I was so stupid.

When I got to the police station, I saw two other women there. I didn't know them. They asked me some questions and then I waited outside for a while. I was taken with one of these two women to Keraterm. We didn't know where they were taking us. When we arrived, we realized that we were in Keraterm — it was a brick-and-ceramic-tile factory. I thought that we two women would stay together, but they separated us.

They locked me in one of the big halls. Offices had earlier been in this building. There were office tables in the room. It was dark. I heard the screams of the men who were tortured and the shouts of their torturers. At about 2:00 a.m., I heard the door being unlocked, and I saw the light of a flashlight. I recognized Zoran Sikirica, who was at that time the commander of Keraterm. He told me that inspectors were coming from Banja Luka in a few minutes and that they would have to ask me some questions. Only a crazy person would believe that any inspectors were coming to interrogate you at 2:00 in the morning. And then he did it. He raped me on one of the tables.

First, he started to insult me. He asked me if I had a husband . . . or a lover. Then he ordered me to take off my clothes. I started to cry, and I told him that I was menstruating. He said he didn't mind and that he would show me how a Serb does it. He tied my hands and then he raped me on the table.

Selima testified that she and Sikirica were the only ones in the room during the rape. She said that she recognized Sikirica's face and voice. After he left the room, three other men entered. Selima said that they did not have flashlights and, therefore, she could not see their faces. She only saw that one of the men had a moustache. She testified that one of the men raped her while the others stood by. According to Selima:

> While one of them was raping me, the other two were laughing, insulting me and cheering him [i.e., the rapist] on. They smelled of alcohol. It was terrible. They bit my legs, which were black and blue for the next couple of days. When they finished, one of them untied my hands, and they were gone. That night I cried a lot, but I never cried again [during my detention.]

The following day, Selima and the other woman with whom she had come to Keraterm[217] were taken to a large hall in the factory. The two women were separated by seven young soldiers, who took Selima to a small room. According to Selima:

> The room seemed as if it was underground. They [i.e., the soldiers] were very young. One of them told me that I had lived long enough and that I would see death coming. They started to insult me, and I thought this was the end. Then [another] soldier came in. I had never seen him before but I would like to know who he is because he saved my life. He shouted at these young soldiers and he cursed them. He said, "What are you doing to this woman?"

> After that, they moved us [i.e., Selima and the other woman] into the large hall, where the male prisoners were kept. The soldiers told us that we should not dare to cry or tell anyone about what had happened. Some

---

[217] The witness identified the woman by name and profession.

other soldiers came later and asked me if anyone had harmed me, but I replied "no" — otherwise, they would have killed me. The commander — the one who raped me — personally sent a soldier the next day [after the rape] to ask me if anyone had molested me.[218] What else could I have done?

Selima was later interned at the Omarska camp, where she claims to have seen her rapist, Zoran Sikirica. According to Selima, many guards from Keraterm also came to Omarska.[219]

Čarakovo

Helsinki Watch and the Women's Rights Project interviewed a young married couple, both Muslims, from Čarakovo. The family of Selim,[220] the twenty-four-year-old husband, had remained in the village, awaiting the return of his brother from a detention camp. A Serbian soldier named Rajko Dragić broke into the house where he was staying with his wife, Senada, his wife's sister and their four-year-old daughter. According to the young man:

> My wife's sister, my wife and I were in the house. First he [Dragić] took our VCR and television. Then he pointed a machine gun at me and forced my wife to undress. He held a knife to her neck. He was alone. Several others were outside but they didn't come into the house. He was yelling and drunk. He shouted at my wife

---

[218] The witness did not indicate how she knew that her assailant had personally sent a soldier to question her.

[219] Selima claims to have recognized some of the guards and soldiers at Keraterm and Omarska. The above section concerning the Keraterm camp identifies some of the guards and soldiers named by the witness and other former detainees interviewed by Helsinki Watch representatives.

[220] Interviewed by Helsinki Watch representatives in January 1993 at the mosque in Zagreb, Croatia. The couple chose to withold their names, and the names used here are pseudonyms.

and told her to leave me and marry him. He said he would kill me. He was wearing a camouflage uniform with bullets around his chest. He may have been wearing a red beret. He was from the "Serbian Army."

I know the man who raped my wife. He is from my wife's village, Rakelići. His name is Rajko Dragić, but people call him "Bokser." He raped her, and then he burned our house. I worked with him at the rail company in Prijedor.[221]

According to Senada, the young woman who was raped:

A man broke into our house and raped me. He was in a green uniform and had a machine gun and a knife. I didn't know him. My husband had to watch while I was raped. I have a four-year-old daughter; she saw the rape. There was no way I could avoid it; he would have killed both of us. He just said, "Your husband has to watch." He was in the house all day and raped me once for two to three hours. He was screaming that he wanted to marry me. He was drunk and breaking our things. He left, and the house was burned. We all had to run away.

The young couple fled with their family after the house was set on fire, but did not report what had happened for fear that they would be killed.

F.S., a thirty-two-year-old Muslim mother of two young children,[222] originally is from the village of Hambarine. During the attack on her village, F.S. and her family fled to the village of Čarakovo, where they spent two months, from late May to late July. After Čarakovo

---

[221] The witness claimed that "Bokser" raped other women in the village, but he provided no evidence to support the assertion.

[222] Interviewed by Helsinki Watch and the Women's Rights Project on January 14, 1993, in a refugee camp in Croatia.

fell to Serbian forces, F.S. claims that the village's inhabitants were threatened with rape. According to F.S.:

> I was in the house with my sister and our children. The soldiers came in and told us to stay inside. The first soldier who came in was polite and just warned us.[223] Others that came in later were drunk and violent. They tried to humiliate us and said, "We should rape these women." We were trembling with fear, trembling as much as if they had raped us, but they left without acting on their words. They stayed about fifteen to twenty minutes and asked me for water. There were twenty soldiers in the yard. I had to give each one water from the well, one by one. Nothing happened to me, but they were making fun of me.[224]

> No women were taken from the village. We formed large groups of women to stay together in houses. The soldiers would come and harass teenage boys. The soldiers would come every day and tell us to leave. They asked where the men were and would take us outside and line us up.

F.S.'s husband was interned in a camp. F.S. and her children eventually moved from Čarakovo to another village closer to Prijedor. During the walk there, F.S. claims to have seen bodies in the street between Čarokovo and Prijedor. F.S. and her children then went voluntarily to the Trnopolje camp, from where they were taken to Travnik. They eventually left Bosnia.

---

[223] The witness did not elaborate on the content of the warning.

[224] The witness asserts that other women in Čarakovo claimed to have been raped, but she did not witness the abuse.

Rakovčani

Munevra is a twenty-year-old Muslim receptionist from the village of Rakovčani, approximately four kilometers from Prijedor.[225] She witnessed the aftermath of a friend's rape after an attack on her village in June. According to Munevra:

> My village was burned, and we were forced to leave. All the men were taken to a camp; some disappeared, some were killed, some survived. The area is mostly Muslim, but we were mistreated. We were told to move out in twenty-four hours. There were many rapes and many robberies. We walked twenty-two hours to [Muslim- and Croatian-controlled territory in Bosnia.]
>
> They came to our homes [and] took what they wanted. If anyone opposed, them they were killed. They were shooting all around our village. They took away the men and raped women and children.
>
> My neighbor, who was born in 1973, went to school with me; she was raped by fifteen men. We had to carry her from the village. She didn't know where she was, didn't even know her own name. She was a virgin. I didn't see her being raped. Her mother came in to our house crying, screaming that she couldn't do anything. She was raped in the basement of her house. We carried her into her house. She was badly bruised. Her mother watched from the window. There was another group too busy looting to join in. She was very beautiful, but they didn't care. As long as you are a Muslim. They scream and yell; are not nice. Our houses are very near. I could hear her screaming and crying and begging: "I'm a virgin." "Well, this is why we chose you," they said. She spent two months in a hospital with the psychiatric cases. I don't

---

[225] Interviewed by Helsinki Watch representatives on January 14, 1993, in the Resnik refugee camp in Croatia. The witness chose to withold her name, and the name used here is a pseudonym.

know if she was pregnant, but if she was, she would not want the baby.

There are women in this camp who were raped, but they are not talking about it. When I meet them I talk about everything else. They want to forget this and lead a normal life. They think they are inferior. Virginity is very important to us Muslims.[226]

Municipality of Ključ

K.S.[227] is a housewife from a village in the municipality of Ključ. She refused to identify the name of her village, fearing that her identity would thereby be disclosed. The woman, who was raped in her home, was born in 1939 and is illiterate. She could not recall the day of her assault but did specify that it had taken place approximately four months before Helsinki Watch interviewed her, probably in late September. She could only identify the approximate month by the farming season at the time of her assault, which she identified as the period during which corn is harvested and potatoes are dug out of the ground. According to K.S.:

> One evening soldiers pounded on our front door. They had already been in our village near Ključ. I do not want to tell you the name of the village. Six of us women and my man [i.e., husband] were in the house. The women were our relatives and neighbors. They had taken refuge in our house because the house had two cement and iron-reinforced floors, so it provided a good shelter. Ours was a two-story house.

---

[226] Helsinki Watch has interviewed scores of men and women who claim to have spoken to victims of rape who recounted their abuse. In many cases, the witnesses told Helsinki Watch representatives the name of the victim and her possible whereabouts. Helsinki Watch was not able to interview such victims and has not been able to confirm many allegations.

[227] Interviewed by Helsinki Watch representatives on January 22, 1993, in a refugee camp in Croatia.

That night, they pounded on the door. I asked: "Who is banging? We are home alone, please don't bang." My mother-in-law's bed was situated exactly below the window. After I'd spoken, they broke the window with their rifle butts. The glass shattered all over my mother-in-law. I opened the front door, and five armed Serbian soldiers came in.

K.S. described the soldiers to the Helsinki Watch representative:

I know they were Serbs. The Muslims wore no uniforms, only the Serbs did. It was them. They wore camouflage [and] they had bullet cartridges and knives tucked in their belts. Around the arms they had some insignia, I do not know exactly what kind, but not ours [i.e, not insignia belonging to the Bosnian Muslim forces]. They had different kinds of caps: berets, hats, baseball caps [but] I do not remember the insignia on their caps; they were pushed down tight on their foreheads. Their faces were not covered [with a mask]. When they led us outside, I saw them well. It was a cloudless night, moonlight. The inside was lit by candlelight. They all were very young, about twenty-five to twenty-eight years old.

K.S. testified that she recognized one of the soldiers who was dressed in fatigues, but did not know his name. She claims that the soldier used to man Serbian barricades in the vicinity of the police station in Ključ. K.S. continued:

They chased us all out of our house, six women and my man. They lined us up in front of the house. With knives hanging from their belts, they thrust guns in our throats, yelled and threatened us. They asked us to give them German marks and cursed at us. They pressed a knife up to my husband's neck and said [to me], "If you want the old man alive, give us gold and marks." Then one of my cousins brought out all her gold [jewelry], so that they would spare my man.

> One of them grabbed me by the chest and pulled me over. "Come here," he said. I was calling for help and begging them to kill me rather than separate me from the rest of my folks. I wept and cried out that we were not guilty of anything. He grabbed me by the shoulders and threw me on the ground. He screamed at me, asking which of the villagers had the most gold and money. I told him that I did not know. Our men have never worked abroad; we were not rich. My man and I have lived on his pension. It took three of my man's pensions [to buy] a sack of flour. He hit me on the shoulder and threw me on the ground again. My shoulder still hurts very much. He started tearing off my clothes. Then, the three of them took turns on me.

K.S. claims that her husband and the other women did not witness the rape but heard what was happening. According to K.S.:

> That man took me behind the house — to the side — while the others remained in front of the house. It all took place on the concrete [floor]. I was cold and sore all over. I pleaded with them, "Children, don't. I could be your mother." Then I collapsed and knew nothing more. When I had regained my senses, they were no longer around me, but I heard their voices and the shouts coming from the front of the house.

K.S. then crawled into the house, only to be found and raped again. According to K.S.:

> I crawled this way [i.e., on hands and knees] into the house. [I] went upstairs, found the room, lay down on the bed and slipped a blanket over my head. Then, one of them came in. I only heard him at first. Then he pulled the blanket, lit my face with a flashlight and roared: "Did you try to hide again? Out with [the German] marks!" I wept while telling him that we had no marks. He then spread my legs and raped me. He was very strong — you cannot defend yourself.

When he was done, he inserted his hand inside me and began pinching me with his fingers, as if he wanted to pull everything out. I screamed, and he grabbed my right breast and twisted it so hard that I screamed again; long afterwards my entire breast was blackened. He thrust the knife to my throat and said that, if I screamed one more time, he would slaughter me. He inserted his fingers inside me again — it hurt tremendously — and then he thrust his hand at my face and I had to lick his fingers clean, one by one. He repeated the whole thing once more.

He lowered his knife down below and said that he would rip me open. He kept cursing at me and shouting: "Where is your [Bosnian President] Alija [Izetbegović] now?" He called me an Ustaša [and cursed at me]. I thought it was the end of me. But then, he left. I do not know why he did not kill me. Before they left, they threatened to burn everything if we told anyone what happened. I was covered with blood all over. Once they left, I vomited. I felt very ill. The women helped me; they washed me up. We were afraid that they would come back again.

K.S. claims that her husband reported the incident to the Serbian police authorities, who sent a car to take K.S. to the hospital. According to K.S.:

[My husband] nursed me; he was very good to me. Even now, he takes very good care of me. The following morning, he informed the police about what happened. They sent a car, which took me to the hospital. The doctor was a Serb; at that time, all Muslim physicians had been fired. He gave me shots and some powders.

K.S. told the doctor and a police officer that she had been raped. However, K.S. claims that perpetrators of such crimes are never brought to justice. According to K.S.:

> [The doctor] said that something like that should not be allowed to happen and that they were going to locate those who did it. But they say one thing and do another. What happened to me has been happening to other women by and large. During the day, they tell you that that ought not to be happening, that they will find those soldiers [responsible for the rapes], and then, at night, the soldiers come again and they act as they please. During the day, the Serbian neighbors greet you and pretend that everything is as usual, but at night, these very same people shoot at windows and raid houses.
>
> The policeman who took me to the hospital was writing something down but they put on a big act, you know. They leave it all alone.

After she returned from the hospital, K.S., her husband and the other women were given shelter by local Serbs. According to K.S.:

> Neighbors took us in — Serbs — and we spent six nights at their place. We feared that they [i.e., the assailants] might return. Ah, the fear is great! We feared they would come back to slit our throats. But I had to tell someone what had happened to me [because] I was very ill. They [the Serbs] are not all the same. Some feel pity for you, but some act out evil [deeds] or talk others into it. I would go to my house during the day, but I was afraid to sleep there.

K.S. believes she was assaulted because her husband had refused to sign over their house to the Serbian authorities. According to K.S.:

> [My husband] said he did not want to leave, although most of the people had left our village by that time.

K.S. surmised that Serbian soldiers had maintained a presence in their village, possibly for several months. According to K.S.:

> I was not aware of the fact that somebody would provide for us in this way [i.e., as in the refugee camp]. I thought

we would be hungry. That's why they did it, so that we would have to leave. The next morning, after that all had happened, my man signed everything of ours over to them, just so they would let us leave.

K.S., her husband and her eighty-five-year-old mother-in-law obtained the necessary papers from the Serbian authorities eight days after the rape. They were evacuated in a Serbian-organized convoy which was bound for the Muslim- and Croatian-controlled town of Travnik. According to K.S.:

> [We left for Travnik] on eight buses and eight trucks.[228] The trucks belonged to them. They crammed us into those trucks and left us above Travnik, on Vlašić mountain. There, we were surrounded by Četniks. They shouted and called us names, they took money and gold [jewelry] from those who still possessed any. We were passing by dead people; at some places one couldn't get through because of all the bags and clothing on the ground. Men, women and children [were] screaming, crying their hearts out. It was a horror!

K.S. said she has medical complications resulting from her assault. She also complained of nightmares and feelings of shame. According to K.S.:

> This shoulder that he grabbed still hurts, my husband keeps rubbing it — and my back, as well. My heart keeps pounding, I often cannot sleep, I fear my own shadow. I keep dreaming about handguns; that they are killing me. I keep awaking with a jerk. That fear cannot be described. I wish that they had gunned me down instead of what they did to me. They denigrated me, which will bear hard upon my body and soul as long as I live. When I arrived here [at the refugee camp], I did not come out of my room for a month. I was ashamed. Whenever

---

[228] The witness described the trucks as large tractor-trailers, covered with canvas, which usually are used for the transport of wood.

somebody looked at me, I thought that he or she knew everything about what I had been forced to do. Sometimes, I wonder, would it be best for me to throw myself under the bus . . . And yet, I would have to have strength to return home some day . . .!? God grant that all of this settles down, but . . . Even this frightens me — this statement that I am giving to you. There are Serbs everywhere, including here. In my hometown there are still some folks left; they are doing now to them what they did to me.

What happened to me, happened to many, but the women keep it secret. It is shameful. Thus, the mother conceals it if it happened to her daughter so she can marry and if it happened to an older woman, she wants to protect her marriage. It is a huge embarrassment, you know.

Vojići

M.C. was born in 1972 and is from the village of Vojići in the municipality of Ključ. She is single and has an elementary-school education. Helsinki Watch representatives interviewed the woman[229] in a hospital, where she had given birth to a child four days earlier. M.C. was impregnated by a rapist in Ključ. According to M.C.:

I went to Ključ on April 25, [1992,] from my village of Vojići, in order to pay a fine concerning our house — something in connection with the land taxes. The shooting had started in Ključ in April, and it was very tense. I took a bus and, while I was riding through the town, I saw four or five Četniks standing in front of a building in a narrow street — I do not know the name [of the street] — in the town's center, near the municipal government building.

M.C. described the soldiers:

---

[229] Interviewed on January 22, 1993, in Zagreb, Croatia.

They were dressed in the olive-green uniforms, with *pionirke*[230] caps. I do not remember if there were any insignia on the caps. But, I do know that they were Četniks. Our young men [i.e., Muslims] wore neither uniforms nor weapons.

After M.C. had paid her fine, she was accosted by one of the soldiers and raped in an office of the municipal government building. According to M.C.:

> One of them — obese, between thirty and thirty-five years old, with a short beard and brown hair — was sitting on a chair. He called to me, "Hey, come back, girl, and behave," and I greeted them and said that I was going to pay a fine. The one who addressed me first told another soldier, "Come on, take her where she should go." I said that this was not needed, but he persisted.

Another soldier followed M.C. to the municipal government buidling. She described him as tall, thin and approximately forty to forty-five years old. She did not know the soldier. M.C. continued:

> I walked in front of him. We came to the municipal government building. I entered through the double door and went to pay a fine in the second-floor office.
>
> [The soldier came] into the building [with me] but not to the office. When I stepped out of the office and into a hallway, he awaited me and then pushed me into another office, holding me by the arm. He covered my mouth and pushed me in there. I struggled against him, but I could not scream because my mouth was blocked. He had a gun; I was horrified.

---

[230] *Pionirke* caps were those worn by the members — practically all elementary-school-age children — of the Yugoslav youth organization, the Association of Pioneers. These caps are navy blue, with a red star. The members of the Yugoslav Army (JNA) wear the same style caps, but they are olive green.

M.C. claims that the room was furnished with two desks which were situated in the center of the office. Some chairs also were in the room. She remembers the room as being bright and sunny and the time as being approximately 1:00 p.m. According to M.C., the soldier said nothing to her when they went into the room, where he raped her against a wall. According to M.C.:

> He raped me. It hurt. He raped me while standing. He bent me against the wall, and he placed his gun next to me. Otherwise, he carried it on his shoulder. I begged him to let me go, but he refused to. He kept quiet and went about his job. I was terrified of him and his gun. He unbuttoned my blouse and the skirt, which had an elastic waist, which he pushed down to my ankles. He only took off his trousers. I was a virgin.
>
> When he was done, he released me. I put myself together, and he let me leave. I stumbled in the doorway. He followed me out to the hallway. Another Serbian soldier was passing by, to whom he boasted, "I've just had a sugary treat!" and the soldier responded, "Fiery are the boys from Ribnik!"

M.C. walked past the group of soldiers again but they said nothing to her. She went home but said nothing to her parents because she claims to have felt ashamed and afraid. She realized that she was pregnant after she missed her second menstrual period. However, she did not seek any medical care because she claims that the non-Serbs were afraid to leave their houses for fear of attack. She also managed to hide her pregnancy until September, when she left Ključ with a convoy. Her parents have been resettled in a third country, and they only learned of their daughter's pregnancy after she gave birth.

M.C. gave birth to a boy, but she does not intend to keep the child. She claims that she has been in touch with her father, who has asked his daughter to join him but to leave the child behind. At the time of the Helsinki Watch interview, M.C. said that she had not seen her child.[231]

Trnopolje

Helsinki Watch has not interviewed any women who were themselves raped in Trnopolje. We have, however, received numerous corroborating reports about a systematic pattern of rape at Trnopolje and we include some of them in this section.

According to witnesses interned at Trnopolje, guards frequently entered the area where women slept in the Trnopolje camp, shining flashlights at the younger women and taking them to unknown destinations. Most of those taken in the evening were returned in the early morning and claimed to have been raped.

---

[231] Hospital files in Croatia contain information about women from northwestern Bosnia who were raped, allegedly by Serbian forces. In January 1993, Helsinki Watch representatives were permitted to examine a report compiled by the Croatian Ministry of Health that summarized the medical cases of rape to which several hospitals in northern Croatia had attended. The medical records also included a summary of the circumstances surrounding the rape of each woman but, because Helsinki Watch was not able to interview all the women, we are citing only information of a medical nature.

- Doctors at the Sisters of Charity Hospital in Zagreb treated a twenty-two-year-old woman who claimed to have been raped during her internment by Serbian forces somewhere between the Serbian-controlled town of Donji Vakuf and the Muslim- and Croatian-controlled town of Bugojno. The woman says that she was abducted in late April and released from detention on or about October 1, 1992. She received medical attention on October 23, when doctors determined that she was in her twenty-fourth or twenty-fifth week of pregnancy and, an abortion was performed.

- The psychiatric clinic at the hospital in the town of Vrapča, Croatia, treated a thirty-one-year-old Muslim woman from the Foča municipality who had been raped in the Manjača camp, in northwestern Bosnia. According to the medical records, burn marks were found on the woman's thighs, presumably "from hot irons."

Aida, a petite eighteen-year-old from Kozarac,[232] was among a group of women and children who were taken to Trnopolje after fighting broke out on May 23, 1992. Aida spent fourteen days in Trnopolje and claims to have gotten very little food. She testified that, during her internment in Trnopolje, soldiers frequently removed women, whom she believes were raped. According to Aida:

> Every night, Serbian soldiers would come to the large room where we were confined. They would take out girls and rape them — at least one girl was taken every night. The women who had babies came back. Some girls never came back. Mothers would hide their daughters under blankets. The soldiers would pull aside the blankets and look at the girls with flashlights.

Aida claims that she was not discovered by the soldiers in the evening because her mother had her belongings in a corner of the room where she was able to hide her well under the blankets, and the soldiers, who searched the darkened room with single flashlights, did not find her.

Aida said that she recognized two of the soldiers who came into the room in the evening looking for women. She testified that the two men had been her highschool teachers. According to Aida:

> One was my physics teacher, Ljubomir Žjelar. He had been my teacher for four years and had always seemed to like me. In the camp, he pretended not to recognize me or the other girls who had been his students. The other was Mišo Radulović; [he was] not a young man. He had been my crafts teacher.

S.S. is a forty-year-old Muslim woman from the village of Trnopolje[233] who was forcibly displaced from her home[234] and

---

[232] Interviewed by Helsinki Watch representatives on February 10, 1993, in Zagreb, Croatia.

[233] Interviewed by Helsinki Watch and the Women's Rights Project on January 16, 1993, in a refugee camp in Croatia.

interned at the Trnopolje camp in late July or early August. According to S.S.:

> We spent the night in a big room in a school. They came at night with flashlights looking for a specific woman, my cousin, A.S. I was at her wedding one year ago. She had an eight-month-old baby and was still breast-feeding. When they came into the room, they were cursing [Muslims]. We knew these men; they used to be our neighbors.
>
> They asked for her [i.e., the cousin] by name. Her mother and mother-in-law said she wasn't there. The soldiers threatened to put a bomb in the room. Her mother screamed, "Don't take her." The men said, "We want her, not you." She gave her baby to her mother and went out with the two soldiers. They were in their uniforms. She was outside for about three hours. When she returned she was stiff and frozen and in shock. They raped her and told her not to talk or they would kill her family.

Z. M.,[235] a twenty-five-year-old Muslim woman, spent fifteen days in the Trnopolje camp between May 26 and June 10, 1992. She remembers being very afraid of rape. Her account appears to corroborate the above account concerning the rape of A.S. According to Z.M.:

> In the Trnopolje camp we were most afraid of rape because drunk soldiers would come and take women out. We had an agreement that girls and unmarried women would stay in the attic. We were hiding our girls. One night a soldier came into the room where we were staying with a flashlight asking for a woman named R.K.

---

[234] See relevant section above for the witness's account of her forced expulsion from her home.

[235] Interviewed by Helsinki Watch representatives in January 1993 in a refugee camp in Croatia.

> I knew her in passing from before the war; we were from the same area. Two soldiers came in, looking for this woman, but they couldn't find her. They shouted, "Give us that girl, or we will take another." They shined a flashlight on a woman breast-feeding her baby and said, "You. Get up." One soldier said, "No, don't take her. She has a baby." The other one said, "I said what I wanted. If you don't come, I'll put a bomb in here." She went out with them for a long time. She returned before dawn. Her face was red, and her trousers were torn. Her sister-in-law told us later that there were six of them that raped her.[236]

A.H., a thirty-six-year-old Muslim woman from Kozarac was interned in Trnopolje for eight days.[237] A.H. claims that elderly men who were detained in the same area as the women and children were beaten. She testified that Serbian soldiers came into the dark hall at night with flashlights, drunk, cursing, pulling aside blankets and choosing girls, kicking them and telling them to stand up. When mothers and mothers-in-law would protest or interfere, the soldiers beat them. According to A.H.:

> One young woman who was six or seven months pregnant was taken out in this way three times. Some nights, the choosing of the women who were to be taken away began at nighfall and might go on until 1:00 a.m. The soldiers brought in a dog one time that snapped at the women.

---

[236] The witness knew the name of the woman who was raped but refused to reveal her identity out of concern for the woman's privacy.

[237] Interviewed by Helsinki Watch representatives on February 10, 1993, in the Resnik refugee camp in Croatia.

Munevra, a twenty-year-old receptionist from the village of Rakovčani,[238] had been interned in Trnopolje. At the time of Helsinki Watch's interview, she said that eighteen men from her immediate family were missing. According to Munevra:

> Very few women were raped in my village. But in the camp in Trnopolje the Četniks chose small children. I hid in a corner because I didn't want to be noticed. I hid there for fourteen days. Some of the Serbs had sympathy for us, but very few. During the day, the ICRC and journalists were around [but] all the bad things happened at night when they were gone. There was one well-developed twelve-year-old; they took her mostly at night.

According to a doctor interned at Trnopolje:[239]

> There was a group of guards who seemed experienced [at abusing the prisoners], but I don't know their names. This group would check and examine people, and they were usually looking for gold and watches. From time to time, they would kick and beat women but not as brutally as they beat the men. There was a group of tank drivers, that would come to the camp in the evening with flashlights and pick out women. The women were aged thirteen and older.

The doctor claims that seven rape victims complained to the camp medical personnel. According to the doctor:

> There was one doctor and a technician who covered all the camps in the area, and these seven women reported

---

[238] Interviewed by Helsinki Watch representatives on January 14, 1993, in the Resnik refugee camp in Croatia. The witness chose to withold her name, and the name used here is a pseudonym.

[239] Interviewed by Helsinki Watch representatives in October 1992 in a refugee camp in Croatia.

their rapes to them. The doctor took their names, and a gynecologist and psychiatrist were also notified that the women had been raped. However, the doctor did not file a complaint with the authorities. After that, women didn't dare to complain anymore. The tank drivers came looking for the seven who complained but, fortunately, the women had left the day before.[240]

Reported Castration

Helsinki Watch conducted separate interviews with men who claimed to have been present in the Omarska camp when one or more men were castrated. All the accounts mention at least one youth — Jasmin Hrnić — who was either castrated or the victim of an attempt to castrate him. The details of the accounts differ, and it remains unclear

---

[240] Seida Velić, a twenty-six-year-old Muslim woman, was held in Trnopolje for over a month, and subsequently was interviewed by foreign journalists. Her testimony indicates that local Serbian soldiers tried to protect women from assaults by soldiers who were not native to the area. *The New York Times* quotes Ms. Velić:

> Women and children were housed separately from the male prisoners. Late one night, a group of drunken men barged into [Ms]. Velić's hall, shouting out that they were Serbian Četniks from Serbia and Montenegro. The men began pacing around the room, shining flashlights into women's faces and selecting women who were taken away.
>
> Some of the guards whe were local Serbs tried to intervene, telling the other guards to leave them alone. When that didn't work, the local Serbs wrested away some of the younger women. Those women who were taken away reported they had been raped when they returned the next morning. Some of the women did not return.
>
> The camp commander, who wore a JNA major's uniform, apologized for what had happened and personally guaranteed their safety. Local Serbian guards were posted around the women's quarters and there was no repeat of the incident. (See Stephen Engelberg, "Refugees from Camps Tell of Agony and Terror," *The New York Times*, August 7, 1992.)

if the witnesses viewed the entire incident, part of the incident or if there was more than one case in which men were castrated in Omarska.

Certain elements of the witness's testimony are identical or similar. The abuse occurred in the late evening in mid-July at the Omarska camp, outside a warehouse-type room in which hundreds of men were held. The order to castrate the man/men was allegedly given by Duško Tadić, a former restaurant owner in Kozarac whose nickname was "Dule." All claim that another prisoner — a youth — was taken from a separate room and ordered to bite the penis of Jasmin Hrnić. Some allege that Hrnić was subsequently castrated by Tadić.

The witnesses interviewed by Helsinki Watch viewed the abuse from different vantage points (e.g., from inside the warehouse, from a window, through a bathroom keyhole in the hallway) and, therefore, their accounts differ in detail. Most, but not all, of those interviewed claim that a second man also was castrated.

Although details of the accounts differ, Helsinki Watch believed that sufficient evidence exists to support the claim that at least one man — Jasmin Hrnić — was sexually violated in the Omarska camp. Helsinki Watch will continue to investigate the incident(s) and will report its findings.

Obstruction of Humanitarian Relief

Bosanska Krupa

On November 19, outside Bosanska Krupa, U.N. troops returned fire for the first time to defend supplies. Despite Serbian assurances of safe passage, French U.N. forces were fired upon for about ten minutes from a Serbian-held hillside. The U.N. troops received commands to return fire using 20-millimeter guns mounted on armored vehicles. The French-protected convoy included six armored personnel carriers and four trucks of relief goods. One truck and one armored vehicle were hit by gunfire, but none of the troops or aid workers was injured.[241]

---

[241] Chuck Sudetic, "U.N. Troops' Role Widens in Bosnia; 2 Towns Get Aid," *The New York Times*, November 20, 1992.

Indiscriminate Use of Force

Jajce

Foreign press reports claim that after the Bosnian- and Croatian-held town of Jajce fell in October 1992, Serbian forces continued to launch attacks on the estimated 40,000 refugees who tried to leave the area for safety. At least seven displaced persons from Jajce died after they arrived at the Travnik hospital; another sixty were treated for injuries. Around November 1, 1992, Nijaza Dizdar, a Muslim woman fleeing with her husband and family from Jajce, was hit while driving down the road to Travnik. She lost both her legs. Her husband, Sejid, drove them another one hundred yards when a second shell exploded nearby. He then carried his wife to the hospital in Travnik because ambulances would not take the risk of driving down the road that was being shelled. A Croatian cameraman working for the British Broadcasting Company (BBC) was killed after Serbian gunners fired at his armored car. According to witnesses, those killed in the shelling were not caught in cross fire but were deliberately targeted for attack. No battles were reported along the escape route from Jajce to Travnik.[242]

---

[242] Peter Maas, "Bosnians Fleeing War Face New Fight for Life," *The Washington Post*, November 2, 1992.

Abuses in Northeastern Bosnia

Bosnia-Hercegovina

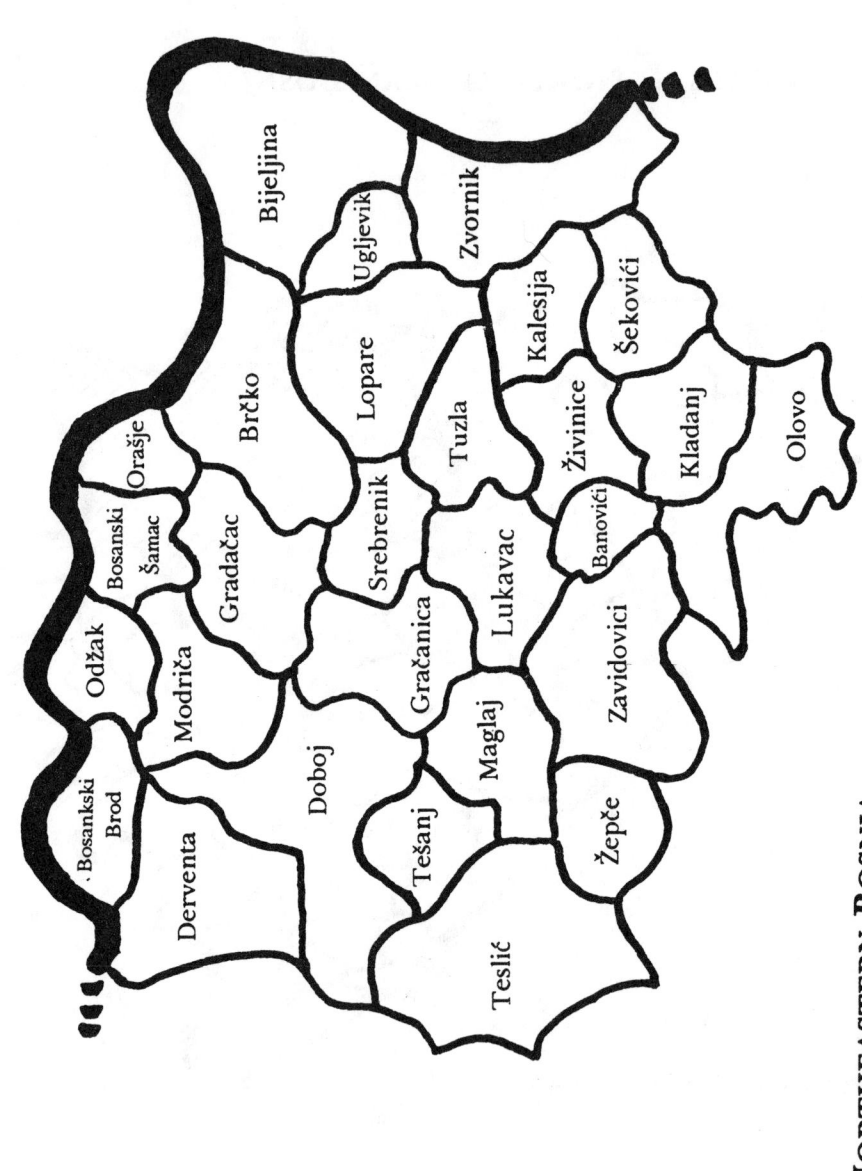

NORTHEASTERN BOSNIA

ABUSES IN NORTHEASTERN BOSNIA

Northeastern Bosnia is the site of heavy fighting between Serbian, Bosnian and Croatian troops, all of which are vying for control over contested territory. Serbian forces hope to consolidate their control over a corridor of territory in northeastern Bosnia that would link Serbian-controlled areas of Croatia and northwestern Bosnia with Serbia proper. The Serbian corridor is frequently attacked from the north and south, by Croatian HVO troops in Orašje and Bosnian Muslim troops in Gradačac, respectively. Croatian and Muslim positions also are subject to attacks by Serbian forces.

This section of the report encompasses the largely Serbian-controlled municipalities of Bosanski Brod, Odžak, Bosanski Šamac, Derventa, Modriča, Bijeljina, Doboj, Ugljevik, Zvornik, Teslić and Šekovići.[1] Muslim forces largely control the municipalities of Gradačac, Srebrenik, Tešanj, Maglaj, Lukavac, Tuzla, Banovići, Živnice, Kladanj, Olova and Kalesija.[2] The municipalities of Zavidovići and Žepće are controlled jointly by Croatian and Muslim forces. This chapter of the report also includes the municipalities of Brčko, Lopare and Gračanica, which are controlled in part by Serbian and in part by Muslim forces. In addition, this section of the report encompasses the Croatian-held municipality of Orašje. In general, the main roads in northeastern Bosnia are controlled by Serbian forces, but these forces are increasingly attacked by Muslim and Croatian troops.

Helsinki Watch representatives have not visited the municipalities under Muslim control in northeastern Bosnia-Hercegovina. The sieges of cities in, or fighting en route to, the area prevented access during Helsinki Watch's visits. Future missions will investigate rules of war and other violations in this region.

The extent of abuses perpetrated by Serbian forces in northeastern Bosnia is not fully known. Continued fighting and heavy paramilitary activity in the region have discouraged journalists and others from thoroughly investigating reports in the area. Some non-Serbs have

---

[1] Although Serbian forces occupy most of the territory in these areas, Bosnian forces control slivers of territory in these municipalities.

[2] Although Bosnian forces control most of the territory in these areas, Serbian forces control strips of territory in some of the municipalities.

fled from areas before they fell to Serbian forces, but many are believed to have been summarily executed or interned in camps. Serbian forces operate a detention camp in the village of Batković in the municipality of Bijeljin. A second known detention camp called Luka, in the municipality of Brčko, was closed during the early summer of 1992. "Ethnic cleansing" practices in the Bijeljina area often are attributed to the forces of Željko Ražnjatović, a.k.a. "Arkan," and Helsinki Watch representatives who have visited the area have also spoken to forces who claim to belong to the paramilitary group founded by Vojislav Šešelj. The self-proclaimed "Army of the Serbian Republic" also operates in the area. Mistreatment in detention, arbitrary killing and summary execution characterize abuses in Serbian-controlled areas of northeastern Bosnia.

Croatian HVO forces in Orašje appear not to be under a clear chain of command, thereby creating fertile ground for the commission of gross abuses, especially of detainees. A similar situation seems to have existed in Bosanski Brod, a municipality that was under Croatian and, to a lesser extent, Muslim, control until it fell to Serbian forces in early October 1992.

ABUSES BY SERBIAN FORCES

Abuses in Detention

Brčko

Helsinki Watch representatives interviewed a Croatian resident of Brčko,[3] who was detained by Serbian forces in May 1992. Zvonko, in his fifties, and his wife, Vesna,[4] had lived in Brčko for over twenty years. Fighting broke out in Brčko in late April, and a bridge linking the city with Croatia was destroyed.[5] The couple remained in their apartment

---

[3] Before the war, the population of the municipality of Brčko was 87,332, of which 44 percent were Muslims, 25.4 percent Croats, 20.8 percent Serbs and 6.4 percent identified themselves as Yugoslavs. The witness claimed that, in the city of Brčko, Muslims comprised the majority of the population (approximately 70 percent). According to the witness, Croats and Serbs accounted for approximately 17 and 11 percent of the city's population, respectively.

[4] The couple was interviewed by Helsinki Watch representatives on October 18, 1992, in Županja, Croatia, but both husband and wife preferred to withhold their names. The names given here are pseudonyms.

[5] For an account of the battles in the Brčko municipality, see Helsinki Watch's *War Crimes in Bosnia-Hercegovina*, August 1992, pp. 69-70, 94-99, 132-33 and 137-39. The destruction of the bridge linking Croatia with Brčko is described in the aforementioned report on pp. 137-39. The gentleman interviewed above recounted the following to Helsinki Watch representatives:

> On April 30 at 4:30 a.m., part of the bridge over the Sava [River] was blown up, cutting communication [between Croatia and Brčko]. A lot of people were killed on the bridge. There were many buses of Bosnian guest workers from Germany who were coming back for the May 1 holiday [i.e., International Workers' Day]. The buses were waiting to cross the bridge at approximately 5:00 a.m. The JNA waited until people from the buses were on the bridge to detonate the explosion. Two men who were wounded on the bridge were [held] in [the detention] camp [where I was held]. I don't know how many people were on the bridge. Survivors were transferred to the Brčko hospital and then to the camp [Luka].

during the battles in Brčko. On May 7, at noon, the husband was in the bathroom when he heard a noise. He saw his wife open the door to six armed persons, two of whom were in police uniforms with berets bearing the Serbian flag, two were in camouflage, and the others wore leather jackets and jeans. According to Zvonko:

> They said they were searching for weapons and pushed my wife and pointed a gun to her back, forcing her to walk in front of them as they searched [the apartment]. They went through the mattresses, shelves, drawers, even the refrigerator. They were carrying weapons, hand grenades, pistols and knives.
>
> I was told to put on my clothes and wait outside by the car while they searched the apartment. They asked about the whereabouts of my son. Then I was put into an all-terrain vehicle [i.e., a Pince-Gauer] with benches in the back and taken to the central police station. The police station was built thirty years ago and it stands in the middle of town, on the main road. I was led to the magistrate's office, where my passport, agenda book and Croatian-English dictionary were confiscated. I was given a half-hour preliminary interview and then they told me that I would have to wait there for further questioning by Major Dragan.

Zvonko waited for about two hours, during which time, a soldier bearing an AK-47 kept him under guard.

> I looked at this soldier, but he thought I was being provocative and he told me not to look at him for both our well-beings. But after two hours there was not much else to look at, so we introduced ourselves and talked a bit and I asked him to help me.

The soldier promised to tell the guards who were to relieve him not to harm Zvonko, at least until after he had been questioned. During this time, other officials came in and out of the room and directed questions at him. According to Zvonko:

> When they found out I was a Croat born in western Hercegovina, they thought they would have to shoot me. One said, "I'm a good shot ... nothing will hurt. It will be very quick." One soldier put his Kalishnikov to my forehead, cursed my Ustaša mother and said, "You're finished." After the usual questions asking who I was and where I was from, another man said, "I'd like to hit you with my iron knuckles, but I won't because you have gray hair like my father."

Zvonko said that he spent twenty-four hours waiting in the magistrate's office before he was transferred to another room furnished with a desk, armchair and bench. He used the books and curtains in the room to make a bed. The guards brought him food regularly, usually whatever they themselves had to eat. Zvonko claimed that, during his detention in the police station, he heard the sound of shooting and screams all around him. According to Zvonko:

> That day [i.e., May 8], at about around 4:00 [p.m.], five young men were killed in the corridor of the police station. Four of them were shot point-blank and a fifth who tried to escape was killed outside. I heard the shots and the shouts and curses of the police officer pursuing the fifth man. I also heard a group of young men singing a Serbian song.[6] I did not realize what had happened until the following day, when another prisoner told me that the men had been killed.

---

[6] Zvonko identified the verses of a popular Serbian national song: "Who says such things? Who is lying that Serbia is small? It's not small, it's not small, it's waged war thrice." ["*Ko to kaže, ko to laže Srbija je mala. Nije mala, nije mala, tri put ratovala.*"]

On May 10, a young man, maybe sixteen years of age, was brought into the office where I was being held. Later, police officers came and told the teenager that his father and uncle had been brought to the police station. He was told that both would be shot if he didn't disclose what he had done with his gun. After a time, the young man heard some shrieks and cries from below and said, "That's my father." There was a shot later. Then the police came in and said, "We aren't going to shoot your father — we'll just send him to be exchanged, but you'll have to be cooperative." The youth lay down on a bench, while I sat at a desk. I heard the police discussing among themselves whether to shoot this youth. One asked why they should do such a thing. Another replied, "Because we've already shot his father and uncle."

Zvonko also reported that he heard several hundred gunshots coming from the other side of the building.[7] He counted the shots. At night, the shots were more clearly heard and increased in number. He reported that, every morning between 4:00 a.m. and 5:00 a.m., a truck would arrive and leave thirty minutes thereafter. Meanwhile, dawn would break and other traffic noise would resume, making it impossible to tell whether other trucks were coming or going.

On May 13, Zvonko's main interrogator, Major Dragan, finally arrived. According to Zvonko:

> Dragan asked me if I was the one he was supposed to interview. He was dressed in camouflage, wearing an army cap. He also wore dark sunglasses. He asked me the same questions: "Who are you?" and "Where are you from?" When he heard that I was a Croat from western Hercegovina, he said, "Oh, you're a special case! I can't

---

[7] The witness had been told by another prisoner who was being released that there were "special compartments in the building which were used for summary executions. The compartments were on the opposite side of the building from where I was held, closer to the Sava River." The witness believes that the shots he was hearing were coming from these "execution compartments" but was unable to provide any firm evidence of their existence.

> let you go just like that." So he took me and a drunk Serbian policeman to a solitary room on the side of the building, from where the shooting could be heard. We went into a large room which did not have proper beds but, rather, some slanted wooden platforms. The drunk went to sleep and I stayed awake all night, waiting to be shot.

While in this room, Zvonko did not witness the execution of prisoners, but he described what he heard in detail.

> First, I heard six shots fired in a steady, slow, rhythmic sequence, [as if] a silencer [was being used]. After the shots, I heard what sounded like a retractable metal elevator grate opening. Then there was a sound that resembled a body falling.[8] An automatic gun would fire into the compartment, and then the elevator would descend, [possibly] with the body.

He reported that he once heard the police shouting, "Where has the elevator operator gone?" Zvonko could not identify the exact location of the elevator, but he felt it was very close to the room in which he was detained. He said that six offices were adjacent to the room in which he was held and that a bathroom was opposite the offices.

On the morning of May 14, Zvonko heard a truck arrive at about 4:00 a.m. At approximately 8:00 a.m., Zvonko knocked on the door and asked to use the toilet. When he returned, there were six to eight new men in the room, two of whom were his friends. At 10:00 a.m., they were ordered to walk outside with their hands behind their backs and they were put in a small van. The drunken soldier was not among them. They arrived at Luka at noon.[9]

---

[8] The witness believed that he heard an elevator, operated by an attendant. He believed that a prisoner or several prisoners were brought up to the floor in the elevator and then shot. Their bodies were then brought down by the elevator operator. Helsinki Watch has not been able to confirm such accusations.

[9] For an account of the man's detention in Luka, see below.

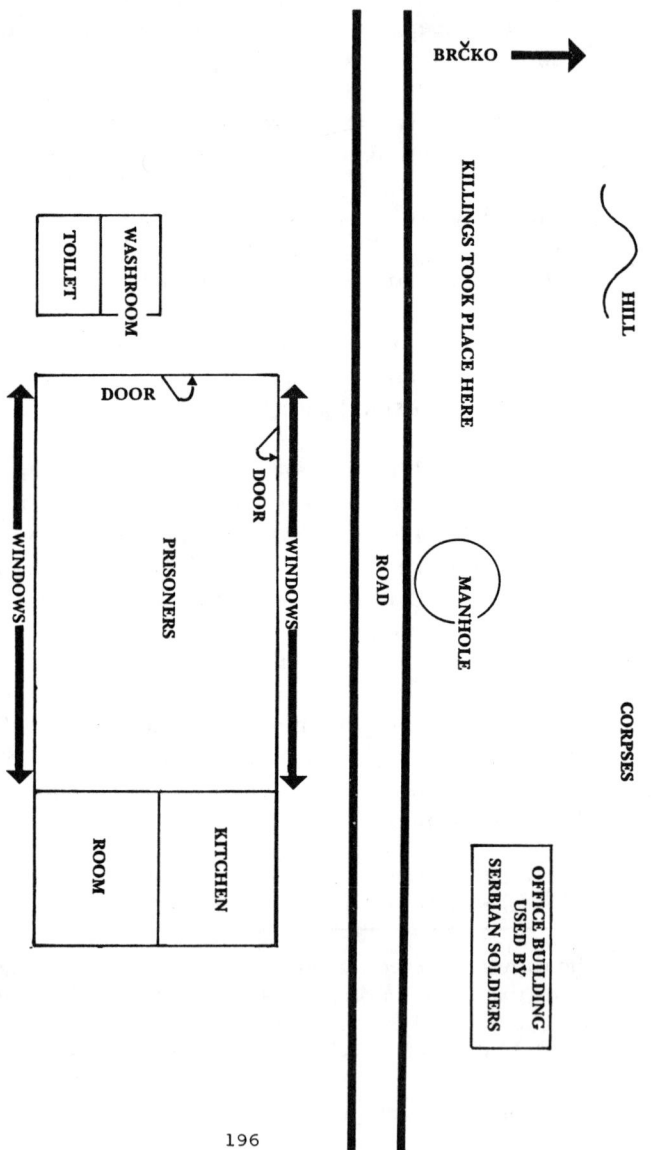

Luka

Between May and July 1992, Serbian forces operated a detention camp, which is commonly referred to as "Luka," near the town of Brčko. According to former prisoners interviewed by Helsinki Watch representatives,[10] detainees taken from the camp were "disappeared" or summarily executed. Luka reportedly was closed in mid-1992 and was never visited by the ICRC.[11] Those detained at Luka are believed to have been transferred to a detention facility in the village of Batković, in the municipality of Bijeljina.[12] Helsinki Watch representatives interviewed three former detainees of the Luka camp, all of whom appeared to have been held in different areas of the camp. Their testimonies confirm that summary executions and beatings in Luka were commonplace.

Many of Luka's prisoners had been forcibly displaced from their homes before their detention. Muhamer, a fifty-two-year-old man,[13] described the aftermath of the fighting in Brčko and his subsequent detention in Luka to Helsinki Watch representatives:

> An attack was launched on April 30, 1992, from Potočara against the settlement of Dizdaruša, and it lasted the entire day. On May 1, there was an attack on the newer settlement of Rosulja within the Kolobora area of town. I lived in this area and went into the basement with six other people [during the battles]. We had no arms and stayed in the basement for three days. The attack was

---

[10] Interviewed in October 1992.

[11] The Luka camp is believed to have operated between May and July 1992. On May 18, an ICRC delegate, Frederic Maurice, was killed during an attack on an ICRC relief convoy in Sarajevo. On May 20, the ICRC temporarily withdrew its delegates from Bosnia-Hercegovina, but resumed work in Bosnia in June. Suspension of the ICRC's activities precluded them from visiting the Luka camp.

[12] For an account of the Batković camp, see the following section.

[13] The witness was interviewed on October 20, 1992, in Zagreb, Croatia, but chose to withhold his name. The name used here is a pseudonym.

launched by the JNA and paramilitary Četnik groups. On May 3, at approximately 4:00 p.m., we heard yelling outside. They were yelling "Come out, Turks! Come out of your rat holes!" Then they fired a volley of gunfire into the windows. They kept shooting and yelling, "Get out or we'll throw a hand grenade."

I took off my shirt, which was white, and gave it to a woman named H.K., who was in the basement with us. She went outside with it and we walked behind her. In total there were seven of us — four men and three women. They grabbed H.K., and three soldiers started to beat her. They hit her in the chest and then they grabbed us and started to beat us. They hit me in the stomach with their truncheons and guns. One of the women, S.Z., fell, and they started to pull her hair. They were dressed in the old [Yugoslav] police uniforms and wore moss green berets, similar to those worn by the JNA, but the red-star insignia had been replaced by the Serbian [national symbol of a cross encircled by] four Ss. They had red berets stuffed in their pockets.

Muhamer said that Serbian soldiers had placed a cannon between the health clinic and the post office and that they were being fired upon from the direction of the post office. However, the shooting stopped after the soldiers yelled, presumably to their colleagues, to stop shooting. The seven were then taken to the health clinic, where the men were separated from the women. According to Muhamer, the women remained at the health clinic and the men were taken to the mosque.

Muhamer said that he spent forty-eight hours in the mosque, where between 150 and 200 men were detained. He was then taken to the "Laser" firm. At approximately 4:00 p.m. on the same day, he and other prisoners, including approximately twenty women and ten children, were taken to the Luka camp. According to Muhamer:

We entered through the gate, and I saw many of the people who had been held in the mosque and many others who were from Brčko. I was in Luka from about May 7 or 8 to June 23. We didn't get food or water for the first four days.

In addition to Muhamer, Helsinki Watch interviewed two other persons who had formerly been detained in Luka. All reported that several large warehouses[14] were lined up in a row. Muhamer said that he was placed in one of these warehouses, which was lit by a single light. Windows lined the length of two walls of the warehouse. A smaller room and a kitchen were at one end of the structure. A toilet and washroom were across the hall from the warehouse's door. The witness reported that a light encircled the area around the warehouse. A road separated the warehouse from a smaller structure, which housed Serbian soldiers.[15] Muhamer claimed that approximately 1,500 people were detained in Luka at the time of his internment. According to Muhamer:

> There were very few women and children among them; maybe ten women — one of whom was pregnant — and about ten children, up to the age of twelve. I was placed in the first warehouse. There were about two hundred to three hundred Croats in the warehouse. A Jew was also among those in the warehouse.[16] But there were many people there whom I did not know.

The witness testified that truckloads of mostly male prisoners arrived at Luka on a daily basis. The few women and children detained at the camp were held in a building that functioned as an office for Serbian camp authorities. There were about one hundred people in the room in which he was detained. According to Muhamer, prisoners were regularly mistreated, some were "disappeared" and several were executed. According to Muhamer:

> The warehouse was huge, and they usually left the door open. We were kept in the dark inside the warehouse, but bright lights illuminated the outdoors, [i.e., enabling him to see what was occurring outside the warehouse]. If

---

[14] The witness used the word *hangar* to describe the warehouse, therefore denoting that it was a large structure capable of holding many prisoners.

[15] See drawing of the Luka camp.

[16] The witness identified the individual by name.

anyone went to the bathroom, they were beaten. At about 8:00 p.m. one evening, they [i.e. Serbian forces] came in with a list [and called out the names of some] people, many of whom were doctors and members of the intelligentsia. These people were taken away.[17]

Muhamer said that Serbian guards summarily executed prisoners in full view of other detainees. According to Muhamer:

I don't know the names of all those killed. A blond man who looked about twenty-two or a little older was shot in the back of the head with one bullet. The executioner — a man named Goran who was wearing a police uniform — stood about two or three meters away from him when he shot. The police officer shot him in front of the full hall, and he fell on his side. He was then taken by the hair to the manhole and his throat was slit. There were about ten people there [i.e, by the manhole]. Another man dressed in a JNA uniform slit the throat of a blond youth who was about eighteen years old. They wore "Arkan's hat," [i.e., a black ski mask or wool hat that was rolled up on the head]. They did not have beards. Those who were killing the prisoners were between eighteen and thirty years old. The killing went on nonstop.

Beatings in detention sometimes resulted in death, according to the witness. A victim of such abuse included a pregnant woman. According to Muhamer:

A pregnant woman named Sefka was among the prisoners. She was about four to six months pregnant, and her stomach had visibly swelled. They beat her for three days and, on the fourth day, she died. They beat her by the manhole, and they killed her father. She was beaten by a police officer. There were about twenty-one

---

[17] Muhamer claims that these people were killed, but he did not witness their killing.

people [who were killed] by the manhole. I counted, but I didn't know any of them.

Goran and a man named Ranko beat me. Three or four times a night they would come in and beat people at random. Men were bestially beaten in another room, and their faces were totally disfigured. No one was on guard duty when they beat us.

The prisoners were also questioned during their detention. According to Muhamer:

Inspectors took us to the police station for interrogation. I was interrogated seven times by men who knew me. Their names were: Dragiša Tesanović (a former colleague of mine), [a man whose surname was] Sarkanović, Boro Kaurinović, Petar Kaurinović, and a man named "Kosta." They asked me if I was a member of the SDA, who had organized the party in my part of town, was I at a military position, where was my money, etc.. Two inspectors were present; one remained outside the door, and another stood by the window.

The witness reported that one of his interrogators, "Kosta," was either the commander or the deputy commander of the camp, with the rank of major or lieutenant colonel. He was also referred to by another nickname, "Kole."[18] According to Muhamer:

It was rumoured that "Kosta" was from Bijeljina. He was dressed in a JNA uniform with an officer's hat and Arkan's woolen ski mask. He was about forty or forty-five years old, had blond hair and was relatively short, about one meter and seventy-five centimeters in height.

---

[18] The witness gave Helsinki Watch representatives the telephone number where he alleged that "Kole" and other interrogators could be reached. Helsinki Watch retains the telephone number in secure files outside the Helsinki Watch offices.

Muhamer said that thirty-five men were brought before the inspectors named Tesanović and Similčić on June 23. A judge who was president of the court and whose surname was Zobenica also was present. The inspectors called out names of some prisoners, and these men were granted permits[19] and were released. Muhamer says that he, too, was released during a prisoner exchange on June 23.

A second inmate, Omer, interviewed by Helsinki Watch representatives[20] spent seventeen days in Luka, arriving on May 17, 1992. According to Omer, approximately 650 or 700 men were transported to Luka in nine buses in one day.[21] They arrived at the camp in the early afternoon but were not allowed to leave the buses for about one and a half to two hours, until night had fallen. The men were then told to leave the buses and were lined up along the side of a large warehouse with their hands behind their heads. They were made to run around to the entrance of the warehouse, during which time a cordon of soldiers beat them. The warehouse they ran into was already half filled with prisoners, most of whom were from Vlasenica, Kalesija, Zvornik and Koraj. The people already in the warehouse were made to lie down, put their hands on their heads and press their faces to the floor while the new prisoners ran into the warehouse. The inmates had their heads shaved to mark them as prisoners. According to Omer, many prisoners were killed.

---

[19] A permit (i.e., *propusnica*) is frequently issued by local military and/or civilian authorities in war-torn areas throughout Croatia and Bosnia-Hercegovina. To varying degrees, all three sides require that visitors to the region report to the local authorities before they move about areas under their control. Serbian civilian and military authorities in Serbian-occupied regions of Croatia and Bosnia-Hercegovina have been particularly stringent about the need for such permits, which can be issued either by their own agents or, in some cases, by the U.N. forces. (The validity of a U.N.-issued pass is usually restricted to Serbian-occupied areas of Croatia, which are nominally under U.N. supervision.) The permits allow the holder to pass through checkpoints and they delineate the purpose, destination and duration of one's travel throughout the region.

[20] Omer was interviewed on October 18, 1992, in Županja, Croatia, but preferred to withhold his name. The name given here is a pseudonym.

[21] It appears that the buses made several trips to transport prisoners to the camp.

> Some of the people would be taken away from the warehouses. Then we would hear shooting — either volleys of gunfire or individual shots. Then a truck would come and remove the bodies.[22] We used to watch through the sliding doors of the warehouse, which didn't close tightly and left a little space through which you could see. We also could see piles of shoes and boots that were collected from people when they were let out to use the toilet. I remember a tall man from Brčko who came to Luka three times. He was looking for gold rings and other valuables, and he took the prisoners' belongings.

The witness claims that 500 men from Brčko and Brezovo Polje were detained in his facility and that a total of ten to twelve warehouses was on the camp grounds. According to Omer:

> One warehouse would be emptied and then filled with new people. But no one was taken from the warehouse in which I was detained. Those of us from Brezovo Polje were separated [from the other prisoners]. We were considered "not guilty" because not a single shot had been fired from our village. [The prisoners in the] other warehouses were not so fortunate — they were considered "guilty" even though they hadn't committed any crime.[23] While I was in Luka, no one in the warehouse in which I was detained was killed. People were beaten if they were accused of something, [for example,] membership in, or support of, the SDA.

---

[22] Omer claims that the bodies were taken away and deposited in holes dug by bulldozers, but it remains unclear as to whether or not he actually saw the bodies being deposited in the graves.

[23] Omer claims that he learned of the treatment of other prisoners at the Batković camp, where he was subsequently detained. (See following section.) In Batković, the witness was reunited with former Luka prisoners who had been detained in other warehouses on the camp's premises. The testimony of the other Luka detainees cited here supports Omer's assertions.

Helsinki Watch representatives also interviewed a married couple, in their late forties or early fifties.[24] The husband, Zvonko, who had been detained at Luka, told Helsinki Watch:

> Luka is a section of Brčko near the Sava River, where there are a lot of warehouses. Prisoners were held in one building which had three big halls, or warehouses; each warehouse was approximately fifty by twenty meters. Offices of two companies were opposite the front of the building. The police and the magistrates worked in these offices. There were three water closets on the premises.

According to Zvonko, new arrivals were placed in the first hall. After they had been interrogated in the offices opposite the building, the prisoners were brought into the second hall. Zvonko claimed that the second hall housed persons who were to be executed or released. Zvonko found some ninety to one hundred men there, sitting on the floor, on cardboard boxes or crates. He said that several women were among the prisoners but that they were released one or two days thereafter. Zvonko described the conditions in the camp:

> I was interrogated by a subordinate who I had hired at the factory.[25] The man was fair. He did not mistreat me and asked, "What are you doing here?" He told me that I could be released, so I was sent to the second hall.
>
> We were fed three regular meals a day at Luka. They gave out mess kits from the prison. Only sixty portions were delivered for about ninety to one hundred men, so we would share the food.
>
> Hygiene was terrible. People had no time to go to the toilet, nor did they have soap or toilet paper. During the day, we were allowed to use the toilets, but at night we

---

[24] Interviewed on October 18, 1992, in Županja, Croatia. The husband had earlier been detained in Brčko, and his testimony appears above.

[25] Zvonko worked as an engineer in a local factory that processed soybeans.

were brought three buckets in which we were to relieve ourselves. You couldn't sleep from the sound of people urinating at night.

The guards would sometimes hit someone in the hall, but those who were to be beaten were taken outside, across to the offices. One man[26] was beaten two hundred times with a nightstick. He was hit on the head with an aluminum bar.[27] A neighbor who had arrived before me was beaten so severely in the face that a week passed before I could recognize him. This man had been asked to accuse someone of something, but he refused. They hit him with iron knuckles directly in the eyes — he thought he would be blinded [but was not]. A young man from Brčko was beaten in such a way and so severely that he urinated blood. Two other men had to carry him [to the bathroom], and a third had to help him to urinate.

Zvonko reported that prisoners were summarily executed in the camp. According to Zvonko:

Six men were shot the day I arrived at Luka [i.e., May 14]. They were killed in the afternoon, at approximately 2:00 p.m. A friend of mine, Stjepan Itrić, was among those who had been executed. On May 15, another twelve men were shot and my friend Adžip Piljić was among them. On May 16, another six were shot.

The police would enter the room, point [at prisoners and say,] "You, you and you, stand up!" Then another officer would come and say, "Let's go." They would be led to a place behind the second hall, and everyone could hear the shots. Then the police would come back and call for three volunteers to take the bodies to another place.

---

[26] The witness identified the victim by name.

[27] The witness claims not to have witnessed the beatings but did see the physical condition of the prisoners after they were returned to the hangar.

These volunteers would return to the room, and then the next person to be shot would be led out. This would happen in the evening, about 9:00 p.m. or 10:00 p.m. Then they would ask four more volunteers to load the bodies onto a truck.

Zvonko testified that one of the aforementioned friends who had been executed was killed while he was loading bodies onto the truck. According to Zvonko, the man — a Muslim — was recognized by the police and shot because his two sons were fighting on the Muslim/Croatian side in the war. Other prisoners tried to dissuade the man from volunteering. The witness said that he learned of his friend's death after one of the other volunteers — an acquaintance of Zvonko's — returned to the warehouse and told him of the man's execution. Zvonko continued:

> The main torturer was a man from Bijeljina, Goran Jelišić, nicknamed "Semberac." He was thought by inmates to have killed about one hundred men. But every guard used to kill people. Among the guards was a man named "Kole" and his fourteen-year-old sister, Monika, a girl with an angelic face. Monika used to carry a plastic bag, and everyone had to empty their pockets into the bag. She left me a digital clock [in which she] had no interest. She used to wear a gun all the time.[28] Other guards were Mišo Čajević and Mišo Hajduković. Another guard's first name was Mile, but he was nicknamed "Bolero" because he was the owner of Cafe Bolero. Mile Bolero had a pistol with a silencer and a Kalashnikov with a sniper sighting. All were killers.

According to Zvonko, the self-styled Bosnian Serb police were in charge of the camp's administration. The witness identified Professor

---

[28] A second witness interviewed by Helsinki Watch representatives also mentioned Monika. According to this witness, Monika was approximately sixteen years old and the sister of "Kole"/"Kosta." She was about one meter, sixty centimeters in height, had short hair and always wore a new set of civilian clothing.

Dragan Vesilić[29] as the commander of the police force in Brčko. Although the Serbian police force was formed after the self-proclaimed "Serbian Republic" was established in Bosnia-Hercegovina, the witness claims that most of the local Serbs from Brčko refused to involve themselves in the killings.

> Some of the men [at the camp] were from Bor in Serbia and spoke with a Serbian *ekavica* dialect.[30] There was another man named "Goran," who appeared in a camouflage police uniform and wore an army cap. All these people were from the same gang [i.e., presumably from the same unit].

According to Zvonko, the incident in which six persons were shot on May 16 was the last of such shootings near the warehouses.[31] On May 20, a man dressed in military uniform with a pistol and a silencer addressed the prisoners. The witness believes that this individual may have held the rank of major. The prisoners were told that, as of May 20, all shooting, killing and maltreatment would cease. According to the witness, another official standing near this "major" said that out of the

---

[29] This does not appear to be the same Major Dragan who had earlier interrogated the witness in Brčko. (See section regarding beatings and mistreatment in detention in Brčko.)

[30] Two major dialects in Serbo-Croatian are the *ekavica* and *ijekavica* dialects. Most residents of Bosnia-Hercegovina, Croatia and Montenegro speak the *ijekavica* dialect, but residents of Serbia speak the *ekavica* dialect. In addition to the various dialects, minor grammatical and etymological variations exist in each of the four republics. Slovenes and Macedonians each speak their own respective languages, which are distinct from Serbo-Croatian.

[31] The witness claims that, although killings ceased in the warehouses, those prisoners slated for execution were taken to the police station, where they were killed. Helsinki Watch has not been able to confirm the allegation.

sixty-five men present,[32] at least twenty-nine should have been killed. Zvonko continued:

> The "major" who announced the cessation of all killings spoke in a Serbian [*ekavica*] dialect and was frequently in the camp. Every time he entered the hall in which I was detained, he would salute and say, "God help you, brothers!" Another officer would carry a mace like object, which we were all forced to kiss. He hit one fellow over the head who failed to perform this obeisance.

Zvonko described the ten days preceding his release on May 30.

> [During] the last ten days [of my detention], we were ordinarily treated. No egregious abuses occurred, although some people were severely beaten in the interrogation room. A retired railway worker — a Muslim — was so badly beaten in the head that his hair was caked with blood. The blood also had flowed down his face, from a cross that had been carved on the left side of his forehead.

Zvonko's wife, Vesna, had stayed in the couple's apartment after her husband was arrested. According to Vesna:

> When my husband was taken away, I stayed in the apartment, terrified, expecting someone to come and pick me up, too. I watched these soldiers from my window every day. The day after my husband was taken, they came to register me, but I was not arrested. I saw one of my husband's former managers and asked him to tell me of the whereabouts of my husband. Two days thereafter, I heard he was [being held] at the police station. I saw him through a window. A week later, I

---

[32] The number of men in the hall had been reduced from approximately ninety-five to sixty-five due to an earlier prisoner exchange in which approximately thirty prisoners had been exchanged for persons captured by Croats and Muslims.

went [to the police station] again, but he was no longer there. At that point, I found out that he had been taken to Luka.

Vesna visited a local Serbian Orthodox priest and cried, insisting that her husband was not guilty of anything. She says that her sons were accused of being in the Croatian military solely because they were graduate students in Zagreb:

> The priest said that he knew that my husband had been taken away, but he said that he could not get him released.

The day after her visit to the priest, Zvonko was released from Luka. Vesna speculated that her colleague's husband, who was a good friend of the police commander, may have intervened on Zvonko's behalf. He had promised that her husband would be released if he was found "not guilty" and if no weapons were found in their apartment. According to Vesna:

> After Zvonko's release, I was afraid even to go into the yard. I only went out before 10:00 a.m., to do chores.

The couple obtained passes which would allow them to leave the area on July 11. The next day, they took a regular bus to Subotica in Vojvodina, the northern region of Serbia. They went to a collection camp in Subotica, where they slept on mats in tents, hoping to obtain travel documents. They purchased false passports for 150 German marks and left Yugoslavia to live in Croatia.

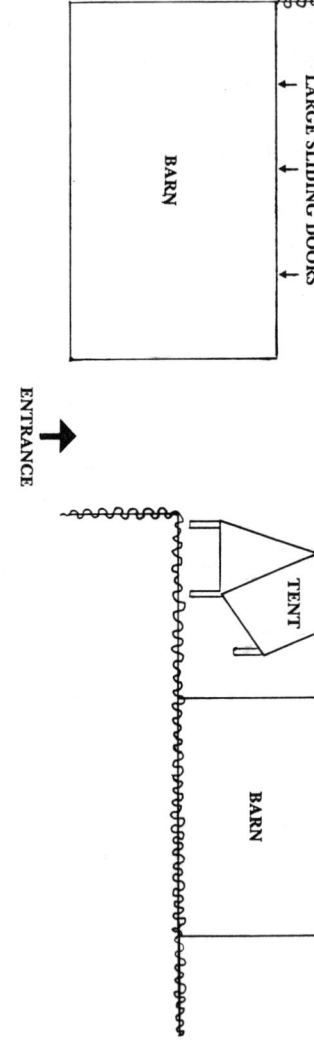

BATKOVIĆ

Batković

The existence of a Serbian-operated detention camp in the village of Batković (municipality of Bijeljina) was confirmed by the foreign press in August 1992.[33] A Helsinki Watch representative visited the camp twice in late August 1992, at which time a Major Mauzer identified himself as the commander of the camp. Helsinki Watch representatives were told that 1,200 men were being detained at the time of their visit. Two thirds of the detainees were said to be former combatants, and the remaining prisoners were civilians who were being held in the camp "for their own protection." The Batković camp was established in mid- or late June 1992. The prisoners were held in two large barns with large sliding metal doors which opened to face a courtyard. The barns had no windows, and the prisoners lay on bales of hay covered by tent canvas. Other barns also were on the premises, but they were used by the Serbian soldiers. Two large tents were used as feeding areas for the prisoners, although some prisoners also appeared to have been detained in the tents. Outdoor toilets and showers were established in the courtyard.[34]

Although Serbian authorities in the Batković camp permitted the Helsinki Watch representative and members of the press to speak with the camp's inmates, the prisoners were visibly terrified and declined to speak with anyone. Helsinki Watch interviewed an individual who was subsequently released from the camp, a grandfather in his sixties named Omer.[35] Prior to his arrest, the man had been a resident of Brezovo Polje, a village in the municipality of Brčko. Initially, he had been detained in the Luka camp for seventeen days[36] but was then

---

[33] See Peter Maass, "The Search for a Secret Prison Camp: Reporters' Queries Provoke Angry Serb Response," *The Washington Post*, August 13, 1992; and Peter Maass, "Illusory Serb Prison Camp Materializes," *The Washington Post*, August 27, 1992.

[34] See drawing of the Batkovic camp.

[35] The witness was interviewed on October 18, 1992, in Županja, Croatia, but chose to withhold his name. The name used here is a pseudonym.

[36] See testimony above.

transferred to the Batković camp on or about July 18, 1992. He spent thirty-three days in Batković and was released on August 20, 1992.

Omer's description of the camp corresponded to what a Helsinki Watch representative had seen during the aforementioned August 1992 visit. Omer described further details of the camp:

> Batković is located on a big farm, with warehouses for field equipment and food storage. There also was a big collective warehouse with twenty toilet holes; no partitions [separated the toilets]. The conditions in Batković were very bad. I was held in a warehouse about seventy by thirty meters, with about 1,200 men. The warehouse was filled with seven rows of military mattresses — one for two men — so we had to sleep on our sides. The pallets were about eighty centimeters wide.

For most of his detention, the second warehouse in the camp remained empty. However, at the time of his release from Batković, the second warehouse was being prepared to house other prisoners.[37] Omer said that a huge military tent about thirty meters long had two rows of pallets and a narrow passage down the middle. When new prisoners arrived, a second tent was erected. Omer said that during his detention approximately 1,700 men were held in the Batković camp. The warehouse and two tents were encircled by wire and prisoners were allowed to walk within that perimeter for specified periods, usually two hours after both breakfast and lunch.

According to Omer, the prisoners received three meals a day. A slice of bread about two inches thick and a piece of butter or an egg was served for breakfast. Lunch and supper consisted of a cooked meal, usually a slice of bread and soup or stew. The witness claims that the portions were not adequate for him and that he believed the total portion of food comprised one and a half or two, as opposed to three, portions a day.

---

[37] At the time of Helsinki Watch's visit to the camp in late August, prisoners occupied the second warehouse.

Two guards were constantly on duty outside the area encircled by wire. Each guard was posted in one of two guard towers, one on each corner of the encircled area. According to Omer:

> The farm was located in the middle of a plain, with no forest nearby. We didn't have any problems with guards, only from soldiers who would come now and then to beat prisoners. There was a period during which the soldiers would come and beat people every night. [The frequency of the beatings] seemed to depend on the soldiers' return to and from the battlefield.
>
> Usually after it got dark in the evening, these soldiers would separate the genuine POWs — there were about five or six of them. Then they would take them outside the enclosure, and from behind the warehouse we could hear cries and screams. The POWs were beaten every night, and the others were beaten from time to time, depending on the mood of the soldiers.

Omer reported that no one was killed by gunfire, although some died from beatings. During his detention, Omer declared, thirteen people were beaten to death.

> We would see them being separated and then we could hear shouts, shrieks, cries. These men would then come back, every part of them blackened, and they would lie down. After a few hours, they would be dead.
>
> Two of the POWs died. Two civilians whom I knew also were killed.[38] Sead Delić was called to work in the barracks, where he was beaten. He fell gravely ill and died in the hospital. All the others died in the warehouse. Smail Buljčević [another civilian that I knew] had been beaten, developed a high temperature and couldn't leave the warehouse.

---

[38] He identified them both by name.

Omer did not recognize any of the perpetrators of the abuse because they often wore stockings to cover their faces. He said that some prisoners did manage to recognize some of the soldiers, who were otherwise dressed in camouflage.[39]

Rape

Obudovac

Helsinki Watch and the Women's Rights Project of Human Rights Watch interviewed a twenty-five-year-old Croatian woman, M.,[40] who was held from the end of October until the first week of January in a house by Serbian soldiers in Obudovac (in or near the municipality of Orašje). M. was seized, beaten and raped on the spot by several Serbian soldiers while she walked between two villages. She was taken to a house in Obudovac where she was raped, forbidden to speak and guarded constantly. According to M.:

> They grabbed me and took me to a house in Obudovac, a Serbian village near Donja Mahala. There were several other women in the place to which I was taken — I am not sure how many, maybe five or six. When they caught me, they beat me and ["]did it to me["].[41] Then they took me to this house, and six men did it to me again. They left me for a while, and then they would do it again. The men changed all the time. It depended from day to day; usually it happened every evening when it

---

[39] The witness claims that local villagers, Serbs from Serbia proper, Romanians and possibly Greeks were among the guards. It appears that he was given such information from the other prisoners who claimed to have recognized the soldiers. Helsinki Watch has not been able to confirm such accusations.

[40] Interviewed on January 13, 1993, in Zagreb, Croatia.

[41] Throughout the interview, the women used the words "did it to me" to describe the fact that she had been raped.

became dark. It happened every day. Each time, about six men [raped me].

Several other women, both Muslim and Croatian, also were kept in the house. All of these women were raped repeatedly by different men. M. believes that most of the men who raped her were Montenegrin.

> I didn't know the other women in the house. They were from other places and we weren't allowed to talk. They beat us if we whispered or made noise. I was lucky because I was not injured in any other way. But others were hurt. I saw what was happening to other women, and I was afraid. I tried to be as invisible as possible. I don't know what happened to the other women after I was exchanged. I feel terrible about those even younger than myself [who were detained and raped] in that place. The youngest there were fourteen, fifteen — maybe younger; just children, and old women, too. They didn't care about age.

During her detention in Obudovac, M. missed her first and second menstrual periods. She visited her family after being released, and then headed for Zagreb to seek an abortion. According to M.:

> It was their aim to make a baby. They wanted to humiliate us. They would say directly, looking into your eyes, that they wanted to make a baby. They seemed to be men without souls and hearts. They are without mercy.

Doboj

Helsinki Watch and the Women's Rights Project interviewed a forty-year-old Muslim woman, B., from Doboj.[42] B. had previously spoken with several journalists, both newspaper and television reporters, but said that she had stopped doing interviews with the press. Helsinki Watch has no reason to doubt the facts of her testimony.

---

[42] Interviewed in January 1993 in Zagreb, Croatia.

She recounted that the occupation of Doboj began on May 1 or 2. People were allowed to leave the city of Doboj, so B. fled with her family to their family home in the village of Grabska. Thereafter, Serbian forces started shelling Grabska and B.'s son, her mother-in-law and sister-in-law were evacuated. B. and her husband chose to stay in Doboj because they had helped to found the local Party of Democratic Action (Stranka Demokratske Akcija — SDA) and felt an obligation to remain. According to B.:

> On May 10, they told us that we had to turn over all weapons by noon. At 11:25 [a.m.], they started shelling [the village]. We didn't surrender any guns because we had no weapons — just guns for hunting. They started first to shell the mosque — seven and a half hours of nonstop shelling. They also used military helicopters.
>
> They [i.e., ground troops] were coming from two sides, forcing everyone to come out of their houses and burning the houses. They forced some women and children to lie down in the main road; they threatened to drive over them with tanks if those in hiding did not emerge.

After everyone had emerged from their houses, the Serbian soldiers gathered them on the main road and separated the men from the women and children. According to B., the Serbian soldiers had lists from which they called out women's names; they directed these women to board buses. Some children appeared to have boarded the buses with their mothers. B. was among those women who boarded the three blue-and-white buses after having her name read from a list. The men were left standing in a group.

The women and children first were taken to a school in Srpska Grabska. They were then transferred to a factory warehouse used by the Bosanska company that produced jams and juices in Doboj. Muslim forces were attacking nearby. B. then was transferred to a high school in the Usara section of Doboj, where she was held for twenty-eight days. According to B.:

> It began there as soon as I arrived. They told us not to look at the soldiers so that we wouldn't remember them.

> We were not allowed to talk with each other. During the day, we stayed in a big sports hall. The guards were always there. If they caught us talking, they would take a woman out, beat her and more than the usual [number of men] would rape her. They liked to punish us. They would ask women if they had male relatives in the city; I saw them ask this of one woman and they brought her fourteen-year-old son and forced him to rape her.
>
> Some of us were selected by name; some would just get chosen. If a man couldn't rape [i.e., if he was physically unable] he would use a bottle or a gun or he would urinate on me. Not all of the men who raped me were the same. Some men came and chose women of their own will and others were forced.

B. remembers that four different types of soldiers were present at different times in the camp: local Serbian militia; the Yugoslav army (JNA); police forces based in the Serbian-occupied town of Knin in Croatia;[43] and members of the "White Eagles" [Beli Orlovi] paramilitary group, who wore an insignia bearing three eagles and a *kokarda* on their hats. B. claims that local Serbs, including several doctors whom she knew from the hospital, also raped women detained at the the high school. According to B.:

> Some of the local Serbs wore black stockings on their heads to disguise their faces because they didn't want to be recognized. [Nevertheless,] I recognized many of them. [They were] colleagues — doctors with whom I worked. The first [man] who raped me was a Serbian doctor named Jodić. He knew I recognized him. He saw my name on the list and called it out. I had known Jodić for ten years. We worked in the same hospital. I would see him every day in the employees' cafeteria. We spoke

---

[43] B. referred to the police forces from Knin as "Martičevci," because their commander is Milan Martić, the interior minister of the so-called "Serbian Republic" of Krajina in Serbian-occupied areas of Croatia. B. also claims that the forces from Knin wore high black hats and insignia on their uniforms.

generally, "Hi, how are you." He was a very polite, nice man. Another doctor whom I had previously known also raped me; [his name was] Obrad Filipović. I wasn't allowed to say anything. Before he raped me he said, "Now you know who we are. You will remember forever." I was so surprised; he was a doctor!

B. claims that women were most frequently raped in the classrooms of the high school.

Once I saw the face of a woman I knew; her daughter was with her. Three men were with them inside [the classroom]. I was brought in by one man, and another four men followed. On that occasion, I was raped with a gun by one of the three men already in the room. I didn't recognize him. Others stood watching. Some spat on us. They were raping me, the mother and her daughter at the same time. Sometimes you had to accept ten men, sometimes three. Sometimes when they were away, they wouldn't call me for one or two days. I wanted nothing, not bread, not water, just to be alone. I felt I wanted to die. We had no change of clothes and couldn't wash ourselves.

B. remembers that the school hall where the women were forced to sit during the day with their knees pulled up to their chests was packed full of women of all ages. A woman sitting close to B. tried to speak with her, but B. feared punishment and did not respond. The guards took the women to the bathroom only at designated times. They also placed a pot in the middle of the room and told the women to use it to relieve themselves. However, the pot was punctured and if the women used it, urine and feces would leak in the area where other women were sitting.

The guards also brought a man who they said was a gynecologist to the school and submitted the younger women to internal exams. Recalls B.:

A gynecologist would come to the hall, to one of the classrooms. They told us that he was a doctor, but I'm not so sure because he didn't realize that I had an IUD and he examined me internally. Only the younger women would see the doctor. I think they were checking to see if we were pregnant because he would say, "You're not pregnant." The Serbs said to us, "Why aren't you pregnant? See how nicely we treat women who are pregnant?" Once they brought girls not older than seventeen into the hall. They were clean and dressed nicely. They said, "See how well we treat them. They are pregnant."

The [pregnant girls] were from outside, and I didn't know them. I don't know if they were pregnant, but they were wearing maternity dresses. I think they were lying, but I didn't pay too much attention. I think they wanted to know who was pregnant in case anyone was hiding it. They wanted women to have children to stigmatize us forever. The child is a reminder of what happened.

B. claimed that the man who oversaw the women's detention in the school was Nikola Jorgić, whose nickname was "Jorga." Before the war, Jorgić is alleged to have served as a commander of the police force in Doboj. B. said that she knew Jorgić before her detention. She also asserts that he introduced himself to the women as "the man in charge."

I think he was proud. I would see him coming in, sometimes in the morning, sometimes every day. Sometimes we wouldn't see him for a while. "Jorga" and Stanković were in charge of the prisoner exchanges and the money. Without "Jorga['s"] permission], no woman was allowed to leave the camp. He would come in with a list and announce who would be released. Soldiers who belonged to [the paramilitary group headed by Vojislav] Šešelj and those who belonged to [Milan] Martić [in Knin] also were present; maybe they were "Jorga's" bosses. I don't think he was the highest-ranking officer [in the area] because items that were stolen were sent to Serbia.

After twenty-eight days in the high school, B. was released. Told that she was released in a prisoner exchange, B. later discovered that her brother had paid 1,000 German marks to secure her release.[44]

Forced Displacement

Brezovo Polje

Helsinki Watch interviewed a family that had been forcibly expelled from Brezovo Polje, a village about fourteen kilometers from the Sava River.[45] The women in the family were Muslims married to Croats. Some of their family members were still interned in the Batković camp at the time of the interview.

According to one of the women:

> Some time after Brčko fell and the killing there stopped, soldiers came to Brezovo Polje and took away the men.

---

[44] Helsinki Watch has received a number of reports that Serbian forces raped women in areas under their control in northeastern Bosnia. Hospital files in Croatia also contain information about women in northeastern Bosnia who were raped, allegedly by Serbian forces. In January 1993, Helsinki Watch representatives were permitted to examine a report compiled by the Croatian Ministry of Health which summarized the medical cases of rape to which several hospitals in northern Croatia had attended. The medical records also included a summary of the circumstances surrounding the rape of each woman but, because Helsinki Watch was not able to interview these women, the information cited here is solely of a medical nature. According to the report, a twenty-eight-year-old Croatian woman from Doboj was raped on several occasions after the town's fall to Serbian forces. She arrived at the Petrova Hospital in Zagreb in the eighteenth week of her pregnancy. A forty-five-year-old woman from Doboj also claimed to have been raped by Serbian forces in the town. On November 14, doctors at the Sisters of Charity Hospital in Zagreb ascertained that the woman was in her twelfth week of pregnancy and performed an abortion.

[45] The family said that the village of Brezovo Polje was predominantly populated by Muslims, although about 5 percent of the residents were Serbs and one or two Croatian families lived in the village, as well. The family was interviewed on October 18, 1992, in Županja, Croatia.

They told the women and children to be ready to leave in ten minutes.

Omer, the grandfather in the family,[46] reported that soldiers entered Brezovo Polje on either May 17 or June 17 and that the men — the youngest of whom was fourteen and the oldest about seventy-eight or seventy-nine years of age — were taken to Luka. Omer said that the soldiers entering the village were not locals but, rather, paramilitaries from Serbia coming from the conquest of Bijeljina. According to Omer:

> Until the soldiers came, we were living quite normally. There had been shooting in Brčko, but all was normal in Brezovo Polje. There were even refugees from Brčko in the village.[47]
>
> Now the houses along the main road have been robbed and stand empty, but the houses off to the side are occupied by Serbian refugee families from Bosanski Šamac.

Omer testified that no executions took place in Brezovo Polje, although looting was rampant. According to one of the women in the family:

> The soldiers confiscated our cars. We women could only take one bag with us. Money and jewelry were taken from us. Around June 23 or 24, we women and children were sent to Čaparde, where we spent the night in a school. The girls were separated from their mothers and

---

[46] The man was held in the Batković camp, and his testimony appears above.

[47] Prior to the expulsion of its inhabitants, Brezovo Polje appeared to have been transformed into a ghetto in which Muslim civilians were held hostage. See Helsinki Watch, *War Crimes in Bosnia-Hercegovina*, August 1992, pp. 69-70.

taken away by soldiers.[48] That night everyone was robbed. The girls returned the next morning, when we continued our trip. We stopped in Kladanj for two days and then we went on to Tuzla.

The women eventually paid 100 German marks to be evacuated from Bosnia.

Zvornik, Cerska, and Konjević Polje

In early February and mid-March 1993, thousands of Muslims were driven from their homes in northeastern and southeastern Bosnia in response to a renewed offensive by Serbian forces in the region. Most of the displaced persons fled to the city of Tuzla and the town of Srebrenica, which remain under the control of Bosnian troops.[49] Two weeks prior to the February expulsions, Serbian forces expelled four thousand Muslims from the municipality of Trebinje, in southwestern Bosnia.[50]

The Serbian offensive appeared to have been caused by a U.N. proposal to divide Bosnia into largely autonomous provinces, in which an ethnic group would retain *de facto* control of designated regions.[51] Despite Serbian offensives on the area, the U.N. plan placed Zvornik and its surrounding villages under Muslim control. Some have claimed that the renewed attacks also were aimed at forcing the displacement of

---

[48] The woman claims that approximately forty young women were taken from the school and that they were raped. She also asserted that the girls visited doctors in Kladanj and Tuzla. Helsinki Watch has not been able to confirm this assertion.

[49] Chuck Sudetic, "Bosnian Peace Plan Said to Spur New Attacks by Serbs," *The New York Times*, February 8, 1993 and Chuck Sudetic, "Serbs Overrun Muslim Enclave in Bosnia's East," *The New York Times*, March 15, 1993.

[50] For an account of the forced displacement of Muslims from Trebinje, see the section on abuses in southwestern Bosnia.

[51] Chuck Sudetic, "Bosnia Peace Plan Said to Spur New Attacks by Serbs," *The New York Times*, February 8, 1993.

Muslims, so as to better consolidate Serbian control over the district prior to the deployment of U.N. peacekeeping troops.[52]

Other Abuses

Incident at Bridge in Doboj Involving Forced Displacement, Killings, Use of Human Shields and Other Abuses

In early July 1992, persons were released from the Trnopolje ghetto in northwestern Bosnia, placed in cattle cars and taken to the town of Doboj in northeastern Bosnia, from where they entered Muslim-controlled territory in Gračanica. Several such deportations appear to have taken place during the first two weeks of July. During one such deportation, when the detainees arrived in Doboj, they were made to throw their belongings over a bridge. As the civilians were crossing over to Bosnian-held territory, they were shot at by the Serbian forces from whose custody they had just been released.

The refugees who were deported from the Trnopolje camp to Doboj had previously been displaced from their homes in northwestern Bosnia. S.S., a twenty-one-year-old woman from Sanski Most,[53] recounted the expulsion of persons in her town and their deportation to Doboj. According to S.S.:

> I was forced to leave my community on July 5. Serbian soldiers went house to house forcing about 3,500 women, children and elderly persons to leave. Men between the ages of sixteen and fifty-five were left behind in a camp in Sanski Most [called] camp Krinis. Women and children were kept in this camp overnight, and then we were put on trucks and buses and transported to Trnopolje.
>
> At Trnopolje, we were transferred to railroad cattle cars. There I saw a woman call out, "Why are you doing this to us?" She was pulled out of the group by the guards.

---

[52] *Ibid.*

[53] Interviewed by Helsinki Watch representatives on February 10, 1993.

Then a man called out, "Why are you taking my wife?" He was pulled out [of the line] as well. Later I heard shots. I think that the couple was killed, but I did not see them shot. I never saw the couple again.

During their journey to Doboj, the displaced were robbed by Serbian forces. Jasmina from Kozarac[54] described the journey to Doboj, via Banja Luka:

> When we left [Trnopolje], twenty-two railway wagons were filled. We went first to Doboj, then to [Bosnian-controlled territory in] Gračanica. The train stopped a few times and soldiers demanded our money.

A.H., a thirty-six-year-old woman from Kozarac,[55] also was transported from Trnopolje to Doboj in a cattle car and was robbed en route. The trains stopped for several hours in Banja Luka, before traveling on to Doboj. According to A.H.:

> From Trnopolje, I was transported by cattle car. They counted off 180 persons in my car; the train had eight cars, each with about the same number [of persons in each car]. On the way to Doboj, the train stopped from 5:30 a.m. until 10:30 a.m. the next day. We remained on the train [during that time.] Soldiers came on board [demanding] our money, gold and jewelry. We had to give everything.

According to A.H., when the detainees reached Doboj, they were met by Serbian soldiers who separated men from ages eighteen through sixty from the others. The remaining detainees appear to have been divided into groups, each of which was told to walk over a bridge.

---

[54] The witness was interviewed by Helsinki Watch representatives in October 1992 in Livno, Bosnia-Hercegovina. The witness chose to withold her name, and the name used here is a pseudonym.

[55] Interviewed by Helsinki Watch representatives on February 10, 1993.

Some witnesses interviewed by Helsinki Watch reported that the clothing of a previous convoy of displaced persons was lying on the ground. According to M.S., a woman from the village of Kamičani in northwestern Bosnia:[56]

> [We left Banja Luka and] they unloaded us by the bridge over the Bosna River, near Doboj. We saw a lot of clothing lying on the ground; it had been taken from the people of the previous convoy, so we thought they would kill us. There were many armed soldiers around us.

According to K.B., a forty-year-old schoolteacher for mentally retarded children:[57]

> They took us off the train near Doboj, and we walked the next seven kilometers. We walked along a carpet of children's clothes and blankets that were left from the previous convoy of refugees [displaced persons]. Some left their old family members along the road, since it was impossible to carry them farther.

Jasmina testified that some were told to jump into a pit after they were taken from the train. According to Jasmina:

> When we arrived in Doboj, we were not allowed [to remain at the train] station. Instead, we had to stop in a coal pit. People were forced to jump into this ditch, and some broke their legs. We then were forced to walk fifteen kilometers to the first Muslim village.

Several detainees interviewed by Helsinki Watch claim that, as they were crossing a bridge in Doboj, Serbian soldiers summarily executed those who refused to throw their belongings into the river.

---

[56] Interviewed by Helsinki Watch representatives in December 1992.

[57] Interviewed by Helsinki Watch representatives in December 1992. For an account of the witness's displacement from Kozarac and her subsequent internment in the Trnopolje ghetto, see the relevant sections above.

According to R.K., an eighteen-year-old student from Kozarac:[58]

> We were taken to the bridge [in Doboj], where the Serbs told us to throw all our belongings into the river. I was about four or five meters away from a woman who refused to throw her things over the bridge. They hit her in the chest with their guns and then shot her in the head, and blood splattered all over.
>
> I started to run and I kept running. I didn't turn back but the guard must have taken out a hand grenade because I heard someone say, "No. She's only a kid." I had run across the bridge.[59]

The displaced persons were sent along various paths to reach Bosnian-controlled territory. Some were made to walk through mine fields, some were used as human shields and others were shot at by Serbian forces as they approached Bosnian-held territory.

The site of the aforementioned woman's execution appears to have been close to the front lines, prompting Bosnian forces to shoot in response to the gunshots fired by the Serbian soldiers. According to S.S.:

> Bosnian soldiers who had been shadowing the convoy from a distance started shooting. The Serbs grabbed

---

[58] Interviewed on October 26, 1992. For accounts of the forcible displacement of Kozarac's residents and treatment in detention in the Trnopolje ghetto, see the chapter on abuses in northwestern Bosnia.

[59] Two witnesses described an incident in which a woman either refused to throw a bag over the side of the bridge or asked to remove something from the bag before she discarded it. One witness said that the woman asked to remove a baby bottle from the bag, while another witness claimed that the woman was carrying the baby in the bag. The bag was then thrown over the side of the bridge, either by the woman or the soldier, who threatened the woman with an automatic rifle. While one witness said that the woman was then shot and her body was thrown over the bridge, another witness claimed that the woman was threatened with execution but not killed. Helsinki Watch will continue to investigate this incident and report its findings.

some young boys and used them as human shields to stop the shooting against them.

Other detainees were made to walk through mine fields. S.S. claims that a Serbian commander forced those who had crossed the bridge to walk through a mine field to reach what she called "free territory." No one stepped on a mine, however; the displaced walked seventeen kilometers before they reached Bosnian-controlled territory.

Yet another group of displaced persons was shot at by Serbian forces shortly after they were released from custody. According to R.K.:

> The bridge led toward [the Bosnian-controlled town of] Gračanica. A man [who acted as our guide] took us toward Gračanica. Then some trucks showed up and someone said, "These are the ones." We had hidden my brother because we were afraid that, since he was a male, he would be killed or taken from us. We were exchanged for some men and other refugees. We kept walking forward, but there were mines all over the place and we had to be careful.
>
> We got to a tunnel, and our guide disappeared. Then we were in the tunnel and we realized that we had been brought here to act as human shields because our side was at the other end of the tunnel. As we approached the end of the tunnel, toward the Muslim side, the Serbs from the other side of the tunnel started to shoot at us and the Muslims started to yell to us to run out of the tunnel as fast as possible. Many women and children were killed then.

ABUSES BY CROATIAN FORCES

Abuses in Detention

Orašje

The town of Orašje[60] is under the control of Croatian HVO forces and has been the scene of heavy fighting for several months. Helsinki Watch is gravely concerned about the treatment of prisoners in Orašje. In particular, we have reason to believe that deaths in detention and mistreatment of prisoners have taken place in Orašje. A clear chain of command appears to be lacking among the Croatian forces in Orašje, which is removed in proximity from HVO headquarters in Mostar (in southwestern Bosnia). Helsinki Watch has reason to believe that the absence of a command structure among the Orašje troops has encouraged individual soldiers, who are not fearful of disciplinary actions on the part of their superiors, to perpetrate abuses in areas under their control.[61]

Rape

Helsinki Watch representatives conducted separate interviews with Serbian women who claim to have been raped by Croatian forces in the municipalities of Bosanski Brod and Odžak, when the area was under Croatian and, to a lesser extent, Muslim control.[62] Although the women had testified on numerous occasions on behalf of the Serbian government, Helsinki Watch found their testimonies credible.

---

[60] Prior to the war, the population of the municipality of Orašje was 28,201, of which 75.3 percent were Croats, 15 percent Serbs and 6.7 percent Muslims.

[61] Helsinki Watch cannot be more specific about the abuses in this report, but has additional documentation kept in secure files outside its offices.

[62] The two victims were introduced to Helsinki Watch representatives by the Serbian government's Commission for War Crimes and Genocide. They were interviewed in January 1993 in Belgrade, Yugoslavia.

Two of the victims had been detained after Muslim and Croatian forces assumed control of their village of Novi Grad. Following a twenty-one-day battle, Serbian forces relinquished their weapons and negotiations began. Both witnesses claim that although the Serbs had been promised safe passage to the predominantly Serbian village of Miloševac, they were detained in the high school in Odžak. According to each of the two women, the men were held in the school gym and the women were detained in the classrooms. The following day, the women and children and some men were released and settled in Odžak, in the homes of Muslims who appeared to have been family friends of the Serbian captives. About two weeks later, the women and children were told that they could return to their homes in Novi Grad. Several Serbian women were then taken from Novi Grad and raped in the village of Posavska Mahala and in the Bulek settlement, near Bosanski Brod.

Posavska Mahala

Helsinki Watch and the Women's Rights Project interviewed two women who were raped on two separate occasions by Croatian forces in the village of Posavska Mahala.[63] The men responsible for both instances of rape appear not to have been members of the Bosnian Croatian forces (HVO) but part of a paramilitary group identified as the "Fire Horses" (Vatreni Konji). The women reported the rapes to the authorities in the town of Novi Grad, but the offenders were never prosecuted.

Gordana, a forty-three-year-old housewife was raped by Croatian soldiers in the village of Posavska Mahala. According to Gordana:[64]

> The first few days [in Novi Grad] were not bad. [However,] for reasons of safety, several families lived together in one Serbian house. The violence started on

---

[63] Interviewed in January 1993 in Belgrade, Yugoslavia. The witnesses were identified by the Yugoslav State Commission on War Crimes and Genocide. See also the section on methodology in the Introduction to this report.

[64] The witness was interviewed in January 1993 in Belgrade, Yugoslavia. The name used here is a pseudonym.

June 20. One day, they took three of us women from the house in which I was living, and four women were taken from another house. They dragged us out of our beds, barefoot, at about 1:00 a.m. There were five of them, men in green uniforms without any insignia. I didn't recognize any of them, and I couldn't really see them anyway because they were shining flashlights into our eyes.

We were taken to a Croatian village, Posavska Mahala, where we were met by another thirty of their soldiers. I know that they were soldiers because I saw their green uniforms in the bright moonlight. One of them grabbed my arm and insisted that I say that I loved only him and no one else in the world. As he was dragging me around, he said that he was from Županja [Croatia]. He brought me to an abandoned barn, and we both had to jump in through the window. He then ordered me to undress. I had 4,000 German marks tied around my waist, and he took this away from me.

He raped me, ordered me to get dressed again and handed me back to the others. Another man took me to the house where the other two women were being raped. I told him that I had AIDS, so instead of raping me, he forced me to perform fellatio. I was forced to do the same to another soldier. All of this happened on a bed, in one of the rooms in the house where [two other women,] M. and D., were being raped. They were in the other rooms.

Several days thereafter, approximately forty-five women and children left Posavska Mahala and returned to Novi Grad. The women visited the Croatian military headquarters in Novi Grad, where they reported the rapes to the military police. According to Gordana, no action was taken to investigate the incident or to arrest or prosecute the perpetrators. According to Gordana:

It was safer in Novi Grad, since the military police were in charge of the headquarters while the rest of town was being raided by the "Fire Horses." We reported the rapes to the military police, who promised to take action against the perpetrators but did nothing. My house was set on fire four days later.

Helsinki Watch and the Women's Rights Project interviewed L.L., a Serbian woman identified by the Yugoslav State Commission on War Crimes and Genocide as a victim of rape.[65] L.L. is thirty-seven years old and originally from Potičanski Lipik, near Odžak. Prior to speaking with us, she talked to numerous journalists and others. She, too, says that she was raped by Croatian soldiers in the village of Posavska Mahala.

L.L. claims that her village was first shelled from the Croatian side of the Sava River on April 18 or 19, 1992. The attack continued for approximately three weeks. On May 8, L.L., her sister, a neighbor and their four children fled to the village of Hasić, where they were taken in by a Muslim man, I.D. According to L.L., Croatian military police officers told the displaced Serbs in Hasić to return to their homes in Potičanski Lipik, where the Serbian women were sexually abused by Croatian forces. According to L.L.:

> The Croatian military police came [to the village of Hasić]. They said we had to go back home. They wore green army uniforms and white belts. They said they would burn the Muslim houses if they kept the Serbs with them. When we got home, we had to work in the fields. The Croatian soldiers — my neighbors — started mistreating women in their homes.

In the early morning hours of June 5, 1992, soldiers broke into the house of D.N., where L.L. had taken refuge with a group of women and children. The Croatian soldiers then forced her outdoors and demanded to know the whereabouts of the Serbian forces. L.L. was then taken to another house and told to call out the names of three women staying there. According to L.L.:

> There were fifteen of them. They called themselves the Fire Horses. They took me to a house that belongs to

---

[65] Interviewed in January 1993 in Belgrade, Yugoslavia.

M.B. They hit me and told me to call out of the house three women who were staying there: M.D., M.N., and S.S.[66]

All four of us were put in the back of a car and we were taken to their headquarters in Posavaska Mahala, where they took us to two separate houses and started to mistreat us. I know that seven of them raped me two times each. I counted seven and then I fainted.

I was in a large room of the house that belonged to J.B. They ripped off my clothes and started raping me. They didn't spare my mouth or my anus. When this man Marijan came [toward me], I asked him, "What are you doing to us?" He [cursed me]. He threatened to kill my sons if I told anyone about the rape.

L.L. identified several of her rapists by name. They were Marijan Brnić, Jozo Barukčić, Jozo's father, Martin Barukčić, another Martin Barukčić, Ilija Jurić, Ilija Glavaš and Pavo Glavaš. According to L.L.:

The fifteen men were going from one woman to another. They kept me there until 5:30 that morning. They made me leave the house naked. Marijan kicked me from behind and told me to walk home through the fields. I said I couldn't, and he cursed me and said, "You survived fifteen of us and you can't walk home?"

L.L. claims that she was abandoned on the side of a road near Novi Grad, where she met her children and a Croatian soldier who offered to help her. According to L.L.:

Someone drove me back to Novi Grad; they dumped me on the road. A Croatian soldier stopped his car and offered to help me. Then my six-year-old son saw me and said, "Mommy, get up." The Croatian soldier gave

---

[66] The witness identified the other three women by name. Their names are kept in secure files outside Helsinki Watch's offices.

my son some chocolate. He insisted that I tell him who raped me so that they could get rid of them. Then my seventeen-year-old son came and took me to D.'s house.

The rapists were my neighbors in uniform. They had the letter U[67] on their hats and crosses hanging on long necklaces around their necks.

L.L. reported the rapes to the Croatian police in Novi Grad. The police took her to a doctor in Odžak and arrested the rapists. According to L.L., Croats[68] accused the police of defending "Četniks" and attacked the police station. The rapists were later released.

Bosanski Brod

M.P., a seventeen-year-old high-school drop-out from Novi Grad,[69] said that the Serbs were not disturbed after they returned to their homes in Novi Grad. However, approximately a week thereafter, destruction of Serbian property caused them to flee to the forest. They were subsequently captured and sexually abused by Croatian forces in Bosanski Brod. According to M.P.:

Since Serbian houses were being set on fire every night, we hid in the forests. They found us there on July 13 and took us to Bosanski Brod, to a warehouse in the Bulek settlement, which has been turned into a prison. Six of us girls were immediately separated from the other, older women.

---

[67] The letter U was used a symbol of the Nazi-aligned Ustaša forces during World War II.

[68] The witness did not specify if the Croats were members of the armed forces, the police or civilians.

[69] Interviewed by Helsinki Watch representatives in January 1993 in Belgrade, Yugoslavia. The witness was identified by the Yugoslav State Commission on War Crimes and Genocide. See also the section on methodology in the Introduction to this report.

According to M.P., the man in charge of the prison was Anto Golubović from Odžak, born in 1969; M.P. claims to have known him before the war. She also identified Golubović's deputy, Josip Tolić, who was born in 1968 and lived in the village of Bijele Bate, near Odžak. According to M.P., Golubović and Tolić took two twenty-one-year-old women to an unknown location. M.P. said:

> The remaining three women[70] and I were picked out by whoever wanted us. I spent one month and two days there [in the prison] and the same thing happened every night.
>
> Five of them slept with me. In addition to those two [Golubović and Tolić], Dorica Božić (born in 1970), Simo Topolović and Ibrahim Libro also raped me. I was never with more than one of them at a time.
>
> They acted as if they were making love to their own girlfriends but, if you tried to resist, they would hit you and it was all the same anyway. They were hiding us from the ICRC until one of the men from the other prison slipped a note to the ICRC saying that we were in the [Bulek settlement].

The witness reported that the ICRC visited the prison and registered the six women who had been sexually abused. According to M.P., forty other women who were detained in the facility had not been raped. A prisoner exchange took place on August 15, in the village of Dragalica, and the women were released.

---

[70] The witness identified by name the other five women who had been raped. Helsinki Watch retains the names of the women in secure files outside the Helsinki Watch offices. Of the three women referred to here, two were in their early thirties and one was seventeen years old.

ABUSES BY UNKNOWN FORCES

Attacks on Aid Convoys

Tuzla

During an absence of U.N. relief convoys, the Bosnian government hired drivers and used local relief agencies to bring supplies to Tuzla. Because these convoys did not receive U.N. protection, black marketeers and checkpoint guards often depleted the relief shipments before they reached their destinations. Some reports cite that 10 percent of the aid was lost to checkpoint guards.[71]

However, on November 19, the first U.N. relief convoy carrying thirty-six tons of food, clothing and plastic sheeting for emergency home supplies reached Tuzla from Vitez (in central Bosnia).[72] The 110-mile journey took ten hours to complete because of winter road conditions, accidents and traffic. On its return trip, the convoy was also fired upon by an anti-aircraft gun from a position a mile up on a mountain.[73] The parties responsible for the attacks have not been identified.

---

[71] Chuck Sudetic, "Grim Lifeline for 700,000 Bosnians: 60 Miles of Mud," *The New York Times*, November 13, 1992.

[72] David Crary, "Fighting Hinders Aid Distribution; Peace Envoys in Croatia," The Associated Press, November 19, 1992, and John F. Burns, "British Convoy Arrives," *The New York Times*, November 20, 1992.

[73] John F. Burns, "On Vital Bosnia Road, Winter Is a Fierce Foe," *The New York Times*, November 22, 1992.

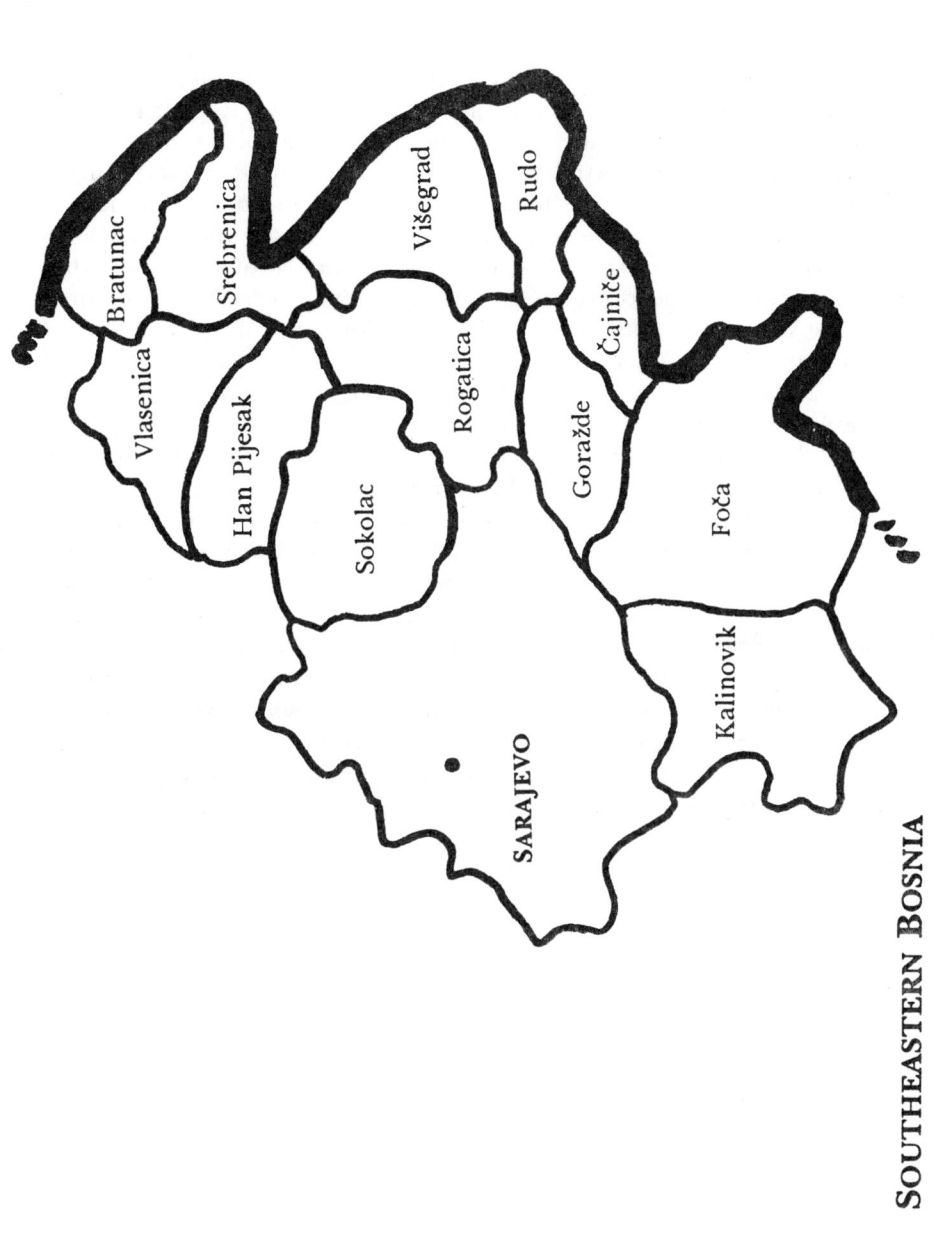

SOUTHEASTERN BOSNIA

ABUSES IN SOUTHEASTERN BOSNIA

This section of the report encompasses the municipalities of Bratunac, Srebrenica, Vlasenica, Han Pijesak, Višegrad, Rogatica, Rudo, Čajniče, Foča, Goražde, Pale, Sokolovac and Sarajevo. Almost all of southeastern Bosnia is controlled by Serbian forces, with the exception of Sarajevo, and pockets of territory in and around the municipalities of Goražde and Srebrenica and the village of Žepa (in the municipality of Rogatica) which are controlled by Bosnian Muslim troops. Parts of the municipality of Sarajevo are controlled by Serbian forces while others, including the city's center, are controlled by forces loyal to the Bosnian government.

Fighting has been most heated in the Sarajevo municipality, where Serbian forces have used the tactics of siege warfare to force the flight of Sarajevo's residents. Similar tactics have been used by Serbian forces in the Srebrenica and Goražde municipalities. In the areas of Foča, Višegrad, and Rudo, Serbian forces have mistreated prisoners and civilians in jails and makeshift prisons. The rape of Muslim women also appears to be widespread in the region. Muslims are continually being expelled from the area in large numbers. The destruction of entire Muslim villages appears to be systematic in parts of southeastern Bosnia.

In January 1993, Bosnian Muslim troops launched an offensive and captured some territory from Serbian forces in southeastern Bosnia. Bosnian Muslim troops are also reported to have attacked Serbian civilians in the region. All parties to the conflict have obstructed the delivery of humanitarian aid to Sarajevo and eastern Bosnia.

ABUSES BY SERBIAN FORCES

Abuses in Detention

Foča[1]

Several detention facilities are operated by Serbian forces in the Foča area. Men are most frequently detained in the main central Foča prison, commonly referred to as the "KP Dom" (i.e., krivični popravni dom). Persons also have been detained in the Foča police station, where women have been held in separate quarters. Women, children and elderly persons also have been detained in the Partizan sports hall.

The most egregious abuses in the region appear to have been perpetrated against women in the Foča police station, high-school and Partizan sports hall and will be described below, in the section pertaining to rape. This section will describe treatment in the Foča prison which does not appear to have been rampant, although beatings did occur. Former detainees interviewed by Helsinki Watch claim to have been given blankets and to have been fed on a daily basis.

A.R.,[2] a fifty-eight-year-old Muslim resident of Foča, told Helsinki Watch representatives that Serbian forces arrested twenty-eight men in late April. According to the witness, the men were detained without charge in the Foča prison.

> I was at home on April 27 when Serbian special forces[3] came to my home. They were dressed in camouflage, but

---

[1] Prior to the war, the population of the municipality of Foča was 40,513, of which 51.6 percent were Muslims and 45.3 Serbs. According to the 1991 census, few appear to have referred to themselves as Yugoslavs or Croats. The remaining 3.1 percent of Foča's population was most probably, but not exclusively, Montenegrin and Albanian.

[2] Interviewed on October 3, 1992, in a refugee camp in Yugoslavia. The name of the refugee camp in which the witness was interviewed is in a secure area outside Helsinki Watch's office.

[3] The witness believes that the special forces were members of the Foča police.

they wore no hat nor did their uniform bear any insignia. One of the police officers was a neighbor of mine, but the rest of the officers were outsiders — they were not residents of Foča. Their accents resembled Montenegrin speech.

I was put on a bus with twenty-seven other men from the area. We were told that we were being taken to a place where we would be required to make a statement. We were taken to the Foča prison, and we remained in detention for four months.

A.R. claims that Serbian police officers and JNA military police were present at the jail. All were armed with pistols and AK-47s. All the men who had been arrested were questioned. According to A.R.:

I was questioned and given a cigarette. My interrogator did not ask me any specific questions at first; he just called me by my first name and told me to talk. I asked him what he wanted me to speak about. The interrogator replied, "To tell you the truth, I don't even know what I am supposed to ask you. I have a paper here in front of me which orders me to conduct an interrogation."

A.R.'s interrogator was a former classmate of A.R.'s twenty-four-year-old son and therefore was amiable toward him. A.R. was told to sign a paper but, because he did not have his glasses with him, he does not know what he signed nor did he ask his interrogator about the content of the document. According to A.R.:

As I was walking out, another guard walked into the office. He asked my interrogator if I had confessed and the latter replied, "Did he confess to what?" The guard then said that if the special forces arrive that I would confess to everything. I was taken to another room and detained in the prison for four months, but I was never charged with a crime.

A.H., a fifty-five-year-old Muslim man from the village of Jelec,[4] in the municipality of Foča, also reported that he was not mistreated during his internment at the Foča prison. A.H. told Helsinki Watch:

> Forty-five men were placed in room number 22. Later, we were individually questioned. A man whose surname was Koprvica asked me questions that primarily concerned the membership of the SDA and the number of weapons in the village. I told him that we had handed over the weapons. My son was with me and he too was interrogated, but neither of us was mistreated.

A.R. reported that, during his detention, the prisoners were fed cabbage, macaroni and water daily. Both A.R. and A.H. said that the prisoners also were given fifteen dekagrams of bread every day but that it had to be divided among twenty prisoners. A.R. stated that the prisoners were fed three times a day. According to A.H., cots and blankets were provided to the prisoners.

A.R. claimed that approximately 560 men were detained in the prison throughout his detention, although the number fluctuated, depending on whether or not prisoner exchanges took place or if new inmates were brought to the prison. A.R. was interned in a room in the prison but reported that other prisoners were detained in jail cells.

> There were seventy-five of us in one room. There was one entrance into an area which was divided into four quarters. I was detained in one of these quarters. We were given a place to sleep, some socks and sponges with which to wash ourselves.

A.H. and A.R. were released from prison and deported from the area on or about August 30. A.H. claimed that 250 men remained in the prison at the time of his release.

---

[4] A.H. was interviewed in a refugee camp in Yugoslavia on October 3, 1992. The name of the refugee camp in which the witness was interviewed is in a secure area outside Helsinki Watch's office. See section concerning forced displacement for an account of the expulsion of Jelec's population.

Helsinki Watch representatives interviewed N.K., a seventeen-year-old Muslim youth,[5] who also had been detained in the Foča prison. Unlike the two previous witnesses, however, N.K. reported that detainees were beaten in the prison during his detention. According to N.K.:

> When I got to the prison [on May 19], they asked me about some people; I knew some but not others. They wanted to know the whereabouts of my father and neighbor and whether they had borne arms, but they never did. They all threatened us, especially the man dressed in civilian clothing, during the interrogation.
>
> For three and a half months, I was kept in one room. During that time, people would come and others would go. They gradually increased the number of prisoners in the room from about thirty to seventy-five.
>
> A police officer would come to the room in the evening and read out the names of some men, who were taken from the room and beaten. Usually, they were taken outside of the cell. The room had seven large windows and, although we could have seen what was going on, we were not allowed to stand by the windows so we only heard the men being beaten. I was not beaten; they just called me an Ustaša. But others were beaten, some severely. At one point, they opened the door to throw one of the men back in the room and I saw that H.K. was being badly beaten by three men. Those who had been badly beaten in the head could not stand up for almost a month. Although some returned to the cell badly beaten, others were never brought back.

---

[5] N.K. was interviewed on October 3, 1992, in a refugee camp in Yugoslavia. The name of the refugee camp in which the witness was interviewed is a secure area outside in Helsinki Watch's office.

The youth was released on August 29 and appears to have been evacuated from Foča at the same time as the two aforementioned witnesses, but on a different bus.[6] According to N.K.:

> On August 29, at about 11:00 a.m., the guards took several people from the cell. We were given some lunch and taken to a different room. En route to Nikšić [Montenegro], we were stopped by the local Četnik paramilitary duke [*vojvoda*], Pero Elez, who was from the Miljevine settlement. Elez ordered the driver to take us back to the prison. The driver did as he was told, and we spent another one and a half hours in the Foča prison. Then two police officers arrived and they read out twenty names and those men were taken from the room. Twenty-five minutes later, the same police officers came into the room and told the rest of us to get back on the bus. In front of the prison, we saw another bus across the street, and the other twenty men may have been in that bus.
>
> We headed toward Montenegro again. When we got to a place called Sčepan Polje, a youth named D.A. was beaten. D.A.'s mother was Croatian and his father was Muslim. He also was from the Foča area and had been in the prison with us. [He did not have a Muslim first name, and] the police officer asked him if he was a Serb. D.A. said no. Then the police officer said, "Then you must be a Croat!" and he let a soldier beat him with the butt of his AK-47.

---

[6] A.H., the previous witness, claims to have been released on August 30. N.K. claims the release took place on August 29, but the events described by the two men were virtually identical, leading one to assume that the evacuation took place on the same day.

Rape

In southeastern Bosnia, Serbian forces use rape as one of many methods of torturing and humiliating women. Many women and their families are forcibly expelled from their villages, their houses are burned and they are either placed in designated detention facilities or interned in villages that effectively serve as ghettos for Muslim civilians. The women are sexually mistreated during their detention, and many are gang-raped on one or more occasions. Many women from the region who were interviewed by Helsinki Watch representatives were held in more than one facility or area during their detention and were often raped in each facility. In particular, rape appears to have been rampant and an accepted mode of behavior for Serbian soldiers in the municipality of Foča. In one case, a commander was aware of, and initially condoned, the gang rape of several women.

Rasima,[7] a thirty-six-year-old Muslim mother of three, was arrested and beaten while in custody in the Foča prison. She and her children were released from the prison but were subsequently detained, during which time Rasima was raped. She recounted the destruction of her village and subsequent detention to Helsinki Watch representatives:

> The Četniks captured my husband, my children and me, and we were taken to the prison in Foča. At the time of my arrest — July 27 — I was at a neighbor's house and about six Četniks dressed in camouflage and JNA uniforms came into the house. Some of them had kokarde on their hats, but others wore no hats. They took all of us to the prison.
>
> When we got to the prison, three guards joined the six Četniks who had initially captured us. One of the guards beat us, but I didn't know him. He beat the children also. There was no electricity in the room, and some held flashlights in our faces. They then beat my husband.

---

[7] The woman was interviewed on October 3, 1992, in a refugee camp in Yugoslavia. The name of the refugee camp in which the witness was interviewed is kept in secure files outside Helsinki Watch's office. The woman preferred to withhold her name. The name used here is a pseudonym.

They kicked him in the face with their boots and beat me and my children.[8] They eventually let me and my children return to the village, but my husband had to remain in the prison.

We returned to our village, Šušjesna, and stayed there for about nine days, which is when the village was attacked. The village was divided into Muslim and Serbian sectors, and the Serbian side of the village attacked the Muslim area. The first mortar fell at about 9:00 a.m. After the village fell, we were taken to a neighboring village called Šukovac. As we were leaving, we watched as the Serbs burned the Muslim houses in the village — the Serbian houses were left untouched.

Rasima and her children remained in the village of Šukovac for two months, during which time she was raped on three occasions in three separate locations by different men.

The men who raped me were part of the army[9] — there were three of them and they wore camouflage uniforms and JNA uniforms; two of them were from Montenegro. They would come to the house that was used for questioning, and then they took us to the village of Trnovača in a car — to a particular house. Two of my neighbors were brought to this house, and we were raped for two to three hours. The three men each took one of us and raped us. I was raped by the one who said he was from Foča. We were then brought back to Šukovac.

Five days later, I was taken to the police station in Foča and placed in a cell for seven days. There were two

---

[8] Rasima had a scar on her nose; the scar resembled those that never properly heal because the injury required stitches, but such treatment was never rendered. She claimed that this scar was a result of her beating in the prison.

[9] The woman was not sure if the soldiers belonged to the regular Yugoslav army (JNA) or the "Army of the Serbian Republic" (of Bosnia–Hercegovina).

guards present: one was an active police officer from the Foča police force, and his name was Dragan; another was a member of the reserve police force. I was held with two other women.

After our fifth day in detention, we were individually questioned in the police station. During my interrogation, I was beaten and raped by two men. They asked me where the Muslims were hiding, they attacked me for bearing Muslim children, they asked if any weapons were left behind and they threatened to cut off my fingers and breasts one by one. They also threatened to kill my children.

After the seventh day of Rasima's detention, a convoy of cars arrived, and the women were asked if they wanted to leave or remain. It is unclear whether the prisoners were given the option to remain in the prison or if they would be released and allowed to remain in Foča. According to Rasima:

I said that I would like to stay until I found my husband. They then told me that if I stayed, they would kill me. I got onto the convoy with my children. I was told that a prisoner exchange had taken place and that some of the prisoners in Foča had been released, but I haven't been able to track down my husband. I don't know where he is.

In addition to the Foča prison and police station, women from the municipality are interned in schools, sports halls and other makeshift detention facilities. Frequently, they are taken from their place of detention and raped in abandoned houses which frequently serve as sleeping or working quarters for Serbian soldiers.

Helsinki Watch representatives interviewed M., a twenty-eight-year-old woman[10] from the village of Mešaje, in the

---

[10] Interviewed on October 3, 1992, in a village in Yugoslavia. In order to protect the witness, Helsinki Watch has omitted the name of the village where the interview took place. The place of the interview is kept in a secure area outside

municipality of Foča. M. reported that her village contained about 155 Muslim households and was surrounded by predominantly Serbian towns. On July 3, 1992, Serbian forces attacked her village. According to M.:

> We slept in the forest, about two kilometers from the village of Trnovača. Seven days before the attack on my village, there had been an attack on the village of Trnovača and all the men aged fourteen and older were taken away. We heard that the men were killed and that their bodies had been thrown into the river. When we heard this news, we were terrified and fled. There was a lot of shooting and burning while we were fleeing. We took refuge in the forest . . . but they eventually found us. They beat the men with rifle butts. We watched as they loaded seven buses with our people. The soldiers were dressed in camouflage uniforms.

Helsinki Watch representatives interviewed Senada, another Muslim woman from the village of Mešaja,[11] who corroborated much of M.'s testimony. According to Senada:

> Our village was attacked from the Foča city center on July 3. There were five busloads of soldiers that came into the village. We had been afraid for some time because, prior to the attack, shots were fired into our village every night, so we slept in the forest. The morning of the attack we were still in the forest, but they knew where we were and came up to us. It was about 6:20 a.m. They started to shoot at us and we started to run. During the shooting, they killed an elderly man called Edhem. They also killed Zahir and Selman and a woman called Selima; I don't know their surnames,

---

Helsinki Watch's office.

[11] Senada was interviewed on October 3, 1992, in a village in Yugoslavia. Because the woman preferred to withhold her name, the name used here is a pseudonym. The name of the refugee camp in which the witness was interviewed is keptis a secure area outside Helsinki Watch's office.

though. They also shot a woman who was carrying her three-year-old child on her back while she was running away.

> They eventually told us to stop running and to surrender, and then they stopped shooting. There were about twenty-four women and an equal number of children who they arrested. They cursed us and [Bosnian President] Alija Izetbegović and called us Ustašas. They rounded up all of us. Three of the women had been wounded in the shooting, and about seven men were also taken into custody.[12] The [wounded] women were taken to the high school in Foča, but the seven men were left behind in the forest with the remaining Serbian soldiers. My husband was among the seven, and he had been wounded in the fighting. People have told me that they were all killed.

The remaining women and children were taken to the construction site of a hydroelectric plant in the settlement of Buk Bijeli, where some women were raped in workers' sleeping quarters. According to Senada:

> We were first taken to the settlement of Buk Bijeli, which is a makeshift area of barracks for workers. The soldiers separated the younger girls — they ranged in age from fifteen to twenty — and raped them. They questioned us, and then they raped women in adjoining barracks. We heard them and saw the girls after their attack.

M. named Gojko Janković, a villager from Trnovača, as one of the main organizers of the attack and subsequent abuses. M. was raped during interrogation. According to M.:

---

[12] It is unclear whether the Muslim men were armed and returning fire, whether the Muslims had initiated the shooting to warrant return fire or whether the Serbian forces had shot indiscriminately and without provocation at the civilians.

They burned houses in the vicinity and eventually arrested us. They took us [from the forest] to the settlement of Buk Bijeli, where we were interrogated by a so-called "duke" [*vojvoda*], but I did not recognize this man. Everyone over the age of eighteen was questioned. They asked me about the whereabouts of my husband and the types of weapons we possessed. They told me to admit that we had hidden weapons. I was questioned by three men in camouflage for about twenty minutes.

Another three men then came and took me away to one of the workers' quarters. A power plant was supposed to have been built at the site, and there were about ten barracks that had been built for the workers. I was raped in one of those barracks by the three men for about thirty minutes.

During M.'s rape, her two children remained outside the door of the barracks.

Senada, M. and M.'s children were then taken to a high school in Foča, where sexual abuse was commonplace. M. was held in the high school for ten days and claims to have been raped every day of her detention. According to M.:

We were put in a classroom, in which others were already detained. They beat a little girl who they mistook for a boy. They asked her to take off her jacket, and then they left her alone.

We were taken to the cafeteria to eat and then back up to the classroom. Some of us women were taken to another room. They would take four to five women at a time from the classroom. On one occasion, four soldiers took three other women and me to the other room. Each of the soldiers raped one of us. They then left, and four other soldiers came and raped us. Then another four came and did the same thing. At one point, one of the men raping me was J.V. — he was an acquaintance.[13] I started to protest and resist, but the men who were raping the other three women in the room started to curse me and called me an Ustaša. These three men demanded that I take off my clothes, and then they raped me.

I was then taken back to the classroom, but another man came and took me away and raped me again. There were other women from my village in the room, and they too were being raped by men. All of the women who were taken from the classroom were later returned.

This type of scenario occurred every night. I was held in the high school for ten days, and every day I was raped. Some of the men who came to take us away and then rape us were familiar to me; others I had never seen before.

Senada was also raped in the high school:

We were taken to the high school in Foča, where I remained for about fifteen days. There were about forty-nine people in the classroom where we were held. Most of the people in the room were women and children, although there were a few elderly persons. The Serbs brought in cameras and taped us, supposedly to show how well treated we were for television audiences. The soldiers would come and take women away. They were raped. I was taken away only once and was raped by only one soldier, although there were many soldiers in the room where I was being raped.

---

[13] M. claims that, although she recognized the man, she did not know his name. She claims that someone later told her the name of the acquaintance who had raped her. Helsinki Watch has refrained from disclosing the individual because M. admitted that she could not have identified her attacker by name if she had not been told his name by others.

The women were then transferred to the Partizan sports hall and sexually abused by Serbian soldiers, almost daily. According to Senada:

> I was raped every night during my stay in the sports hall. The men who raped me were always different — the same man never raped me twice. Three girls were taken away, but they never came back. The soldiers who were raping us were locals from Foča, and others were from Montenegro. They told us that they were from Nikšić [Montenegro], and they did not hide their accents[14] or their identities.
>
> The night before we were to be evacuated from Foča — it was August 14 — a bus of soldiers from Serbia arrived. Days before, we were told that reinforcements were coming from Serbia. A Serbian woman who had been my neighbor came to see us. She was supposed to check on us before we left, but she broke down and started to cry.

M. spent thirty days in the sports hall and was raped frequently. According to M.:

> In the sports hall, rape was a daily occurrence. The men who raped me and the other women were Serbian soldiers. A variety of men raped us, and we were rarely — if ever — raped by the same man.
>
> There were about seventy-two people who were being held in the Partizan sports hall at the time of my detention. There were about four elderly persons, and the rest were all women and children. They took the women out of the hall and brought us to abandoned Muslim houses. This time I did not resist. They would make us laugh before they raped us. If we didn't laugh, they threatened to kill us. Not all the women were taken from the hall, but some who were taken never returned.

---

[14] Montenegrins and Serbs speak the same language but with different dialects, i.e, *ijekavica* and *ekavica*, respectively.

Four women were taken from the hall, allegedly because they were to participate in some type of negotiations, but I never saw them again.[15]

Selima,[16] a fifty-three-year-old woman, also was detained in the Foča sports hall and corroborated the other two women's accounts. Selima and her severely handicapped twenty-six-year-old son were detained in the Foča sports hall, where Selima witnessed women being taken from the hall, some of whom returned claiming that they had been raped. According to Selima:

In early August, I was taken to the camp for fifteen days. The camp was the Partizan sports hall in the city center. My son was brought with me; they brought him on a board. The hall detained primarily women, children and the elderly. We were guarded by soldiers who worked in shifts — at all times, there were three guards present. Every night, men would come into the hall with their guns, cursing us and calling us Ustašas. We were usually fed once a day, although there were days when we received no food at all. Every night they would take the younger women — usually those who were sixteen or seventeen years old — from the sports hall, and many never came back. I know the names of two such girls.[17] A third girl was taken away with them that night and she never returned, but I don't know her name. Some of the

---

[15] M. also was forced to act as a messenger for the Serbian forces on a subsequent occasion. See below.

[16] Selima was interviewed on October 3, 1992, in a refugee camp in Yugoslavia. The name of the refugee camp in which the witness was interviewed is in a secure area outside of Helsinki Watch's office. Because she chose to withhold her name, the name used here is a pseudonym.

[17] The witness identified the two young women by name. Most of those interviewed by Helsinki Watch who had been detained in the sports hall recounted the incident in which the three women were removed from the hall. They all claimed not to have known the fate of the women.

women who were taken away did come back, and they claimed to have been raped by five or six men.

One night, one of the men told me to go outside, and he threatened to kill me if I didn't get out. I refused, and he eventually relented and left me alone.

M. was forced to act as a negotiator for the Serbian forces. She was taken from the hall, to the village of Djindjicima, near Goražde, and told to deliver a message to Bosnian forces and to return with their reply. M. was forced to cross battle lines twice, eventually returning to Serbian-held territory. She was taken to the Foča prison, from where she was removed and gang-raped in the sports hall and, again, at the workers' barracks. According to M., a commander was present during the rape in the workers' barracks but, initially, he did nothing to intervene. The commander demanded that his soldiers stop mistreating the victims only after they had been thoroughly brutalized. According to M.:

> On August 12, some foreigners came to the prison, and the Serbs were told that they had to release us. On the evening between August 12 and 13, a thirty-year-old woman and I were taken away and we were raped on the benches of the sports hall. The number of men who came to rape us increased. First there were three, then four and five. I eventually counted twenty-eight different men who raped me that night, but I lost consciousness after that. They must have thrown water on me, because I was all wet when I awoke.
>
> We were taken back to [the workers' quarters at] Buk Bijeli, and there I was gang-raped again by four men dressed in camouflage. The other woman who was being raped started to cry; the soldiers started to yell at her. They started to scream, "Your guys are doing the same things that we are doing!" A man took me to a room, and he told the other soldiers not to bother me for the next hour. This man did not rape me, but it was clear to me that he was a commander of some sort. He knew what the soldiers had been doing to us. He said that his name

was Boro and that he was born in Valjevo [Serbia]. He told me that he was going to evacuate us at 5:00 a.m.

There was banging at the door, and then Boro started yelling at the soldiers. He cursed them and said, "Isn't it enough! Look what you've done to them!" He then started to speak with me. He told me his name and said that he was married and had two children. Then the banging on the door started again, and four shots were fired. Boro then walked out. I was still lying on the floor at that time, and then Boro came back and told me to get dressed.

M. was then returned to the Partizan sports hall, where a guard watched over her. According to M.:

This guard was visibly upset. He claimed that his fellow soldiers had just taken away a twelve-year-old girl. This soldier told me to call for Boro and to tell him about this little girl. He said, "Boro will listen to you." I did what he told me and then shortly thereafter, five soldiers came back with the little girl. I do not know what happened to her.

M. was evacuated from Foča with her children, but she does not know of her husband's whereabouts.

Some of the aforementioned women received medical attention after their release. Helsinki Watch representatives spoke to a gynecologist[18] who treated Senada and M. in late August. The doctor's medical records confirm that the women were raped and that one of them had become pregnant but had suffered a miscarriage. In addition to the women interviewed by Helsinki Watch, the gynecologist's medical records indicated that the doctor had treated nine other women who had been raped while detained in the Foča area. Of the doctor's additional

---

[18] The doctor was interviewed on October 3, 1992, in a city in Yugoslavia. To protect the identity of the doctor, the site of the interview remains in secure files outside Helsinki Watch's office.

nine patients, two women had become pregnant as a result of rape and had terminated their pregnancies. Two women suffered uterine or ovarian complications as a result of their abuse. The doctor said that most of the women examined had been raped during the first week of July and that they were examined in late August. Most of the medical records were dated August 21, 1992.[19]

Mutilation

Helsinki Watch representatives interviewed Nihada,[20] a widow, who had been threatened with death and was tattooed by a Serbian soldier. Helsinki Watch representatives visited a refugee camp unannounced and interviewed Nihada's eleven-year-old daughter, who directed the representatives to her mother. Nihada was ill and lying on a cot, wrapped in blankets, with surgical tape placed on various sections of her arms. When she pulled back the blankets to stand up and greet her visitors, the Helsinki Watch representatives noticed that she had surgical tape on her inner thighs. In addition to the eleven-year-old daughter,

---

[19] Hospital files in Croatia also contain information about women from southeastern Bosnia who had been raped, allegedly by Serbian forces. In January 1993, Helsinki Watch representatives were permitted to examine a report compiled by the Croatian Ministry of Health, which summarized the medical cases of rape to which several hospitals in northern Croatia had attended. The medical records also included a summary of the circumstances surrounding the rape of each woman but, because Helsinki Watch was not able to interview all the women, the information cited here is solely of a medical nature. The Petrova Hospital in Zagreb treated a thirty-year-old Muslim woman from the Goražde municipality who became pregnant as a result of her rape. She arrived at the hospital in her twenty-eighth week of pregnancy and, due to the advanced stage of the pregnancy, the woman was expected to give birth to the child. Helsinki Watch has also obtained an affidavit taken by a Serbian group which recounts the case of a Muslim woman who had been raped in the Serbian-controlled area of Grbavica in Sarajevo. To protect the security of the woman and the group, Helsinki Watch has chosen not to disclose further the contents of the affidavit.

[20] Nihada was interviewed in October 1992 in a city in Yugoslavia. She chose to withhold her name, so the name used here is a pseudonym.

Nihada had two other daughters, ages thirteen and eighteen. Nihada identified herself as a Muslim. According to Nihada:

> The Serbs provoked us for four months, so the people from my village slept and basically lived in the forest during that time — we were afraid that the Serbs would come to kill us. My husband had died ten years ago. The children were hungry and thirsty, so we went back to our house to get some food. I turned on the oven and was going to make a cake. I heard gunfire outside, and then went to the door and walked out. A Četnik then came into the house. His name was Rade Dolaš, and he was from the predominantly Serbian village of Mokronoga. He showed me a piece of paper that looked like an official document, a warrant or order of some sort. He said, "I have been ordered to kill you . . . [and] your children as well." I told him that he could kill me but begged him to leave my children alone. He told me to go into the house, and he put a hand grenade on the table. He then threw a fistful of bullets on the floor and started loading his gun, a large gun with a bayonet at the end.
>
> He then said, "Listen closely to what I am going to tell you. I am going to cut a Serbian cross into your face and throw salt in your face." I told him that he couldn't do that, and then he said that he would tattoo me "with sixty-four letters." I told him that he was crazy. He then got angry and said he was going to kill my children, that he was going to cut the fingers from my children's hands and make a necklace out of them.[21] I got scared and I let him tattoo my body.

Nihada removed the pieces of surgical tape on her arms and inner thighs. Her attacker, Rade Dolaš, had tattooed his name and the

---

[21] All sides in the war have made the assertion that opposing forces are cutting the fingers from infants' hands, which are then worn as necklaces by combatants and extremists. Similar stories circulate about the amputation of ears. Helsinki Watch has received no evidence to support such assertions.

following words on her body: "Rade–husband" [*Rade, muz.*] and "Rade. Don't forget me." [*Rade. Ne zaboravi me.*] The tattoos were written in bluish–gray ink and resembled the type frequently seen on sailors and soldiers from the Yugoslav Army (JNA). The writing was sloppily encircled, and it appeared to have been written hastily.

After the soldier had tattooed Nihada, he turned on her eleven–year–old daughter and shaved her head:[22]

> She had beautiful long hair, but he tried to shave a Serbian cross on her head. Otherwise, he did not touch my daughters, although I feared that he would rape them. He then said, "You're the wife of M.B. I won't do anything to you anymore." He asked me if I would be "faithful" and if I would promise not to go out of the house. He said, "I have to shoot at the next house," and then he crossed the street and I saw him shooting at the house. While he was shooting up the house, we fled through the field and hid among the corn stalks.

Nihada hid until approximately 5:30 p.m., when she saw another woman walking around. Nihada and her daughters decided to return to their house, which had been ransacked. According to Nihada:

> The entire house had been destroyed. My walls were full of bullet holes, and everything was demolished. I collected all my documents, one bag and then went to my neighbor's, D.'s, home. But the shooting started again and then someone yelled, "There's the Chinaman! [*Kineza*]," which is the nickname we used for the Četniks. There were men dressed in camouflage, wearing red berets with kokarde. D. jumped over a fence and I started to run toward the cornfields. A Četnik started to shoot all over the village. D. was wounded in the back. All this happened in early August.

---

[22] Initially, Helsinki Watch representatives mistook the girl for a boy. Her hair was very short and growing in all directions, as if it had, in fact, been shorn.

According to Nihada, there had been about thirty-seven Muslim houses in her village of Mioće, which was divided into two sections called Gornji (upper) Mioće and Donji (lower) Mioće. She claims that all the Muslim houses in Donji Mioće were destroyed and that all but eight Muslim houses in Gornji Mioće were demolished. Nihada believes that about six men, eight women and some children remained in the eight Muslim houses that had not been destroyed in Gornje Mioće. She stated that the Serbian houses in the village were untouched. Nihada alleges that the Serbs took furniture and other belongings from the Muslim houses in the village and that they confiscated the cattle and crops belonging to the Muslim families. A Helsinki Watch representative asked why she had remained in the village after all the violence. She replied:

> I was among the last people there in the village. I was poor, and I thought that they wouldn't touch the poor people. I was wrong.

Summary Executions

Serbian forces in southeastern Bosnia have destroyed Muslim villages and arbitrarily executed their inhabitants. The destruction of Muslim villages and property in southeastern Bosnia appears to have been systematic. Helsinki Watch has received accounts of summary executions and forced displacements of Muslims and the pillage of their property.

Skelani

Farima, a mother of three, from the village of Skelani, in the municipality of Srebrenica, witnessed the arbitrary execution of men in her village by Serbian troops.[23] On a prior occasion, Helsinki Watch interviewed survivors of the Skelani massacre whose accounts corroborate

---

[23] The woman's husband appears to have been one of the victims of the executions. During Helsinki Watch's interview in October 1992, in a refugee camp in Yugoslavia, the woman did not indicate that her husband had been executed, but her son later stated that his father had been killed. See below.

the testimony taken from Farima.[24] According to Farima, Serbian troops attacked the village on May 8, 1992:

> The shooting started at about 4:00 p.m., but we were surrounded and could not escape. They finally entered the village at 8:00 p.m. and immediately began setting houses on fire, looking for men and executing them. When they got to our house, they ordered us to come out with hands raised above our heads, including the children. There were four men among us, and they shot them in front of us. We were screaming, and the children cried as we were forced to walk on.
>
> I saw another six men killed nearby. The bodies were taken to two houses [which] were set on fire. All the Muslim houses were burned, but the Serbian homes remain untouched.

When Farima's child was asked about the whereabouts of his father, the child replied: "He's in the yard, dead."

Farima reported that she and her children were taken to the police station, where they were insulted but not harmed physically. Approximately thirty women and children were detained at the station and were guarded by soldiers who had previously been their neighbors. The women and children spent the night in the police station and then were transported from Bosnia.

Rudo

According to a sixty-year-old woman from the village of Gaučići[25] in the municipality of Rudo, Serbian forces "disappeared" one of her sons and summarily executed another, a young man in his early twenties. The woman told Helsinki Watch representatives:

---

[24] See Helsinki Watch, *War Crimes in Bosnia-Hercegovina*, August 1992, pp. 60-62.

[25] Interviewed on October 5, 1992, in a refugee camp in Yugoslavia.

My son S. was killed on July 30. He had served his tour of duty in the JNA and had returned only two months earlier. He was in front of his house when two Četniks — our neighbors — killed him. I was in the house, and I heard a gunshot. I went outside to find that Dragan Savić, from the Višegrad municipality, "Cojo" Radjan, from Mršova and Petar Micević, also from Mršova, had killed my son. These men were our neighbors. Savić had helped my husband build our house.

The Četniks organized themselves. The day before my one son's murder, my other [twenty–seven–year–old] son H. was arrested and taken in the direction of Rudo. I do not know where he is.

Forced Displacement

Foča

Selima, a fifty–three–year–old woman,[26] and her severely handicapped twenty–six–year–old son were driven from their home in Foča in early April 1992. According to Selima:

They attacked Foča on April 7 and 8. They had called my husband, M., over the telephone and the voice said, "M., give up your weapons." The three of us then went into the basement. They were shooting into the windows, and when they got to the house they found us. I ran into the stable. They looked for a gun and found it. They took the gun and left. Then a mortar hit our house while we were all inside. They chased us away, and then they burned the house. We ran into another house and watched as they burned our belongings. There were

---

[26] Interviewed on October 3, 1992, in a refugee camp in Yugoslavia. The woman was subsequently detained at the Foča sports hall, where she corroborated the testimony of other women who had been raped at the hall. See relevant section above.

> about five or six men dressed in camouflage who entered
> our house and started burning everything, but I did not
> recognize them.
>
> A few days later they came back to the house and took
> my husband away. A few days later, a police officer came
> to the house and told me to go up to the attic. It was
> dark, and I asked him why I had to go to the attic. He hit
> me in the head with his gun and then beat me with the
> gun. An ambulance came to get me, and my son came
> with me — a doctor took him with me and put him in the
> ambulance.[27]

Selima and her son were detained in the Foča sports hall for approximately four months and then were deported from Bosnia on August 18.

A.S., a thirteen-year-old resident of Foča,[28] described the pillage of her city by Serbian forces to a Helsinki Watch representative. She reported that fighting in the city broke out on April 8, 1992, and that people were arbitrarily arrested and "disappeared." According to A.S.:

> The shelling in Foča started on April 8, and three days
> later the [Serbian paramilitary group known as the]
> White Eagles and Serbian guardsmen picked up all the
> men. My father was taken away on April 11. My mother
> was taken away on June 8 by Drago Radanović, who is
> nicknamed "Srce." I never heard from them again.

A.S. recounted her observations of Foča after its fall to Serbian forces:

> I used to live thirty meters away from the Foča prison
> where the men were held. The women were taken to the

---

[27] Selima claimed that when Serbian forces assumed control of Foča, all Muslim doctors, nurses and patients were expelled from the hospital. She said that this took place some time around August 1, 1992.

[28] Interviewed on October 5, 1992, in a refugee camp in Yugoslavia.

Partizan sports center. There are about seventy women there, ages between nine and seventy. They are being raped.[29]

We were all taken to prison on April 11 but B.D., our Serbian neighbor, got us out three days later. It wasn't bad — this was only the beginning.

Bodies came down the river from Miljevina and Brod and, since they would get caught up in the wires hanging off the bridge, the soldiers would throw hand grenades at them.

My house burned down on May 22, so I stayed at my aunt's thereafter and eventually left Bosnia.

Šukovac

Helsinki Watch representatives interviewed S.Z., a mother of a ten-year-old girl, from the village Šukovac in the Foča municipality. According to the woman, Serbian soldiers burned Muslim homes as they searched houses in her village. According to S.Z.:

The soldiers were dressed in green camouflage uniforms and ordered us to come out of the basement. I was there with my mother and my daughter. One soldier wanted to kill my mother, and when I jumped at him, he turned around and started hitting me and he kicked my mother in the head. They looked for the men, searched the houses and set them on fire. As we were leaving the village, the soldiers were threatening to kill us all. Some said that they would burn us alive, but a few of them wanted to let us go. They took me to the police station

---

[29] The girl claims only to have heard of the rapes and was neither a victim of, nor a witness to, such abuse. However, the fact that women were raped in the Partizan sports hall is supported by testimony contained in the preceeding section.

in Foča, where I was held for five days. They did not beat me while I was there.

Godijevno

Helsinki Watch interviewed a seventeen-year-old Muslim, N.K.,[30] from the village of Godijevno in the municipality of Foča. According to the youth, his village was attacked on April 22 at 6:00 a.m. Mortars were launched from the opposite side of the river, from the village of Brušna. According to N.K.:

> My mother woke me up, and we all got dressed and ran to the forest. I locked the house, and a mortar fell not far from me, so I ran toward the forest. Another mortar fell near me, and this time I was wounded in the head and feet. The mortars kept falling, so I crawled into a nearby house. There were about twenty women and children from the village already hiding in the house. They wrapped my wounds, and we all went into the basement.
>
> Later, the Serbian army surrounded the house, and they told us to come out. They said they would not harm us, but we were scared. They had ski masks over their heads. Then they shot off seven bullets and killed Nura Hadjimešić, who was about fifty years old. A woman named S.H., who was about fifty-five years old, was wounded. They opened the door and told us to get outside. They shot into the air, threatened to kill us and called us Ustašas. There were about ten soldiers who came to the basement door and the rest — about thirty soldiers — were scattered about the village. They were burning houses in the village. I saw one soldier kick open the door to my house, and then I saw smoke coming out of the house. They claimed that they came looking for weapons. A reserve police officer carrying an AK-47 took

---

[30] Interviewed by Helsinki Watch representatives on October 3, 1992, in Yugoslavia.

us back to the basement and told us to stay there, but no one came back for us that day.

N.K.: After the attack, the youth again fled to the forest. According to

At about 4:00 p.m. the next day, I went to the forest to find my family. I went to the nearest Muslim village, but some of the houses had already been burned there as well. The Serb[ian forces] had already gone through this village, but some of the villagers had returned. I took shelter in one of these houses, and at nightfall, my father and brother found me in that house. My sister and mother were still in the forest.

At about 8:00 a.m. the next morning, my father asked a Serbian neighbor to take me to the hospital in Foča. This Serbian man[31] was good to me and he took me to the hospital, where I spent twenty-five days.[32]

The youth was then taken to the Foča prison and detained for three and a half months.[33]

---

[31] The witness identified the man by name.

[32] On the basis of interviews conducted with several Foča residents, it appears that the Foča hospital was held by the Muslims until April 29, during which time persons sought refuge from the fighting. However, it remains unclear whether Bosnian forces were returning fire from the hospital or whether it was used solely as sanctuary for civilians. Helsinki Watch interviewed a woman who was in the hospital on April 29. She claimed that Serbian forces assumed control of the hospital and transferred most of the men to the Foča prison.

[33] See above section on abuses in detention for an account of the youth's internment in the Foča prison.

Jelec

In late April, Serbian forces began taking steps to displace the Muslim population in the village of Jelec in the municipality of Foča. According to fifty-five-year-old A.H.,[34] the village was populated by about 450 Muslim households and approximately fifty Serbian homes.

> On April 25, the leaders of the Serbian Democratic Party [SDS] in our village visited our homes and asked that we surrender our weapons. They asked that we Muslims surrender any armaments we had, and negotiations between the Serbs and the Muslims lasted for five days. Finally, it was agreed that we would give up our arms — most of which were hunting rifles — and that we would bring these guns to the local headquarters of the [predominantly Muslim] Party for Democratic Action [SDA].

On May 1, the Muslims relinquished fifteen hunting rifles at the SDA headquarters, where soldiers dressed in military uniforms without any insignia collected the weapons. The soldiers were armed with AK-47s. On May 2, mortars fell on Jelec from the villages of Miljavina, Trešnjavo Brdo and Kalinovik.[35] The attack lasted until 10:00 a.m. on May 4. During the two-day attack, many villagers fled the area. According to A.H.:

> We fled into the hills, from where I watched the attack on the town.[36] After the mortars stopped falling, the village was blockaded, and infantry units entered the village. The people who could not or would not flee were killed and the Muslim homes were burned, including the

---

[34] Interviewed on October 3, 1992, in a refugee camp in Yugoslavia. The man was later detained in the Foča prison. See relevant section above.

[35] According to the witness, a military base was located in Kalinovik.

[36] The witness said that he viewed the attack through his binoculars, which he otherwise used for hunting.

stables. The next day, on May 5, the men who had fled into the hills went back to the village, but I did not go with them.[37]

On May 6, the people who had taken refuge in the hills returned to their village, only to find that their homes had been burned. They headed toward Sarajevo but abandoned the plan when they realized that they would not have safe passage into the city. They then reached an area called Jazići, near the town of Kalinovik, where they were met by the police forces of the self-proclaimed "Serbian Republic."

> There were about twenty police officers, all of whom were armed with AK–47s. They told us not to move and that a bus would come to pick us up. The bus came shortly thereafter and took one group toward Kalinovik. The same bus made four trips, and eventually all of us were brought to Kalinovik, where we were questioned at the police station. I was questioned by the police commander, who was known to me as Željaja, and by his interrogator, Rajko Višnjevac. Željaja was dressed in camouflage and Višnjevac was in civilian attire. Neither man was armed during the interrogation. They questioned me briefly and asked me to recount what happened in the village. I was not mistreated in any way during the interrogation.

---

[37] The witness said that the men who returned to the village reported that the following people were among those killed: five brothers belonging to the Srnja family and three of their sons (their bodies allegedly were found in a creek and bore gunshot wounds); Enver Srnja, a man in his mid-fifties, and his Montenegrin wife, Jelena; Edhem Hadžić, his wife, Fata and their daughter; Edhem Šljivo, an elderly man who was approximately seventy years old; Camil Tuzlak, approximately ninety years old; Mustafa Tuzlak, approximately sixty years old; Hasna Hadžić, approximately eighty years old; Hadjira Srnja, approximately eighty years old; Hakija Sabas approximately fifty-six years old; Osman Zameča, a man in his mid-forties; Djemajle Sajdinovič; Jusuf Djinić; and Nasuf Ljezanović. The witness claims that all the aforementioned persons were killed by Serbian forces. Helsinki Watch has not been able to confirm the deaths of these individuals or whether they were killed by cross fire, summarily executed or, in some cases, if any of them were combatants.

After his interrogation, A.H. was brought to the gym of the local school in Kalinovik, where approximately 250 persons were detained. He was held in the school for three days, during which time the detainees were fed by officers of the Yugoslav Army [JNA]. On May 1, women and children were released and forty-five men were taken to a military camp in Bileća. They were subsequently brought back to the Foča prison and released on August 30 and expelled from Bosnia via bus. According to A.H., the city of Foča had been pillaged and property and cultural monuments had been destroyed.

> We drove through the city of Foča, much of which had been burned, and it was full of Bosnian Serb army officers. We passed through Tito street [Titova ulica], and the mosque there was burned and damaged by what appears to have been a bulldozer.

Zagradje

According to a witness from Zagradje in the municipality of Rudo,[38] the Muslim and Serbian police officers in Rudo had refused to work together in early May. According to the witness, Serbian forces had taken control of the police station in Zagradje and disarmed the Muslim police officers. Serbian forces then terrorized and arbitrarily arrested the village's Muslim population, forcing many to flee. The witness told Helsinki Watch:

> The Serbs kept shooting to scare us away from our village and they were arresting people en masse. In May, we had started to flee to the forest when we got scared but in June and July, we stayed there permanently. The Serbs would not let us pass through the Uvac border point in Priboj, so I fled through the hills [and left Bosnia.]

Helsinki Watch representatives have interviewed forcibly displaced persons from the Rudo municipality who reported that Serbian

---

[38] Interviewed by Helsinki Watch representatives in October 1992, in a city in Yugoslavia.

paramilitaries in Uvac (in Bosnia) and Serbian police officers in Priboj (Serbia) controlled the border between the two republics. The refugees claimed that the Serbian paramilitaries regularly mistreated Muslims trying to flee through the Uvac border point.

Velika Daljegošta

Helsinki Watch interviewed a thirteen-year-old girl[39] from the predominantly Muslim village of Velika Daljegošta in the municipality of Srebrenica. According to the girl:

> Our village had about fifty mostly Muslim homes. One day in early May, the Serbs came to collect our weapons. They collected about ten handguns and rifles. They took the weapons to the police station in Bajina Bašta [in Serbia] and told us that if someone attacked, they would defend us. Well, the next day there was an attack. It started at about 4:00 p.m. and the mortars appeared aimed at the mosque, but it was not hit. The mortars came from the villages of Mustajnić and Božić [in Bosnia-Hercegovina]. We fled to another area, and we hid near a creek. The attack lasted one night and, in the morning, we returned to our homes.
>
> The next day, a man called "Boban" came dressed in civilian clothing carrying an AK-47. I do not know his last name, but I know that he is from the village of Crvice. He told us that we had to move out in five or six days and, if we refused, there was a possibility that we would perish. Two days later, he came back to our village in a car and he called all the villagers together. He then read from some type of document and told us that we had to leave immediately. He said that those who did not leave by 3:00 p.m. would be killed.

---

[39] Interviewed by Helsinki Watch representatives in October 1992 in a city in Yugoslavia.

The girl claimed that she and her family feared for their lives and decided to leave the area. They were escorted from their village by Yugoslav Army (JNA) reserve soldiers. The inhabitants of three other villages were deported the same day. According to the girl:

> There were about five hundred people fleeing. Most were Muslims from the villages of Velika Daljegošta, Mala and Tursanovići. We went over the bridge to Bajina Bašta, in Serbia. We got to the bridge at about 5:00 p.m. but stayed there until 9:00 p.m. We were in eight buses and one truck. The JNA soldiers escorting us were dressed either in camouflage or in green uniforms. When we crossed the bridge, many men wearing four Ss [i.e., the Serbian national symbol used by several paramilitary groups] were on the Serbian side [of the bridge]. There were many such soldiers; they were armed with AK–47s and they drove regular [civilian] cars. The JNA escorted us halfway through Bajina Bašta, and then we were left on our own.

Skelani

Anticipating an attack on the village of Skelani, some of the village's residents had fled to the forest. According to E.T., a fifty-eight-year-old Muslim woman:[40]

> We were hiding in the forest for three days. At one point my husband wanted a cup of coffee so desperately he said he would die for it, so we went back to our house. As I poured the coffee, Zlatan Marčetić, Dušan's son, came to our door dressed in fatigues and told us we had to leave immediately, since everything would be burning within an hour.

---

[40] Interviewed by Helsinki Watch representatives in October 1992 in a refugee camp in Yugoslavia.

According to the witness, the soldier organized safe passage for the couple, but the village was subsequently attacked and partially burned in early May.

Mioća

A resident of the village of Mioća, in the Rudo municipality, told Helsinki Watch representatives that Muslims were ordered to leave the area by local Serbian authorities. According to the witness:[41]

> The president of the municipality of Rudo, Vojo Topalović, ordered us to leave on or about August 13. Before that, the Četniks would roam the streets with AK-47s, hoping to scare us into fleeing.

The Use of Siege Warfare in Sarajevo

Serbian forces, in particular, have laid siege to heavily populated towns and cities, where they have used force indiscriminately and disproportionately to terrorize and thereby effect the displacement of non-Serbian civilians from territory that they hope to control. Sarajevo is the best known, but by no means the only case, in which Serbian forces have used siege warfare to facilitate their policy of "ethnic cleansing." According to a Bosnian Serb journalist interviewed by Helsinki Watch representatives:[42]

> In Sarajevo, the minute the Serbian forces see people assembled in a group — waiting to buy bread, forming a line outside a store, walking in a group across the street — they start to shoot.

---

[41] Interviewed by Helsinki Watch in October 1992 in a refugee camp in Yugoslavia.

[42] Interviewed on October 1, 1992, in Belgrade, Yugoslavia. The journalist voluntarily remained in Sarajevo during its siege and was eventually evacuated in mid-August.

In February, two women and a child were killed in Sarajevo by an exploding shell as they waited in line at a water station.[43]

Before the war, Sarajevo and its environs had a population of some 600,000 of whom about 400,000 lived within the city itself. Today, a year after the start of the siege at the beginning of April 1992, the latter number has dwindled to fewer than 300,000. The reduction in the population is due to flight by a part of the population, including a portion — but by no means all — of its residents of Serbian ethnic origin; sporadic evacuations; deaths due to shellings and sniper fire; and deaths due to the combined effects of hunger, cold, lack of adequate medical care and public health problems attributable to the siege.

Press accounts of the siege regularly report ten, twenty or thirty civilian deaths a day due to shelling and sniper fire. This suggests several thousand deaths over a twelve-month period due to indiscriminate bombardment by the besieging forces. As is to be expected in such circumstances, the number of those severely injured in this manner is far greater.[44]

Electricity and running water have been cut off from Sarajevo during most of the siege, and the supply of food has been limited because of impediments placed in the way of airlifts and ground convoys.[45] The consequences have been great privation for the residents, including the elimination of civilian transportation within the city because of the lack of fuel and such difficulties as an absence of elevator service in high-rise apartment buildings. Inevitably, of course, the old, the very young and the infirm have suffered the most.

By late August, cases of such water-borne diseases as hepatitis, abdominal typhus and gastroenteritis increased 10 percent because the water systems no longer work properly.[46]   In early September,

---

[43] Chuck Sudetic, "Serbian Artillery Shells Sarajevo but Some Relief Flights Resume," *The New York Times*, February 9, 1993.

[44] A chronology of the siege of Sarajevo is contained in Appendix F.

[45] For a further account, see below section on the obstruction of humanitarian aid and attacks on relief personnel.

[46] Blaine Harden, "Sarajevo Looks Grimly Toward Menacing Winter," *The Washington Post*, September 1,1992.

U.N.-assisted attempts at restoring electricity and water failed. Doctors also reported an epidemic of dysentery in the city. Encircling Serbian forces have repeatedly hindered power line repairs.[47]

The supply of coal and other heating fuels has been minimal, and most heating stations have also been shelled into disrepair.[48] Until late January 1993, U.N. relief shipments did not include heating oil, and most wood in Sarajevo has been harvested by the city's residents.[49]

In late November, the UNHCR estimated that the average person in Sarajevo had lost ten to twenty pounds since April and that 10 percent of the population was "moderately malnourished."

Water has been obtained from underground wells, but it must be carried through the streets for long distances and up dark flights of stairs in plastic jugs. The effects of the severe cold of winter have been exacerbated considerably by the destruction of virtually every pane of glass in the city by the constant bombardment. In the course of a brief visit to Sarajevo in early January, Helsinki Watch saw hardly a residential, religious, cultural or commercial building that had not been damaged by the bombardment. Many buildings had been destroyed or rendered uninhabitable, requiring the survivors to find new quarters in which to try to survive the siege. Other buildings that had been severely damaged were still inhabited, but the difficulties of staying warm were exacerbated by gaping holes in the walls.

---

[47] Blaine Harden, "Missile Said to Down Plane in Bosnia," *The Washington Post*, September 5, 1992.

[48] John F. Burns, "Reserves of Flour in Sarajevo Dwindle to a 2-Week Supply," *The New York Times*, August 11, 1992.

[49] Blaine Harden, "'Winter Is Here and Hope Is Lost,'" *The Washington Post*, November 23, 1992 and Peter Maass, "Sarajevo Grapples with a New Enemy – Winter," *The Washington Post*, December 29, 1992.

ABUSES BY MUSLIM FORCES

From April to August, Bosnian-held areas in southeastern regions of the country were heavily besieged by Serbian troops. In August, Bosnian forces in the Goražde, and later in the Srebrenica municipality, began launching offensives against Serbian positions.[50] Hit-and-run raids and guerrilla tactics were used widely by Bosnian forces.[51] During these attacks, Bosnian troops appear to have fired on and summarily executed disarmed Serbian combatants and, in some cases, civilians.

---

[50] In August 1992, Bosnian Muslim forces claimed to have launched a successful offensive to break the siege of Goražde and have since consolidated their hold over territory in the municipality. Bosnian Serb leader Radovan Karadžić claimed that the withdrawal of Serbian forces from parts of the Goražde municipality was part of a Serbian decision to lift the siege of Goražde. After Bosnian forces captured greater swaths of territory in the Goražde municipality, offensives were launched against the Serbian-held areas of Foča, Višegrad and Bratunac. (See Tim Judah, "Muslim Offensive Turns War Against Serbs in Bosnia," *The Times of London*, September 28, 1992.)

[51] In addition to counterattacks, the Serbian response to the Bosnian offensive was the blockade of humanitarian aid to Bosnian-controlled municipalities in southeastern Bosnia in early 1993. (The following section of this report describes the obstruction of deliveries of humanitarian relief to the region.) After a Bosnian attack on the Serbian-occupied village of Skelani in mid-January 1993, Serbian forces from northern Bosnia reinforced the local troops in the Bratunac area. The Bosnian-held town of Kamenica fell to Serbian forces in mid-February 1993. (For accounts of the fighting between Bosnian and Serbian troops between August 1992 and February 1993, see Tim Judah, "Muslim Offensive Turns War Against Serbs in Bosnia," *The Times of London*, September 28, 1992; Tim Judah, "Serb Forces Move South to Bolster Creaking Defences," *The Times of London*, December 30, 1992; Tim Judah, "Belgrade Accuses Muslims of Attack and Returns Fire," *The Times of London*, January 18, 1993; "Skelani: 18. - 25. januara 1993," *Vreme*, January 25, 1993; Donald Forbes, "Serbs Claim Men Were Tortured by Moslems in Eastern Bosnia," Reuters Information Service, February 17, 1993; and Tim Judah, "U.N. Help Arrives Too Late to Save Muslim Enclave," *The Times of London*, February 18, 1993.)

Summary Executions of Disarmed Combatants and Civilians

Near Bratunac

On December 14, 1992, Bosnian Muslim forces descended on two villages near the town of Bratunac and executed sixty-three people, mostly civilians.[52] Videos of the corpses suggest that "after being shot, some of the victims were hacked . . . with knives or blunt objects and one man was castrated."[53]

Kamenica

Bosnian forces controlled the town of Kamenica (municipality of Višegrad) for approximately four months. After the town fell to Serbian forces in mid-February 1993, bodies of Serbian combatants and possibly civilians were found in three mass graves and a pond.[54] One grave contained between eighteen and twenty-three bodies.[55] According to foreign journalists who were at the site of the exhumation, one corpse was decapitated and the feet of another were tied with wire.[56] Although

---

[52] Tim Judah, "Serb Forces Move South to Bolster Creaking Defences," *The Times of London*, December 30, 1992.

[53] *Ibid*. Helsinki Watch has received no information that would supplement foreign press accounts of the massacre. Helsinki Watch has requested medical evidence from Serbian authorities in Bosnia and Serbia proper. Helsinki Watch will continue to investigate the massacre and report its findings.

[54] Donald Forbes, "Serbs Claim Men Were Tortured by Moslems in Eastern Bosnia," Reuters Information Services, February 17, 1993.

[55] Foreign press accounts differ on the number of victims. *The Times of London* claims that eighteen bodies were exhumed, and *The New York Times* cites twenty-three victims. See Tim Judah, "U.N. Help Arrives Too Late to Save Muslim Enclave," *The Times of London*, February 18, 1993, and "Serbs Unearth 23 Bodies from Mass Graves," *The New York Times*, February 18, 1993.

[56] Donald Forbes, "Serbs Claim Men Were Tortured by Moslems in Eastern Bosnia," Reuters Information Services, February 17, 1993, and Tim Judah, "U.N. Help Arrives Too Late to Save Muslim Enclave," *The Times of London*, February

most of the victims appear to have been combatants, some also may have been civilians.[57]

The circumstances under which the victims were executed remain unknown. However, the fact that the feet of one of the victims had been tied with wire raises the possibility that the victim was summarily executed, and possibly tortured, after he had been disarmed. On February 17, 1993, the corpses found in one grave were exhumed and reportedly were taken to the town of Zvornik for an autopsy. Helsinki Watch has requested copies of the autopsy reports from Serbian officials in Bosnia and Serbia proper and will further investigate the killings.

Attacks on Civilian Targets

Goražde

In late August 1992, Serbian forces lifted the siege of Goražde briefly, only to renew their offensive in early September. Serbian sources justified the renewed attacks by pointing to an incident in which Serbian civilians were killed by Bosnian forces. According to the accounts, as the Serbian forces began lifting their siege of Goražde on August 27, several hundred Serbian inhabitants from the town began to travel north by bus, truck and car toward the Serbian–controlled town of Rogatica.[58] Near the village of Kukavice, three hundred people were alleged to have been

---

17, 1993.

[57] Press accounts about the identity of the victims differ somewhat. According to *The Times of London*, "almost all [the victims] wore the rotting remnants of pieces of military uniform." (See Tim Judah, "U.N. Help Arrives Too Late to Save Muslim Enclave," *The Times of London*, February 18, 1993.) According to *The New York Times*, the bodies "were clothed in Serbian uniforms, others in civilian dress and others naked." (See "Serbs Unearth 23 Bodies from Mass Graves," *The New York Times*, February 18, 1993.)

[58] Roger Cohen, "Siege Is Resumed in Bosnian Town," *The New York Times*, September 9, 1992.

killed by Muslim machine-gun fire.[59] Portions of Serbian press accounts of the incident reportedly "were based on reports of a recent United Nations humanitarian convoy into the town."[60]

---

[59] *Ibid.*

[60] *Ibid.* Press accounts do not give the name of the report issued by representatives who were part of the United Nations convoy.

ABUSES BY ALL PARTIES

Obstruction of Humanitarian Aid and Attacks on Relief Personnel

According to the UNHCR, 380,000 people are at high risk of exposure, starvation and endemic diseases in Sarajevo. An additional 100,000 people are at similar risk in eastern Bosnia, most particularly in the besieged areas of Goražde, Žepa, and Srebrenica.[61] Despite the dire needs of these communities, U.N. humanitarian relief flights and convoys to the city of Sarajevo and to eastern Bosnian towns have been obstructed, attacked and harassed by all parties to the conflict but, most particularly, by Serbian forces. Between October and mid-January, the United Nations documented fifty-four incidents of attack on convoys and personnel. The U.N. also has experienced numerous thefts of supplies and delays at manned checkpoints.[62]

The Bosnian government has been critical of U.N. efforts in Bosnia claiming, among other things, that the U.N. has not forcefully dealt with Serbian forces that obstruct the delivery of humanitarian aid to Muslims in besieged areas. On February 12, 1993, the Bosnian government announced that the residents of Sarajevo would boycott all humanitarian relief to their city unless the U.N. escalated efforts to deliver aid to towns in eastern Bosnia, which have had little or no aid delivered since the outbreak of war in 1992.[63] At the time, the Bosnian government claimed that the towns and villages of Žepa, Cerska and

---

[61] United Nations High Commissioner for Refugees, Office of the Special Envoy for former Yugoslavia, "Information Notes on Former Yugoslavia," January 22, 1993, and John F. Burns, "Bosnians Tell U.N. They'll Refuse Relief Aid Shipments to Sarajevo," *The New York Times*, February 13, 1993.

[62] John F. Burns, "Most Relief Operations in Bosnia Are Halted by U.N. Aid Agency," *The New York Times*, February 19, 1993.

[63] John F. Burns, "Bosnians Tell U.N. They'll Refuse Relief Aid Shipments to Sarajevo," *The New York Times*, February 13, 1993.

Konjević Polje are in dire need of humanitarian and medical relief.[64] Frustrated by the Bosnian government's denial of aid to Sarajevo and the refusal of Bosnian Serbs to let aid convoys travel to besieged towns, the U.N. High Commissioner for Refugees, on February 17, 1993, suspended most operations in Bosnia until agreements made with forces on all sides were honored and convoys carrying food and medicine were allowed safe passage.[65]

On February 19, U.N. Secretary General Boutros-Ghali resumed relief efforts across Bosnia-Hercegovina and implied that the blockade of supplies would be lifted as early as the next day.[66] On February 21, UNHCR officials asserted that discontinuing aid to Bosnia had resulted in Serbian concessions to allow delivery of aid. In late February, Serbian leaders proposed that UNHCR officials provide supplies and building materials to "ethnically cleansed" towns in exchange for safe passage of convoys to besieged Muslim and Croat areas.[67]

In order to provide relief to areas unreachable by convoy, the United States, in consultation with its European allies and the United Nations, announced a plan to airdrop relief supplies to outlying areas of Bosnia on February 24. The planes would fly high enough to avoid

---

[64] Letter to George Bush, President of the United States of America, from Hakija Turajlić, Deputy Prime Minister of the Republic of Bosnia-Hercegovina, Sarajevo, dated December 28, 1992. Cerska and Konjević Polje have since fallen to Serbian forces.

[65] John F. Burns, "Most Relief Operations in Bosnia are Halted by U.N. Aid Agency," *The New York Times*, February 19, 1993 and David Ottaway, "U.N. Halts Relief Operations in Bosnia," *The Washington Post*, February 18, 1993.

[66] John F. Burns, "Bosnia Cheering Boutros-Ghali's Decision on Aid," *The New York Times*, February 20, 1993.

[67] David B. Ottaway, "Serbs in Bosnia Demand Aid for Allowing Trucks Through," *The Washington Post*, February 27, 1993.

antiaircraft fire, but low enough to drop supplies within a few miles of the town.[68]

The first airdrops began on March 1, 1993, and targeted the enclaves of Cerska, Žepa and Goražde.[69] Serbian forces stepped up attacks and the enclave of Cerska fell on March 2.[70]

Attacks on Sarajevo Airport and Relief Flights

Although Sarajevo's Butmir Airport generally has remained open, the grounds, planes, support vehicles and personnel have all been attacked. Aircraft carrying supplies have been shot at, on the ground and in the air. U.N. soldiers charged with unloading humanitarian cargo or otherwise stationed at Sarajevo's airport have been wounded by shrapnel. Trucks carrying food and medicine have also been fired on.[71] Mortars and bullets have been fired onto the runways of the airport, damaging a hangar and the control tower. In addition, Serbian forces have threatened to react "with all means" at their disposal if planes fly over their positions en route to Butmir Airport.[72]

Canadian U.N. troops have experienced several attacks on their tour of duty in Bosnia. Two Canadian UNPROFOR soldiers were

---

[68] Ruth Marcus and Barton Gellman, "Britain's Leader Endorses U.S. Airdrop After White House Talks with Clinton," *The Washington Post*, February 25, 1993 and Daniel Williams, "Clinton and Boutros-Ghali Agree on U.S. Airdrop of Aid to Bosnia," *The Washington Post*, February 24, 1993.

[69] Stephen Kinzer, "Much Bosnian Aid Missed Its Target," *The New York Times*, March 2, 1993; Stephen Kinzer, "U.S. Planes Start Dropping Relief Supplies to Bosnians," *The New York Times*, March 1, 1993; and Peter Maass, "U.S. Launches 2nd Airdrop After First Misses Muslims," *The Washington Post*, March 2, 1993.

[70] John F. Burns, "Enclave in Bosnia Reported to Fall After U.S. Airdrop," *The New York Times*, March 3, 1993.

[71] John F. Burns, "The Food Gets Through, A Brave but Small Step," *The New York Times*, July 16, 1992.

[72] John Daniszewski, "Aid Routes in Bosnia Imperiled," The Associated Press as reported in *The Washington Post*, July 26, 1992.

wounded by shrapnel, and six U.N. trucks were destroyed on the airport tarmac in July 1992.[73] In a separate incident, a Canadian soldier, stringing barbed wire around a U.N. bunker, stepped on a land mine and lost his right foot.[74] Canadian troops have answered with defensive fire on several occasions. In one episode, a Canadian officer fired six shots at a sniper who had been firing on aid convoys for several days; the Canadian soldier's fire was not returned.[75]

Relief flights were suspended on August 18 because of threatening actions taken by Bosnian and Croatian troops. A British C-130 transport plane's instruments picked up radar signals, indicative of antiaircraft fire, while flying over a Croatian-controlled area of Bosnia. Although the pilot reported seeing smoke from the ground, there was no evidence that the plane had been hit.

In addition, a U.N. convoy encountered mines as it returned to Sarajevo's airport along a road held by Bosnian forces. Similarly, a convoy returning from Goražde also encountered Bosnian-laid mines.[76] Because U.N. officials felt that the roads were unsafe, they suspended all relief efforts in and around the airport. The airport reopened two days later, after Serbian and Bosnian forces provided assurances that the relief shipments would not be hindered.[77]

On September 3, an Italian U.N. relief plane was shot down near Jasenik, twenty miles west of Sarajevo, in Croatian-controlled territory, killing all on board. Two American helicopters encountered small-arms

---

[73] "Sarajevo Aid Cut Off," Associated Press article carried by *New York Newsday*, July 21, 1992.

[74] Peter Maass, "Canadian 'Yank' Fires on Sniper in Sarajevo," *The Washington Post*, July 29, 1992.

[75] *Ibid.*

[76] Stephen Engelberg, "Fearing Attack by All Sides, U.N. Halts Sarajevo Airlift," *The New York Times*, August 19, 1992 and "Aid Flight Reportedly Targeted at Sarajevo Airport, London Press Association, August 18, 1992, as reported in Foreign Broadcast Information Service, August 19, 1992.

[77] John Pomfret, "Relief Airlift to Resume in Sarajevo," The Associated Press as reported in *The Washington Post*, August 20, 1992.

fire as they flew a rescue mission to the site of the plane crash.[78] Results of an Italian-led preliminary investigation showed that the plane had been hit by at least one shoulder-fired heat-seeking missile. Their conclusion was based on the fact that the wreckage was scattered over a large area, indicating that the plane had been heavily damaged before hitting the ground.[79] On September 15, the Pentagon announced that the helicopters involved in the rescue attempt had indeed been hit by small-arms fire. Croatian troops in Bosnia said that they had fired at the helicopters because they thought they belonged to Serbian forces.[80] Due to the attack on the U.N. plane, relief flights were suspended until October 2, 1992.[81]

On September 8, U.N. officials reported that two French U.N. soldiers, who were part of a U.N. convoy near Sarajevo airport, had been killed and at least two wounded by heavy machine-gun fire that lasted for at least five minutes.[82] A U.N. report on the incident later confirmed

---

[78] Chuck Sudetic, "U.N. Relief Plane Reported Downed on Bosnia Mission," *The New York Times*, September 4, 1992; Blaine Harden, "Missile Said to Down Plane in Bosnia," *The Washington Post*, September 5, 1992; and Chuck Sudetic, "Downed Plane: Serbs and Bosnians Trade Charges," *The New York Times*, September 5, 1992.

[79] Blaine Harden, "Missile Hit Aid Plane, Initial Report Shows," *The Washington Post*, September 17, 1992.

[80] Michael Gordon, "Pentagon Says a Rescue Helicopter Was Fired on in Bosnia," *The New York Times*, September 16, 1992.

[81] John M. Goshko, "Humanitarian Supply Airlift to Sarajevo to Resume Soon," *The Washington Post*, October 2, 1992.

[82] John Pomfret, "Two French Soldiers Slain in Bosnia," The Associated Press as reported in *The Washington Post*, September 9, 1992; and "2 French Troops Killed in Attack on U.N. Convoy," The Associated Press as reported in *The New York Times*, September 9, 1992.

that the U.N. convoy mistakenly drove into cross fire between the warring Serbian and Bosnian forces.[83]

On September 10, Bush administration officials said that Serbian warplanes were using relief flights as cover for military operations. The U.S. asserted that such action by Serbian forces jeopardized the safety of U.N. relief flights because it drew ground fire from opposing Bosnian and Croatian forces. A near-collision between U.N. and Serbian aircraft occurred on August 28, when a Serbian plane passed in front of a French aircraft.[84] Because of such practices, the U.N. Security Council began discussions of establishing a "no-fly zone" over Bosnia.[85] In addition, the U.N. Security Council voted in favor of increasing the number of troops provided for the peacekeeping operation in Bosnia from 1,500 to 6,800. The additional troops arrived in late November 1992.[86]

---

[83] Chuck Sudetic, "Angry U.N. General Says Bosnia Attacked Convoy," *The New York Times*, September 10, 1992; Blaine Harden, "Muslims Fired on French Convoy, U.N. General Charges," *The Washington Post*, September 10, 1992; and Patrick Moore, "Bosnian Update," Radio Free Europe/Radio Liberty *Daily Report*, No. 176, September 14, 1992.

[84] Michael Gordon, "U.S. Says Serbian Warplanes Use Relief Flights as 'Cover,'" *The New York Times*, September 11, 1992, and "Croatian Official: Serb Fighters Flew Under Cover of Humanitarian Flights," The Associated Press, September 11, 1992.

[85] On October 2, then-U.S. President George Bush asked the United Nations to adopt a resolution that would impose a ban on all military flights over Bosnian airspace, excepting U.N. relief flights. Several days later, the United Nations Security Council voted fourteen to zero, with China abstaining, to impose a ban on military flights. (Kurt Schork, "Serb Planes Said to Strike Bosnia, Defy U.N. Ban," Reuters Information Service as reported in *The Washington Post*, October 11, 1992.) On October 10, 1992, nineteen people were killed and thirty-four wounded in an air attack on Gradačać, less than twenty-four hours after the U.N.-imposed flight ban. Western journalists reported hearing and seeing aircraft in the area. (Chuck Sudetic, "Serbian Planes Said to Kill 19 After U.N. Ban," *The New York Times*, October 11, 1992.)

[86] "U.N. Sending More Peacekeepers to Bosnia, with More Powers," The Associated Press, September 15, 1992.

On October 16, the main road from the airport was barricaded by Bosnian soldiers, who claimed that the road would be unsafe because of an expected Serbian offensive in the area. The U.N. declined to use an alternate route known to be extremely hazardous.[87] The barricades were removed two days later, with the agreement that the U.N. would monitor the road to ensure that it not be used by Serbian forces for military purposes.[88] After relief flights were resumed, fighting between Croatian and Muslim troops again suspended relief flights into Sarajevo on October 21.[89]

Relief flights were resumed but were again threatened with suspension on November 26, after a French plane was fired on as it landed. Damage was minimal, and the plane departed without mechanical problems.[90] Similarly, a U.S. plane was hit by gunfire in early December, causing the suspension of relief flights for three weeks.

In February, relief flights to Sarajevo were suspended indefinitely after U.N. peacekeeping troops witnessed an attack on a German transport plane. The propeller of the plane was hit by a 23-millimeter antiaircraft weapon set up in the village of Kosijersko Selo, in Serbian-held territory.[91] One crew member was injured in the incident. At the request of the UNHCR, Zagreb was replaced by an Italian air base on the Adriatic as the point of departure for relief flights to Sarajevo.[92]

---

[87] "Aid to Sarajevo Cut — by Defenders," Reuters Information Service as reported in *The Washington Post*, October 17, 1992.

[88] "Sarajevo Relief Blockade to End," *The Washington Post*, October 18, 1992.

[89] Peter Maass, "Muslim-Croat Battle Halts Sarajevo Airlift," *The Washington Post*, October 22, 1992.

[90] Blaine Harden, "Two U.N. Relief Convoys Fail to Reach Isolated Muslim Towns," *The Washington Post*, November 26, 1992.

[91] Chuck Sudetic, "Serbian Artillery Shells Sarajevo but Some Relief Flights Resume," *The New York Times*, February 9, 1993, and "Sarajevo Flights Halted," The Associated Press as reported in *The New York Times*, February 7, 1993.

[92] "Italy Takes Over Zagreb's Role on Mercy Flights," Reuters Information Services, February 9, 1993.

Attacks on, and Obstruction of, Aid Convoys

Efforts to transport supplies have been thwarted on several occasions by mined roads, direct attacks by forces on all sides, cross fire and pilfering.

Initial arrangements for bringing supplies to Sarajevo's airport did not provide for the transport of supplies to besieged and remote towns and villages in eastern Bosnia-Hercegovina where food supplies have been low since the outbreak of the war in April 1992. Moreover, eastern Bosnia has been particularly hard-hit by the Serbian practice of "ethnic cleansing," and many of those who have been forcibly displaced from their homes in the region have sought refuge in besieged pockets of territory still under the control of Bosnian troops. The influx of displaced persons and dwindling supplies of food and medicine have exacerbated the already-dire humanitarian situation in the eastern region.

Despite a statement by the Yugoslav government "guarantee[ing] free and safe passage for any humanitarian convoy intended for the civilian population in Bosnia-Hercegovina,"[93] repeated attacks have occurred on relief convoys with and without U.N. military escorts.

Goražde

In late July, the UNHCR sent three supply trucks to Goražde, escorted by a U.N. armored personnel carrier. Although the trucks carried some food, the trip was largely focused on determining the level of accessibility into the town.[94]

A second convoy sent to Goražde returned to Sarajevo after running into land mines and small-arms fire. The convoy carried twenty tons of food and medicine and included two trucks, one light vehicle, two U.N. armored personnel carriers, and later added one Serbian personnel

---

[93] "Free, Safe Passage Guaranteed for Aid to Bosnia," Tanjug Yugoslav News Agency report of August 13, 1992, as translated in Foreign Broadcast Information Service, August 14, 1992.

[94] John Daniszewski, "Gorazde Hammered, Defenders Appeal for Help," The Associated Press, July 23, 1992.

carrier.[95] At the insistence of the Serbian troops, the convoy took back roads. Near the village of Mesići, the convoy encountered an overturned car containing dead Serbian soldiers. While removing the car from the road, the convoy was attacked by small-arms fire from unidentifiable forces. The convoy left the area, and the lead personnel carrier hit a land mine, slightly injuring an interpreter. The convoy again moved forward. After a few yards, one of the supply trucks hit another land mine that blew the wheels off its left side. The relief workers spent the night by the roadside, fearing a repeated attack.[96]

In mid-August, Ukrainian U.N. troops escorted a relief convoy carrying eight truckloads of food and medicine to Goražde, making the first delivery to the 70,000 people trapped in the city. On its return trip, the convoy encountered cross fire thirteen miles out of Goražde and, farther along, had to remove land mines from a bridge.[97]

In November, Serbian forces repeatedly obstructed relief convoys destined for the Bosnian-controlled areas of Srebrenica and Goražde. In reaction to the Serbian forces' actions, the UNHCR Special Envoy, José Maria Mendiluce, threatened to stop all relief shipments to Serbian areas in eastern Bosnia if humanitarian-aid convoys headed to Bosnian-controlled areas were not allowed to reach their destinations. If these conditions were not met, Mendiluce threatened to ask the U.N. Security Council for further action. He also commented that the aid cut off from Serbian areas would not cause any great suffering and that the people in Goražde and Srebrenica were at greater risk. He did not, however, restrict his censure only to Serbian forces; he acknowledged that Croatian and Muslim troops were also interfering with aid deliveries.[98]

---

[95] John Daniszewski, "Aid Routes in Bosnia Imperiled," The Associated Press as reported in *The Washington Post*, July 26, 1992.

[96] John F. Burns, "U.N. Suggests Airdrops to Bosnian Town," *The New York Times*, July 27, 1992.

[97] Peter Maass, "U.N. Relief Reaches Bosnian City," *The Washington Post*, August 16, 1992 and Stephen Engleberg, "Serbs Following a Twin Strategy," *The New York Times*, August 16, 1992.

[98] Blaine Harden, "U.N. Halts Food Aid to Serbs," *The Washington Post*, November 24, 1992.

Despite these steps, convoys to Goražde and Srebrenica were kept from their respective destinations. The convoys were to travel on a road that had been inspected previously by a French reconnaissance mission. However, a fifteen-vehicle convoy headed to Goražde was forced to stop after a French-manned armored personnel carrier hit a land mine five miles away from the town. Although both convoys encountered difficulties, they received orders from their U.N. commanders to remain until they reached the towns and their missions were completed.[99] Goražde was reached after the mines were cleared and, after three days' delay, the convoy to Srebrenica reached its destination (see below).

Other relief efforts have met with practical obstructions. For example, aid convoys destined to reach various towns in eastern Bosnia in early February were delayed because the local refugee agency had run out of fuel.[100]

On February 24, Serbian troops halted a twelve-truck convoy carrying food and medicine at a checkpoint in Rogatica. Serbian commanders said that they suspected that the convoy was carrying ammunition and weapons and proceeded to examine the contents of each truck carton by carton. Only six of the trucks had been inspected by nightfall.[101] The convoy finally reached Goražde eleven days after it had left a United Nations depot in Belgrade 200 miles away. This convoy was the fourth to reach Goražde since the war began.[102]

Sarajevo

On June 2, 1992, a U.N.-escorted convoy carrying dried milk, baby formula and other foods to the suburb of Dobrinja was attacked

---

[99] Blaine Harden, "Two U.N. Relief Convoys Fail to Reach Isolated Muslim Towns," *The Washington Post*, November 26, 1992.

[100] Christine Spolar, "Overcoming the Odds in Sarajevo," *The Washington Post*, February 4, 1993.

[101] John F. Burns, "Serbian Forces Halt Land Convoy Taking Aid to Besieged Bosnians," *The New York Times*, February 25, 1993.

[102] John F. Burns, "Serbs Free Another Convoy to Besieged Muslims," *The New York Times*, February 26, 1993.

from all sides by Serbian machine-gun fire. A driver and a passenger on one of the buses were seriously wounded. U.N. officials reported that Serbian forces later drove off with the two wounded people, the supplies and the convoy's vehicles. The convoy had been organized by a Sarajevo charity, and all forces in the area had been notified and had guaranteed the convoy's safe passage.[103]

On September 6, a U.N. supply truck carrying blankets was struck by mortar fire outside a Sarajevo warehouse. There were no deaths or injuries.[104]

On October 10, 1992, a U.N. troop carrier struck a land mine in between Stup and Ilidža, killing a Ukrainian U.N. soldier and wounding three others.[105]

On November 1, the United Nations Children's Fund (UNICEF) succeeded in sending a convoy of children's relief supplies to Sarajevo, encountering resistance only from the Bosnian government, who denounced efforts to send children's clothing made in Serbia as insensitive and insulting. A cease-fire negotiated for the delivery held for the length of the journey.[106]

U.N. relief efforts were virtually nonexistent for elderly persons in a nursing home in Nedžarići, on the outskirts of Sarajevo. Sniper and mortar attacks hampered access to the area, and U.N. personnel preferred to focus their relief efforts in the center of Sarajevo. Over a two-day period in early January, ten elderly persons died from the cold at the unheated nursing home. Another woman at the home, riddled with frostbite and suffering from infections, was near death. A week earlier, seven of the home's residents had died within five days, again due to the cold. Because of the deaths, U.N. airlifts began carrying wood, coal,

---

[103] Blaine Harden, "Serb Forces Attack Bosnian Food Convoy," *The Washington Post*, June 3, 1992.

[104] "Mortar Fire Hits U.N. Truck Delivering Aid to Sarajevo," Reuters Information Services as reported in *The Washington Post*, September 7, 1992.

[105] Chuck Sudetic, "Serbian Planes Said to Kill 19 After U.N. Ban," *The New York Times*, October 11, 1992.

[106] Paul Lewis, "First Convoy of Children's Aid Reaches Sarajevo," *The New York Times*, November 2, 1992.

stoves, sleeping bags and blankets to try to combat the near-zero temperatures.[107] On January 7, U.N. officials prepared to evacuate the residents of the home for the elderly. In the meantime, French U.N. troops arrived with the first of five wood-burning stoves to heat the home, and food shipments were increased. Of the 302 residents at the home at the start of the siege, seventeen had died from sniper and mortar fire and 167 had succumbed to exposure, lack of medicine or other causes due to the war.[108]

In early February, U.N. forces again made attempts to restore Sarajevo's electricity and heating. Sniper bullets barely missed the repair crew, and Bosnians returned fire with grenades that fell only yards from the U.N. troops. Most repair missions usually are abandoned because of breaches in cease-fires to allow the repairs.[109]

A privately organized relief convoy from a group based in Alsace, France, reported that Serbian troops in Iližda had forcibly unloaded six trucks of a sixty-vehicle, 523-ton convoy bound for Sarajevo. The pilfered supplies included 1,000 pairs of shoes and boots, 2,000 track suits and about thirty tons of food and medicine.[110]

Srebrenica

In early November, the UNHCR attempted to send an aid convoy to the Serbian-controlled town of Bratunac and the Bosnian-controlled town of Srebrenica. Nineteen trucks carrying food and other supplies were rerouted to the Serbian towns of Loznica, Užice and Šabac because Bosnian Serb demonstrators near Bratunac would not allow the shipment

---

[107] John F. Burns, "Bosnia's Elderly Fall to a New Enemy: Cold," *The New York Times*, January 6, 1993.

[108] John F. Burns, "Battle to Save Bosnians from the Cold," *The New York Times*, December 8, 1992.

[109] Christine Spolar, "U.N. Repairmen Bow to Sarajevo's Chaos," *The Washington Post*, February 2, 1993.

[110] John F. Burns, "Serbs Free Another Convoy to Besieged Muslims," *The New York Times*, February 26, 1993.

through to Srebrenica. The U.N. refused to deliver aid to only one of two prearranged towns.[111]

Despite steps taken by the UNHCR to ensure the delivery of supplies to Goražde and Srebrenica, a twenty-five-vehicle convoy headed to Srebrenica was halted at a Bosnian Serb roadblock, where U.N. soldiers were told that they were not allowed to pass.[112] Like the convoy headed for Goražde mentioned above, the UNHCR convoy was ordered to hold its ground.[113] After three days' delay, the convoy, with its Belgian escort, reached Srebrenica in late November without incident. The 70,000 people in the town include refugees from nearby areas and about 25,000 children. The supplies were lacking in much-needed medicine, due to an unexplained oversight.[114]

In the Srebrenica hospital, 320 people have died because of a lack of medicine. Surgeons have operated without anesthesia and antibiotics. Blood for transfusions also is unavailable.[115]

On March 16, Lieutenant General Philippe Morillon, commander of the U.N French forces assigned to Bosnia, announced that he would not leave the besieged city until Bosnian Serbs allowed the relief convoy he led to enter the town.[116] On March 19, the convoy, carrying 175 tons of food and medical supplies, was allowed passage into Srebrenica,

---

[111] "U.N. Convoy Gives Up Attempt to Reach Muslim Town," Reuters Information Service, November 6, 1992, and Terry Leonard, "Bosnians Block Exodus of 6,000 from Sarajevo," The Associated Press as reported in *The Washington Post*, November 7, 1992.

[112] Blaine Harden, "Two U.N. Relief Convoys Fail to Reach Isolated Muslim Towns," *The Washington Post*, November 26, 1992.

[113] *Ibid.*

[114] Chuck Sudetic, "After 8 Months, First Relief Reaches One Bosnian Town," *The New York Times*, November 29, 1992.

[115] *Ibid.*

[116] John F. Burns, "U.N. General to Stay in Bosnian Town," *The New York Times*, March 17, 1993.

after Morillon negotiated with Serbian forces for several days.[117] A day later, Morillon supervised the evacuation of 680 Muslim residents of Srebrenica, one hundred of whom were seriously wounded, to the town of Tuzla.[118] In addition, General Morillon also sought to make a trade-off with Serbian forces. In exchange for safe passage of relief convoys to Srebrenica, Morillon promised the evacuation of about 250 Serbs from Tuzla.[119]

Žepa

Žepa has been under siege for twelve months, and no U.N. shipments have reached the town. Ham radio operators have reported that lack of food, medicine and the cold have caused the deaths of scores of people.[120] On January 15, a sixteen-vehicle U.N. convoy, carrying eighty tons of aid, came within 500 yards of the Muslim village of Žepa, before it was turned back by a Serbian-manned log barricade.[121] At a prior barricade, six cars carrying journalists were refused passage and 100 boxes of aid were confiscated by Serbian guards, allegedly because they were in excess of the authorized amount of aid. Serbian forces also deliberately sent the U.N. convoy down a road known to be blocked by

---

[117] John F. Burns, "Aid Trucks Arrive in a Bosnian Town After Serbs Yield," *The New York Times*, March 20, 1993.

[118] John F. Burns, "U.N. Evacuates Bosnian Muslims from a Town Besieged by Serbs," *The New York Times*, March 21, 1993.

[119] John F. Burns, "U.N. Aid Seeks Deal on Stranded Serbs," *The New York Times*, March 22, 1993.

[120] Tony Smith, "Convoy Stranded Outside Žepa," The Associated Press, January 16, 1993; Peter Maass, "A Cry of Help from a Frozen Hell," *The Washington Post*, January 13, 1993; John F. Burns, "U.N. to Ask NATO to Airdrop Supplies for Bosnians," *The New York Times*, January 12, 1993; and Peter Maass, "U.N. Convoy to Isolated Bosnian Town Blocked by Serb-Erected Barricade," *The Washington Post*, January 17, 1993.

[121] John F. Burns, "The Longest Ride: Serbs Hinder Aid," *The New York Times*, January 18, 1993.

fallen trees and, later, by land mines, in order to prolong their arrival.[122] The convoy turned back to spend the night in Borike, twelve miles away. On January 17, the U.N. convoy finally reached the town.[123]

The convoy members found the town's doctors in the hospital amputating limbs with a carpenter's saw, administering liquor to surgical patients for lack of anesthetics and cauterizing surgical wounds with a heated wire. The surgeons' instruments, two scalpels and the carpenter's saw, were kept in a wooden box. Conditions were very unsanitary and operations were performed on a kitchen table. Adults were given liquor to dull the pain while children were not given any anesthetics. Seventeen patients had developed gas gangrene and sixteen patients had died. Food supplies, prior to the convoy, had consisted of dried meat from animals slain during the siege, vegetables left from the fall harvest and bread made from straw.[124] Unlike Sarajevo, heating homes was possible due to an ample supply of firewood. However, as in Sarajevo, Žepa is without electricity, running water, central heating or gasoline due to the Serbian siege.[125]

After several days of intense negotiations with Serbian military officials, a second U.N. convoy reached Žepa on February 21. The convoy carried sixty-five tons of food and medicines for 30,000 residents.[126] The convoy reached Žepa a week after it had left Sarajevo with supplies. The convoy was held by Serbian forces near Rogatica. After it left Rogatica, the convoy encountered a large mortar crater in the road leading to Žepa. French combat engineers and a bulldozer were brought in to fill the crater. The bulldozer hit a land

---

[122] *Ibid.*

[123] *Ibid.*

[124] John F. Burns, "Primitive Bosnian Clinic Appalls Convoy," *The New York Times*, January 19, 1993.

[125] Peter Maass, "Convoy Brings Food, Hope to Besieged Bosnian Town," *The Washington Post*, January 19, 1993.

[126] Peter Maass, "U.N. Officials Dispute U.S. Airdrop Proposal," *The Washington Post*, February 22, 1993.

mine, and the convoy was again delayed. After clearing away land mines, fallen trees and other obstacles, the convoy finally reached Žepa.[127]

Cerska

In February 1993 a ten-truck U.N. relief convoy carrying sixty-five tons of food and medicines was prevented from reaching the besieged village of Cerska by Serbian forces.[128] Despite negotiations with a local Serbian commander identified as Major Pandurović, U.N. officials were unable to persuade Serbian forces to let the relief vehicles pass.[129] Although Serbian authorities reportedly told the U.N. that they would issue the necessary commands allowing the convoy passage, they also stated that final clearance would depend on local commanders' assessments.[130] In mid-February, a ten-truck U.N. convoy with a Ukrainian escort was delayed in Loznica outside of Cerska because Serbian forces refused to let the shipment pass.[131] After four days of negotiations, U.N. High Commissioner for Refugees Sadako Ogata recalled the convoy to Cerska and called off all relief operations to eastern Bosnia and Sarajevo, citing interference from Serbs primarily.[132]

The 20,000 estimated residents of Cerska have received no assistance since the beginning of the war in April 1992. Approximately

---

[127] John F. Burns, "Convoy Finally Reached Besieged Bosnian Town," *The New York Times*, February 22, 1993.

[128] David Ottaway, "U.N. Halts Relief Operations in Bosnia," *The Washington Post*, February 18, 1993.

[129] John F. Burns, "U.N. Aid Convoy in Bosnia Blocked by Serbs for Third Day," *The New York Times*, February 18, 1993.

[130] *Ibid.*

[131] Peter Maass, Bosnia Acts to End Aid Boycott," *The Washington Post*, February 21, 1993, and John F. Burns, "Convoy Halted by Serbs Looms as Test Case in Bosnia," *The New York Times*, February 16, 1993.

[132] Peter Maass, "Bosnia Acts to End Aid Boycott," *The Washington Post*, February 21, 1993.

6,000 people were encouraged by Serbian forces to leave Cerska and flee to Tuzla. At least thirty people, some of them children, are said to have died on en route.[133]

On March 2, one day after U.S.-sponsored airdrops of supplies were dropped near the town, the Cerska enclave fell to attacks by Serbian forces.[134]

Attacks on Medical Personnel and Hospitals

Sarajevo

In June 1992 Serbian artillery reportedly hit a hospital bus in Sarajevo, killing a doctor and injuring two nurses.[135] In July, a doctor escorted by U.N. forces bringing medical supplies to one of Sarajevo's hospitals came under sniper fire. The sniper stopped after the Canadian U.N. troops returned fire.[136]

In October, the Koševo Hospital in Sarajevo suffered extensive damage from artillery shelling and bullets. The functioning of the hospital was severely hampered by the shortages of electricity and water. Ambulances have been shot full of holes as they race through the city carrying wounded. Dozens of patients in the hospital have been wounded by shelling.[137]

Muamera Puska, a front-line nurse in Sarajevo, has been wounded five times in the course of duty. She has been hit in the thigh by shrapnel, shot in the right arm by a sniper, hit in the shin by a

---

[133] *Ibid.*

[134] John F. Burns, "Enclave in Bosnia Reported to Fall After U.S. Airdrop," *The New York Times*, March 3, 1993.

[135] "Serbs' Guns Hit Sarajevo Hospital Bus," Sarajevo Radio broadcast cited by the Reuters Information Service as reported in *The Washington Post*, June 25, 1992.

[136] Charles Lane, "The Siege of Sarajevo," *Newsweek*, July 6, 1992.

[137] John F. Burns, "A Sarajevo Hospital Works in 'Horror Beyond Anything,'" *The New York Times*, October 18, 1992.

ricocheting bullet, hit in the knee by shrapnel and her heel was sliced open by a tank shell.[138]

In early March, an architect named Munira was killed while surveying mortar damage to Koševo Hospital. Eight others were injured. Her husband, Tajib, also an architect, has mapped ninety-six direct mortar hits on the hospital and eighty-one shells that landed near the building. Tajib and others who work at the hospital have observed that shelling of the hospital increases around noon, during visiting hours.[139]

---

[138] Peter Maass, "Amid War, Bosnia Honors its Heroes," *The Washington Post*, February 27, 1993.

[139] Peter Maass, "Noon Visiting Hours Prove Deadly as Serbs Target Sarajevo Hospital," *The Washington Post*, March 10, 1993.

ABUSES IN SOUTHWESTERN AND CENTRAL BOSNIA

BOSNIA-HERCEGOVINA

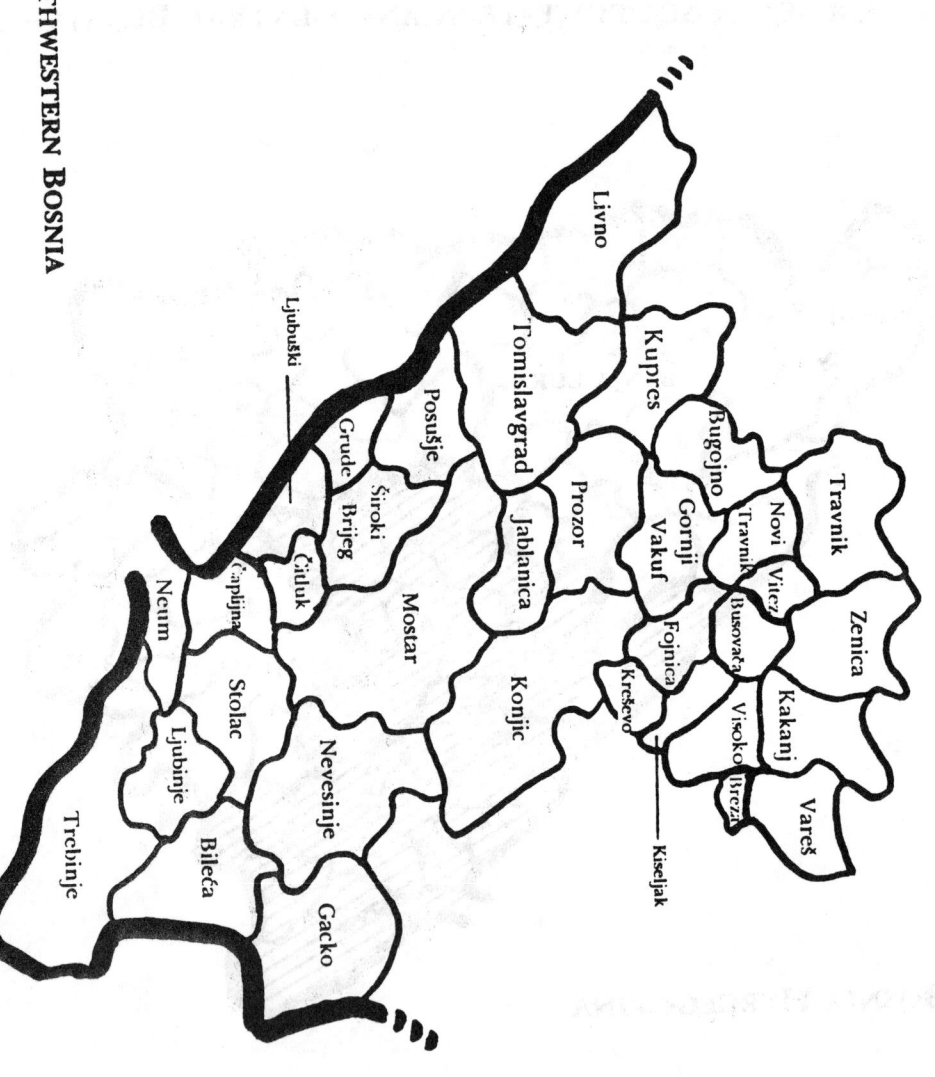

ABUSES IN SOUTHWESTERN AND CENTRAL BOSNIA

This section of the report includes the Hercegovina and central regions of Bosnia. Hercegovina is commonly divided into two sectors — western Hercegovina,[1] populated predominantly by Croats, and eastern Hercegovina,[2] populated predominantly by Serbs. Muslims comprise a portion of the population in both western and eastern Hercegovina, particularly in the municipalities of Mostar, Prozor, Jablanica, Konjic and Stolac.

Bosnian Croatian forces known as the Croatian Defense Council (Hrvatsko Vijeće Obrane — HVO) control most of western Hercegovina, including the municipalities of Neum, Čapljina, Ljubuški, Čitluk, Široki Brijeg, Grude, Posušje, Tomislavgrad[3] and Prozor. In central Bosnia, Croatian forces generally control the municipality of Kiseljak.

Muslim forces control the municipalities of Visoko and Breza. Forces loyal to the Bosnian government are predominantly, but not exclusively, Muslim. Formerly part of local territorial defense (*territorialna odbrane* — TO) units, these predominantly Muslim forces now are known as the Army of the Republic of Bosnia-Hercegovina and are under the nominal control of the Bosnian government. However, due to a breakdown in communications and the encirclement of Sarajevo by Serbian forces, the Bosnian Army generally is commanded on a regional basis. The Army of the Republic of Bosnia and Hercegovina is divided into five corps which are based in Sarajevo, Tuzla, Zenica, Mostar and Bihać.

Several paramilitary and local vigilante Muslim and, to a lesser extent, Croatian forces operate in Bosnia. Some of these groups are

---

[1] Western Hercegovina is composed of the following municipalities: Jablanica, Bugojno, Konjic, Kupres, Čapljina, Čitluk, Ljubuški, Grude, Široki Brijeg, Mostar, Posušje, Neum, Tomislavgrad, Livno and Prozor.

[2] Eastern Hercegovina includes the municipalities of Stolac, Trebinje and Ljubinje.

[3] The municipality was originally referred to as Duvno but, in recent years, its name has been changed to Tomislavgrad. The latter is used in this report to identify the municipality.

headed by local warlords, and others are self-organized and conduct black-market operations. Several Muslim militias, weakly linked to Bosnian government forces, operate primarily in central Bosnia.[4] During the early stages of the war, Muslim paramilitary units actively participated in military operations alongside Bosnian TO forces. When the Army of Bosnia-Hercegovina was proclaimed, Bosnian political and military leaders sought to bring many of the paramilitary groups under their control. However, Muslim, Croatian and Serbian paramilitary activity remains rife throughout Bosnia-Hercegovina.

The municipalities of Zenica, Kakanj, Konjic, Donji Vakuf, Vitez, Travnik, Novi Travnik, Fojnica, Vareš, Busovača, Bugojno, Kreševo, Jablanica and Mostar are under the nominal joint control of Muslim and Croatian forces. However, some of these areas are controlled to much larger extents by Muslim or Croatian forces,[5] while others are under strained joint control.[6]

Bosnian Serb forces control most of eastern Hercegovina, including the municipalities of Ljubinje and Trebinje. Serbian forces also control the municipalities of Nevesinje, Bileća, Gacko and Kupres, which are also covered in this section of the report.

The municipalities of Stolac and Livno are partially controlled by Croatian forces and partially by Serbian forces. Although generally under Serbian control, western parts of the Trebinje municipality and southern parts of the Kupres municipality are controlled by Croatian forces. Although mostly under joint Croatian and Muslim control, a small portion of territory in the easternmost parts of the Mostar and Konjic municipalities is under Serbian control.

On July 3, 1992, Mate Boban, the head of the Croatian Democratic Union (Hrvatska Demokratska Zajednica — HDZ) in

---

[4] Some of these groups are known as the "Green Berets" (Zelene Beretke); MOS (Mulimanske Obrambene Snage), a variation of the Croatian "HOS" force; the "Green Legion" (Zelena Legija); and the "Young Muslims" (Mladi Muslimani).

[5] Muslim forces retain supremacy in Zenica and Kakanj, while Croatian troops have stronger control in Vareš, Busovača, Travnik, Bugojno, Kreševo and Mostar.

[6] Vitez, Novi Travnik, Donji Vakuf, Fojnica, Konjic and Jablanica are under joint Muslim-Croatian control but, due to recent fighting between the two forces, relationships remain strained.

Bosnia–Hercegovina, proclaimed the establishment of the "Community of Herceg–Bosna," an autonomous Croatian territory within the republic of Bosnia–Hercegovina.[7] The main Croatian armed group fighting in Bosnia — the HVO — is composed of Bosnian Croats and generally fights on behalf of the self-proclaimed "Community of Herceg–Bosna."[8]

In addition to the HVO forces, a Croatian paramilitary group that also includes Muslims — the Croatian Defense Forces (Hrvatske Obrambene Snage — HOS) — has participated in hostilities in Bosnia. HOS is the armed wing of the ultra-right-wing Party of Rights (Hrvatska Stranka Prava — HSP), a political party that advocates the inclusion of Bosnia–Hercegovina in a "Greater Croatia."[9] HOS forces were responsible for brutal abuses in the Mostar and Čapljina municipalities during the summer of 1992. Although most HOS forces have since been incorporated into either the HVO or Bosnian Army, HOS troops continue to operate in Croatian- and Muslim-controlled areas, particularly in central Bosnia.

Although HVO, HOS and the Bosnian government forces fought together during the early stages of the war in Bosnia, tensions have arisen among all three parties. In early August, Blaž Kraljević, the leader of HOS troops in Bosnia, and seven other HOS members were assassinated at a Croatian checkpoint in Hercegovina, presumably by

---

[7] For an account of the Croatian position and a detailed description of Croatian armed forces fighting in Bosnia–Hercegovina, see Helsinki Watch, *War Crimes in Bosnia–Hercegovina*, August 1992, pp. 32–35 and 41–46.

[8] In the early stages of the war, members of the regular army of the Republic of Croatia (Hrvatska Vojska — HV), participated in the fighting in Bosnia. The HV eventually withdrew from Bosnia, but Croatia continues to supply military, humanitarian and other aid to Croatian and, to a lesser extent Muslim, forces in Bosnia–Hercegovina.

[9] During World War II, Bosnia–Hercegovina was incorporated as part of the Nazi puppet "Independent State of Croatia" (Nezavisna Država Hrvatska — NDH). The Croatian Party of Rights and its armed wing advocate the establishment of similar borders.

HVO forces.[10] Shortly thereafter, HVO troops disarmed many of the HOS troops, thereby diminishing the fighting capabilities of the paramilitary organization.[11] Currently, most prisoners held by Croatian forces in Bosnia are under HVO jurisdiction.

In addition to the dispute between the HVO and HOS in Bosnia, relations between Croatian and Muslim forces have been severely damaged in recent months. In October 1992 and January 1993, fighting between HVO troops and Bosnian government forces weakened the alliance between Muslim and Croatian troops in Bosnia-Hercegovina. In some cases, human rights abuses appear to have taken place, primarily against Muslims.[12]

Croatian and Muslim forces most frequently imprison detainees in existing prisons or jails. Prisoners also are detained in deserted schools, military facilities and other public buildings that have been transformed to serve as detention facilities. Bosnian Muslim forces operate a detention facility in former Yugoslav Army (JNA) barracks in the village of Čelebići, in the municipality of Konjic. Croatian and Bosnian Muslim forces are responsible for beatings and other mistreatment in detention. Both sides have arbitrarily arrested and detained civilians. Many civilians held against their will are hostages under international law.[13]

Serbian forces in Trebinje are responsible for abuses against non-Serbs in that municipality, most recently for the forcible eviction of

---

[10] Zoran Batusic, "The Rights of the Croatian Party of Rights," *The East European Reporter*, November/December 1992, pp. 57-59. See also the section concerning assassinations.

[11] In some cases, Muslims have joined HOS forces. The preference for HOS over HVO among the Muslims lies in the fact that HOS advocates the retention of Bosnia-Hercegovina as an entity within a "Greater Croatia." HVO troops, on the other hand, largely protect only those parts of Bosnia that have been proclaimed the territory of the "Community of Herceg-Bosna," i.e., western Hercegovina and parts of central Bosnia.

[12] For an account of these abuses, refer to relevant section below.

[13] Refer to the relevant section concerning patterns of abuse for a definition of "hostages" and the prohibitions against holding such persons under international law.

Muslims from the area. Serbian forces also have used indiscrim[inate force] against Bosnian and Croatian civilian targets, most notably i[n ...]

ABUSES BY CROATIAN FORCES

This section describes violations of the rules of war and human rights abuses perpetrated by the Croatian Defense Council (HVO) and Croatian Defense Forces (HOS). It documents abuses committed by HOS forces during the summer of 1992, when most of its troops were Croats. Helsinki Watch has no evidence of abuses committed by Muslim or Croatian members of HOS after August 1992.[14]

Mate Boban, the head of the Croatian Democratic Union (HDZ) in Bosnia-Hercegovina and president to the self-proclaimed "Community of Herceg-Bosna"[15] claims that HVO was formed as a [para]"military organ" of Bosnian Croats in the fall of 1991. According to Boban:

> HVO was formed in September or October 1991. We formed it in 1991 because thirteen Croatian villages in the municipality of Trebinje — including Ravno — were destroyed and the Bosnian government did nothing thereafter. HVO [units were] formed in all of Hercegovina.[16]

---

[14] Abuses committed by predominantly Muslim forces are discussed in the following section.

[15] Interviewed by Helsinki Watch representatives on October 23, 1992, in Grude, Bosnia-Hercegovina.

[16] During the war in Croatia, Serbian and Yugoslav forces attacked Croatian civilian and military positions — particularly in the Dubrovnik area — from Trebinje. The seat of the JNA barracks in Mostar also served as a base for these forces. In early 1991, JNA reservists and Serbian paramilitaries terrorized the non-Serbian population in the Trebinje area and destroyed homes and property belonging to Muslims and Croats. Helsinki Watch is not aware of any action taken by the Bosnian government to protest these abuses on its territory to the Yugoslav or Serbian governments or to the Yugoslav Army (JNA).

According to Boban, HVO was proclaimed to be an "official" military force on April 3, 1992.

Boban acknowledged that the armed forces of the Republic of Croatia (Hrvatska Vojska — HV) send food and uniforms to HVO forces in Bosnia-Hercegovina. He denied that Croatian Army (HV) units fight in Bosnia-Hercegovina. According to Boban, "HVO fights alone." Boban claimed that military service in HVO forces is compulsory only for Croats. Serbs and Muslims can join voluntarily but are not conscripted.[17]

Boban said that HVO troops assumed control over detention facilities operated by HOS forces in the Čapljina municipality in August 1992. He said that old military barracks existed in the southern area of Mostar (*južni logor*) but that no prisoners were held at that site. Rather, prisoners were held in the central prison in Mostar, near the heliodrom, which also was the main prison on the territory of the self-proclaimed "Community of Herceg-Bosna." According to Boban:

> The central prison detains Croats — i.e., military soldiers — and Muslims and Serbs who are suspected of working against us. We have a department in charge of criminal investigations. All the people in the prison are under investigatory detention. Then they are set free, and it is decided whether or not they will be brought before the military court. Most of the time, we are looking into whether or not [the prisoner] was in possession of weapons. We have a military prosecutor in Mostar. There are laws governing all these offices and their functions.

Virtually every Croatian military and police official interviewed by Helsinki Watch representatives stressed the legal basis for the arrests

---

[17] Helsinki Watch representatives interviewed several Serbian residents of western Hercegovina who confirmed that Serbs were not being conscripted into HVO forces. Helsinki Watch has received reports that Muslim men between the ages of eighteen and fifty-five are being forcibly repatriated to Bosnia-Hercegovina, where they are being conscripted into the HVO. Helsinki Watch has not been able to confirm whether Muslim residents in western Hercegovina are drafted into the HVO.

and investigation of prisoners.[18] Many claimed that the self-proclaimed "Community of Herceg-Bosna" recently had adopted a panoply of laws regulating the conduct of the law-enforcement officers, the courts and governing bodies. Various individuals explained that these laws were identical to the laws of the Republic of Bosnia-Hercegovina, excepting deletions in which references to the socialist economic or political system of the former Yugoslavia are mentioned, e.g., regulations dealing with

---

[18] According to a deputy of Valentin Ćorić, the head of the HVO military police in Mostar, the criminal division of the military police was established in early October to conduct investigations of the accused prisoners. A criminal report was forwarded to the court and prosecutor, who then decided whether to issue an indictment and take the case to court. At the time of Helsinki Watch's visit, no prisoner had yet stood trial. A tribunal was being formed, and persons who served as professional judges before the war were asked to serve on the court. According to Ćorić, two Serbian judges from Mostar were asked to participate, but both declined.

According to Ćorić, all prisoners are entitled to a trial before sentencing or release. Ćorić explained that both a military and civilian court system operate in Mostar, but the tribunal before which a prisoner is tried depends on the nature of the offense, not whether or not the defendant is a member of a military force. Therefore, if a civilian is accused of a military offense — such as possessing weapons without a license — he or she would be tried by the military court. Moreover, Ćorić justifies the use of military courts to try civilians by claiming that all men between the ages of sixteen and sixty are subject to military duty and are therefore treated as soldiers. He mentioned that about fifteen manslaughter (i.e., negligent homicide) cases were pending before a court, presumably in Mostar.

Ćorić claimed that a trial of Serbs would begin shortly after Helsinki Watch's visit, although the defendants were accused of "collaborating to incite a rebellion" as early as June 1991. The evidence gathered thus far included possession of fifty to seventy rifles, machine guns and hand grenades. According to Ćorić, organizers of the "rebellion" would be treated differently from accomplices. The court also would take into account whether war crimes were committed against civilians. Defendants will be able to choose their own lawyer, but they doubt that any lawyer will accept their cases, so the court will appoint a defender from a list of lawyers and give them every opportunity for defense. When asked whether the defendants would be allowed to contact lawyers and others outside of Mostar to help with their case, Ćorić said that this would be permitted, although he stated that it was almost impossible to reach areas outside of Mostar by telephone because of the war's disruption of communications.

self-management of the Yugoslav economy,[19] insulting the president of Yugoslavia, etc.

Although an obvious effort is being made to establish some semblance of legality, the investigatory and judicial procedures were still in disarray and, at the time of Helsinki Watch's visit, those imprisoned appear to have been held for military or ethnic, not legal, reasons. Moreover, under international law, due process must be guaranteed to a defendant standing trial.[20] Given the current political climate in

---

[19] The Socialist Federal Republic of Yugoslavia based its political and economic systems on the concept of worker self-management. This concept purports to give workers the right to act as collective owners of their place of employment and to decide how the fruits of their labor would be allocated. According to the 1974 Yugoslav Constitution:

> [M]an's inviolable status and role shall be based on:
>
>> social ownership of the means of production which precludes the return of any kind of system of exploitation of man, and which, by ending the alienation of the working class and working people from the means of production, in the distribution of the product of labor, and in guidance of the development of society on self-management foundations; (See *Constitution of the Socialist Federal Republic of Yugoslavia (Ustav Socijalističke Federativne Republike Jugoslavije)*, translated by Marko Pavičić (Belgrade, Jugoslavenski stvarnost, 1989).

Despite Yugoslavia's purported adherence to socialist self-management, most major enterprises were owned and indirectly operated by the League of Communists of Yugoslavia (LCY).

[20] According to Article 75(3) and (4) of Protocol I of the Geneva Conventions:

3. Any person arrested, detained or interned for actions related to the armed conflict shall be informed promptly, in a language he understands, of the reasons why these measures have been taken. Except in cases of arrest or detention for penal offences, such persons shall be released with the minimum delay possible and in any event as soon as the circumstances justifying the arrest, detention or internment have ceased to exist.

4. No sentence may be passed and no penalty may be executed on a person found guilty of a penal offence related to the armed conflict except pursuant to a conviction pronounced by an impartial and regularly constituted court respecting the generally recognized principles of regular judicial procedure, which include the following:

>a. the procedure shall provide for an accused to be informed without delay of the particulars of the offence alleged against him and shall afford the accused before and during his trial all necessary rights and means of defence;
>
>b. no one shall be convicted of an offence except on the basis of individual penal responsibility;
>
>c. no one shall be accused or convicted of a criminal offence on account of any act or omission which did not constitute a criminal offence under the national or international law to which he was subject at the time when it was committed; nor shall a heavier penalty be imposed than that which was applicable at the time when the criminal offence was committed; if, after the commission of the offence, provision is made by law for the imposition of a lighter penalty, the offender shall benefit thereby;
>
>d. anyone charged with an offence is presumed innocent until proven guilty according to law;
>
>e. anyone charged with an offence shall have the right to be tried in his presence;
>
>f. no one shall be compelled to testify against himself or to confess guilt;
>
>g. anyone charged with an offence shall have the right to examine, or have examined, the witnesses against him and to obtain the attendance and examination of witnesses on his behalf under the same conditions as witnesses against him;
>
>h. no one shall be prosecuted or punished by the same Party for an offence in respect of which a final judgment acquitting or convicting that person has been previously pronounced

Bosnia-Hercegovina, it is doubtful that any party to the conflict — including the Croats — can ensure a defendant of the opposing side an impartial and fair trial. This assertion was indeed voiced by several Croatian military and police officials with whom Helsinki Watch spoke. According to Jozo Perić, a police investigator in Livno, whether or not trials would be held depended on "the political situation, the releases of detainees and whether an amnesty was granted to the Serbian prisoners." Perić assumed that an amnesty would be granted to those who sided with the Serbian forces. According to Perić:

> An amnesty law will probably be passed. A large number of people should be tried but, given the current political climate, due process could not be guaranteed and the legal proceedings would probably be a farce. Nevertheless, the top leaders should be punished.

Boban claims that HVO forces have been instructed to respect human rights and the rules of war. According to Boban:

> From the first day, we gave orders that all Croats in the armed forces in Bosnia-Hercegovina [sic] adhere to the rules of war, to stop abuses when they see them being perpetrated and to protect moral dignity [of the community]. Despite the war, we think we've had a pretty good record. Everyone is responsible for these abuses.

---

under the same law and judicial procedure;

i. anyone prosecuted for an offence shall have the right to have the judgment pronounced publicly; and

j. a convicted person shall be advised on conviction of his judicial and other remedies and of the time limits within which they may be exercised.

Abuses in Detention

Helsinki Watch representatives interviewed prisoners detained in the municipalities of Mostar, Livno and Tomislavgrad in October 1992. Former detainees from the Čapljina municipality also were interviewed. Some of the detainees were Serbian men or women who had been arrested after many unregistered weapons were found in their homes. Other Serbian men and women prisoners appear to be civilians who were arbitrarily arrested and imprisoned on the basis of their ethnic affililation. Still other prisoners included several Muslims — primarily from the municipality of Trebinje — who fought with the Yugoslav Army (JNA) and who had been captured during combat. The last category of prisoners included Croatian soldiers who were interned for breaches of discipline.

Most of the detainees interviewed by Helsinki Watch representatives in mid- and late October 1992 reported that beatings and general mistreatment had been commonplace in August. They said that the mistreatment stopped in September and October and that their general treatment improved. Croatian authorities also are operating a semi-furlough program in some detention facilities, in which prisoners are allowed to go home for a day to shower, change clothes and visit family members. They are permitted to go home in the morning and are required to return to the prison in the evenings; both during their departure from, and return to, the prison, the detainees are not escorted by Croatian guards. Although Helsinki Watch welcomes these improvements, we are still concerned that abuses continue to take place in Croatian-controlled prisons in western and central Bosnia. Helsinki Watch representatives have interviewed persons who did not want to speak about their experiences, and it is possible that further abuse is occurring.

Although Helsinki Watch welcomes the fact that HVO soldiers are detained for breaches of conduct, such soldiers are interned for no more that fifteen days and are not prosecuted for serious abuses. Helsinki Watch believes that those HVO soldiers found guilty of torture, willful destruction of civilian property or other abuses should be prosecuted for such offenses.

HVO forces operate detention facilities in the central Mostar prison, the police station and school in Livno and in a school in Tomislavgrad. HOS paramilitary forces operated detention facilities in a former JNA clinic in Mostar and former JNA barracks in the village of Dretelj, in the municipality of Čapljina. HVO troops subsequently closed the HOS-operated detention facilities and either released, exchanged or transferred their prisoners to the central Mostar jail.

Abuses By HVO Forces

Mostar

The Mostar prison is operated by the HVO military authorities. An investigatory judge, a warden and others oversee the prison. The jail detains mostly men and some women. The guards who attend to the female prisoners are women, and the women prisoners are detained in an area separate from the male prisoners. After HVO assumed control over HOS forces in western Bosnia in August 1992, many prisoners held by HOS were brought to the Mostar prison. Similarly, most of the prisoners held by HVO forces in smaller jails in the area also were transferred to the Mostar prison at approximately the same time.

Most of the detainees interviewed in the Mostar prison reported that their treatment there was satisfactory at the time of Helsinki Watch's visit in October. However, they did report that abuse had taken place in the past and that certain guards were more brutal than others. None appeared to bear signs of torture or malnourishment. Some of the women prisoners were wearing makeup and no one appeared frightened to speak.

Rooms in the Mostar prison were crowded with double-bunk beds but otherwise clean and heated. There are windows in every room inspected by Helsinki Watch representatives. Each wing of the jail has two or three large rooms, which contain approximately forty or fifty prisoners per room. A barred door separates the wings from the central part of the building. A bathroom was located in each wing. Prisoners could go to the bathroom or sit out at tables in the halls in each wing, without much supervision by the guards.

According to Valentin Čorić,[21] the chief of the HVO military police in Mostar, the prison in Mostar is the central prison for Croats, Serbs and Muslims accused of military offenses. At the time of Helsinki Watch's visit in late October 1992, both Čorić and his deputy claimed that, as of September 21, 1992, 392 prisoners were held in the Mostar

---

[21] Interviewed by Helsinki Watch representatives in October 1992 in Mostar, Bosnia-Hercegovina.

jail. Some were subsequently released and 269 remained in late October.[22] Most of the prisoners were from the municipalities of Čapljina, Ljubuški, Grude, Stolac, Tomislavgrad, Livno and Bugojno. According to Ćorić's deputy, five categories of prisoners are interned in the Mostar prison:

> 1. Serbian combatants captured during the course of a battle and for whom a criminal indictment is being considered: some are locals from Mostar, others are from Bijelo Polje, Nevesinje, Gacko and Trebinje. Approximately twenty-two prisoners — including a Muslim who had fought with the Serbian forces — were interned in the prison. After a judicial system is reestablished, members of this group for whom a criminal indictment is issued will stand trial.
>
> 2. "Collaborators with the enemy": this group includes persons on whose premises long-barreled guns were found and/or the proprietors of homes in which Serbian forces are alleged to have sought refuge. Those who possessed short-barreled guns reportedly were not imprisoned, but their arms were confiscated.[23]
>
> 3. Those kept for exchange purposes: this group includes persons who have family members who have sided with Serbian forces in the war. These prisoners were arrested on the basis of citizens'

---

[22] Helsinki Watch representatives inquired about the type of criteria used to determine whether to release a prisoner. Citing the laws of Bosnia-Hercegovina which have been incorporated into the statutes of the self-proclaimed "Community of Herceg-Bosna," Ćorić explained that an investigation was conducted to determine the availability of credible evidence to implicate the imprisoned in a crime. After an investigation was completed, if sufficient evidence did not exist to implicate an individual's "cooperation with the enemy," the individual was released. Similar procedures are followed for Croatian soldiers accused of disciplinary infractions. He claimed that most soldiers served a sentence of five to fifteen days of imprisonment for disciplinary infractions.

[23] Other HVO officials later told Helsinki Watch representatives that some were charged with illegal possession of a weapon.

reports. An investigation is being conducted to determine whether criminal charges will be filed against such persons.[24]

4. Common criminals: those guilty of common crimes not related to the war. Ćorić's deputy claims that fifteen instances of murder not related to the armed conflict had taken place in the area but that the military authorities were responsible for investigating the crime.

5. Croatian soldiers: at the time of Helsinki Watch's visit, about forty HVO soldiers reportedly were detained in the Mostar prison for breach of discipline. According to Ćorić, none of the Croatian prisoners interned in the prison were army deserters; all were military personnel imprisoned for disciplinary infractions, such as drunkeness and destruction of property. Both Boban and Ćorić claimed that Croatian authorities of the self-proclaimed "Community of Herceg-Bosna" are not seeking deserters. They believed that the issue of desertion should be dealt with after the war.

Prisoners were assigned work duty. According to Ćorić, work hours were strictly regulated: prisoners worked eight hours every other day. According to the prisoners and former detainees interviewed by Helsinki Watch representatives, most interned in the central Mostar prison were required to work every day. Ćorić said that an afternoon rest period usually was allowed the prisoners every day.

When asked about the behavior of the guards in the prison, Ćorić said the guards are not allowed to talk to prisoners about the reasons for their internment. He claims that approximately five guards had quit and that most of the guards were soldiers who had recently returned from the front lines. He asserted that persons with criminal records were not permitted to act as prison guards. Ćorić claims that special attention is paid to any criminal records and that a background check is conducted by the secret police.[25] Ćorić claims that the only problem reported by the

---

[24] Helsinki Watch considers those who have been detained without legitimate cause to be hostages, including all those who fall into this category.

[25] Helsinki Watch has not been able to confirm this assertion.

prisoners involved an instance in which local civilians started to beat the prisoners while they were on work duty.[26] He explained that, in such a case, the guards on duty are held responsible for the prisoners' safety, even if they are not the attackers.

Many of the prisoners held in the Mostar central prison earlier had been held in an older prison facility on Šantićeva street in Mostar. Treatment in the older prison generally appears to have been satisfactory. Most of the prisoners held in the Šantićeva jail were transferred to the central Mostar prison in August and September, although a few people remained interned in the former. Prisoners interviewed by Helsinki Watch claimed that the Šantićeva jail was being prepared to house common criminals.[27]

Several prisoners interviewed by Helsinki Watch representatives claim to have been beaten during their initial internment in the Mostar prison. At the time of Helsinki Watch's visit, Boris[28] had been badly beaten and injured on the head and legs. He had been confined to his room. He said that some guards in the Mostar prison were amiable and treated the prisoners well but that others were brutal and mistreated prisoners.

Predrag was arrested in June 1992, and reported that his home was destroyed on April 8. He said that others were arrested with him and that one was beaten so badly that he was taken to the hospital.[29] Predrag initially was held in the jail on Šantićeva street but subsequently was transferred to the main Mostar prison. Predrag was questioned and required to give a statement on three occasions. The day of his arrest in

---

[26] A prisoner who was present during the attack was interviewed by Helsinki Watch representatives and confirmed that HVO guards prevented the civilians from further beating the prisoners. For a more detailed account, see the testimony of Dejan below.

[27] Helsinki Watch has not been able to confirm this assertion.

[28] Interviewed by Helsinki Watch representatives on October 24, 1992, in Bosnia-Hercegovina. Because some of the people in this section were in detention at the time of Helsinki Watch's visit, all names and other identifying information have been deleted to ensure the witnesses' safety. The information remains in a secure place outside Helsinki Watch's office.

[29] The witness identified the man by name.

June 1992, he was abused by guards who beat him during the interrogation and made no effort to record his statement. In July, he gave a statement that was "correctly" recorded and no one beat him. Seven days prior to Helsinki Watch's visit, he gave a similar statement, which he described as "correct and complete." According to Predrag:

> On the day of my arrest, I was beaten almost to death; it's a wonder how I'm still alive. I received medical treatment from a male nurse, but there's a lack of medicine.

Predrag said, "Each of us has mementos," as he showed Helsinki Watch representatives the scars on his leg. He continued:

> I also was hit severely in the ribs and kidneys. The leaders [at the main Mostar prison] do not allow the guards to beat prisoners.

Predrag suggested that prisoners had been beaten earlier. He said that prisoners were beaten when individual guards were on duty. Predrag reported that prisoners were not being beaten in the Mostar prison at the time of Helsinki Watch's visit, but he did know of earlier cases in which a man from Ljubuški was beaten. He claimed that an older prisoner had scars which would indicate that he had been beaten in the past.[30] He described current conditions in the prison:

> Prisoners can move around the area, up to the bars in the hallway, and go to the bathroom. The food is the minimum to survive; everyone has lost at least fifteen kilograms. We get three meals per day. Breakfast consists of two slices of bread, tea or white coffee or cocoa;[31] lunch is two slices of bread and soup or souplike food; two slices of bread and about five or six spoonfuls of soup are served for dinner. We work very hard in the

---

[30] Predrag did not name the two men.

[31] In the former Yugoslavia, a common breakfast includes coffee or cocoa added to hot milk, i.e., "white coffee."

villages, the city and here [in the prison]. We have to
clean buildings, load and unload materials, build bunkers
on the front lines. We usually work every day — from
7:00 a.m. to nightfall — and sometimes even during the
night, but not regularly. Today, a lot of people are in the
jail because of the rain. The ICRC has visited us a few
times. A few days after our arrest, we were shown to a
few journalists — mostly Croatian — and an Australian
television crew.

Milan,[32] a combatant, was captured by Bosnian Muslim and Croatian forces. He was first interned in the jail on Šantičeva street and then in the central Mostar prison.

Milan described the conditions of the prison to Helsinki Watch representatives:

At the Mostar prison we can freely walk about in the
hallways — we don't have to stay in our cells. There are
about twenty to twenty-five soldiers on duty. There had
been one or two guards who would enter our cells and,
when we all stood to attention, they beat people at
random with their feet and hands. They were familiar
faces.

This is the central jail in Herceg-Bosna [sic]. All the jails
have been consolidated into this one. No one touches us
here. We do some work, I think near the front lines
because you can hear the fighting. We construct bunkers,
fill bags with sand and things like that, usually in areas
near Podvaležje and Rožci. We do some cleaning in the
city, too. Guards are present while we work.

Milan said that he was questioned twice but that he had not been charged with a crime. According to Milan:

---

[32] Interviewed by Helsinki Watch representatives on October 24, 1992, in the central Mostar prison in Bosnia-Hercegovina. The witness chose to withhold his name, and the name used here is a pseudonym.

I have not been given a formal indictment. I made a statement twice; once in Šantičeva and once here. I was interrogated by a military inspector [in the central Mostar prison.] There is no mistreatment here, and we are treated very correctly. I have relatives in Mostar, but none of us POWs have had any visitors.

Dejan,[33] a combatant who surrendered to Croatian and Muslim forces, reported that most of the guards behaved properly toward the prisoners but that individual guards were not "correct." He was not beaten during the course of his detention, but he claims that other prisoners had been beaten elsewhere. He said that the administrators in the prison did not allow mistreatment of prisoners. Dejan confirmed that the prisoners have been accosted by civilians while they were on work duty. According to Dejan:

> We've had problems with civilians attacking us while we were working, but the guards actually saved us from the civilians. Now that the war is winding down,[34] even the civilians treat us better, sometimes even giving us a little food and drink — although there's not much food around for anyone.
>
> We work every day — sometimes hard work, sometimes less arduous. Employers come in the morning to ask for ten people or so, and then they go off. After lunch, we are free until dinner if there are no other urgent jobs. After dinner, we are free and go to sleep. Some people will go to work tonight.

---

[33] Interveiwed by Helsinki Watch representatives in October 1992 in Bosnia-Hercegovina. The witness's name has been withheld to protect his safety, and the name used here is a pseudonym.

[34] The fighting around Mostar had subsided somewhat in October but soon began again.

> The food could be much better. I usually weigh 106 kilograms but I've lost about twenty-five or thirty kilograms since I've been here.
>
> There is no difference in the way guards treat the POWs and the civilian suspects. In fact, sometimes it's easier for the POWs because we have better rapport with the guards as military men.

Helsinki Watch representatives also interviewed, Damir,[35] an HVO soldier detained in the Mostar prison. He was serving his fourth day of a five-day sentence for leaving his guard's post. He said that he and a friend were "fooling around" and shot off a few rounds in the front of the command station. He said there was a misunderstanding — they were just "horsing around" and wouldn't dare shoot *at* the command. He was dressed down by his deputy commander and thought that would be the extent of his punishment. However, after his commander discovered what he had done, he decided to make Damir, a veteran soldier, an example to the younger men in the platoon.

Damir reported that the other soldiers in his wing were imprisoned for offenses ranging from burglary to "accidental killing." He said that Croatian and other civilians[36] were detained in his wing and that, unlike the other prisoners, none were assigned to work duty. He reported that the prisoners slept in two large rooms and had access to a living room, presumably in their wing of the prison. They were allowed to go out to the barred door and walk outside for thirty minutes each day. He said that not everyone knew when he or she would be released, including some of the soldiers who are under investigation for the more serious offenses. Damir reported that the treatment by the prison guards was "super" but that the food was "pretty bad," with little meat and small portions.

---

[35] Interviewed by Helsinki Watch representatives in October 1992 in Bosnia-Hercegovina. Helsinki Watch has used a pseudonym to protect the witness.

[36] Helsinki Watch did not confirm whether Croatian civilians were held in the prison. If they were, they may have been interned for the commission of common crimes.

Stojan,[37] a combatant arrested by Bosnian Muslim forces, was held in the HVO-controlled jail on Šantičeva street from June to mid-September, during which time he reported no mistreatment. In late September, Stojan was transferred to the central Mostar prison:

> On September 21, after a failed exchange attempt, we were brought here, to the heliodrom.[38] The commander [of the prison] is good toward us. I would commend him. Here and there, you come across beatings, but the commander doesn't allow such treatment. The conditions are fine, and the behavior of the guards is correct, although there are cases in which someone has a bad surname[39] and there is some conflict. But if a guard beats a prisoner, he is punished and removed. There is order in this jail, especially during the past two months.
>
> There are about thirty men in a room. About 90 percent of the people in the prison are Serbian civilians from the Mostar environs, and I think HVO needs people for exchange. There are only about twenty soldiers here.

Indeed, although some prisoners in the Mostar jail had been combatants or admitted to possession of large stocks of weaponry, many appeared to be civilians who were detained because they were Serbs.

When asked why she was in detention, Tanja,[40] another prisoner, replied, "Because I'm Serbian, like the rest of the women

---

[37] Interviewed by Helsinki Watch representatives on October 24, 1992, in the central Mostar prison in Bosnia-Hercegovina. The name used is a pseudonym to protect the witness.

[38] The central Mostar prison is also the site of a heliodrom.

[39] Presumably, if someone has a Serbian name.

[40] Interviewed by Helsinki Watch representatives in Octoer 1992 in Bosnia-Hercegovina. The name is a pseudonym used to protect the witness.

prisoners." Tanja reported that she had not been charged with a crime. According to Tanja:

> They said it's simpler to hold me [in custody] because it's easier to investigate and prosecute us. Every day someone or other is being investigated, but I haven't been [questioned] yet.

Tanja claims that, at the time of Helsinki Watch's visit in October, between fifty-one and fifty-four women were held in the main Mostar prison, and most were between the ages of thirty and forty. She said that three women were responsible for housework in the prison. She also asserted that three women were still detained in the old jail in Šantićeva street but that that jail was practically empty and would be used to detain common criminals. Tanja said that women who had been kept in the Šantićeva jail had earlier been held by HOS forces who raped and physically abused women in their custody.[41] Tanja reported that guards at the main Mostar prison behaved properly toward the women in detention. In addition to the three women who are responsible for the housework in the prison, Tanja said that other women detained in the prison were also given work duty.

> From the moment I arrived, I was made to work. Fifty days ago, I stepped off a chair on which I was standing and I broke my arm. I got medical attention and I seem to be recovering.

Tanja described the conditions in the prison:

> We get three meals a day without meat — but still, it's three meals. The worst part of detention for us is the fact that we hardly have any clothing. Women were allowed to go back to our homes to get something, but in some cases others had moved into their homes. Some women went back to their apartments and found absolutely nothing inside.

---

[41] For Helsinki Watch interviews with women who were raped by HOS or HVO forces, see section on rape below.

There are mothers with young children detained here but they have no contact with the children. Husbands and wives can't contact each other, except indirectly when the ICRC visits.

Tanja said that Serbs were being driven from their homes in the area:

We don't have rights. This is a dirty war, and we had nothing to do with it. If they are able to detain old ladies, then anything is possible.

Snežana[42] was transferred from the old jail in Šantičeva street in Mostar to the main Mostar prison in late September 1992. She said that her home had been destroyed while she was in detention. According to Snežana:

I came [to the Mostar prison] on September 25. I don't know why, but we were all transferred here. The doctors come and take care of us and we are not mistreated. All are good to us here, and the food is fine.

But I feel terrible here. I asked to go home and get some clothes, and a neighbor told me that my house, and all the Serbian houses, had been burned down. The exchange didn't work out. I got to the exchange point, but I did not want to go over to the other [i.e., Serbian] side. I expressed my wish to stay, and then I was brought back here. I want to stay here. My family is still here, and I'm Serbian.

---

[42] Interviewed by Helsinki Watch representatives on October 24, 1992, in Bosnia-Hercegovina. The name used here is a pseudonym in order to protect the witness.

Livno Police Station

Two prisons operate in the town of Livno: one is administered by the local police and the other by Croatian military authorities (HVO). This section deals with treatment in the former prison; the latter is discussed in the next section.

According to Jozo Perić,[43] who described himself as "a competent police authority," 106 Serbs in Livno were investigated and conditionally released.[44] He said that local Serbian representatives, at the request of the police, conducted a poll of the Serbs in Livno and found that twenty Serbs wished to cross over to Serbian-controlled territory. At the time of Helsinki Watch's visit, Perić reported that twenty-eight prisoners were held in the jail at the Livno police station for "rebellion." A common criminal and one Croat who "wishes to join the

---

[43] Mr. Peric did not wish to disclose his affiliation. He was interviewed by Helsinki Watch representatives on October 27, 1992, in the police station in Livno, Bosnia-Hercegovina.

[44] Perić claimed that 1,200 rifles were found in Livno, "a place where only the police had guns." He said that the local Serbs were preparing an armed rebellion against the local authorities. He showed Helsinki Watch representatives a list of names which he claimed were persons detained for possessing weapons. Perić also asserted that local Serbs had formed an illegal armed unit on January 31, 1991.

When asked if the local authorities retained any evidence to support his claims and to justify the detention of local Serbs, Perić showed Helsinki Watch representatives a document dated October 5, 1991, which delineated the organization of volunteer units for the region known as Bosanska Krajina, the north-central area in western Bosnia, of which Livno is on the periphery. The document bore the stamp of the Serbian Democratic Party (SDS) of Bosnia-Hercegovina. He also exhibited minutes of a meeting held on December 6, 1991, to the same effect; the document was a survey of weapons and a list of people connected with the Serbian local militia in the town of Bosansko Grahovo in Bosnia and in the town of Knin, in Croatia. The municipalities and towns of Bosansko Grahovo and Knin are controlled by Serbian forces and are contiguous, although they are in two separate republics.

Several Serbian prisoners interviewed by Helsinki Watch representatives admitted to possessing weapons or having known of their distribution to Serbs in the Livno municipality. According to these witnesses, the Serbian Democratic Party (SDS), in conjunction with the Yugoslav Army (JNA), organized the distribution of the weapons on a local and municipal basis.

other side" also were in custody in the prison. He asserted that no prisoners had yet been tried by the court.

Helsinki Watch representatives were permitted to interview the prisoners detained in the Livno jail privately and to inspect their quarters. The women prisoners were held in one cramped room, with mattresses on the floor. Most of the women were middle-aged or elderly. The men were held in rooms that bordered a courtyard. Four to six men were held in each room. The rooms were small, cramped and covered in blankets because they were unheated. The prisoners had an electric hot plate, on which they heated any canned food they received. Hygiene also appeared poor.

As in the case of the central Mostar prison, detainees in the Livno police station were beaten during the earlier stages of the war but treatment generally improved thereafter. Prison visits also were suspended for an undetermined length of time but, at the time of Helsinki Watch's visit, prisoners reported that they were allowed visits. One prisoner claimed that he was fed only once a day while another asserted that the prisoners were fed twice daily. All concurred that the food was poor and the portions meager. Prisoners at the Livno police station also were assigned to work duty but with less frequency than in the Mostar prison.

Jovan[45] spent two and a half months in the civilian prison and three and a half months in the Livno school building.[46] He stated that, during his detention in the police station, prisoners were beaten and were not allowed visitors. He also reported that he lost twenty kilograms in the jail. Jovan reported that, in the police station, "We were given nothing to eat and later we received only one tin of food a day."

Jovan reported that his wife was found murdered in his house and that his house had been burned while he was in prison. When his wife was killed, he asked for Valium or a sedative but his request was refused. He reported that none of the prisoners were allowed visits.

---

[45] Interviewed by Helsinki Watch representatives in October 1992 in Bosnia-Hercegovina. The name given here is a pseudonym used to protect the witness.

[46] The witness was later held in the Livno school, and his account is contained below.

Prison conditions appear to have improved after Jovan's transfer from the jail.

Viktor,[47] another prisoner at the police station, reported that the prisoners were allowed visits. He said that visits were suspended for several days during an escalation in fighting but that they had been restored thereafter. Viktor described the food the prisoners received:

> We never get any hot food — just canned food. We always get two meals during the day. [We are fed] in the morning at about 8:30 a.m. or 9:00 a.m. During the summer [we eat a meal] at 6:00 p.m. and in the winter, at 5:00 p.m.. Now we can get food and clothes from home. They can bring it every day; at any time. We always get a quarter of a loaf of bread — a total of half a loaf a day — some canned foods, cheese, jam and some sweets.

Nebojša,[48] a Serbian prisoner in his sixties, described the behavior of the guards in the jail and the prisoners' work duties:

> During the first few days everything was going on, but later it became better. I was beaten when they tried to force me to admit to "rebellion," but they didn't succeed. Now there is a lack of food, but the guards are treating people fine. I've only been called to work once — [I had to] unload trucks. Work is assigned depending on needs. The younger people have been digging trenches.

---

[47] Interviewed by Helsinki Watch representatives on October 27, 1992, in the police station jail in Livno, Bosnia-Hercegovina. The name used here is a pseudonym in order to protect the witness.

[48] Interviewed by Helsinki Watch representatives in October 1992 in Livno, Bosnia-Hercegovina. The name used here is a pseudonym to protect the witness.

Viktor was detained at the Livno police station for three days, questioned at the HVO military headquarters[49] and then returned to the police station in late April. Viktor said that he was abused once in the police station because he did not confess to possessing weapons. He also stated that he was beaten by a soldier who had lost a friend or relative due to the fighting:

> I was hit only once because I didn't want to confess that I had weapons. A soldier had come into the jail and beat us because one of his friends or family members had been killed or hurt. He wanted to get in [to my cell] but the guards wouldn't let him. He pushed them aside and walked into our cell. He was called "Bolotin" but he came back and later excused himself for his behavior. He was very humane when he came to apologize. He said that someone dear to him had been killed but he didn't know me and should not have taken his frustrations out on me.

Viktor said that, after he confessed to possessing weapons, his treatment in the jail improved. According to Viktor:

> When I finally admitted that I had weapons, they treated me okay. I was questioned, but by soldiers not police officers. Those who admitted that they had guns and handed them over were treated according to international law [sic]; there were no problems. All they wanted to do was to collect and supervise the weapons.

Viktor said that all the prisoners held in the jail had been beaten at one point during their detention in various parts of western Hercegovina:

> All of us were beaten, but I haven't been beaten very badly. But they are okay. They even get us some things without seeking any money.... We get newspapers. We

---

[49] For an account of the witness's treatment in the HVO military headquarters in Livno, see relevant section below.

know all the people. They know we're not to blame.
Those of us who stayed are generally not to blame.

Nebojša described the conditions in the jail:

We are held in cells which hold only four people. There
used to be thirteen [to a room], but now there are just
six in my room. Three of the rooms have six inmates,
and another has just five. Some people were released;
some were moved to the school.[50] There's no heating.
Because people have left, they've taken their blankets.
There's a courtyard in the back that we can walk around
in. The rooms are ten by five meters or twelve by five
meters in size.

Nebojša reported that the ICRC had visited the jail on four occasions. He also said that he had not been told of the charges against him, whether he would stand trial or of his general fate.

Nataša[51] was first arrested on June 25 and held in custody in the Livno police station for one month:

During the first month of my detention [i.e., from June
25 to late July], we had good relations with the guards in
the jail. But to stay in prison was a terrible thing because
all the time we [women] are in one room, only able to go
out twice a day to go to the toilet.

After her release, Nataša stayed in Livno; she was afraid to go back to her village for fear of "disappearing during the night." She reported that several people had "disappeared."

Nataša was released in late July, but was rearrested twice thereafter. She was held in the Livno school the third time she was

---

[50] The school in Livno was also used as a detention facility and was operated by HVO forces at the time of Helsinki Watch's visit in October 1992. See following section for a description of the treatment of the prisoners in the school.

[51] Interviewed by Helsinki Watch representatives in October 1992 in Livno, Bosnia-Hercegovina. The name used here is a pseudonym to protect the witness.

arrested and was transferred to the civilian Livno prison twenty days before Helsinki Watch's visit. She described the conditions in the jail:

> Twenty days ago we were moved from the school to a little wood-paneled office in the police headquarters. Four other women, who are relatives of important SDS party members, [also are detained in the Livno police station]. It's very cold, and all of us have been sick with the flu. There's no heating. We get one blanket from the guards, and we sleep on the floor. We can get clothing.
>
> The behavior of the guards toward the women is very correct here. My mother comes every day and asks the guards to give me the things she brings.

Nataša stated that those people who had been released were required to report to the police station every day and, in some cases, their relatives were also required to report to the station. Ivan,[52] a sixty-one-year-old prisoner, reported on the conditions of the prison:

> I'm being held downstairs in the jail. Conditions are okay. We get bread and cheese in the morning, and we can get water or go to the bathroom when we ask. I have an apartment in Livno, and my son brings me food. I'm the only person in my room. I haven't been beaten [in the Livno jail].

Livno School

This detention facility is operated by HVO forces in a school in the town of Livno. As in most other Croatian-controlled prisons in western Hercegovina, prisoners were beaten routinely during the summer of 1992, but treatment improved thereafter. During the summer, prisoners were detained in the Livno school, and the men detainees were beaten by guards. Many prisoners were later released, and the remaining

---

[52] Interviewed by Helsinki Watch representatives in October 1992 in Livno, Bosnia-Hervegovina. The name used here is a pseudonym to protect the witness.

women prisoners were taken to the jail in the Livno police station.[53] At the time of Helsinki Watch's visit to the detention facility in the school, approximately thirteen or fourteen men remained in detention.

Security in the facility was minimal. Prisoners were held in an unheated gymnasium, where they had pallets and blankets on the floor. At the time of Helsinki Watch's visit, three prisoners were cleaning the guards' guns, which they claim to do almost on a daily basis. No guards supervised the prisoners during this time.[54] A large hallway, in which drawings from schoolchildren still hung, separated the gymnasium from the lounge used by the military police officers. The lounge — in which children's stuffed animals remained — was the only heated room in the school and had earlier been the place where science exhibits were housed. Just in front of the entrance to the gymnasium was a passageway lined on each side with several barred cells, which were vacant at the time of Helsinki Watch's visit.

According to the commander of the detention facility in the Livno school,[55] a roundup of Serbs took place in August, and 168 people — all Serbs — were arrested.[56] The commander stated that many of those intially arrested had been released. He stated that the remaining prisoners in the Livno school and others held in the Mostar prison would

---

[53] For an account of the conditions at the Livno police station, see preceding section.

[54] Two Helsinki Watch representatives told one of the prisoners cleaning the soldiers' guns that they found this curious. The prisoner replied, "Oh, this is nothing. Yesterday I was cleaning a loaded gun, and I could have killed some of them. But they're nice guys, so what's the point?"

[55] Interviewed by Helsinki Watch representatives in October 1992 in Livno, Bosnia-Hercegovina. The commander was a member of the HVO and did not give his name. A prisoner identified him as Mohamed Ibrahimović, a Muslim member of the HVO.

[56] The commander said that documents were found indicating that those currently held in detention were in possession of large quantities of weaponry. The prison commander, who claims to have participated in the roundup, stated that "enough weapons to arm a whole battalion" were found, primarily in homes belonging to elderly women.

shortly be released, pending a directive from the Croatian authorities in Mostar.[57]

Fourteen men reportedly were detained in the school at the time of Helsinki Watch's visit. The commander stated that prisoners were not POWs and that they were treated "fairly." He reported that the prisoners were allowed to go to their homes to shower without an escort but that they had to return to the school by a designated time.[58] He reported that the cells are cleaned once a week and that the prisoners cleaned the bathrooms. He asserted that the detainees ate the same food as the guards and soldiers. He stated that prisoners can request to go to town to purchase items such as cigarettes and are permitted to do so. He also said that the prisoners receive visitors daily. Seriously ill detainees reportedly were released and allowed to go home. He reported that the prisoners are not required to do any physical labor other than clean the jail. According to the commander:

> There are far many more people accused than are actually held here, because there's not enough space to keep them. The people under special investigation are under a form of house arrest and have to report here at 9:00 a.m. and 5:00 p.m. every day.

In late April, a two-week roundup of Livno's Serbian population was organized by local HVO forces. An unknown number of men and women were detained in the Livno school. Most were subsequently released, but some of the men were beaten during their detention. The beatings took place in classrooms on the ground floor, and possibly on the first floor, of the school. Conditions in the school subsequently

---

[57] It is unclear whether the prisoners were scheduled to be released or exchanged. During Helsinki Watch's visit, many prisoners held throughout Croatian-controlled territory in western Hercegovina were waiting to be exchanged on October 26 for prisoners held by Serbian forces. Although some Serbian prisoners to whom Helsinki Watch spoke stated that they wanted to go to Serbian-controlled territory, many claimed that they would refuse to be exchanged and would prefer to remain in Livno or Mostar. Most of those who wanted to leave were detained in the Tomislavgrad municipality.

[58] This was confirmed by the prisoners.

improved, and treatment of prisoners appeared satisfactory at the time of Helsinki Watch's visit in October 1992.

Dragana[59] was detained in the Livno school in early August[60] at a time when men were beaten in the prison. According to Dragana:

> I was in the custody of the military police; we were all kept in one big room in the school. We were able to walk to the toilets and get water but endured terrible mistreatment. My husband was almost beaten to death, but I wasn't harmed. The military police didn't touch the women, but they beat the men.

Veran[61] described his arrest:

> Sometime between April 24 and 27, I was in the shelter because of an [air or general warning] raid. There were about two hundred or three hundred of us in the shelter. About three HVO military police officers came in and called people out of the shelter by their names. They said that we were needed. I was taken to my apartment, and they showed me a search warrant. They proceeded to search my apartment but found nothing. I had already given my weapons to the local police. Earlier, they had broadcast a request over the radio asking that we all give up our weapons to the local police.
>
> [After they searched the apartment,] I was taken to the local police station and put in the jail. There were about ten or fifteen police officers and hundreds of us. When

---

[59] Interviewed by Helsinki Watch representatives in October 1992 in Livno, Bosnia-Hercegovina. The name used here is a pseudonym to protect the witness.

[60] The witness had been detained before and after her internment at the Livno school. For her accounts, see preceding section concerning the Livno police station.

[61] Interviewed by Helsinki Watch representatives in October 1992 in Livno, Bosnia-Hercegovina.

they were conducting an investigation, I was questioned. I was questioned by investigatory judges who were dressed in uniforms and were armed. I was usually questioned by one or two judges. I've been in the school for two and a half months and have only been questioned twice during my stay here.

Veran refused to talk about his treatment, saying only that there are "some good guys around." He appears to have been beaten or tortured in the past and was on the verge of tears but refused to elaborate about his treatment.

Veran confirmed that prisoners were allowed to leave the prison for family visits. However, when Veran returned to his apartment, he found someone living in his home. According to Veran:

> We can go out. I went home and saw that a widow had moved into my apartment. Her husband was a soldier and he had recently been killed.

Lazar[62] was arrested while walking home from work in Livno. He was taken to the military headquarters of the local territorial defense unit,[63] where he was beaten during interrogation. Lazar described his arrest:

> On May 7, I was at work and then I went home. A military police officer stopped me in the street and said that his commander was looking for me. He didn't have a warrant or anything like that. I went to the TO [i.e., the office of the territorial defense unit] and two men came and took my biographical information. They said that they would force me to tell them where the guns were, and I said that I didn't know anything about that. I was physically maltreated by the police officers. A man

---

[62] Interviewed by Helsinki Watch representatives in the Livno school on October 27, 1992.

[63] It is unclear if the headquarters housed Croatian or Muslim forces or both. The witness implied that both Muslim and Croatian forces used the headquarters.

— who I assume was their commander — questioned me, but a soldier also beat me. At first, only one man beat me, but then a second man came and joined him.

The following day, Lazar was taken to the Livno school, where he was beaten again. According to Lazar:

The next day, I went with them to show them what I had. I had hidden it, but I couldn't find the weapons; someone must have taken them. I was then brought to the school and was mistreated in a classroom. I was mistreated in the study hall, on the ground floor. Two military police officers beat me, but I don't see them around anymore. One of them said he would rape my daughter before my eyes.[64] They beat my hands. Their commander was not present during the mistreatment.

Lazar was then taken to the Livno police station, where he remained until August 9. He claims not to have been mistreated but complained of the lack of hygiene and food in the police station. He was subsequently returned to the school. According to Lazar:

I was at the police station until August 9, and then I was brought [to the school auditorium]. In the beginning, from time to time and case to case, there was some maltreatment. The food was bad, but then it got better. Those who were punished wouldn't get food for one or two days. Those who wouldn't tell them where they hid weapons would not get fed.

The maltreatment stopped after the ICRC visit. Now it's great. We're like free citizens. There was a roundup of all Serbs, but they're all home now. There are fourteen of us here, and most are close to sixty. I don't know why we're here. We're old and sick. No doctor comes here. When we were held in the police station, we had a

---

[64] He claimed to know the name of one of the soldiers but refused to disclose that information.

doctor. The soldiers don't get us doctors, but they bring us our medicines.

I am not maltreated here. I know most of the guards and police officers here. The food is good; it's like home. I go to see my wife; I went yesterday. My wife is afraid and she stays in the house, but she is okay. She works in a kiosk that sells pastries. No one has bothered her.

Saša[65] was detained in the Livno police station for two and a half months and for three and a half months in the school. He described the conditions in the facility as good:

We often drink coffee with the commander, and we can go home and take a shower. We have access to radio, television and newspapers. You saw we even clean the guns for the police here. We get all kinds of cooked food for lunch and dinner and a normal "dry" meal [i.e., sandwiches] of bread and cheese in the morning. We can even cook coffee. I've gained back seven kilograms since I've been here. Only the military police have access to us.

Helsinki Watch representatives asked if the cells outside the gymnasium were ever used to house prisoners. Saša replied that Croatian soldiers, for example, who had gotten drunk were held in the outer cells.

Saša said that sixty to seventy prisoners had been held in the school earlier but most were released in September. Others were released somewhat later, after they had been questioned.

---

[65] Interviewed by Helsinki Watch representatives in October 1992 in Livno, Bosnia-Hercegovina. The name used here is a pseudonym to protect the witness.

Livno HVO Headquarters

Viktor[66] was arrested on April 26:

[On the day of my arrest,] I had gone to my sister-in-law's house to celebrate Easter, and the sirens started to wail.[67] We went into the shelter, and they picked us out of the basement. It was Orthodox Easter — April 26 — at about 8:00 p.m., when the sirens went off. We were in the shelter of a business firm; there were some workers and neighbors — about thirty people of all three nationalities in the shelter.

Men in camouflage uniforms without any insignia arrived in a police car. They were probably members of the military police, but I didn't know anyone. Three of them entered, and they were armed only with handguns. They said they were looking for [Viktor], and I said that was me. They told me to go with them, and I asked why. They said I had to go to the police station. I asked if they had a warrant, and they said that they did not but that I had to go with them nevertheless. They didn't mistreat me [en route to the police station].

Viktor remained in a cell at the Livno police station for two or three days; during this time he was not questioned or mistreated. Thereafter, Croatian military police officers arrived and he was taken to the local military headquarters, where he was interrogated and beaten. He was then returned to the police station. According to Viktor:

---

[66] Interviewed by Helsinki Watch representatives on October 27, 1992, in the police station in Livno, Bosnia-Hercegovina. The name used here is a pseudonym in order to protect the witness.

[67] Sirens are sounded throughout Croatia and Bosnia-Hercegovina to warn the population to take shelter from the fighting. The sirens either signify an air-raid alert or a general safety alert.

The military police arrived. The war had started, and they took me to the military police headquarters. I was questioned by a police officer and beaten. There were more than ten men in uniform and one in civilian clothing. They beat me with their hands, feet and truncheons for a long time, and then I was taken back to the police station. The next day, the legal proceedings started, and I was questioned at the police station.

Tomislavgrad School

Approximately fifty men were detained in a local school at the time of Helsinki Watch's visit to Tomislavgrad. All the detainees were part of a work unit. Weather permitting, the prisoners worked eight-hour days; otherwise they were not given any exercise. The prisoners were allowed to receive visitors. Many of the detainees had family in the village of Raščani,[68] who sent them cigarettes and clothing.

Drago Banović, the head of the military police in Tomislavgrad,[69] described the Serbian men held in the school as "terrorists caught with weapons supplied by the Yugoslav Army (JNA) or as preparing rebellion."[70] Banović said that a large number of the prisoners wanted to be exchanged and that they would have to choose their destination when the ICRC organized their release. Banović said that the civilian police administered the detention facility in the

---

[68] Serbian civilians are held hostage in the village of Raščani by Croatian forces. See relevant section below.

[69] Interviewed by Helsinki Watch representatives in October 1992 in Tomislavgrad, Bosnia-Hercegovina.

[70] Banović showed Helsinki Watch representatives a list of prisoners alleged to have possessed weapons and several handwritten confessions. According to Banovic:

> Most of the prisoners believe they are innocent. They were forced to accept weapons from the Yugoslav Army [JNA] or they wouldn't be considered good Serbs.

Tomislavgrad school, an assertion that was confirmed by prisoners detained in the school.

At the time of Helsinki Watch's visit, prisoners were held in three large rooms in the school — two on the first floor and one above. The guards and Drago Banović remained in another room on the first floor — just next to the first cell — where they were playing cards at the time of Helsinki Watch's visit. Some prisoners were walking in the hall and a woman had come to visit someone. The rooms themselves have large windows but were unheated. The prisoners had fashioned sleeping platforms and covered them with blankets. Most were asleep or huddled together to keep warm.

The atmosphere was fairly relaxed. Because no private room could be found, most of Helsinki Watch's interviews with the prisoners were conducted in a group.[71] The men were unwilling to discuss past abusive behavior. The ICRC first visited the prisoners on August 24, 1992, and then regularly thereafter. The prisoners also had been visited by members of the European Community Monitoring Mission[72] and various journalists.

Approximately fifty men were held in one room in the school; they had been detained from four to seven months. One prisoner, who had been a member of the HVO, had been released earlier.

The prisoners complained of hygiene in the school, saying they were not given sufficient opportunity to wash; the first time they were allowed to bathe was nearly four months after their internment. They claimed not to have access to hot water. The prisoners said that they had been allowed to go to the village of Raščani, where their families were

---

[71] See section on methodology in the Introduction to this report.

[72] An EC monitoring mission which was launched in Croatia was gradually expanded to include parts of Bosnia-Hercegovina. The EC monitors, most of whom are members of their countries' armed forces, were dispatched to Bosnia-Hercegovina to monitor compliance with cease-fire and other EC-negotiated agreements. After a member of the EC monitoring mission was killed near Mostar on May 2, 1992, the EC suspended its mission to Bosnia-Hercegovina the following day. ("EC Suspends Action," Paris, Agence France Presse report on May 3, 1992, as reported in FBIS, May 4, 1992.) On May 12, the last twelve EC monitors withdrew from Sarajevo, declaring that it was too dangerous to stay in the capital.(Laura Silber and Judy Dempsey, *The Financial Times*, May 13, 1992.)

confined, on two occasions. They were given two hours to bathe and then were ordered to return to the prison. The prisoners visited Raščani fifteen days before Helsinki Watch's visit.

The prisoners reported that, although families could visit, their access depended on the disposition of the guards on duty. Others claimed that only men whose wives were not Serbian were allowed visits. The prisoners also complained that they did not know the reasons for their detention. They claimed that no one had been charged with a crime, and when they inquired as to the reasons for their detention, they were told that their cases were under investigation.

Their meals were acceptable, according to the prisoners, and they were fed three times a day. They confirmed that they worked in a field about two kilometers away from the prison tending to agricultural chores, such as harvesting potatoes. Some said that, due to bad weather and the inability to use machines in the field, they had to dig up the potatoes with their bare hands. The prisoners said that they usually worked from 9:00 a.m. to 6:00 p.m., seven days a week.

In the group interviews conducted by Helsinki Watch representatives at this site — in circumstances in which the prisoners would not know whether their comments would be disclosed by any of those present — they described the treatment by the guards as "excellent." They claimed that there had been problems earlier, but they did not care to elaborate on these, other than to say that these were "individual" problems. They claimed only to have contact with members of the civilian police forces and, when they worked, with members of HOS.

The prisoners were eager to find out when they might be released. Some said that they would prefer to stay in the area rather than be exchanged to the Serbian side. However, they expressed dismay that the village of Eminovo Selo had been destroyed,[73] and one man claimed that HVO soldiers were living in his apartment.

---

[73] See the section below concerning the pillaging and destruction of villages and cultural objects.

Abuses By HOS Forces

Mostar

Among the most brutal abuses by Croatian forces in Bosnia-Hercegovina were those committed by HOS forces in Čapljina and Mostar. HOS forces operated a detention facility in a military clinic formerly used by the Yugoslav Army (JNA) in Mostar and a former JNA facility in the village of Dretelj in the municipality of Čapljina. The police station in Čapljina was also used as a place of internment for Serbs. Most HOS-operated facilities in western Hercegovina have either been closed, or control was handed over to HVO forces in August 1992. Many prisoners in HOS facilities were released, exchanged or transferred to HVO-controlled jails.

N.S., a fifty-six-year-old Serbian accountant from Mostar,[74] was arrested in his apartment the evening of July 16, 1992, by HOS forces and detained in Mostar before his transfer to a detention facility in the village of Dretelj, in the municipality of Čapljina.[75] N.S. described his detention in a former military clinic in Mostar:

> They placed me in a cell, where I found another ten to fifteen people. The next morning, another prisoner and I were ordered to tend the roses in the yard. They made me wear an officer's cap because I was a reserve captain in the Yugoslav Army (JNA). The guard was threatening to kill me. Since he was telling passersby that we were Četniks captured at the front, they [those who passed by] were saying that he should beat us. I spent three days there. We were receiving food and were not questioned or beaten, only insulted.

---

[74] Interviewed by Helsinki Watch representatives on February 8, 1993, in Belgrade, Yugoslavia.

[75] For an account of his treatment in Dretelj, see the following section.

Dušan, a twenty-five-year-old man from Mostar,[76] appears to have been held in the same facility as N.S. Dušan was arrested by HOS forces, whom he claims were all Muslims. According to Dušan:

> I was probably arrested because HOS wanted to take over my apartment or because they needed people for the purposes of exchange, but the Serbs have refused the exchanges.

Dušan was taken to what the witness referred to as "the HOS military police station" in Mostar. He described his arrest:

> At about 4:00 p.m. or 5:00 p.m. on August 3, five HOS soldiers came to my apartment. My father and I lived there, and my sister and mother had left in April. They [the soldiers] were dressed in black uniforms with HOS insignia and armed with automatic weapons. They rang the bell and told me that they had been ordered to come and get me. I knew two of the soldiers, and they were both Muslims.
>
> They had a warrant for our arrest and a search warrant. It's actually a universal paper with no names on it and anyone can use it. They took my father and me to Mostar for one day, and then we were taken to Dretelj, near Čapljina.[77]

Dušan described his treatment at HOS headquarters in Mostar:

> We were taken to the HOS military police station, which was near the military hospital. A man took down some general documentary information about us and took our belongings. They put us in a room, in which ten people

---

[76] Interviewed by Helsinki Watch representatives on October 24, 1992, in Mostar, Bosnia-Hercegovina.

[77] For an account of the witness's treatment in the Dretelj detention facility, see relevant section below.

were already detained. Through the course of the night, an additional ten arrived. There was a total of about twenty prisoners in the room. Several women also were among the prisoners. We spent the night in that room, and no one touched me, but others were beaten by [a soldier] who came and kicked or hit the prisoners — it was nothing major. We slept on some type of wooden board with a pillow.

B.K., a fifty-seven-year-old retired elementary school teacher from Mostar,[78] was arrested by HOS forces on July 31, 1992, at approximately 3:00 p.m. B.K. described her arrest:

On July 31, [at] about 3:00 p.m., three HOS soldiers came to my door. They came for me only because I am Serbian. I recognized one of them. He was Sergej Belović. They searched my apartment looking for gold and hard currency, but I didn't have any. They broke everything. Sergej wanted to rape me, but I told him that he should be ashamed of himself, since I am old enough to be his mother. He was very angry and called me a Četnik. He then threw me out of my apartment, locked it up and wrote "HOS" on the door.

B.K. was taken to the HOS-operated detention facility in Mostar, where she was interrogated and beaten. According to B.K.:

They put me in their Mercedes and took me to the prison, which was in the former military hospital in downtown Mostar. I spent the next half hour in a cell by myself, but I was soon brought out and questioned by Ivo Zelenika. I knew him from before the war; he lived on

---

[78] Interviewed by Helsinki Watch representatives in January 1993 in Belgrade, Yugoslavia. The witness was provided by the Yugoslav State Commission on War Crimes and Genocide. This witness had been interviewed on numerous occasions prior to the Helsinki Watch interview. The witness's account was corroborated by other testimony received by Helsinki Watch. See also, section on methodology in the Introduction to this report.

Šantićeva Street in Mostar. He only asked for my name and address but he beat me with a rubber stick and cursed at me.

After this, I was taken to a cell in the basement where there were an additional ten women. The guards asked if I knew any of them, and I said that I didn't, although I recognized some of them. At about 10:00 p.m. on the same day, they took six of us out to the courtyard, including [a woman][79] who was brought there on the same day as I. There were seven male prisoners there, and we were ordered to line up against them.

The guards started to beat the men with fists and rifle butts and to kick them in the stomach. The younger women were forced to act as if they were lesbians, and we had to watch.

Then they tied the women together in a line, so that each one of us was tied to two others. We were ordered to get on a truck, while about ten HOS soldiers stood around with their guns pointed at us. Once we got on, we realized that we were sitting on a pile of blood-stained civilian clothes. As we were driving through Mostar, they were hitting us at random with rifle butts and forcing us to sing Ustaša songs.

B.K. and the other women were driven from Mostar through Čitluk, Grude and Ljubuški. The truck stopped in a forest at the Dretelj detention facility, near Čapljina, where the prisoners remained.[80]

---

[79] The witness identified the woman by name.

[80] For an account of the witness's treatment in Dretelj, see following section.

Dretelj

N.S., a fifty-six-year-old Serbian accountant from Mostar,[81] was arrested in his apartment the evening of July 16, 1992, by HOS forces. N.S. was detained in Mostar for three days and then was transferred to a detention facility in the village of Dretelj, in the municipality of Čapljina. The Dretelj detention facility had been a former Yugoslav Army (JNA) barracks. N.S. described his arrest:

> I was arrested by HOS [soldiers] — three young men and a young woman, all [of whom] were in uniform. They took my watch and threatened me not to tell anyone that they had taken my belongings. They put me in a car and drove me to the prison in Mostar, which is a former military health clinic.[82]

N.S. spent three days in detention in Mostar and then was taken to Dretelj with seven other men prisoners and four women detainees.

P.S., a forty-year-old man from Mostar,[83] was arrested by HOS troops and detained at the Dretelj detention facility. Prior to his detention, P.S. claimed that he was forced to sign a loyalty oath to the Bosnian government. According to P.S.:

> On May 3, I was forced to sign a loyalty oath to Bosnia-Hercegovina and [Bosnian President] Alija Izetbegovic. I didn't

---

[81] Interviewed by Helsinki Watch representatives on February 8, 1993, in Belgrade, Yugoslavia.

[82] For an account of the prisoner's detention in Mostar, see relevant section below.

[83] Interviewed by Helsinki Watch representatives on January 19, 1993, in Belgrade, Yugoslavia. The witness was provided by the Yugoslav State Commission on War Crimes and Genocide. The witness had been interviewed on numerous occasions by newspaper, magazine and television reporters. See also section on methodology in the Introduction to this report.

want to sign it, but I had to in order to save my life and the lives of my children.

P.S. was arrested on July 2 and was detained briefly in a jail in Mostar.[84] He described his arrest and brief internment in Mostar to Helsinki Watch representatives:

> I was arrested in front of my children by HOS, the Croatian Defense Forces. I was taken from my house barefoot, in a tee shirt and shorts because they arrested me at night. I still have the tee shirt. They were beating my children as well. I have six-year-old twins and an eleven-year-old daughter. They took me to the prison in Mostar. They told me that they raped my eleven-year-old daughter. She wasn't raped, but I believed it at the time.
>
> In Mostar, they threw us into the basement and killed a man called Dragan Djursović in front of me. After ten days of terrible torture in Mostar, they took us to a camp in Dretelj.

N.S. reported that, upon their arrival at the Dretelj facility, he and the other prisoners were met by Blaž Kraljević, the head of HOS forces in Bosnia-Hercegovina, who was assassinated — presumably by HVO forces — in early August 1992.[85] N.S. described his arrival at Dretelj:

> [In Dretelj], we received a "welcome lecture" by Blaž Kraljević, the self-proclaimed HOS general. He said that nobody would harm us and that we would only be interrogated. There were another twenty very young Ustašas around him — all dressed in black, armed with machine guns, knives, pistols and clubs. They separated the men from the women and took us to a warehouse —

---

[84] The witness did not specify to which jail in Mostar he was taken. Presumably, he was interned in the HOS-operated detention facility in a former JNA clinic. (See preceding section for accounts of the treament in the clinic.)

[85] See section concerning assassinations below for an account of Kraljević's murder and the disarming of HOS by HVO forces.

there was one [warehouse] for the men and one for the women.

About forty men were in my warehouse. They lined eight of us up and three or four of them beat us for an hour, hitting us with rubber truncheons, fists and rifle butts. The old prisoners [i.e., those who had been there before N.S.'s arrival] had to teach us the house rules, which [included] addressing the guards as "sir."

The next morning, they ordered us to clean the area, and then we received breakfast. We would receive two or three meals a day — a slice of bread and a few beans or a bit of rice. Everyone could hit us, and we were not given water. If we asked for water, we would be beaten.

This continued after lunch. They would force us to sing Ustaša songs, to bark like dogs, bleat like sheep. The guards were not from Mostar, but from Stolac, Čapljina and Ljubuški. Their nicknames were Max, Dugi, Sapa, Tonći, Vinci and Idriz. At about eight at night, we would be taken back to the barracks.

Dušan[86] was arrested by HOS forces, whom he claims were all Muslims. He was taken to what the witness referred to as "the HOS military police station" in Mostar and then to the detention facility in Dretelj. Dušan described the Dretelj detention facility:

In the morning [of August 4], they said that we were going to Dretelj and that we would be exchanged there. At about 12:00 noon, thirteen men and six women were put on a truck and taken to the village of Dretelj, which is in the municipality of Čapljina. We were held in the storage warehouse of a Yugoslav Army [JNA] garrison. We were lined up in the warehouse. The women were

---

[86] Interviewed by Helsinki Watch representatives on October 24, 1992, in Mostar, Bosnia-Hercegovina. The name used here is a pseudonym to protect the witness.

put in a different warehouse. There was no interrogation; we just slept and ate. We couldn't walk outside and there was a total of about seventy [men] in the warehouse and, after more prisoners arrived, a total of about ninety-four prisoners were detained in the warehouse.

N.S. reports that prisoners were regularly mistreated and humiliated in Dretelj. According to N.S.:

At night, they used to call prisoners out and beat them. There were three or four women guards who were worse than the men. Their names were Suzana, Marina, Irena — I don't remember the fourth.

They forced us to kiss and touch each others' genitals. Once, they offered me a cigarette and when I lit it, a guard beat me, saying a Četnik should not smoke. Then he put the burning cigarette into my mouth, and I had to eat it.

P.S. recounted a similar tale:

The easiest torture was when they made me bite off the top of a lit cigarette and eat it. I will show you my medical reports. We used a pot as a toilet. They made me drink from it.

The men in the camp were from the same army unit, HOS, as those in Mostar. They wore the letter U[87] on their uniforms as well as [the] HOS [insignia].

---

[87] The letter "U" was used as an insignia by the Croatian fascists (Ustašas) aligned with Nazi Germany during World War II. Ante Pavelić was the head of the Nazi quisling state called the Independent State of Croatia (Nezavisna Država Hrvatska - NDH). Dobroslav Paraga is the current leader of the ultra-right wing Croatian Party of Rights (Hrvatska Stranka Prava - HSP). Although HSP leaders disavow the atrocities perpetrated by the Ustaša during World War II, the party does not condemn the existence of the NDH, which it views as an independent "Greater Croatia."

People were kept there for four months. No hygiene; the dirt was terrible. They would undress a man, line the rest of us up and make us perform oral sex on him, another prisoner. There were two Ustaša women, sisters, who liked to force us to do this: Marina and Gordana Grubišić. They would make fifty to sixty of us do this. We would throw up and faint. This is how days would go by; at any moment you would expect death.

N.S. said that prisoners were routinely beaten in Dretelj. According to N.S.:

Two prisoners died of beatings — Nenad Marković and X.[88] They were beating Balaban and when he could no longer stand, they tied him to a chair and beat him until he fainted. He was calling for his wife, Sofia, who was being held in the other warehouse. He died a few hours later. He was about sixty years old; [and had been] a flight controller in Mostar. Nenad Marković was about forty-five years old and also was from Mostar. Jovan Pejanović was taken to the hospital in Split. We don't know what happened to him.

B.K., a fifty-seven-year-old retired elementary school teacher from Mostar,[89] was arrested by HOS forces on July 31, 1992. She was detained in the HOS-operated detention facility in Mostar[90] and then

---

[88] The witness identified the other victim by name. P.S. and B.K. also identified the same victim in seperate interviews. Because the victim's family remains in a Croatian-controlled area of Hercegovina, the victim's name is withheld here to protect the victim's safety.

[89] Interviewed by Helsinki Watch representatives in January 1993 in Belgrade, Yugoslavia. The witness was provided by the Yugoslav State Commission on War Crimes and Genocide. This witness had been interviewed on numerous occasions prior to the Helsinki Watch interview. The woman's account was corroborated by other testimony received by Helsinki Watch. See also section on methodology in the Introduction to this report.

[90] For an account of the witness's treatment in Mostar, refer to preceding section.

was transferred to Dretelj. According to B.K., Dretelj had been a fuel depot that was used by the Yugoslav Army (JNA). B.K. claims that there was torture and abuse in Dretelj:

> Women [prisoners] were taken into one set of barracks and the men into the other. There were about fifty other women in the barracks. In the morning, I discovered that I had gone deaf due to the shock. My hearing recovered ten days later. We were questioned about our political involvement, the whereabouts of our children, etc. They were irritated with me because I couldn't hear anything.
>
> Later, it was terrible. We heard the screams from the other barracks during the night, and they told us to line up against the wall. Those minutes were the most difficult because we always thought that they would execute us all. However, all the women from my barracks survived. The night of August 2 was the most difficult one. X was killed in the yard between the barracks. They were beating him with clubs until he died.
>
> The food was terrible. We got a can of liver pâté to share between three of us at 9:00 a.m. At 5:00 p.m., we would get the leftovers from their lunch but they would pour hot water into it. We got little water to drink and none to wash. There were female guards. They would shout a lot, threatening us.

P.S. also described the abuses perpetrated in Dretelj:

> There were one hundred women[91] and one hundred men [detained in Dretelj]. We don't want to talk about what happened because they forced us to beat each other. If they told me to beat myself, I didn't mind that. They told me to hit my head two-hundred times and would make me do it until I did it hard enough to satisfy them.

---

[91] B.K., a woman prisoner, claimed that fifty women were detained at Dretelj. (See previous testimony.)

> We had five knives and five spoons for one hundred of us [prisoners], all [of whom were detained] in one room. They fed us nothing, maybe two pieces [presumably, of bread] per day. We were forced to sit in one room with our heads down and our knees drawn up to our chests. Half of us couldn't get up from this position and we were not allowed to help each other. The room was fifty by thirty meters; it used to be a storage room for fuel. I was there for forty days.
>
> I know the people who tortured me in the camp. They did this to me because I am a Serb. I don't understand this; I would like to meet these guards and talk with them. One man was my great friend, he couldn't hit me, but he told others to hit my tailbone. One of the Ustaša, Luka Nezić, would sometimes bring me water. He said, "I fight with a gun, not against helpless men."

Dušan also reported that prisoners were regularly mistreated in Dretelj:

> I was in Dretelj for twelve days, and we were fed twice a day. Mistreatment did take place. We were perpetually being kicked — some more than others. Five or six guards would come in when the commander wasn't around and kick us. The commander had forbidden that such things take place. Some people's backs were black and blue from the kicking with boots and the hitting with truncheons.
>
> We weren't allowed to go out for two days, but otherwise, we dug ditches around the shelter. They [i.e., the soldiers] were afraid of being attacked.[92] Three of four days we had normal activity. I didn't know the guards at Dretelj. There was, however, some type of

---

[92] Presumably, the HOS soldiers feared attack by HVO forces. Čapljina is somewhat removed from the arena of fighting. However, during the witness's detention, HOS's leader had been assassinated, presumably by HVO forces.

disagreement between HVO and HOS, and then HVO disarmed HOS.

N.S. claimed that the ICRC never visited the detention facility at Dretelj. The only outside visitors were a Dutch television crew. N.S. claims that during their visit, the guards threatened the prisoners and told them not to talk about mistreatment in the barracks.

According to N.S., after Blaž Kraljević was assassinated, HOS soldiers mistreated the prisoners, who subsequently were transferred to HVO custody and taken to a detention facility in Čapljina:

> After Kraljević's funeral on August 8 or 9, the guards came back and beat us. They said, "Our general was killed, and you will not survive either." In the morning of August 18 or 19, Kraljević's deputy came and ordered us to collect our belongings. HVO policemen arrived in two buses and transferred us to Čapljina. Here I had my first shower, and I got a haircut and a shave. They kept us in the Grabovina army barracks. Seventy men and twenty-six women [were detained] in three rooms. They were giving us cigarettes and newspapers, and we were allowed to sleep or volunteer to work.

Dušan confirmed N.S.'s account of Dretelj's closure by HVO forces and the prisoners' subsequent transfer to a detention facility in Čapljina. According to N.S.:

> On the evening of August 16, a HOS officer said that the older and sick people should be put on a truck. There were about seventy people who were then taken to Žitomislić. The next day, on August 17, two buses of HVO soldiers arrived. HOS soldiers took out all of the remaining prisoners from the warehouse and placed us in the custody of the HVO soldiers. We were loaded onto the bus and taken to the HVO-controlled Grabovina military barracks in Čapljina. They put us in a room, and we were fed three times a day. A judge questioned us in Čapljina, which HVO had recently taken over from HOS. No one touched us and there were no problems.

On August 16, B.K. and approximately fifty other prisoners were transferred to HVO control. The following day, they were released during a prisoner exchange in the town of Stolac. According to B.K.:

> On August 16 they read a list of about fifty names — both men and women — and ordered us to get on a truck. We were left on a main road, which links Mostar with the coast, near Žitomislić. The HOS soldiers left and about fifteen minutes later, HVO soldiers drove by. They took us to a destroyed elementary school building in Suna. We were not given any food or water.
>
> On August 17 they put us on a bus and drove us back to Mostar, to an HVO-operated prison on Šantičeva Street. At about 5:00 the next morning, all fifty of us from Dretelj and another six hundred from the HVO prison were put on buses and exchanged in Stolac.

Rape

Mostar

Snežana[93] left her village with two Serbian men, possibly combatants, in a car. They were attacked, arrested and questioned by HVO forces on June 20. According to Snežana:

> I got in the car, and they shot at the car from the right bank of the Neretva [River]; I think it was HVO that attacked us and shot at the car. I ran out of the car, and we fled through the vineyards to the HVO military police. After one and a half hours of fleeing, I wanted to return to my home. But I was never indicted, and no one told me why I had been arrested.
>
> We surrendered to the HVO, and that was the first time I saw the HVO insignia on a uniform. There were about fifteen soldiers. I was questioned in a garage, and my hands were tied with wire. I was questioned by one man named Josip. We were questioned all together. They behaved correctly toward us. They took my identification card, bus pass and my checks.

Snežana and the two male prisoners were placed on a bus with other detainees and taken to the university in Mostar. A driver and HVO soldiers also were on the bus, and an HVO car followed the bus. Prisoners were beaten en route to Mostar. According to Snežana:

> When I went into the bus, my neighbor [a HVO soldier] said he knew me. I asked them where we were going. A man from Mostar beat me in the bus and asked me, "Where are your sons?" The bus was full of men who had been arrested and HVO soldiers. I was the only woman.

---

[93] Interviewed by Helsinki Watch representatives on October 24, 1992, in Bosnia-Hercegovina. The name used here is a pseudonym to protect the safety and privacy of the witness.

They beat all of us. They didn't touch me until my neighbor — who was a HVO soldier — told his colleagues not to touch me, but they didn't listen to him. They beat us over our heads with their truncheons, insulted us and called us Četniks.

When the prisoners arrived at the university, they were beaten. Snežana was robbed of her belongings and twice told to strip. The first time she was told to remove her clothing, she claims that HVO military police demanded that three other prisoners rape her. She later was told to remove her clothing but a commander came into the room, thereby preventing any further abuse. According to Snežana:

> At the university, we were terribly mistreated. They took 500 American dollars and 500 German marks from me and the keys to my house and garage. I was not given a receipt. This man [nick-]named Didja took my things. All of us were put in a classroom, which was full of HVO soldiers. They told me twice to strip naked in front of everyone. I was raped in front of everyone. The HVO police told the other detainees to rape me, and three of them did so. I was beaten before all the men with the butt of a gun and I was punched in the eye. They also beat the others and this lasted for about five hours. The second time they told me to take off my clothes, one of their commanders came into the room and told me to get dressed immediately.

Snežana was then taken to the Čelovina jail, located on Šantičeva Street in Mostar, where she remained for three months and claims to have been treated properly. According to Snežana:

> I was then brought to the Čelovina jail on Šantičeva, which is the old jail. There I got protection. I felt like I was in my own house, that's how well I was accepted. There was no maltreatment from anyone, including the guards, the guards' commander, the director of the prison or the deputy director [of the prison]. They treated all the women very well, especially me because they all saw that I had been mistreated.

Hostage-Holding

Raščani

Generally, prisons operated by Croatian military authorities confine men between the ages of seventeen and fifty-five. In at least one case, Serbian women, children and elderly persons were taken to a designated village which was used as a detention area. One detention area that Helsinki Watch investigated was the village of Raščani in the municipality of Tomislavgrad. Those held there were not abused and were allowed to move freely about the village, but they were not allowed to leave the area. In sum, they were held hostage.

On November 1, Mate Boban, the "president" of the self-proclaimed "Community of Herceg-Bosna," ordered the release of all prisoners detained by Croatian forces. Prisoners were indeed released, but those Serbian civilians held in Raščani were not allowed to leave.[94] Despite Boban's decree, the mayor of Tomislavgrad — the municipality of which Raščani is part — refused to release the Serbs held in the village until Serbian forces released Croats from Tomislavgrad who had been captured during the battle for Kupres in April 1992.[95]

Raščani is the smallest of the Serbian villages in the Tomislavgrad area. It is about a kilometer long, on a ridge of stony ground lined by

---

[94] Helsinki Watch visited Raščani one day before the anticipated evacuation, which never took place.

[95] The city and much of the municipality of Kupres fell to Serbian forces in April 1992. Prior to the war, the population of the municipality of Kupres was 50.7 percent Serbian, 39.6 percent Croatian; and 8.4 percent Muslim. It remains unclear if all those Croats detained by Serbian authorities in Kupres were combatants. Although Helsinki Watch is aware that Serbian forces commit abuses against Croats and Muslims in areas under their control, this does not give Croatian forces the right to mistreat Serbian disarmed combatants and civilians in areas under their control. Helsinki Watch is concerned that Croatian and Muslim forces are holding Serbian civilians hostage for the purpose of exchanging them for their combatants held by Serbian forces. This also amounts to hostage-taking, and is strictly forbidden under international law.

Croatian and Muslim forces retain a significantly smaller number of prisoners than do Serbian forces. Regardless of the numbers held, each side is independently responsible for compliance with the rules of armed conflict.

stone houses crowded with displaced Serbian families, in addition to their original inhabitants. At the time of Helsinki Watch's visit, each house had about fifteen residents and a total of approximately 250 people remained in the village. A short, unpaved road joins with the main road below the village; near the juncture of these two roads stands a house in which a Croatian policeman was on guard. Below the town, near the building that houses the guards, was a line of red tractors belonging to the Serbian families in Raščani. Their cars had been confiscated by the Croatian military authorities, who required the Serbs to sign statements claiming that they "voluntarily" donated their vehicles "for the war effort."

Several of the people held in Raščani reported that they were forced from their homes in nearby villages by armed men. They were interned in the local school for several days or weeks and then brought to Raščani. A man from Eminovo Selo said that HVO police collected everyone — including children — in one house to "hold a conference." After four days, the residents were taken to a school in Tomislavgrad where some three hundred were held for approximately six weeks, at which point the younger men were transferred to another school in Tomislavgrad and the rest were confined to Raščani.

Those interviewed by Helsinki Watch claim that, of the five villages populated by Serbs in the Tomislavgrad area, only Raščani had not been destroyed.[96] The day after people were forced to leave, their houses were burned. In Raščani, Helsinki Watch representatives saw a partially built house that had been burned. On the approach to Raščani, Helsinki Watch representatives noticed burned houses around the village of Guber.

According to those interviewed in Raščani, a gang of Croatian soldiers who had returned from the battlefield in Vukovar destroyed the Serbian homes in the area.[97] Relief workers also said that they had

---

[96] Prisoners held in the Tomislavgrad school said that the approximately 250 people confined to Raščani orginally were from the villages of Eminovo Selo, Oplećani, Mandino Selo, Lipa, Raščani and Tomislavgrad.

[97] Vukovar is a city in eastern Croatia that fell to Serbian forces in November 1992. When Serbian and Yugoslav forces destroyed the city, hundreds of residents were summarily executed after the fighting, and thousands remain missing. During the war in Croatia, Bosnian Croats voluntarily joined the Croatian Army (Hrvatska Vojska — HV).

earlier difficulties with members of the "gang." Those in Raščani have since been told that this group had left town. The soldiers were alleged to have come to Raščani, where they beat Serbs, killing two. According to some of the villagers, the local police tried to prevent the soldiers from abusing people, but the police were just "outnumbered and overpowered." Moreover, the soldiers allegedly "forced" the local police to go from house to house, pointing out where someone had something worth stealing. According to those interviewed by Helsinki Watch, the following men were killed in the area:

- Milan Karan, from the village of Raščani, was killed on June 10 while tending sheep.

- Slobodan Karan, from the village of Raščani, and Simo Milisav, from the village of Mandino Selo, were killed on June 24.

- Goran Milisav of Eminovo Selo was killed on June 22.

The circumstances surrounding the deaths of the four men are not known to Helsinki Watch.

The villagers in Raščani also claimed that twenty men were taken to a prison in Ljubuški. Sixteen were released in a prisoner exchange, two were released during a subsequent exchange and the whereabouts of the remaining two men — Milorad Andrijašević and Pero Važić — remain unknown.

At the time of Helsinki Watch's visit, friends and family in neighboring areas were allowed to visit the Serbs in Raščani, but the villagers held there were not permitted to leave. They reported that they were allowed to leave the village for medical reasons, however. In order to visit a doctor, a permission slip had to be granted; some said that the permission slip identified them as "prisoner." The villagers claim that the local authorities told them that they were confined to the village for "their own safety."

The Serbs held in Raščani were not subjected to continuing physical mistreatment and said they were not threatened with criminal charges. Nevertheless, some reported that Croatian soldiers came periodically to the village to take their cars, tractors, televisions and videocassette recorders.

They reported that the local authorities were distributing packages of food — about enough for a breakfast meal — to each family in the village. Some had brought food with them earlier, and neighbors bring food to Raščani. At the time of Helsinki Watch's visit, younger Serbian men were interned in a school in Tomislavgrad.[98] The villagers in Raščani were allowed to send the men such items as fresh clothing. Some said they could not visit these young men.

Donje Selo

When Helsinki Watch representatives visited Donje Selo, a Croatian-controlled village in the municipality of Konjic, night had fallen, there was no electricity in the area and the entrance to and from Donje Selo was guarded by two HVO soldiers — one man and a woman. On the basis of an interview with one Serbian family,[99] it is unclear whether Serbs in the village are prevented from leaving. Most of the Serbs in the village were either indigineous to Donje Selo or were displaced from nearby areas. Helsinki Watch interviewed members of a Serbian family forcibly displaced from the village of Bradina, approximately thirteen kilometers from Sarajevo, after Muslim and Croatian forces attacked the village. The family members — all women — apparently asked to be brought to Donje Selo, where they took shelter in a friend's weekend home. The family said that Serbs in the village were not mistreated and could freely visit male relatives detained in a nearby Muslim-controlled prison.[100]

A Helsinki Watch representative asked one woman in the family if their physical security had been threatened during their stay in Donje Selo. The woman answered:

---

[98] For an account of the treatment in the Tomislavgrad school, see relevant section above.

[99] Helsinki Watch representatives were forced to leave the village because hostilities between Muslims and Croats had commenced in the area and Serbian forces were shelling the municipality. See also section on methodology in the Introduction to this report.

[100] For accounts of the treatment in detention by Bosnian Muslim forces, see relevant section below.

> We have no problems here except fear. We can walk about freely. You hear an occasional slur, but I don't think that's such a big deal. We get our food from [the Catholic charity] Caritas, which consists mainly of flour, oil and some other basic staples. The house in which I'm living now belongs to people in Sarajevo and this is their weekend home. I know the owners of this house but I haven't had the opportunity to ask them if it's okay if we use their house but I don't think they'd mind. There are many local Serbs still here, and there are a few abandoned houses. Anyone who has a family generally has not left the area.

Nevertheless, during the interview, an armed, elderly Croatian civilian walked into the family's temporary home claiming he wanted to escort the Helsinki Watch representatives to their car because of a lack of lighting in the area. The man did not knock before entering the house with a flashlight and a hunting rifle.

Helsinki Watch also interviewed Momir, a fifty–two–year–old man from the village of Bradina,[101] who had been held in detention facilities in the village of Čelebići and the town of Konjic.[102] According to Momir, some male residents were required to work in Donje Selo:

> In Donje Selo, two or three people died of natural causes or of exhaustion. Every day, more displaced persons arrived in Donje Selo.
>
> Zoran Čečez was head of the encampment. He was from the village of Pavo, and he had given orders that we work in the fields. I gained my health back, and two of us tried to get out. We spent four of five days in the

---

[101] Interviewed by Helsinki Watch representatives on October 6, 1992, in Belgrade, Yugoslavia. The witness was supplied by the Yugoslav State Commission on War Crimes and Genocide. See also the methodology section in the Introduction to this report.

[102] For the witness's accounts of treament in both facilities, see relevant sections below.

forest. We took some canned food with us so that we wouldn't be hungry. We went to Serbian-controlled territory in Iližda [in the municipality of Sarajevo].

Svetlana, a twenty-five-year-old Serbian mother of a three-year-old daughter from the village of Bradina,[103] was released from detention in the school in Bradina.[104] She then came to Donje Selo and lived with a cousin for one month. Svetlana reported that all was quiet during her stay in Donje Selo and that "no one bothered us while we were there."

Svetlana visited her village of Bradina while she was in Donje Selo. According to Svetlana:

> There was no problem moving about. A Croat went with me [to my village of Bradina], but I had to pay him. The HVO would take us if we wanted. The relations between the HVO and [predominantly Muslim] TO seemed to be okay. The TO controlled most of the area, but they let us go through the barricades.
>
> After I spent a month there [i.e, in Donje Selo], we left with the Croats' help. Eight of us — all women and children — left, and we had to pay a total of 1,500 German marks to be evacuated. A Croat dressed in an HVO uniform took us Blažuja, which is a Serbian-controlled village near Hadžići. He drove us in an orange HVO truck with HVO license plates. We spent five days [in Blažuja] and [eventually left Bosnia-Hercegovina].

---

[103] Interviewed by Helsinki Watch representatives on October 6, 1992, in Belgrade, Yugoslavia. The witness was seven months pregnant at the time. The witness was supplied by the Yugoslav State Commission on War Crimes and Genocide. See also the section on methodology in the Introduction to this report.

[104] See relevant section below for the witness's account of the treatment in the school.

Assassination

Forces belonging to the Croatian Defense Council (Hrvatsko Vijeće Obrane — HVO) have eliminated political and military opponents in areas under their control. In August 1992, HVO forces are alleged to have assassinated the leader of the Croatian Defense Forces (Hrvatske Obrambene Snage — HOS). Shortly thereafter, HVO and the self-proclaimed governing council of the "Community of Herceg-Bosna" assumed almost exclusive military and political control over western Hercegovina.

The Croatian Defense Force (HOS) is the armed wing of the ultra-right-wing Croatian Party of Rights (Hrvatska Stranka Prava — HSP), which has branches in Croatia and Bosnia-Hercegovina. HSP leaders have criticized officials of the Bosnian and Croatian governments and the leaders of the self-proclaimed "Community of Herceg-Bosna" for their alleged ill-preparedness for, and laxity toward, Serbian armed forces in Croatia and Bosnia-Hercegovina. HSP and its armed wing, HOS, advocate the establishment of a "Greater Croatia," which would include all of present-day Bosnia-Hercegovina. HSP and HOS are critical of HVO because they believe that HVO forces are interested only in preserving territory claimed by the self-proclaimed "Community of Herceg-Bosna" (i.e., south-central Bosnia) and not all of Bosnia-Hercegovina. Some Muslims have joined HOS forces, believing that only HOS has been committed to the maintenance of Bosnia's borders, albeit within a "Greater Croatia."

During the early weeks of the war in Bosnia, HOS forces cooperated — both on the battlefield and otherwise — with Bosnian Muslim and HVO troops. During this time, HOS established its own detention centers in the municipalities of Čapljina and Mostar, where prisoners were brutally mistreated.[105] By the summer of 1992, relations between HVO and HOS had soured. On August 9, 1992, HOS commander Blaž Kraljević and seven other HOS members — six Croats

---

[105] For descriptions of the treatment in HOS-operated facilities in Čapljina and Mostar, see relevant sections above.

and a Muslim — were killed at a police checkpoint in the village of Kruševo, reportedly by HVO forces.[106]

Shortly after Kraljević's assassination, HOS units were disarmed by HVO troops diminishing HOS's military capabilities in western Hercegovina. HVO assumed control of, or closed, HOS-operated detention facilities. HVO officials in Mostar said that HOS formally was dissolved on August 23, 1992, when HOS and HVO officials signed a document indicating that HOS members would be absorbed into the HVO.[107] Remaining HOS units in Bosnia-Hercegovina reportedly have been recognized by the Bosnian government as a segment of the official defense forces.[108]

Unlawful Searches and Seizures and Arbitrary Dismissal from Employment

The treatment of Serbs not held in detention in Croatian-controlled areas of western Hercegovina varies. Croatian civilian and HVO military police officers search the houses of people suspected of arms possession. Helsinki Watch interviewed several persons who had their homes searched by such officers, and almost all stated that the police officers had warrants for the searches. Helsinki Watch also interviewed several Serbs who claim that HVO soldiers confiscated their cars or tractors and other belongings. Some were given receipts stating that the HVO was using their vehicles, and others were not given any document attesting to the confiscation.

Although some Serbs interviewed by Helsinki Watch claim that they continued to go to work and that they were not harassed, others

---

[106] See Zoran Batusic, "The Rights of the Croatian Party of Right," *East European Reporter*, November-December 1992, pp. 57-59, and Vanessa Vasic Janekovic, "Croatian Forces Play Insidious Game," *Balkan War Report*, No. 14, September 14, 1992, p. 10.

[107] Interviewed by Helsinki Watch representatives by telephone in March 1993.

[108] Zoran Batusic, "The Rights of the Croatian Party of Right," *East European Reporter*, November-December 1992, pp. 57-59.

have been dismissed from their jobs by Croatian civilian authorities, apparently due to their ethnic affiliation.

B.R.[109] was dismissed from his job on April 6, 1992. His notice of dismissal designates his successor but does not give a reason for his removal. Helsinki Watch examined B.R.'s notice of dismissal which stated:

> On the basis of Article 60, clause 3, of the decision of the executive council [izvršni odbor] of the municipality of Livno, B.R. is relieved of his duties as director of the Livno affiliate of the state recording office (službe drustvenog knjigovdstva — SDK) and is replaced by J.U., an economist from Livno. This decision takes effect immediately.
> Signed: Zdravko Mihaljević, president of
> the executive council, municipality of
> Livno, April 6, 1992.

B.R. was arrested for weapons possession on May 12; Helsinki Watch does not dispute the local authorities' right to investigate and prosecute persons suspected of illegal arms' possession. However, B.R. was dismissed one month before his arrest and no reason was given for his dismissal, thereby implying that he was removed from his job on the basis of his ethnic affiliation.

ABUSES BY MUSLIM FORCES

Abuses in Detention

In western and central Bosnia, predominantly Muslim forces belonging to the Army of the Republic of Bosnia-Hercegovina reportedly control detention areas in the municipalities of Konjic, Jablenica, Zenica, Tuzla and Visoko. Because of the fighting in and around many of these areas, Helsinki Watch has not been able to investigate detention facilities in all these areas.

---

[109] Interviewed by Helsinki Watch representatives on October 27, 1992, in Livno, Bosnia-Hercegovina.

In October 1992, Helsinki Watch representatives interviewed former inmates of a detention facility in the village of Čelebići, in the municipality of Konjic. The Čelebići detention facility is a former Yugoslav Army barracks, and most of the detainees appeared to be disarmed Serbian male combatants. Former detainees claim that they were held for one to two days in underground manholes, causing some deaths due to suffocation. Others claim that the guards beat prisoners with baseball bats, killing some.

Detainees have also been held in the jail in the town of Konjic. Family members are allowed to visit their brothers, sons and husbands who are detained in the Čelebići barracks and the Konjic prison. Helsinki Watch interviewed several family members who had visited relatives in these detention facilities; some said that their family members were treated fairly, while others alleged that their husbands, brothers or sons had been beaten.

Čelebići

After the Yugoslav Army (JNA) withdrew from its barracks in the village of Čelebići, in the municipality of Konjic, in May 1992, Bosnian Muslim forces assumed control and used the facility to house Serbian prisoners. Prisoners were bestially beaten in the Čelebići barracks, and many died as a result. Treatment appears to have improved since the ICRC first visited Čelebići between August 12 and 14, 1992.

In naming persons whom the U.S. government believed should be investigated for the commission of war crimes in Bosnia-Hercegovina, then Acting Secretary of State Lawrence Eagleburger said that those responsible for the abuse in the Čelebići camp should be prosecuted.[110] Helsinki Watch endorses the call to bring to justice those guilty of the abuses and deaths in Čelebići. United States officials' reports have indicated that the Čelebići detention facility is controlled by Croatian forces.[111] On the basis of Helsinki Watch interviews with international relief workers, Serbian advocates in Belgrade and former detainees, however, it appears that the Čelebići detention facility initially was

---

[110] Elaine Sciolino, "U.S. Names Figures to be Prosecuted Over War Crimes," *The New York Times*, December 17, 1992.

[111] *Ibid.*

controlled by Croatian forces and manned by Muslim guards, but shortly thereafter, Muslim forces assumed control. None of the former detainees or their families interviewed by Helsinki Watch indicated that Croatian forces were present in the Čelebići camp. The commander of the Čelebići facility was identified as a tall, well-built man named Hazim Delić; the U.S. government has identified the commander as Adem Delić.[112]

Ljubomir, a twenty-one-year-old Serb[113] from the village of Brdjani, in the municipality of Konjic, described his arrest and subsequent detention at the Čelebići camp to Helsinki Watch representatives:

> Muslims and Serbs lived in the village of Brdjani — there were no Croats there. While I was serving my military duty in the Yugoslav Army (JNA) in 1990, political parties were formed in the villages, but the relations between the [predominantly Muslim Party of Democratic Action] SDA and the [Serbian Democratic Party] SDS were okay. A territorial defense unit was activated in March [1992] but that [action] left the village divided.

The young man said that Serbs did not join the territorial defense (TO) unit. He also asserted that the Muslims had erected barricades at which they controlled entrance and exit to the village. According to Ljubomir:

> The head of the TO was Commander Hagan Ramić from Brdjani. Weapons were not displayed openly in the streets, and the TO presence was not public. The Muslims started taking over the military objects in the area. Some Croatian forces also were involved, but the bulk of the troops were Muslim. Five or six anti-aircraft guns were put around my village, and the Muslims

---

[112] *Ibid.*

[113] Interviewed by Helsinki Watch representatives on October 6, 1992, in Belgrade, Yugoslavia. The witness was supplied by the Yugoslav State Commission on War Crimes and Genocide. The witness chose to withhold his name, and the name used here is a pseudonym. See also the section on methodology in the Introduction to this report.

attacked Ljuta, which is a munitions-producing factory. The Yugoslav Army [JNA] then left the area. We [Serbs] were then left alone.

Ljubomir reported that the Yugoslav Army had been stationed in barracks in the nearby village of Čelebići, withdrawing in early May 1992. Muslims and Serbs in the village tried to resolve their disputes, according to Ljubomir, but with little success. Fighting between Serbs and Muslims broke out soon thereafter. According to Ljubomir:

> There were various pressures we endured. I worked with the train company in Sarajevo. I had to travel about forty kilometers to get to work every day. The barricades were all over the place and I had problems getting to work. We held meetings with the Muslims. Sometime around May 10 at about noon, we had the last such meeting with them. They asked us to join the Bosnian territorial defense unit, but we could not fight against our own people. I was at that meeting. The Muslims wanted to negotiate with us and we with them but it didn't work. At about 3:00 p.m. or 4:00 p.m., the attack on Brdjani began.
>
> I was at home when the attack [on Brdjani] began. At first, mortars were launched. The women and the children were evacuated in six or seven tractors to Bradina. They shot at the tractors, but only one man was wounded. The trip to Bradina is about three or four kilometers from Brdjani. I also left for Bradina, and we didn't fight back. When we got to Bradina, we felt tensions there as well. There was conflict in Donje Selo, and fighting had broken out there also. We collected some old rifles and handguns. We spent fifteen days in Bradina.
>
> Then at about 12:30 p.m. on May 25, there was a mortar attack on Bradina. About two thousand people were in the village at the time of the attack. We had noticed that Muslims were being evacuated from Sunje, Zukići, Repovica and Brastelica. The battle lasted all day. We

were attacked and as we retreated, we saw flames in the village. We were attacked from the Veleka and Suljina side of the village. About three thousand Muslims attacked, and they took over all the positions. The next day, shooting and mortar attacks [were launched] all day, but we didn't resist much.[114] Seven people from my village were killed during the battle.

Ljubomir, who appears to have been a combatant, fled to the forests with the other Serbian soldiers but eventually surrendered to the Muslim troops. According to Ljubomir:

> On May 26, I fled to Brdjani, to the forest, during a lull in the fighting. We had no guns and spent two or three days in the forest. We hid in our houses [in Brdjani] but the Muslims controlled the village then. Only older Serbs had stayed behind, and they were afraid. You could hear gunfire, but no one appears to have touched them. The Muslims came to our older people and parents, and they told them that we had to surrender or that they would burn the entire village [i.e., Brdjani] and kill everyone. But they promised not to hurt anyone if we surrendered. So we surrendered on or about June 1 to Hagan Ramić and his forces in Brdjani. Two or three of us had guns, but we handed those over. Ten of us were held under house arrest in our homes in Brdjani. They would check on us in our homes, and we had to make a statement to the TO [headquarters of the territorial defense unit]. There was some provocation during my questioning; they said that they would shoot at the Serbian houses. I couldn't sleep in my house [out of fear]. The houses weren't guarded all the time, so I could leave and sleep elsewhere.

Ljubomir remained in Brdjani for approximately ten days, when he and other men were questioned and then taken to the former

---

[114] According to the witness, the Serbs were armed "with guns and one or two automatic weapons."

Yugoslav Army (JNA) barracks in the village of Čelebići. According to Ljubomir:

> At about 11:00 a.m., Hagan Ramić came with a list of people who had to report to the soldiers on duty. About forty men, ranging in age from sixteen to eighty, from the village of Brdjani were told to give statements and that we should all gather in one area. We had started to believe that the Muslims weren't too bad. They lined us up, took our names and dates of birth and brought us to a truck with a cover. No one said anything, and we all got into the truck. The drive was terrible; the driver drove badly. They took us to an unknown destination, to some type of a camp. I realized that we'd gone to Čelebići to the old JNA barracks.

Helsinki Watch also interviewed Momir, a fifty-two-year-old man from Bradina,[115] who also was taken to the Čelebići detention facility. Momir described the battles in his village and the subsequent arrest of its men:

> I was with approximately fifty women and children in a house. We took shelter from the mortars until they got to the house after they had taken over all positions. About forty-five to fifty of them came to the door with guns and told us to get out, which we did.

According to Momir, the soldiers who came to their door all wore camouflage but different hats and insignia. Some wore a fez, a red hat. Others wore a camouflage headband and still others wore a green hat with crosslike insignia. The witness said that the soldiers had insignia patches on their arms. He could not determine to which army the troops

---

[115] Interviewed by Helsinki Watch representatives on October 6, 1992, in Belgrade, Yugoslavia. The witness was supplied by the Yugoslav State Commission on War Crimes and Genocide. The witness chose to withhold his name, and the name used here is a pseudonym. See also the section on methodology in the Introduction to this report.

belonged. He said the insignia patches also varied. The soldiers then took a group of men toward Konjic. According to Momir:

> They told us to line up in the street. Women and children were lined up on one side of the street, and the men were lined up on the other side. Those of us who had a hat on had to remove it and put our hands on our heads. There were about 150 to 200 men in the column. Only that column left the village; I don't know what happened to the women and children. Then we walked one kilometer in a line. The minute we started walking, the hitting began. They hit men with the butts of their guns.

The witness claims that one of the prisoners fell and was stabbed, but he could not see by whom. The wounded prisoner was left on the side of the road.

Momir and the other prisoners were taken to the police station in Konjic and then to the detention facility in Čelebići. According to Momir:

> We got into a truck and were hit as we were getting on. We were all bloody from the beatings. They took us to Konjic, in front of the police station. As we got off the truck, we were hit again. Perko Mrkajić was killed [by the beatings with rifle butts.] They took us into a room and said, "It was a mistake that you came here." They then loaded us back into the truck.
>
> Then we went to the military base in Čelebići. It was night by the time we arrived. When we were getting out of the trucks, they made us put our hands against a wall. There, we were beaten again. They read some type of a prayer. I only understood "Allah..." something or other and then we had to repeat whatever was said by him [i.e. the soldier reciting the prayer]. We repeated it, and he made us say it louder. They made us take off our jackets and shoes. We went into a military warehouse without any coats. Then I was hit in the head and fell unconscious.

Ljubomir, who had been taken from Brdjani in a truck, described his arrival at the Čelebići barracks:

> It was June, and it was hot. We heard machine-gun fire and cursing at Četniks and Serbs. After ten minutes, they took the cover off the truck, and I saw about twenty soldiers of the Muslim army. They were dressed in camouflage and had a half-moon-and-star insignia on their uniforms. They told us to get out one by one and to line up against a nearby wall. They cursed at us and hit us as we got out of the truck. We had to put our arms up against the wall and make the "V" sign.[116] They hit us while we lined up against the wall. We stayed against the wall for about thirty minutes, during which time we had to take everything out of our pockets and take off our belts. They took our gold and watches. They threatened to kill us if we didn't relinquish our belongings or thoroughly empty our pockets.

Ljubomir and six other prisoners were placed in underground manholes, where they remained for two days. According to Ljubomir:

> They then told us to turn left and to keep walking forward with one hand behind our back and the other hand on the shoulder of the person in front of us. They took us to the direction of the manhole, which was two by two meters wide and seven meters deep in the ground. It had a large vent and gas was stored here. A soldier picked up the steel cover and told five of us to go down. It was black and had a ventilation duct and several inches of water. We went down into the chest, and he shut the cover above us. We were quiet for about thirty minutes; we couldn't believe this. We heard voices above us [and the voice of] a guard. Then another man was brought into the manhole three or four hours later. He

---

[116] The Serbs have a three-fingered salute, whereas the Muslims, Croats and Albanians make the "V"-for-victory sign. The making of such a sign has become a means of national expression.

was about thirty years old and had been very badly beaten. We spent two days in the manhole without food, water or hygienic conditions. I heard people being beaten above us, and some of the men were suffocating because they had asthma, and so they opened another manhole. On the second day, we heard people yelling above us. After two days, they took all of us out of the manhole and I saw blood on the wall we were lined up against.

Ljubomir claims that he was held in a military storage facility or warehouse in Čelebići for forty days. According to Ljubomir:

Cars and other vehicles were kept in front of the military warehouse made of corrugated steel. They took groups of five men in[to the warehouse] at a time. I was among the later groups to go in. People were sitting on the concrete. There were about two hundred people in there, and they were all looking at the floor. No one was allowed to look at the soldiers. Some of the people were from Bradina, and had been in detention for about twenty days.

Momir claims that the prisoners were required to relinquish their belongings to the guards. According to Momir:

There were only men in this warehouse. In the evening, they would come with a flashlight, and a military helmet was passed around. They shut off the light, and we passed around the helmet and had to deposit all our money, watches and similar belongings into the helmet. After a while, they turned on the light again and took the helmet. We then waited for morning to arrive.

Ljubomir described the conditions in Čelebići:

We went outside in the morning and evening to go to the bathroom, but we were not allowed any exercise or movement outdoors. We were fed, at a maximum, two times a day but this was rare. Sometimes three or four days went by without any food. We were fed bread and a little water. I weighed eighty-four kilograms when I went into the camp and came out weighing sixty-seven kilograms.

Ljubomir claims that prisoners in Čelebići were beaten regularly and some died as a result of their injuries. Other prisoners had been summarily executed. According to Ljubomir:

> All the men in the camp were Serbs, and we were beaten regularly. Hazim Delić beat us the most. It was a daily beating. A young soldier, who was between eighteen and twenty, also beat us. He was nicknamed "Zenga" but he was a Muslim.[117] We were beaten with baseball bats and shovels and hoes. I got by okay, though. They rarely hit us in the face; usually they beat us in the stomach, kidneys and chest. We had a designated place where we had to sit and we had to be in our place the entire time of our detention — we couldn't get up — period. There were no guards inside [the warehouse] but about twenty patrolled outside.
>
> After my third day in the warehouse, I saw my first killing. Simo Avramović was beaten for about fifteen minutes with boots and baseball bats in front of us by three or four men. This so-called Zenga took him out and beat him to death. His body was brought back into the room and left among us for twenty-four hours. Nedjo Milošević — a man in his fifties or sixties — also was killed through the same methods. On Bairam,[118] the Muslims were celebrating, and they were shooting off

---

[117] During the early stages of the war in Croatia, "Zenga" was a nickname that was attributed by Serbs to the Croatian National Guard (Zbor Narodne Garde — ZNG), the precursor to the Croatian Army (Hrvatska Vojska — HV).

[118] The lesser Bairam (*Id al-Fitr*) and the greater Bairam (*Id al-Adha*) are two major Muslim feasts. Bairam is a three-day feast which concludes the fast of Ramadan.

their guns. They killed a man nicknamed Čorba. His surname was Kuljani, and he was about twenty-three or twenty-four years old. He was shot in front of us. They brought in a chair, in which he had to sit. They then shot him in the back of the head in front of his brother and me. There were about four or five of them. This guy Zenga pulled the trigger. Čedo Avramović, a professor, died of fear — of a heart attack. Miroslav Vujčić also was killed. Boško Samouković, an older man in his late sixties, was killed in front of his two sons.

Ljubomir claims that he was held in warehouse number six, which was referred to as *Šestica*.

Fifteen days after [we arrived in Čelebići], the last group of Serbs came to the camp from Zukići. A father and his two sons were beaten every day. Zenga would bring a mirror after he beat them and asked them if they could recognize themselves in the mirror. They burned the legs of a man named Momčilo. The ICRC did not visit the camp while I was there, and there were other prisoners who were held in warehouse number nine.

Momir also reported that prisoners were bestially beaten in the Čelebići detention facility. He also said that after he was beaten, he was taken to see a doctor. According to Momir:

They opened the door [of the warehouse] and someone said, "See what they did with these civilians." They took us to see a doctor. Four of us would be taken out at a time, and the doctor asked us what was wrong. We were examined and our wounds were bandaged. We were then taken back to the warehouse, but we were not fed at all that day. The next day, we got some tea and bread. I was there for one month and we were not allowed any exercise except when we went to the bathroom, which was outside. Two or three of us were taken to the bathroom at a time.

Ljubomir claims that a television crew visited the Čelebići barracks and that prisoners were beaten as a result. According to Ljubomir:

> While we were in detention, an Arab television crew came and the badly beaten men were taken out of the warehouse. When the television crew arrived, some of the prisoners blurted out things and they later were beaten mercilessly. Five days later, the same television crew came back and Delić was with them. He beat people as he walked between the rows [of prisoners]. The Arab [television crew] taped this. They asked a man named Branko, who was in his sixties, to make a statement. He said that the Muslims attacked his village and then they beat the hell out of him. They also beat his sons because of this as well.

On July 25, Ljubomir was released during a prisoner exchange in the village of Fojnica, between Konjic and Sarajevo. He said that he and an unspecified number of prisoners were exchanged for four or five people from Hadžići who had been held by Serbian forces. Momir was held in the Čelebići barracks for a month and then was transferred to the sports hall in the town of Konjic.

Svetlana, a twenty-five-year-old Serbian mother of a three year-old daughter from the village of Bradina,[119] lived in Donje Selo for a month after having been displaced from her home. While in Donje Selo, Svetlana visited her twenty-nine-year-old husband, who had been interned in Čelebići. According to Svetlana:

> I saw my husband in the camp. He was held in warehouse number six. He was there when I left [Donje Selo]. Because Čelebići is next to Donje Selo, I went to

---

[119] Interviewed by Helsinki Watch representatives on October 6, 1992, in Belgrade, Yugoslavia. The witness was seven months pregnant at the time of the interview. The witness was supplied by the Yugoslav State Commission on War Crimes and Genocide. The witness chose to withhold her name, and the name used here is a pseudonym. See also the section on methodology in the Introduction to this report.

see my husband several times, but did not see him. On Friday, August 23, I saw my husband walk out of a warehouse made of corrugated steel. About 250 people were inside [the warehouse]. I saw him two months after he had been arrested, and he looked very skinny and sallow. He was wearing the same clothes as when I last saw him. He asked me if we were okay. After the ICRC came on July 12, we were allowed to bring food three times a week. We brought food on Mondays, Wednesdays and Fridays. Sometime around July 15 was the first time we brought them food.

Konjic Sports Hall

Momir, a fifty-two-year-old man from the village of Bradina,[120] was transferred from the Čelebići barracks to a detention facility in the sports hall in the town of Konjic. Momir described the conditions in the sports hall:

There were over two hundred people in the sports hall and there were people already there when we arrived. The food was bad. Our family members would bring us food but they were turned back and we were not allowed to speak with them. Occasionally, someone would smuggle some food in.

A mortar shell had fallen in the sports hall, and it hit the wall.[121] Ten of the men were killed, and many were wounded. They took out the dead and wounded, and they

---

[120] Interviewed by Helsinki Watch representatives on October 6, 1992, in Belgrade, Yugoslavia. The witness was supplied by the Yugoslav State Commission on War Crimes and Genocide. The witness chose to withhold his name, and the name used here is a pseudonym. See also the section on methodology in the Introduction to this report.

[121] The mortar round fell on the hall during the fighting. The witness did not indicate that the sports hall had been targetted for attack by any party to the conflict.

brought us rags so we could pick up the blood. Then ten or fifteen days later, they wrote down the names of all who were in the hall.

The prisoners were interrogated and then released and taken to the village of Donje Selo. According to Momir:

> One day, nine of us were called out and questioned by an interrogator who was a judge. He asked me where I had been at the time of the attack. They then let us go to our homes. They said we weren't guilty of anything and that we could go to our houses. We were released and put on a truck and taken to Donje Selo.

Momir said that he did not go to Bradina because he had been told that all the houses were burned down.

Gordana, a thirty-six-year-old Serbian woman from Sarajevo,[122] was forcibly displaced from her family home in Bradina, and her brother was detained in the municipality of Konjic. Gordana's brother was held in the Muslim-operated Čelebići detention facility for eleven days and was then transferred to the Konjic sports hall. At the time of Helsinki Watch's interview in October 1992, Gordana said that she was allowed to visit her brother in the sports hall three times a week. She was permitted to bring him food, clothing and other necessities. She said that the Bosnian Muslim forces controlled the detention facility in the Konjic sports hall. When Helsinki Watch asked Gordana how her brother was being treated in the Konjic sports hall, she replied:

> He has no problems there. About 150 people [are interned in the sports hall]. Some were released last night, and more were released tonight, but I don't know what criteria one has to meet in order to be released. My brother just turned nineteen, and they are releasing youths younger than twenty-one.

---

[122] Interviewed by Helsinki Watch representatives on October 25, 1992, in Bosnia-Hercegovina. The witness chose to withhold her name, and the name used here is a pseudonym.

Bradina School

Svetlana[123] reported that Serbian familes were displaced and detained after Muslim forces assumed control of their village. According to Svetlana:

> The first attack took place on May 25. I was in the basement with my husband and his family during the mortar attack. My mother and father-in-law, my husband, his two brothers, their two wives and four children were in the basement. There was a total of four children in the basement with us. The shooting lasted for twelve days; occasionally we would go upstairs to get something to eat. The second day of the attack, they came and took our cars away. They came into the basement and took our guns, which were hunting rifles. All of the soldiers were Muslims with green headbands and "TO" written on their camouflage uniforms. They wore gloves, but I didn't recognize any of them. They took three of our cars — they belonged to my husband and brother. One of the cars was a Ford 101. They wired the cars to get them started.
>
> On the afternoon of June 5, four or five men arrived in a truck. I recognized one of them — his name was Halilović, and he was from Brdjani. Four of them came into the basement and took the men, allegedly to give a statement, but they never came back. They took my husband, his two brothers and my husband's father. We [women and children] then went upstairs.

Svetlana said that Bosnian Muslim soldiers frequently searched the village. Eventually, Svetlana and her family were told to leave their

---

[123] Interviewed by Helsinki Watch representatives on October 6, 1992, in Belgrade, Yugoslavia. The witness was seven months pregnant at the time. The witness was supplied by the Yugoslav State Commission on War Crimes and Genocide. See also the section on methodology in the Introduction to this report.

house and go to the local school, where others were being detained. According to Svetlana:

> They came three of four times a day and searched the house; they dug around the house. There were usually four of five of them, and they came in various shifts — always different guys. They were armed with automatic weapons. Most were dressed in TO uniforms and others were dressed in civilian clothing but had a headband on their heads. Most of them were young.
>
> They kept coming until July 7, when Osman Karić and Mirsun Rizvić came to my house. They told us to take a blanket and our children and to go to the school — that there was a group of people there already. We took the short road instead of the long road. [They appear to have evacuated us because] they said that Četniks were hiding in the forest and that someone [from the village] was bringing them [i.e., the Serbian forces] food. All the women and children from the village were taken to the school.

Svetlana reported that women, children and elderly persons were held in classrooms, where some were mistreated. According to Svetlana:

> Some women were arbitrarily hit in the classroom [where we were held]. There was no furniture, and we sat on the floor. Throughout the day, more women and children arrived. There also was an old man and three old women who were in the classroom with us. My sister's daughter, who is three years old, was sitting next to me, and she was crying. A guard started to hit her and said, "If I hear your voice, I'll break all your teeth." They asked us who gave food to the Četniks.
>
> They took some women out of the room and they [the women] came back badly beaten. The [soldiers] were all Muslims from [the villages of] Repovci, Sunji, Zukići and Bale. I knew most of them: Agan Ramić, Osman Karić,

Hajro Karić, Mehmedalija Rizvić, Mirso Rizvić, Nusret Ajanović and others. There were many of them.

There were about 250 to 300 women and children held in three classrooms. We were given no food or water. They made the children of two brothers beat one another. Then someone came, and there was a fight between the soldiers and, until dawn, no one bothered us again.

Svetlana stated that Muslim soldiers shot into the school and that several people were injured. According to Svetlana:

The next day, there was shooting all day. We weren't allowed to go to the bathroom. At about 5:00 p.m., they started to shoot at the school. They were shooting at the windows from outside, and we all hit the floor. A little girl was wounded. A bullet hit my purse, and my child fell unconscious. We ran into the bathroom after the shooting stopped, and I splashed water on her. Thirty minutes later they came and said that some of their men had been hurt [in battle]. They claimed that they shot at the school out of revenge and promised that it would not happen again.

The next day we heard shooting again, and at 5:00 p.m. we got scared. We feared that they would shoot at the school again, and we went into the hallway. They started shooting again, but no one was hurt this time. The next day, we had to read some type of prayer.

We started to cry in the morning of our fourth day of detention — we had no food, we didn't know of our fate. They said that if we had family in Konjic, we were free to leave. I went to my cousin's in Donje Selo for one month.

Zenica

Miloš, a forty-six-year-old Serbian man from Zenica,[124] was arrested there on June 3, held in a local school for a day and later transferred to the former prison in Zenica. He reported that he was beaten during detention in the school and in prison. According to Miloš:

> I was arrested on June 3. They came to my apartment, took me to the school and beat me for several hours. We were arrested only because we are Serbs. The army — the Patriotic League[125] — surrounded the house and came into the apartment. I didn't know them; they send people you don't know to arrest you. My sixteen-year-old son and I were taken to the "Manojlo Polić" school, which is the headquarters for the Patriotic League.
>
> I was in the school for only one night but, while there, they beat me from 8:00 a.m. until 2:00 p.m., holding a knife to my throat. I was beaten with rifle butts. They were asking me where the weapons were [kept].

Miloš was transferred to a prison in Zenica, and his son was released the following day. He asserts that his son was later kicked out of his apartment but did not specify by whom. Miloš described the treatment and conditions in the Zenica prison, which he referred to as "a camp:"

> Then they took me to the camp; I was there for five months. The camp is a former prison. The camp was bad [and] the food was bad. At night, they would take you down to the basement and beat you. There were

---

[124] Interviewed by Helsinki Watch representatives on January 18, 1992, at the Mikulja refugee camp near Smederevska Palanka, Serbia, Yugoslavia. The witness chose to withhold his name, and the name used here is a pseudonym.

[125] The Patriotic League is one of several paramilitary groups with weak ties to the Bosnian Army that operates in Muslim-controlled areas of Bosnia-Hercegovina.

fifty-two of us in the room and they would pick several — "you, you and you." Mostly, they kicked us. There were several inches of water on the basement floor. There were six or seven of them; they didn't say anything but they wanted us to admit that we had weapons and to tell them where the weapons were [being kept].

Miloš reported that three women also were detained in the prison, but that they were not mistreated. He said that one of the women had been accused of being a sniper. The women were taken from the prison but Miloš did not know their fate or whereabouts. Miloš surmised that between 250 to 300 men, of an average age of twenty-five, were still held in the Zenica prison at the time of his release in late November or early December.

ABUSES BY CROATIAN AND MUSLIM FORCES

Forced Displacement

Bradina

Gordana, a thirty-six-year-old Serbian woman,[126] had worked as a cashier at a bank in Sarajevo. She is not married and does not have any children. Her family lived in the village of Bradina, which is thirteen kilometers from Sarajevo. Gordana was visiting her family in Bradina when the siege of Sarajevo commenced, so she could not return to her home in the city and remained in the village.

Gordana said that members of her family were scattered about the village at the time of the attack on Bradina. She acknowledged that she was not present when her brother — who appears to have been a combatant — was arrested. Nevertheless, Gordana stated that the Bosnian

---

[126] Interviewed by Helsinki Watch representatives on October 25, 1992, in Bosnia-Hercegovina. The witness chose to withhold her name, and the name used here is a pseudonym.

army and "probably" HOS arrested her brother and several other men who had surrendered.[127] According to Gordana:

> [My brother is detained] probably because he's a Serb. He didn't want to join the Bosnian Army. He was arrested in his village. Everyone armed their own village. All the young men were arrested. They[128] told us to guard our village, but they came and surrounded the village.

Gordana explained her forced displacement from Bradina and the destruction of her family's home. She said that she did not see the houses burned in her village. However, her testimony suggests that Bosnian troops forced people from a shelter in an apartment building and ordered them to return to their homes to gather their belongings. According to Gordana:

> We don't have our house anymore. My house had been burned and I had to leave. Some army or police forces burned it. They didn't physically abuse us, but they burned our houses. The first attack took place on May 25. After May 26, most of the men fled.
>
> The second attack took place on July 12. We were in a private apartment and we couldn't see who burned the houses. We were in the garage — in the shelter — because of the attack. The men were not with us, but my brother came later. While we were in the garage, the TO burned our house. There had been some incident where nine police officers were killed and, for retribution, they came and told us to get out of our houses. We took a few rags [i.e., belongings].

---

[127] At the time of Helsinki Watch's visit, the witness did not report that her brother was being mistreated in detention in the Konjic sports hall. See section above for her comments.

[128] It is unclear if the witness is referring here to Serbian, Croatian or Bosnian authorities.

Soldiers with a *ljiljan* [i.e., a *fleur-de-lis*][129] came in a police car. I knew one of the soldiers. A second soldier came into the room. They did not have a warrant. He shot in the air with an automatic weapon.... The village's men had been taken away long ago, and they put the women and the children in the school.

Gordana claims that, while the women and children were detained in the local school, Bosnian and, possibly, Croatian forces continued to burn Serbian homes in Bradina. Gordana said she did not see any of the burned houses because she was taken to the Muslim- and Croatian-controlled municipality of Konjic after the fall of her village:

We were not in the school for long, though. We were taken to another building and they asked us where we wanted to go.

The witness and her family asked to be transferred to a village in the municipality of Konjic, where they stayed in the home of a family friend. Gordana said that others detained in the school were evacuated from Bradina by train.

Pillaging and Destruction of Villages and Cultural Objects

Čapljina

Helsinki Watch has received reports that Croatian and Muslim forces burned the village of Prebilovac on June 7, 1992. A crypt, containing the remains of victims of the Nazi-aligned Croatian Ustašas of World War II, was allegedly destroyed as well. According to Max Bošković, the commander of the local Serbian militia in the village of Tasovčići in the municipality of Čapljina,[130] a joint Croatian and

---

[129] *Fleurs-de-lis* are part of the Bosnian coat of arms and the insignia by which Bosnian forces are identified.

[130] Interviewed by Helsinki Watch representatives on October 1, 1992, in Belgrade, Yugoslavia. The witness was supplied by the Yugoslav State Commission on War Crimes and Genocide. See also section on methodology in

Muslim armed force[131] attacked military positions in his village on June 7, 1992, from the direction of Metković, in Croatia. According to Bošković:

> We were on armed guard when they attacked us. We fled toward Dubrave, and then Muslim forces from Stolac attacked us. We fled to a mountain, which is about one kilometer away from Prebilovac, and we could see what they were doing in the village. They looted the homes and burned the bones in the crypt. This happened at about 4:00 in the afternoon. In the course of three days, all the Serbian homes in the village were burned.

According to Bošković and a second witness interviewed by Helsinki Watch,[132] Croatian and Muslim forces also destroyed the predominantly Serbian villages of Tasovčići and Klebci in the Čapljina municipality.

Livno and Tomislavgrad

Helsinki Watch representatives interviewed several Serbian residents from the municipalities of Livno and Tomislavgrad who asserted that predominantly Serbian villages and property were destroyed. Serbs held hostage in Raščani claimed that Croatian soldiers, returning from the battle in Vukovar, were responsible for the destruction in the following villages in the municipality of Tomislavgrad: Eminovo Selo,

---

the Introduction to this report.

[131] Bošković asserted that Bosnian Muslim forces, armed forces belonging to the Army of Croatia (HV) and members of the HOS paramilitary group participated in the attack, but that HVO forces were not involved.

[132] Interviewed by Helsinki Watch representatives on October 1, 1992, in Belgrade, Yugoslavia. The witness was supplied by the Yugoslav State Commission on War Crimes and Genocide. See also section on methodology in the Introduction to this report.

Oplećani, Mandino Selo and Lipa. Homes belonging to Serbs in Livno reportedly were also destroyed.[133]

Others interviewed by Helsinki Watch could not identify the perpetrators of the destruction. Most surmised that Croats burned the houses in the villages but were not sure if the arsonists were members of a military, paramiltary or police unit, or civilians.[134]

Bradina

Svetlana, a twenty-five-year-old Serbian mother of a three-year-old daughter from the village of Bradina,[135] lived in Donje Selo for a month after having been displaced from her home. She claims

---

[133] These assertions were made by detainees as hostages in the village of Raščani and by some inmates of Croatian-controlled detention facilities. See the section above for their accounts.

[134] Helsinki Watch representatives interviewed a Serbian resident of Livno who claims that Serbian homes were burned during a Catholic holiday in June. Helsinki Watch is not disclosing the person's name in order to protect him/her from reprisals. The witness acknowledges not being present at the following events contained in his/her testimony but heard that his/her father died as a result of the assault.

> On St. John's Day in June, the Catholics burn fire (*pali se vatre*). That's when the mistreatment of Serbs in Livno began. That's when someone started to burn Serbian houses. Most of the buildings in two villages in the Livno suburbs — Zaštinje and Guber — were burned. My father was killed two or three days later in the village of Zaštinje; he was eighty-three and sick. I heard of his death from other[s]. He appears to have been beaten to death with a blunt object.

Helsinki Watch was not able to corroborate independently this hearsay testimony.

[135] Interviewed by Helsinki Watch representatives on October 6, 1992, in Belgrade, Yugoslavia. The witness was seven months pregnant at the time of the interview. The witness was supplied by the Yugoslav State Commission on War Crimes and Genocide. She withheld her name, and the name used here is a pseudonym. See also the section on methodology in the Introduction to this report.

that she returned to her home in late August or September, to find that it had been burned and looted. According to Svetlana:

> While I was in Donje Selo, I went back to my house in Bradina. My house had been burned but not completely. I saw that many of my belongings had been taken. During the first attack on the village of Bradina [on May 25], I saw them burn the houses and cattle [while carrying] little cans. It was done purposely. Only Muslims were involved and I saw this with my own eyes.

Mostar

N.S., a fifty-six-year-old Serbian accountant from Mostar,[136] was arrested in his apartment the evening of July 16, 1992, by HOS forces. He was subsequently detained in Mostar, Dretelj, Ljubuški and, again, in Mostar.[137]

During his second detention in Mostar, N.S. reported that prisoners had to collect the debris of destroyed Serbian villages in the area. According to N.S.:

> We were held in a former military high school that was used as a HVO prison. Some of the guards were Dragan Rebac, Ivica Pujić, Vinko and Dragan Sesar. We awoke at 6:00 a.m. and went to bed at 9:00 p.m. We worked every day, mostly on clearing the destroyed buildings in the Serbian villages of Buna and Ortjes. We collected usable construction materials and we also packed bags full of sand for the Croatian frontlines. It was difficult work — more difficult for us because we were hungry.

---

[136] Interviewed by Helsinki Watch representatives on February 8, 1993, in Belgrade, Yugoslavia.

[137] For an account of the witness's treatment by HOS forces in Dretelj and a former military clinic in Mostar, see relevant section above. The witness also was detained in HVO-operated detention facilities in Mostar and Ljubuški, where he said that he had not been mistreated.

N.S. was released in a prisoner exchange on October 30, in the town of Zelenika, under the auspices of the ICRC.

Livno

Nebojša,[138] a sixty-two-year-old Serbian salesman from Livno, had been in detention since May 25, 1992, at the time of Helsinki Watch's visit in October. Nebojša said that, on his way to work duty one day, he asked the guards to take him to his house, and they obliged. He claims that his house had been looted. According to Nebojša:

> They took everything from the house — right down to the light switches and the floorboards. I couldn't bear to look; everything was taken away. I had lived there since 1963.

Željko[139] was arrested on August 9 in the town of Livno. He reported to have been wealthy and claimed that five of his houses had been burned. He said that his brother was burned in his home on August 5, 1992, but that the perpetrators remain unknown. He was arrested the previous April, when interethnic tensions surfaced in Livno:

> We were told that all three parties [i.e., Serbs, Muslims and Croats] were arming themselves, though we weren't sure ourselves. I accepted a weapon from the [Serbian Democratic] party but I surrendered it when the police came to search for weapons. It was a rifle. They asked for weapons, I gave [the rifle] to them and, at that point, I was arrested and brought here. I used to live here with my wife, son, daughter-in-law and grandchild, but they all left Livno before the fighting started. I thought nothing was going to happen, but my son, a salesman,

---

[138] Interviewed by Helsinki Watch representatives in October 1992 in Livno, Bosnia-Hercegovina. The name used here is a pseudonym to protect the witness.

[139] Interviewed by Helsinki Watch representatives in October 1992 in Livno, Bosnia-Hercegovina. The name used here is a pseudonym to protect the safety of the witness.

lost his job. We lost our jobs because we were Serbs lots of people did, beginning in April.

I had a house with two floors, a car, a garage — it was all stolen or burned while I've been in jail. The most houses were burned in this part of Livno, and only a few remain — only those where someone was actually in the house.

Fighting Between Croatian and Muslim Forces in Central Bosnia

Helsinki Watch is concerned that abuses of the rules of war have taken place during the October 1992 and January 1993 fighting between HVO troops and Bosnian Army forces.

Full-scale combat between Croatian and Muslim forces first erupted in October 1992[140] and continues sporadically and with varying intensity. Helsinki Watch is concerned that heavy artillery and, in particular, antiaircraft guns, have been used against civilian targets by both Muslim and Croatian forces in the October 1992 and January 1993 battles. Helsinki Watch representatives were in western Bosnia when the fighting between Bosnian Croats and Muslims broke out in October but were unable to travel beyond Konjic toward central Bosnia. Helsinki Watch therefore has not completely investigated reports of abuses by either Croatian or Muslim forces but intends to do so on future missions.

The reason for the outbreak of fighting in October remains unclear. Some claim that HVO forces attacked the Muslim forces as a reprisal for the killing of two HVO soldiers. Others claim that a dispute concerning the division of weapons and fuel led to the fighting. Most of the fighting in October was centered around the towns of Novi Travnik and Prozor, although gun battles were fought in various enclaves in

---

[140] Conflicts between Croatian and Muslim troops and paramilitaries had taken place earlier, particularly in or near Sarajevo. The conflicts appear to have been caused by disagreements on how to divide black-market goods and did not involve sustained artillery attacks, as was the case in October 1992 and January 1993. Bosnian Muslim troops have argued with HVO forces over the latter's unwillingness to help break the siege of Sarajevo.

west-central Bosnia. According to foreign journalists[141] who traveled to the Prozor region in October, Croatian forces attacked civilian targets in Prozor, possibly with the intent to displace the Muslim population.

According to the journalists, on October 23, HVO forces began shelling the Muslim parts of the town of Prozor, one-third of whose population of 15,000 were Muslim. When the reporters went through the town several days after the attack, virtually all Muslims had left the city, though reports indicated that some remained in the suburbs. The reporters encountered hundreds of civilians in the hills above Prozor, where they had been wandering for days without food or shelter. The civilians were on a side road (near the village of Grančanica), off the main road linking Prozor with Jablanica. These people were wandering around the small, hillside villages. One woman reportedly stated that she was looking for a cave in which her family could take shelter.[142]

In January 1993, under the joint auspices of the European Community and the United Nations, a Conference on Yugoslavia, co-chaired by Cyrus Vance and Lord David Owen, proposed a map which would reconstitute Bosnia-Hercegovina into a loose confederation of ten separate provinces. One of the three main constituent groups would retain primary control in nine of the proposed provinces and the tenth region, an area around the city of Sarajevo, would be declared a free zone. Bosnia-Hercegovina would be governed by a transitional

---

[141] Helsinki Watch representatives spoke to journalists from the Associated Press and Reuters after they returned to Split, Croatia, from the Prozor area in Bosnia-Hercegovina.

[142] A Helsinki Watch representative who was in Konjic during the fighting in Prozor witnessed extreme tensions between HVO and Bosnian Army forces in the town. At the same time, Serbian forces began shelling the town. Muslims in the area were frightened and many remained in their homes and were preparing to flee. Both the foreign journalists and Helsinki Watch representatives returned to Split, Croatia, from two separate points in Bosnia, where relations between Muslims and Croats were tense and abuses against Muslims were becoming evident. Nevertheless, upon their arrival in Split, they saw misleading news reports on Croatian Television about the fighting in and around Prozor. The television reports tried to smooth over the tensions and to minimize the damage done to Muslim areas. The television accounts did not correspond with what Helsinki Watch, Reuters, and Associated Press representatives witnessed in those areas.

nine-member, multiethnic council until elections could take place throughout the country.[143]

Under a Bosnian peace proposal presented by Cyrus Vance and Devid Owen, U.N. and E.C. negotiators for the former Yugoslavia, co-chairmern of the joint U.N.-E.C. sponsored International Conference on the Former Yugoslavia, Croats and Muslims would be represented in two south-central provinces, although Croats would be in the majority and, therefore, primary power would reside in their hands. After the proposed map of these provinces was released in January 1993, Bosnian Croat military leaders demanded that Bosnian Muslim troops submit to their authority in areas where Croats were a majority and that, according to the Vance-Owen plan, would come under Croatian control. The Bosnian Muslims refused, and fighting between the two forces commenced in Gornji Vakuf and then spread eastward, toward Kiseljak and Busovača.[144] During the January fighting between Muslim and Croatian forces in central Bosnia, press reports indicated that Croatian forces "attacked and burned villages in Busovača in an effort to drive Muslims from the area."[145]

Attacks on Aid Convoys

Vitez

On October 20, U.N. relief workers came under attack near the town of Vitez, near Zenica and Travnik. The aid workers were caught in cross fire between Croatian and Bosnian forces. That evening, four U.N.

---

[143] John F. Burns, "Dim Hope for Bosnia," *The New York Times*, January 23, 1993.

[144] John F. Burns, "Croats vs. Serbs vs. Muslims: Guns Define Borders," *The New York Times*, February 1, 1993.

[145] *Ibid.*

armored personnel carriers, manned by French troops, set out to rescue the relief party.[146]

ABUSES BY SERBIAN FORCES

Forced Displacement

Trebinje

Trebinje is one of the largest towns in the Serbian-controlled area of eastern Hercegovina.[147] It has been under the control of Serbian forces since the fall of 1991, when it was used as a major command and artillery base by Yugoslav and Serbian troops attacking Dubrovnik in Croatia. During that time, according to the predominantly Muslim Party for Democratic Action (SDA), an estimated five hundred Muslim men fled the region to avoid being drafted by the Yugoslav Army (JNA). Others were conscripted and fought with JNA forces in Croatia and, later, in Bosnia-Hercegovina.

As the political crisis mounted in Bosnia, Trebinje was declared the seat of the self-proclaimed "Serbian Autonomous Region of Eastern Hercegovina" (*Srpska Autonomna Oblast Istočne Hercegovine*, hereinafter "SAO Eastern Hercegovina.")[148] The government of self-declared SAO Eastern Hercegovina is headed by Božidar Vučurević, the local leader of the Serbian Democratic Party [SDS] and of Trebinje's municipal government.

According to the SDA, another thousand Muslims, mostly draft-age men, fled Trebinje when the war erupted in Bosnia. However,

---

[146] John F. Burns, "U.N. May Have to Close a Key Relief Warehouse," *The New York Times*, October 21, 1992 and Peter Maass, "Muslim-Croat Battle Halts Sarajevo Airlift," *The Washington Post*, October 22, 1992.

[147] Prior to the war, the municipality of Trebinje had a population of 30,879: 69.3 percent Serbs, 17.9 percent Muslims and 4 percent Croats.

[148] Prior to the wars in Bosnia and Croatia, Serbian insurgent leaders proclaimed the establishment of Serbian "autonomous regions" in both republics. These "autonomous regions" later were unified as part of the "Serbian Republic of Krajina" and the "Serbian Republic of Bosnia-Hercegovina."

most of Trebinje's Muslim men spent up to eleven months fighting with the local Serbs against local Croats and other Muslims. These Muslims also fought against regular Croatian Army troops (i.e., from Croatia proper) that drove Serbian forces back from the Dubrovnik area in November 1992.

Helsinki Watch representatives interviewed Ekrem, a Muslim resident of Trebinje and a member of the Yugoslav Army (JNA).[149] Ekrem was mobilized into the JNA in November 1991 and was sent to Mostar, and participated on the side of Serbian and Yugoslav forces attacking Dubrovnik. He returned home to Trebinje in June 1992, only to join the Yugoslav Army again during the war in Bosnia-Hercegovina. Although Ekrem stated that he voluntarily joined the JNA in June 1992, he implied that he did so under pressure from local Serbian authorities in Trebinje. He refused to use a weapon and was assigned the post of telephone and radio operator with his battalion. He was captured by Bosnian Muslim forces and detained in the HVO-operated central prison in Mostar.[150] Ekrem described the conditions in Trebinje in late 1991 and 1992:

> I'm apolitical and I have a wife and two children. The political situation in Trebinje was such that I wasn't forcibly told I had to go into the army, but indirectly I had to join — my wife was fired from her job, local pressure, things like that. In Trebinje, the Serbian Democratic Party (SDS) was powerful. In the "SAO Hercegovina" at the end of April or in early May 1992, pressure and police raids took place. People were forcibly mobilized — they were grabbed while in a cafe. They couldn't fill up their ranks, so they needed more men.

When Ekrem returned from his four-month tour of duty in Mostar, he did not have a job and implied that he rejoined the JNA for economic reasons, as well as in reponse to local pressure.

---

[149] Interviewed on October 24, 1992, in Mostar, Bosnia-Hercegovina. The witness chose to withhold his name, and the name used here is a pseudonym.

[150] For an account of the witness's treatment in the central Mostar prison, see relevant section above.

At first, I was mobilized for four months in the Mostar area, and then I went home to Trebinje but I had no work; the economy was in shambles. So I rejoined again in April [1992].

Between April and June 15, I went home intermittently, and the situation got worse. On May 19, 1992, the JNA ceased to exist and passed over the [local] Serbian [militia].

When asked if any changes took place after nominal withdrawal of the JNA from Bosnia in May 1992, Ekrem replied:

The changes made were that we no longer had a star on our hat. The active officers went back to Serbia but the reservists remained, particularly those from Nevesinje. Later, they were all locals.

In January 1993, Serbian troops began to harass and forcibly displace Trebinje's Muslims. Muslims interviewed by Helsinki Watch representatives claim that the forcible displacement of Trebinje's Muslims was in response to the proposed Vance-Owen peace plan, which seeks to divide Bosnia-Hercegovina into ten semiautonomous units each dominated by a particular ethnic group. Under the plan, Trebinje would be Serbian dominated. Many of the Muslims interviewed by Helsinki Watch representatives[151] claim that Serbian authorities sought to consolidate their control over Trebinje, ridding the area of its non-Serbian population.[152] Those Muslim men who fought on the Serbian side were all demobilized and disarmed.

Mme. Sadako Ogata, the United Nations High Commissioner for Refugees, expressed concern about the situation in Trebinje publicly and raised the matter with Radovan Karadžić, the leader of the Bosnian Serbs. Karadžić ordered the deployment of special police units from Pale (the seat of government for the self-proclaimed "Serbian Republic") to

---

[151] Interviewed from February 4 through 6, 1993, in Yugoslavia.

[152] See also Chuck Sudetic, "Serbs Expel 4,000 from Bosnian Town," *The New York Times*, February 7, 1993.

Trebinje, allegedly to protect Muslims in the area. According to UNHCR officials, the special police were withdrawn from Trebinje and sent to front line positions after the Croatian Army launched its surprise offensive against Serbian-occupied territory in Croatia in late January. This permitted local Serbian militia forces to renew their harassment of Muslims.

The Muslims interviewed by Helsinki Watch representatives cited several examples of harassment: threatening phone calls, hand-grenades thrown into their yards and Serbian soldiers barging into Muslim homes and confiscating money, gold, cars and furniture. Reportedly, on or about January 27, the Osman Pasha Mosque, the largest in Trebinje, was burned down. Muslim homes, shops and cultural and religious monuments also were burned. On January 25, Muslims staged a protest in front of Vučurević's office in the city council building, demanding protection from further attacks. In a public speech, Vučurević reportedly responded that the local government was not able to secure the safety of Muslims. This sparked an exodus of approximately four thousand Muslims from Trebinje.[153] Reportedly, several hundred Muslims remain in the Trebinje area.

Enisa, a forty-one-year-old Muslim housewife,[154] believed that the Muslims in Trebinje would not be threatened or expelled because most of the Muslim men — including her husband — had complied with Serbian mobilization orders and served in Serbian armed forces. According to Enisa:

> I lived in a state-owned apartment complex in which several Muslim families lived. For Serbian New Year, [i.e., January 13], they were yelling in front of the house. They said that we should not wait any longer to leave and that they would rape us. They were shooting in the air.

---

[153] Chuck Sudetic, "Serbs Expel 4,000 from Bosnian Town," *The New York Times*, February 7, 1993.

[154] Interviewed by Helsinki Watch representatives on February 5, 1993, in Yugoslavia. The witness chose to withhold her name, and the name used here is a pseudonym.

On January 29, many Muslims protested in front of the town hall because some of the Muslim neighborhoods already had been "cleansed." We wanted guarantees [for our safety]. They [i.e., the Serbian authorities] said that they did not insist that we leave, but that they could not guarantee our safety.

Enisa claimed that several police formations operated in Trebinje. Muslims who sought protection from attacks would approach these police forces, but no security was provided. According to Enisa:

There were five police groups [operating in Trebinje]: the military police, the regular civilian police, special police forces from Pale, the party police of the Serbian Democratic Party [SDS] and some others. You didn't know who was who. If anyone tried to seek protection from one police group, they would tell them to try the others. No one was responsible.

All the Muslims took their names off their front doors. Some people — civilians — came to my front door and said they were going to move in. I managed to sell a few things from my apartment: a new washing machine for one hundred German marks.

A.R., a twenty-three-year-old laborer,[155] supported Enisa's report about the array of Serbian police forces in Trebinje. According to A.R.:

When my garage was set on fire, I called the police. They said they could not do anything, and they gave me the number of the other police. By the time I had called them all, my garage had burned down. The police of the "Serbian Republic" cooperate with the paramilitary formations, and none of those police officers protect Muslims and Croats because they are all Serbs.

---

[155] Interviewed by Helsinki Watch representatives on February 5, 1993, in Yugoslavia.

> In October 1992, murders and looting started. Police arrived from Pale. They acted correctly, but they left later. Some other police came recently, and they were harassing people. [Paramilitary leader Vojislav] Šešelj's men were also there — the "White Eagles" — and some volunteers, mostly from Serbia, but some were from Montenegro.
>
> Apartments were broken into. Property was inventoried, and some was taken away. The mosque was burned down on January 27. I sold my two cars, and I left.

F.K., a thirty-three-year-old mechanic,[156] had fought with Serbian forces in Croatia in the summer of 1992. He was captured by Croatian forces in July[157] and returned to Trebinje after a prisoner exchange. According to F.K.:

> We were disappointed after we returned to Trebinje. We found that our families were being harassed and they were told that we had joined the Ustaša and that we were drinking coffee in Dubrovnik [when, in fact, we had been fighting and imprisoned in Croatia].
>
> The harassment got worse in January [1993]. Some Serbs from Trebinje risked their lives to protect us. They slept in our houses with us. I put my Serbian friend's name on my door a week before I left. [A Serbian man][158] was

---

[156] Interviewed by Helsinki Watch representatives on February 5, 1993, in Yugoslavia.

[157] The witness claims that he was wounded during the fighting, captured by Croatian forces and taken to the military hospital in Split, Croatia. He was then transferred to the Croatian military prison in the Lora port in Split, where he was a victim of, and eyewitness to, the beating of prisoners by guards.

[158] Helsinki Watch is not releasing the name of the individual, in order to protect him from reprisals, but retains his name and profession in a secure place outside its office.

protecting the Muslims, and somebody threw a hand grenade at him.

All the Muslim houses were shot at, and our cars were smashed. The mosque was burned. I decided to leave when my cousin's house was set afire. I called the military police four times. I called a fifth time, and they told me that I would burn with my house if I called them again.

Several people interviewed by Helsinki Watch confirmed that paramilitary and vigilante violence was rife in Trebinje. According to Velida, a retired fifty-four-year-old Muslim woman:[159]

> I lived by myself and had decided to stay in Trebinje. Two men came to my door last Saturday [i.e., January 30] — one was in uniform, the other was a civilian. One held a gun to my chest and said, "Give us the keys. The apartment is ours or I will shoot." The civilian used to work in the same factory as I.[160] He said he needed an apartment.
>
> They came back a couple of times over the next few hours, and then I left. I grabbed a few personal belongings and fled to my sister's house.

According to Velida's sister, Aziza:[161]

---

[159] Interviewed by Helsinki Watch representatives on February 6, 1993. The witness chose to withhold her name, and the name used here is a pseudonym. This witness asked that the place of the interview remain confidential, and that information is kept in secure files outside Helsinki Watch's office.

[160] The witness did not wish to identify the accused.

[161] Interviewed by Helsinki Watch representatives on February 6, 1993. The witness chose to withhold her name, and the name used here is a pseudonym. This witness asked that the place of the interview remain confidential, and that information is kept in secure files outside Helsinki Watch's office.

They were shooting every night, and all the Muslim shops were destroyed. Five men — they had two teeth between them — came to my house a week ago, and I sold them my bedroom furniture for one hundred German marks. Those who had apartments already were buying furniture from us for very little money, and those who moved into Trebinje — i.e., Serbian displaced persons — were seizing apartments and houses.

A few days later, five other Četniks came, saying that they wanted to "cleanse" Trebinje of Ustašas. One was friendlier and suggested that we convert to the Orthodox religion. They gave us a few hours to leave, and one of them said, "Put my name on the door."

Mustafa, a Muslim man,[162] had recently returned from the battlefield where he had fought on behalf of Serbian forces. Faced with harassment in Trebinje, he chose to leave the area. To leave, he had to relinquish his weapons and obtain a pass which permitted his exit from the municipality. According to Mustafa:

I received a receipt for returning my weapon from the army. After I was given a receipt, I received permission to leave town. I left the town twenty-four hours after leaving the front. I tried to drive, but I was stopped. They wanted to take my car. I told them I needed it and they replied, "You need your head even more."

Enisa claims that, on January 31, five buses from the Autoprevost Trebinje bus company left Trebinje with Muslim residents. She claims that each bus ticket cost 106,000 dinars [about U.S. $15 at the time of Helsinki Watch's interview]. According to Enisa:

---

[162] Interviewed by Helsinki Watch representatives on February 6, 1993. The witness chose to withhold his name, age and occupation, and the name used here is a pseudonym. This witness asked that the place of the interview remain confidential, and that information is kept in secure files outside Helsinki Watch's office.

We could not bring anything with us. The buses were searched on the border with Montenegro. Men had to have passes from the president [of the local town council, i.e., Božidar Vučurević] in order to leave the area.

Summary Executions

Trebinje

Helsinki Watch representatives interviewed several people who claim that three Muslim civilians were summarily executed in Trebinje. None of those interviewed witnessed the executions, but the following witness claims to have heard the gunshots and the arriving ambulance.

Mizreta is a thirty-five-year-old electrical engineer from the village of Pridvorci, approximately four kilometers from Trebinje.[163] She reported that, in January, a Serbian teacher, Veljko Popović, scolded a Muslim student, Adis Topčibašić, for having long hair. The student's brother, Elvis Topčibašić, was fighting with Serbian forces at the time and went to see the teacher. He asked Popović to stop bothering his brother about the length of his hair. This apparently started a feud and involved members of the local armed forces.

According to the witnesses interviewed by Helsinki Watch, Veljko Popović and four men in uniform — one armed — drove in a car without license plates to the house of the boy's uncle, Hasan Topčibašić. The uncle mistakenly believed that they had come to search the house. He showed them a piece of paper stating that he would be relieved of military duty in three days. Popović and the four other uniformed men allegedly tore up the document, killed the family dog and threatened to kill Hasan and his family. Popović and the four men then ordered Hasan to show them the house of his brother, Huso — presumably the father of Popović's student, Adis. According to Mizreta:

---

[163] Interviewed by Helsinki Watch representatives on February 4, 1993, in Yugoslavia. The witness chose to withhold her name, and the name used here is a pseudonym. This witness asked that the place of the interview remain confidential, and that information is kept in secure files outside Helsinki Watch's office.

[When they arrived at Huso's house,] Huso and his wife, Hatidža, ran out of their house. But, they ran straight into the four soldiers, who shot all three of them. Huso died later that night. Hasan died on the spot and Hatidža died a day later.

Hasan's wife, Milena, is a Serb, but she did not see this. We called the police. Two special police officers came. One of them was Jugoslav Tabaković, from Bileća. He and his group searched Muslim houses and took their weapons. He searched my house as well. The investigation never went any further.

Indiscriminate and Disproportionate Use of Force

Mostar

The battles in Mostar[164] were fiercest during the early stages of the war — especially in April and May — and have continued, to varying degrees, until the present. The battles in April and May were fought between HVO and Bosnian Muslim forces on the one hand, and Yugoslav Army (JNA) and Serbian militia forces on the other. The JNA had a strong presence in Mostar prior to the war, and many of the attacks on Mostar's city center were launched from the JNA's southern barracks in Mostar.

Croatian and Muslim forces attacked military targets in Mostar in April and May 1992.[165] The JNA and Serbian forces responded by

---

[164] Prior to the war, the population of the municipality of Mostar was 34.8 percent Muslim, 33.8 percent Croatian and 19 percent Serbian. Ten percent identified themselves as Yugoslavs.

[165] See Chuck Sudetic, "Croat Towns Bombed in Bosnia and Herzegovina," *The New York Times*, April 8, 1992; "General Blames Road Blocks on Mostar Clashes," Belgrade Radio Broadcast on April 15, 1992, at 1300 hours, as translated and reprinted in Foreign Broadcasting Information Service (hereinafter FBIS), April 16, 1992, p.30; "Army Launches Artillery Attack on Mostar," Sarajevo Radio Broadcast on April 19, 1992, at 1700 hours, as translated and reprinted in FBIS,

attacking civilian targets in Mostar and other areas in Hercegovina.[166] After the JNA's nominal withdrawal from Bosnia in mid-May, Serbian "irregulars, armed with heavy weapons left to them by the Yugoslav Army as it withdrew," attacked the Muslim quarter of the city, forcing many to flee. After Serbian forces had forced the flight of Muslims in part of the city, they began shelling the Croatian quarter, across the Neretva River.[167] The Croats armed themselves and, with reinforcements from

---

April 20, 1992, p. 30; "Shelling 'Systematically Destroying' Mostar," Sarajevo Radio Broadcast on April 29, 1992 at 700 hours, as translated and reprinted in FBIS, April 29, 1992, p.38; "Sporadic Fighting Rocks Bosnia and Croatia," Reuters Information Services, April 29, 1992; and "'Infantry Clashes' Continue," Belgrade Radio Broadcast on May 6, 1992, at 1300 hours, as translated and reprinted in FBIS, May 6, 1992, p. 34.

[166] See Chuck Sudetic, "Croat Towns Bombed in Bosnia and Herzegovina," *The New York Times*, April 8, 1992; John F. Burns, "Truce Collapsing in Yugoslav Area," *The New York Times*, April 30, 1992; "Army, Serbian Territorial Units Shell Mostar," Tanjug Yugoslav News Agency, May 1, 1992, as translated and reprinted in FBIS, May 1, 1992, p. 29; and M. Sutalo, "Situation Update in Mostar as JNA Leaves," *Borba*, April 17, 1992, as translated and reprinted in FBIS, May 15, 1992, pp. 33-34.

A JNA officer stationed in the Mostar barracks during the attack on the city subsequently switched his allegiance and joined the Bosnian forces. According to the officer, villages in the municipalities of Stolac and Čapljina were attacked and then looted by JNA reserve officers. According to the officer:

> After the tank unit under my command pushed through the defense lines, the reservist units followed. They looted house after house in Divolje Brdo, Domanovići and other villages.

(See M. Sutalo, "Situation Update in Mostar as JNA Leaves," *Borba*, April 17, 1992, as translated and reprinted in FBIS, May 15, 1992. See also Maristela Lucić, "JNA Colonel Switches Allegiance to Bosnia," *Borba*, April 16, 1992, as translated and reprinted in FBIS, May 15, 1992, pp. 34-35.)

[167] Stephen Kinzer, "A Bosnian City is Rubble, and Riven by Hate," *The New York Times*, August 19, 1992.

Croatia proper, they forced back Serbian troops attacking Mostar.[168] Serbian forces were dislodged from their positions by mid-June and retreated to the surrounding hills, from where they continue to shell Mostar. Before withdrawing from their positions in the city, the Serbian troops reportedly "planted explosives under six of the town's seven bridges and detonated them by remote control."[169]

Like the siege of Sarajevo, the indiscriminate and disproportionate use of force in Mostar left much of the city — particularly the Muslim quarter — in ruins. Muslims who returned to their homes in Mostar after the siege was broken reportedly were so enraged by the destruction that they set ablaze a Serbian Orthodox Church.[170] According to foreign journalists, Serbian forces had destroyed "six bridges, burned hundreds of homes and businesses and wrecked both of the principal religious centers, a modern Catholic cathedral and a stately fifteenth-century mosque."[171] The fighting induced over three-fourths of Mostar's population to flee the city. In three months' time, 90,000 of the city's 120,000 residents had fled as a result of the attacks.[172]

---

[168] *Ibid.*

[169] *Ibid.*

[170] *Ibid.*

[171] *Ibid.*

[172] Michael T. Kaufman, "A Bridge Over Bosnia's Desperation," *The New York Times*, July 13, 1992.

Appendix A

**Memorandum of Law
Elements of the International Crime of
"Crimes Against Humanity"
Applied in the Former Yugoslavia**

Human Rights Watch (HRW), of which Helsinki Watch is a division, understands the legal elements of the crime under customary international law known as "crimes against humanity" as follows.[1]

Crimes against humanity are defined as:

> (i) Such crimes as murder, extermination, enslavement, deportation, and rape, and other similarly inhumane acts; or
> (ii) persecutions on political, racial, or religious grounds, but which are carried out by means of crimes either the same as or of a nature not less serious than the crimes described in (i);
> (iii) committed against any civilian population whether in conformity with or in violation of domestic law governing such civilians; and
> (iv) committed on a mass scale.

This definition is drawn from the Charter of the International Military Tribunal (the "Nuremberg Tribunal"), article 6(c), which reads as follows:

> [Crimes against humanity are] murder, extermination, enslavement, deportation, and other inhumane acts committed against any civilian population, before or during the war, or persecutions on political, racial, or religious grounds in execution of or in connection with any crime within the jurisdiction of the Tribunal,

---

[1] For an example of HRW making a finding of crimes against humanity in another setting — the treatment of the Kurds in Iraq — see Middle East Watch/ Physicians for Human Rights, *The Anfal Campaign in Iraqi Kurdistan: The Destruction of Koreme*, January 1993.

whether or not in violation of the domestic law of the country where perpetrated."[2]

The definition in (i) to (iv) above takes into account limiting interpretations of certain terms in the final Judgment of the Nuremberg Tribunal, as well as limitations of certain terms found in the decisions of other Second World War Allied war crimes tribunals interpreting similar language. It is thus narrower than the definition in article 6(c) would otherwise provide.[3] Rape is specifically enumerated as a crime in (i), rather than being a crime included by reference to "other inhumane acts" as in the article 6(c) definition, under the precedent of Allied Control Council Law No. 10's definition of crimes against humanity, which formed the jurisdictional charter and substantive law of the secondary Nuremberg war crimes tribunals. Control Council Law No. 10 specifically enumerates rape, and remains precedent today.[4]

It is the opinion of HRW that the definition of crimes against humanity does not include a necessary connection to war or armed conflict, meaning that it is possible for adjudicable crimes against humanity to occur in times of peace. HRW believes that the Nuremberg Tribunal's refusal to adjudicate alleged crimes against German nationals — e.g., German Jews — by the German government prior to the outbreak of war in 1939 was by reason of the Nuremberg Tribunal's understanding of the limits of its jurisdiction under the Nuremberg Charter, and not

---

[2] Article 6(c) of the Nuremberg Charter, as amended by the Berlin Protocol, 59 Stat. 1546, 1547 (1945), E.A.S. No. 472, 82 U.N.T.S. 284.

[3] The scholarly literature on crimes against humanity is voluminous. See generally Bassiouni, "International Law and the Holocaust," 9 *Cal. West. Int'l. L.J.* 201 (1979); Schwelb, "Crimes Against Humanity," 23 *Brit. Y.B. Int'l.L.* 178 (1946); and Clark, "Crimes Against Humanity," *The Nuremberg Trial and International Law*, ed. Ginsburgs and Kudriartser (1990)("Clark").

[4] See Orentlicher, "Settling Accounts: The Duty to Prosecute Human Rights Violations of a Prior Regime," 100 *Yale L.J.* 2537, 2585 (1991) ("Orentlicher"). Rape, in any case, is a war crime and an "inhumane act" within the meaning of article 6(c); that rape is liable to prosecution as a grave breach of the Geneva Conventions of 1949 and the 1977 Protocol I Additional to the 1949 Geneva Conventions as well as actionable as a constituent crime of crimes against humanity and genocide is axiomatic.

because it understood crimes against humanity, as an international crime, to exist by definition only in time of war. A tribunal otherwise competent to hear crimes against humanity is not disabled solely on the ground that the acts alleged as crimes against humanity did not occur in connection with war. The so-called "war-nexus" is thus not included in the definition of crimes against humanity appearing in the text above.[5]

The war in Bosnia-Hercegovina is today an international armed conflict, and so the controversy over the so-called "war nexus" does not arise, except insofar as prosecution is sought for acts otherwise meeting the definition of crimes against humanity occurring prior to the outbreak of international war. In the view of HRW, the definition of crimes against humanity may be applied equally in time of peace as in time of war. The importance of the category of crimes against humanity, and the principle reason it was adjudicated at Nuremberg, was in order to give the Tribunal jurisdiction over crimes committed by a state against its own citizens. Without this category, international adjudication of such crimes as "ethnic cleansing" committed, for example, by the Republic of Serbia against Moslem and ethnic Croat nationals indisputably living in and subject to the sovereignty of the Republic of Serbia may be impaired, because such crimes are not necessarily "war crimes."[6]

The Judgment of the Nuremberg Tribunal and related precedents establish plainly that individuals incur criminal liability for committing crimes against humanity, and that an individual is not shielded from liability for committing crimes against humanity by acting under color of the state. Likewise, individual members of groups, such as armed

---

[5] In support of the view that the "war-nexus" is either no longer legally relevant or was, at the time of the Nuremberg trial, jurisdictional only and not definitional, see Orentlicher at 2590; Clark at 195-6; and the Fourth Report on the Draft Code of Offenses Against the Peace and Security of Mankind by Mr. Doudou Thiam, 38 U.N. GAOR C.4 at 56, U.N. Doc. A/CN.4/398 (1986) ("...the separation of crimes against humanity from war crimes has now become absolute. Today, crimes against humanity can be committed not only within the context of an armed conflict, but also independently of any such conflict.")

[6] It is possible, however, that a tribunal could hold that in an ethnic war, where a state commits abuses against those of its inhabitants of the ethnicity of the enemy, "nationality," for purposes of determining liability for war crimes, may be assessed by ethnicity rather than by residence. In that case, liability for these crimes could be found on a basis alternative to crimes against humanity.

insurgents or militias, that take on attributes of the state thereby subject themselves to criminal liability where they commit crimes that, if committed by agents of a state, would constitute crimes against humanity.

In the view of HRW, organized militias, paramilitary organizations and self-declared states operating in the territory of the former Yugoslavia have either taken on sufficient attributes of the state or are sufficiently agents of a recognized state in the former Yugoslavia that their members are subject to individual criminal liability for crimes against humanity. HRW does not address the question of whether crimes against humanity may only be committed, as a matter of definition, by individuals acting as agents of a state or an organization that has assumed sufficient attributes of a state.

It is the view of HRW that the systematic and widespread crimes committed in the territory of the former Yugoslavia described in the preceding report constitute a sufficiently "mass scale" to be crimes against humanity in many instances, and deserve judicial prosecution against the appropriate parties as such. HRW believes that any international tribunal established by the United Nations or other body ought, under the Nuremberg precedent, to include crimes against humanity as a substantive crime for adjudication. This is particularly important in order that crimes by a state against its own nationals will not go unpunished because they might not fit the definition of "war crimes."

HELSINKI WATCH

Appendix B

☐ 485 FIFTH AVENUE, NEW YORK, NY 10017-6104 TEL (212) 972-8400 FAX (212) 972-0905
☐ 1522 K STREET NW, #910, WASHINGTON, DC 20005-1202 TEL (202) 371-6592 FAX (202) 371-0124

Jonathan Fanton, Chair
Alice H. Henkin, Vice Chair
Jeri Laber, Executive Director
Lois Whitman, Deputy Director
Susan Osnos, Press Director

Robert L. Bernstein, Founding Chair

COMMITTEE
M. Bernard Aidinoff
Roland Algrant
Kenneth Anderson
Hans A. Bethe
Charles Biblowit
Gladys Chang-Brazil
Roberta Cohen
Lori Damrosch
Drew S. Days III
Istvan Deak
Adrian W. DeWind
E.L. Doctorow
F. Robert Dhruv
Stanley Engelstein
Frances Tarlton Farenthold
Alan R. Finberg
Bernard D. Fischman
Marvin E. Frankel
Ellen Futter
Willard Gaylin, M.D.
John Glusman
Victor Gotbaum
Hanna Gray
Jack Greenberg
John Oufreund
Rita E. Hauser
John Hersey
Elizabeth Holtzman
Lawrence Hughes
Susan Jacoby
Tamar Jacoby
Robert James
Anne M. Johnson
Russell Karp
Rhoda Karpatkin
Stephen Kass
Bentley Kassal
Marina Kaufman
Joanne Landy
Margaret A. Lang
Norman Lear
Leon Levy
Leon Lipson
Wendy Luers
Elizabeth J. McCormack
Theodor Meron
Arthur Miller
Toni Morrison
Daniel Nathans
Mathew Nimetz
Eleanor Holmes Norton
John B. Oakes
Jane Olson
Yun Orlov
Bruce Rabb
Shaun Robinowitz
Felix G. Rohatyn
Donna E. Shalala
Stanley K. Sheinbaum
Jerome J. Shestack
Sanford Solender
George Soros
Susan Weber Soros
Michael Sovern
Svetlana Stone
Rose Tyron
Jay Topkis
Liv Ullman
Gregory Wallace
Rosalind Whitehead
Jerome R. Wiesner
Roger Wilkins

August 7, 1992

President George Bush
The White House
Washington D.C. 20010

Dear President Bush:

Helsinki Watch, a division of Human Rights Watch which has closely monitored and reported on the conflicts in Bosnia-Hercegovina and other parts of the former Yugoslavia, calls on the United States to take the lead internationally at the United Nations in seeking action that is "appropriate for the prevention and suppression of acts of genocide" as provided in Article VIII of the 1951 Convention on the Prevention and Punishment of the Crime of Genocide. In addition, we call on the United States to take the lead in calling on the United Nations to establish an international tribunal to investigate, prosecute and punish war crimes, or "grave breaches" of the 1949 Geneva Conventions and the 1977 Protocol. The evidence that Helsinki Watch has gathered from victims and witnesses to the conflict, as well as the reports by the independent media, demonstrate that international action to prevent and suppress genocide in Bosnia-Hercegovina is required; and that those who have the highest level of responsibility for the most egregious war crimes in the conflict must be prosecuted and punished.

Early next week, Helsinki Watch will publish a major report based on investigations that we have conducted in Bosnia-Hercegovina since the beginning of April. Our report documents forcible expulsions, arbitrary detention, disappearances, indiscriminate killing and summary executions that have victimized hundreds of thousands of people on the basis of their religion or ethnicity. Most of our research was undertaken prior to the recent outcry about abusive detention camps. Though we join in the worldwide demand that all these camps must be opened for inspection by the International Committee of the Red Cross in accordance with the Geneva Conventions, our call on you to act decisively to stop the atrocities in Bosnia-Hercegovina is independent of what may be discovered when the truth about these camps is fully

Helsinki Watch is a division of Human Rights Watch   Robert L. Bernstein, Chair • Adrian W. DeWind, Vice Chair • Aryeh Neier, Executive Director
Kenneth Roth, Deputy Director • Holly J. Burkhalter, Washington Director   Helsinki Watch is affiliated with the International Helsinki Federation for Human Rights

known. In our view, the information that Helsinki Watch and the independent media have gathered about "ethnic cleansing," and the manner in which this has been carried out, itself necessitates international action to prevent and suppress genocide and to prosecute and punish war crimes.

In the report that we are now completing for publication, Helsinki Watch will identify some of those whose responsibility for war crimes should be investigated by an international tribunal.

We are pleased that Deputy Secretary of State Lawrence S. Eagleburger issued a public call on August 5 for a war crimes investigation. Though that was a step in the right direction, we believe that more is required. Secretary Eagleburger's call was not coupled, as we believe it should be, by a proposal for the establishment of an international tribunal with authority to prosecute and punish such crimes. The authority that such a tribunal would have is recognized in United States law (see Section 404, Restatement (Third) of the Foreign Relations Law of the United States (1987)) and by the principles that have been accepted in international law since the establishment of the Nuremberg Tribunal in 1945. Also, Secretary Eagleburger did not refer to the Genocide Convention. As a party to the Convention, the United States has committed that it will "undertake to prevent and to punish" this crime (Article I). In addition, the Convention authorizes the United States to call upon the United Nations to take appropriate action under the Charter "for the prevention and suppression of acts of genocide." It should be noted that the Convention specifies that genocide means acts "committed with intent to destroy, in whole or in part, a national, ethnical, racial or religious group (Article II); and that the acts that are punishable under the convention include genocide itself; "conspiracy to commit genocide; direct and public incitement to commit genocide; attempt to commit genocide; complicity in genocide" (Article III).

It is beyond the competence of Helsinki Watch to determine all the steps that may be required to prevent and suppress the crime of genocide. Whether or not military force is required is not our province. Helsinki Watch believes that it is the responsibility of the Security Council to resolve this question. Helsinki Watch's position is that, however the question of military force is resolved, those responsible for genocide and other war crimes must be held accountable for their crimes, and must become aware that they will be held accountable. It is to this end that we call on you to seek action by the United Nations to prevent and suppress genocide and to establish a tribunal to investigate, prosecute and punish war crimes.

Members of the staff of Helsinki Watch have been in touch with the Department of State about the evidence that we have gathered on acts of genocide and other war crimes. We will continue to furnish information to the State Department and trust that this will be useful to you in dealing with these urgent matters.

We look forward to your response to the calls we have made upon you.

Sincerely,

Aryeh Neier
Executive Director
Human Rights Watch

Jeri Laber
Executive Director
Helsinki Watch

HELSINKI WATCH

485 FIFTH AVENUE, NEW YORK, NY 10017-6104 TEL (212) 972-8400 FAX (212) 972-0905
1522 K STREET NW, #910, WASHINGTON, DC 20005-1202 TEL (202) 371-6592 FAX (202) 371-0124

Appendix C

Jonathan Fanton, Chair
Alice H. Henkin, Vice Chair
Jeri Laber, Executive Director
Lois Whitman, Deputy Director
Susan Osnos, Press Director

Robert L. Bernstein, Founding Chair

August 11, 1992

Hon. Boutros Boutros-Ghali
Secretary General
United Nations
New York NY 10017

Dear Mr. Secretary General:

On behalf of Helsinki Watch, a division of Human Rights Watch, we hereby submit to you our report on "War Crimes in Bosnia-Hercegovina," one in a series that Helsinki Watch has published during the past two years on the armed conflicts in the former Yugoslavia. With the publication of this report, we are calling upon the United Nations to take the following measures to stop the commission of war crimes and to hold those responsible for such crimes accountable.

First, in accordance with Article VIII of the 1951 Convention on the Prevention and Punishment of the Crime of Genocide, we call on the United Nations to take action that is "appropriate for the prevention and suppression of acts of genocide." It is beyond the province and competence of Helsinki Watch to say whether military force must be a component of such action. On the other hand, we believe that the United Nations, through the Security Council, should address this question and determine whether military force is required to prevent and suppress genocide.

Second, we call on the United Nations to establish a tribunal to investigate, prosecute, adjudicate and punish war crimes, or "grave breaches of the Geneva Conventions and First Protocol," in Bosnia-Hercegovina in accordance with internationally recognized principles of due process of law.

Our report sets forth the basis for these calls to the United Nations. We stand ready to provide further details, based on the research leading to the publication of this report, to an appropriate United Nations body that might act on these recommendations.

Helsinki Watch is a division of Human Rights Watch   Robert L. Bernstein, Chair • Adrian W. DeWind, Vice Chair • Aryeh Neier, Executive Director
Kenneth Roth, Deputy Director • Holly J. Burkhalter, Washington Director   Helsinki Watch is affiliated with the International Helsinki Federation for Human Rights

Copies of this letter and our report are being sent to all members of the Security Council.

We trust that the United Nations will address these important issues with the urgency that they warrant.

Best regards.

Sincerely,

Aryeh Neier
Executive Director
Human Rights Watch

Jeri Laber
Executive Director
Helsinki Watch

Appendix D

AFRICA WATCH • AMERICAS WATCH
ASIA WATCH • HELSINKI WATCH
MIDDLE EAST WATCH • FUND FOR FREE EXPRESSION

☐ 485 FIFTH AVENUE, NEW YORK, NY 10017-6104 TEL (212) 972-8400 FAX (212) 972-0905 TELEX 910240 1007 FFFEXPSN NY
☐ 1522 K STREET, NW, SUITE 910, WASHINGTON, DC 20005-1202 TEL (202) 371-6592 FAX (202) 371-0124

ROBERT L. BERNSTEIN
Chair
ADRIAN W. DeWIND
Vice Chair
ARYEH NEIER
Executive Director
KENNETH ROTH
Deputy Director
HOLLY J. BURKHALTER
Washington Director
ELLEN LUTZ
California Director
SUSAN OSNOS
Press Director
JEMERA RONE
Counsel

EXECUTIVE DIRECTORS
OF THE
WATCH COMMITTEES

AFRICA WATCH
RAKIYA OMAAR
AMERICAS WATCH
JUAN E. MÉNDEZ
ASIA WATCH
SIDNEY R. JONES
HELSINKI WATCH
JERI LABER
MIDDLE EAST WATCH
ANDREW WHITLEY
THE FUND FOR
FREE EXPRESSION
GARA LAMARCHE

PROJECT DIRECTORS

PRISONERS' RIGHTS
JOANNA WESCHLER
WOMEN'S RIGHTS
DOROTHY Q. THOMAS

HAMILTON FISH
Managing Director
STEPHANIE STEELE
Operations Director

RACHEL WEINTRAUB
Special Events Director

January 14, 1993

Honorable Boutros Boutros Ghali
Secretary General
United Nations
New York NY 10017

Dear Mr. Secretary General:

On behalf of Human Rights Watch and its Helsinki Watch division, we write to you and to members of the United Nations Security Council to call for an expansion of the mandate of United Nations Protection Forces in Bosnia-Hercegovina. On August 13, 1992, Security Council Resolution 770 called on states to take "all measures necessary," nationally or through regional organizations, to facilitate, in coordination with the U.N., the delivery of humanitarian aid to Sarajevo and elsewhere in Bosnia-Hercegovina by the U.N. and others. In our view, the "measures necessary" require that U.N. forces should protect the delivery of humanitarian assistance to noncombatants of all ethnic and religious groups whose lives are at risk due to sieges which have the purpose and effect of killing them or driving them from their homes and communities as part of the policy and practice of "ethnic cleansing." These include the residents of Sarajevo, Gorazde, Srebrenica, Cerska, Zepa and other besieged communities identified by the United Nations High Commissioner for Refugees as particularly endangered.

We make this call because our own monitoring of the situation on the ground in Bosnia-Hercegovina has made plain to us the dire urgency of the delivery of humanitarian assistance and because the obstruction of the delivery of such assistance constitutes a gross violation of international humanitarian law.

Our monitoring of Bosnia-Hercegovina has been continuous since the beginning of the war last April. We also monitored Bosnia-Hercegovina during the war in Croatia, when combatants and refugees sought refuge in Bosnia. Representatives of the Helsinki Watch division of Human Rights Watch have visited many communities in Bosnia and conducted extensive interviews with victims of the conflict. Lask week, we had an opportunity to visit Sarajevo and to witness first hand the way that the icy

EXECUTIVE COMMITTEE: ROLAND ALGRANT, LISA ANDERSON, PETER BELL, ROBERT L. BERNSTEIN, WILLIAM CARMICHAEL,
DOROTHY CULLMAN, ADRIAN W. DeWIND, IRENE DIAMOND, JONATHAN FANTON, JACK GREENBERG, ALICE H. HENKIN, STEPHEN KASS,
MARINA KAUFMAN, JERI LABER, ARYEH NEIER, BRUCE RABB, KENNETH ROTH, ORVILLE SCHELL, GARY SICK, SOPHIE C. SILBERBERG,
NADINE STROSSEN, ROBERT WEDGEWORTH

cold, the shortages of food, the cut-off of electricity and running water, the damage and destruction of buildings including virtually every pane of glass in the city and the indiscriminate shelling, sniping and machine-gunning have combined to imminently threaten the survival of the city's 300,000 or so remaining residents. The reports we have received about conditions in such communities as Srebrenica, Cerska and Zepa which we could not visit because of the sieges by Serbian forces suggest that their circumstances are even worse. The most severe emergency of all may be in Zepa. Hakija Turajlic, the Deputy Prime Minister of Bosnia-Hercegovina, told us this four days before he was murdered. Another source, independent of the Bosnian government, who had travelled extensively on foot in eastern Bosnia to examine disaster conditions, predicted that all the inhabitants of Zepa, last reported at 25-30,000, would soon die because no relief had been getting in. Also, we note that Jose-Marie Mendiluce, the UNHCR official who directs relief operations in Bosnia, has now called for airdrops of supplies into these towns (The New York Times, January 12, 1993).

The requirements of international law are clear. In Resolution 2444 of December 18, 1969 on Respect for Human Rights in Armed Conflict, adopted unanimously, the General Assembly of the United Nations stated in pertinent part:

b. that it is prohibited to launch attacks against the civilian population as such;

c. that a distinction must be made at all times between persons taking part in the hostilities and members of the civilian population to the effect that the latter be spared as much as possible....

Among the many provisions of the Geneva Conventions of 1949 and of Additional Protocol I of 1977 which are relevant to the conduct of Serbian forces, we note particularly Article 54 of Protocol I which provides in pertinent part:

1. Starvation of civilians as a method of warfare is prohibited.

2. It is prohibited to attack, destroy, remove or render useless objects indispensable to the survival of the civilian population, such as foodstuffs, agricultural areas for the production of foodstuffs, crops, livestock, drinking water installations and supplies and irrigation works, for the specific purpose of denying them for their sustenance value to the civilian population or to the adverse party, whatever the motive, whether in order to starve out civilians, to cause them to move away, or for any other motive.

The actions of the Serbian forces conducting sieges of several communities in Bosnia with predominantly, but far from exclusively, Muslim populations are exactly those that are forbidden by these requirements of international law. In this connection, we note that Article 54 of Protocol I is widely accepted as having the status of customary international law. Accordingly, it is binding on all parties to the conflict regardless of whether they have expressly acceded to Protocol I.

In our call for an expanded mandate for United Nations forces, we take no position on any form of military action that would go beyond the protection of the delivery of humanitarian assistance to civilian noncombatants whose lives are at risk as a consequence of means and methods of warfare that are prohibited under international law.

In making this call, we note the unprecedented statement of the International Committee of the Red Cross of December 4, 1992 by its Director of Operations, Jean de Courtens, also calling for an expansion of the mandate of United Nations forces and urging that they should provide protection to ethnic groups under threat.

We call on the United Nations to act promptly as the severe Bosnian winter is already taking a heavy toll and several communities, with hundreds of thousands of residents, are suffering greatly and the lives of those residents are at immediate risk.

Best regards.

Sincerely,

Robert L. Bernstein
Chairman
Human Rights Watch

Aryeh Neier
Executive Director
Human Rights Watch

Jonathan Fanton
Chairman
Helsinki Watch

Jeri Laber
Executive Director
Helsinki Watch

HUMAN RIGHTS WATCH

Appendix E

AFRICA WATCH • AMERICAS WATCH
ASIA WATCH • HELSINKI WATCH
MIDDLE EAST WATCH • FUND FOR FREE EXPRESSION

☐ 485 FIFTH AVENUE, NEW YORK, NY 10017-6104 TEL (212) 972-8400 FAX (212) 972-0905 TELEX 910240 1007 FFFEXPSN NY
☐ 1522 K STREET, NW, SUITE 910, WASHINGTON, DC 20005-1202 TEL (202) 371-6592 FAX (202) 371-0124

ROBERT L. BERNSTEIN
Chair
ADRIAN W. DeWIND
Vice Chair
ARYEH NEIER
Executive Director
KENNETH ROTH
Deputy Director
HOLLY J. BURKHALTER
Washington Director
ELLEN LUTZ
California Director
SUSAN OSNOS
Press Director
JEMERA RONE
Counsel

EXECUTIVE DIRECTORS OF THE WATCH COMMITTEES

AFRICA WATCH
RAKIYA OMAAR
AMERICAS WATCH
JUAN E. MÉNDEZ
ASIA WATCH
SIDNEY R. JONES
HELSINKI WATCH
JERI LABER
MIDDLE EAST WATCH
ANDREW WHITLEY
THE FUND FOR FREE EXPRESSION
GARA LaMARCHE

PROJECT DIRECTORS

PRISONERS' RIGHTS
JOANNA WESCHLER
WOMEN'S RIGHTS
DOROTHY Q. THOMAS

HAMILTON FISH
Managing Director
STEPHANIE STEELE
Operations Director
RACHEL WEINTRAUB
Special Events Director

February 2, 1993

Mr. Cyrus Vance
c/o The United Nations
New York NY 10017

Dear Mr. Vance:

Human Rights Watch and its Helsinki Watch division write to at this moment of impasse in the Bosnia-Hercegovina peace negotiations to call on you to take certain steps that we believe are urgently required to protect the lives of endangered civilians.

In making this call, we do not underestimate the difficulty of the task that you have undertaken or your own dedication to a just settlement and the protection of the lives and well-being of those noncombatants who face great dangers. We have great respect for your efforts. At the same time, we believe the time has come for a new approach.

The steps that we call on you to take are to state publicly that peace negotiations with respect to constitutional and territorial arrangements will not continue unless and until:

o a neutral body, such as the International Committee of the Red Cross, certifies that the "grave breaches" of the Geneva Conventions, or war crimes, that are known collectively as ethnic cleansing, have been halted;

o the parties allow and facilitate the delivery of humanitarian assistance to civilians in besieged communities.

We attach a copy of a letter that we sent recently to Secretary General Boutros Boutros Ghali and to members of the Security Council on this latter question.

In addition, we call on you to take whatever public steps are necessary to ensure that individuals who ultimately may stand trial for war crimes do not appear to derive undeserved legitimacy from continued public association with you and other officials of the United Nations in the peace negotiations.

EXECUTIVE COMMITTEE: ROLAND ALGRANT, LISA ANDERSON, PETER BELL, ROBERT L. BERNSTEIN, WILLIAM CARMICHAEL, DOROTHY CULLMAN, ADRIAN W. DeWIND, IRENE DIAMOND, JONATHAN FANTON, JACK GREENBERG, ALICE H. HENKIN, STEPHEN KASS, MARINA KAUFMAN, JERI LABER, ARYEH NEIER, BRUCE RABB, KENNETH ROTH, ORVILLE SCHELL, GARY SICK, SOPHIE C. SILBERBERG, NADINE STROSSEN, ROBERT WEDGEWORTH

We have closely monitored the war in Bosnia-Hercegovina from its start. Our main concerns have been to collect information on violations of the laws of armed conflict; to seek accountability for these violations by pressing for the establishment of an international war crimes tribunal to prosecute and punish those principally responsible for grave breaches of the 1949 Geneva Conventions and Additional Protocol I of 1977[1]; and to call on parties to the 1951 Convention on the Prevention and Punishment of the Crime of Genocide and the United Nations Security Council to fulfill their duty under Article VIII of the Convention to take effective action for the "prevention and suppression of acts of genocide."

We have not considered it within our scope and competence as a human rights organization to comment on many aspects of the peace negotiations that you have conducted. We express these views at this time because we are concerned that without the steps that we propose, Serbian forces in particular are using the peace negotiations as a cover to continue unlawful killing, sieges of civilians and horrifying practices of ethnic cleansing.

As you are aware, the sieges of Sarajevo and of perhaps a dozen towns elsewhere in Bosnia have been maintained throughout the peace talks. The lives of more than a half million noncombatants are gravely endangered by these sieges which, in varying degree, have cut off food, fuel, electricity, running water and medical supplies and which have been marked by indiscriminate shelling, and machinegun and sniper fire. Also while the peace talks have been underway, "ethnic cleansing" has progressed in other parts of Bosnia. This has been accomplished by murder, rape, torture, pillage and deportation. Perhaps another half million combatants, non-Serbs still residing in Serbian controlled areas, are imminently threatened by these practices. In addition, we are concerned that Serbian civilians have been held hostage in areas controlled by Croatian or Bosnian forces.[2]

---

[1] Your own endorsement of the establishment of a war crimes tribunal is important to us.

[2] Human Rights Watch/Helsinki Watch have monitored the conduct of the war according to the standards set forth in the laws of war, specifically, the Geneva Conventions of 1949 and Additional Protocol I of 1977. The main provisions of these agreements are also customary international law and, therefore, are binding on all parties to the conflict whether or not they have ratified the Conventions and Protocol. We note here some of the relevant international law requirements.

With respect to the sieges, Article 54 of Protocol I provides in pertinent part:

1. Starvation of civilians as a method of warfare is prohibited.

2. It is prohibited to attack, destroy, remove or render useless objects indispensable to the survival of the civilian population, such as foodstuffs, crops, livestock, drinking water installations and supplies and irrigation works, for the specific purpose of denying them for their sustenance value

We note that the International Committee of the Red Cross has itself issued an unprecedented call for an expansion of the mandate of United Nations forces in Bosnia-Hercegovina to protect vulnerable ethnic groups in their places of residence.

Finally, we note a precedent in United Nations sponsored peace negotiations that

> to the civilian population of the adverse Party, whatever the motive, whether in order to starve out civilians, to cause them to move away, or for any other motive.
>
> Many provisions of the Fourth Geneva Convention and Protocol I deal with the delivery of relief supplies. Among them are Article 70, Section 2 of Protocol I which provides:
>
>> The Parties to the conflict and each High Contracting Party shall allow and facilitate rapid and unimpaired passage of all relief consignments, equipment and personnel provided in accordance with this Section, even if such assistance is destined for the civilian population of the adverse Party.
>
> The shelling, machine-gunning and sniper fire against the besieged residents of Sarajevo and other towns is expressly prohibited by Article 51 of Protocol I which provides in pertinent part:
>
> 1. The civilian population and individual civilians shall enjoy general protection against dangers arising from military operations. To give effect to this protection, the following rules, which are additional to other applicable rules of international law, shall be observed in all circumstances.
>
> 2. The civilian population as such, as well as individual civilians, shall not be the object of attack. Acts or threats of violence the primary purpose of which is to spread terror among the civilian population are prohibited.
>
>   ....
>
> 4. Indiscriminate attacks are prohibited....
>
> 5. Among others, the following types of attacks are to be considered indiscriminate:
>
>   (a) an attack by bombardment by any methods or means which treats as a single military objective a number of clearly separated and distinct military objectives located in a city, town, village or other area containing a similar concentration of civilians or civilian objects; and
>
>   (b) an attack which may be expected to cause incidental loss of civilian life, injury to civilians, damage to civilian objects, or a combination thereof, which would be excessive in relation to the concrete and direct military advantage anticipated.
>
> The ethnic cleansing that is taking place in Serbian-controlled areas of Bosnia has expulsion, or deportation, as its object. Article 147 of the Fourth Geneva Convention provides that deportations and population transfers are "grave breaches," or war crimes. The methods used to bring about deportations, such as "wilfull killing," "torture or inhuman treatment," "wilfully causing great suffering or serious injury to body or health," "unlawful confinement of a protected person," "taking of hostages" and "extensive destruction and appropriation of property, not justified by military necessity and carried out unlawfully and wantonly" are also designated as war crimes under Article 147.

may be helpful. One of the important achievements of the United Nations in recent years was the peace settlement in El Salvador. Prior to negotiating a ceasefire and the political elements of the peace agreement, the United Nations mediators negotiated a series of agreements designed to ensure respect for human rights. One element of those agreements was the establishment of a United Nations agency, ONUSAL, in El Salvador, which brought in international human rights monitors. Despite some reservations about the work of ONUSAL, in general we believe it has been a great success. The likelihood that the United Nations peace settlement will hold in El Salvador after a dozen years of bitter and brutal warfare has been greatly enhanced by first negotiating and implementing an agreement on human rights. We believe that, as in El Salvador, respect for human rights must be made a precondition for continued participation in peace discussions.

In our view, your authority to demand compliance with an agreement on human rights in Bosnia-Hercegovina before proceeding further would be great. The Serbian forces are aware that the maintenance of the negotiations has been an important factor in holding off external military intervention or other sanctions, such as the lifting of the arms embargo on Bosnia-Hercegovina. The alternative would be to permit unlawful killing, sieges of civilians and horrifying practices of ethnic cleansing to continue under the cover of further peace negotiations.

We trust that this expression of our views will be helpful and that you will understand that we have only the greatest admiration for your steadfast determination to bring this awful war to end.

Best regards.

Sincerely,

Robert L. Bernstein
Chairman
Human Rights Watch

Aryeh Neier
Executive Director
Human Rights Watch

Jonathan Fanton
Chairman
Helsinki Watch

Jeri Laber
Executive Director
Helsinki Watch

APPENDIX F

A CHRONOLOGY OF THE SIEGE OF SARAJEVO

The chronology that follows is largely based on press accounts.

1992

April 4–5	Fighting breaks out around Sarajevo.
April 6	Serbian forces shell a Muslim quarter of Sarajevo.
April 10	Sarajevo television transmitter shelled but broadcasting continues.
April 16	U.N. special envoy Cyrus Vance meets with Muslim, Croatian and Serbian leaders in Sarajevo in an effort to end fighting. Intensified shelling and machine-gunning erupts after his departure that evening for Zagreb.
April 18	Seven reportedly killed in shelling of Sarajevo. Two U.S. relief flights arrive at Sarajevo airport.
April 21	Intense fighting in Sarajevo. The television center repeatedly hit by mortar shells. Bodies reported lying in the streets.
April 22	Extensive shelling of Sarajevo reported. Fighting between Serbian and Muslim militias reported in the streets of Sarajevo. At least four reported killed and a dozen wounded. A hospital in Sarajevo and a hotel housing sixty European Community monitors in Ilidza, about two miles west of the city limits, are among the targets of shelling and machine gun fire.

April 30	Muslim neighborhoods reportedly bombarded from dusk to dawn. Two persons said to be killed and fifteen injured.
May 1	At least thirteen reported killed in Sarajevo.
May 2	All-out war in Sarajevo involving tanks, machine guns and rocket-propelled grenades. Government buildings on fire. Bodies reported lying in the streets. City's old Muslim quarter shelled. Sarajevo cut off.
May 5	Heaving shelling reported. Buildings in old Turkish quarter ablaze, and many dead and wounded reported lying in the streets. U.N. envoy Marrack Goulding unable to enter city.
May 7	Officials at Sarajevo morgues report that 115 bodies had been collected from the streets and shelled buildings. The Associated Press reports seeing "scores of corpses tangled on the tiled floor, some headless" at a morgue. Hospital reported targeted.
May 10	*The Washington Post* reports seventeen corpses in morgue at emergency medical center. Serbian forces reported to have seized western suburbs, periodically shooting into cars from high-rise buildings overlooking a highway. Serbian forces reported preventing relief deliveries. Muslim high school reported closed for first time in 453 years. General Ratko Mladić announced as commander of the federal army forces at Sarajevo.
May 12	European Community monitors leave Sarajevo for security reasons.
May 14	Fierce street fighting reported. "Artillery fire from powerful Serbian forces ringing the city

rained down on nearly every neighborhood," according to *The Washington Post*. U.N. headquarters hit by five mortar rounds, and twelve U.N. trucks destroyed by Serb shelling. U.N. says it will withdraw its 300 personnel for security reasons. Casualties uncounted because ambulances cannot travel across lines of fire.

May 18   ICRC director in Sarajevo, Frederic Maurice, killed and two others wounded in ambush by unknown assailants.

May 19   Extensive shelling reported, especially of *Oslobodjenje*, Sarajevo's newspaper.

May 20   ICRC withdraws from Sarajevo.

May 27   At least seventeen reportedly killed and more than a hundred wounded in mortar shelling of people in a breadline in a marketplace. *The New York Times* reports that Serbian units hijacked eleven UNHCR food trucks the previous week. General Mladic recorded as ordering his forces to "bombard Veselice [a Sarajevo neighborhood]. Burn it all."

May 29   Fiercest shelling of siege reported. Parts of city in flames, and electricity and water cut in certain neighborhoods.

June 1   *The New York Times* reports that 734 Serbs, including 486 women and children and 248 officers and teenage cadets, trapped in Marshal Tito barracks in Sarajevo for two months, "hostages to the heavy bombardment of the city by Serbian artillery."

June 3   Shelling of medieval district and machine-gunning of two buses distributing food escorted by U.N. armored vehicles as they entered Dobrinja, a suburb near the airport. One driver killed.

June 6 Most sustained bombardment since siege began. *The New York Times* reports that "every few minutes, 120-millimeter artillery shells, 82-millimeter mortars and volleys from multiple rocket launchers poured down from the slopes of the 5,345-foot Trebević Mountain overlooking the city," and that "nobody appears to have any estimate of the number killed and wounded. But the figure must be high." Also, it is reported that the 734 Yugoslav officers, cadets and dependents confined in the Marshal Tito barracks were permitted to evacuate in an eighty-vehicle convoy. After they left, Serbian gunners shelled the barracks, killing two men and a boy in a passing car and severely wounding two women. *The Washington Post* reports that starvation is beginning in Sarajevo.

June 8 At least fourteen reported killed and 350 wounded in heavy bombardment. A Muslim counterattack on Serbian positions reported but denied by the Bosnian Serb leader, Radovan Karadžić.

June 11 U.N. negotiators arrive to try to open Sarajevo airport to relief flights. *The New York Times* reports, "The gunners today were hitting targets seemingly at random, blasting apartment buildings, churches and mosques." The *Times* also reports that "for a week, there have been no fresh supplies of bread, and Serbian forces moved earlier in the week to cut off the pumps that supply water to much of the city. . . . Almost all districts in the city, excepting those on the periphery that are Serbian-held, lost electrical power."

June 12	Bosnian forces counterattacked Serbian positions. Serbian artillery barrages reportedly killed a dozen people in civilian districts. Twenty brought to the neurosurgery ward of the hospital with brain injuries.
June 14	Continuing Bosnian counterattack reported.
June 15	Cease-fire goes into effect, but three persons killed by mortars and sniper fire.
June 17	Cease-fire collapses and bombardment resumes with mortar batteries and tanks blasting Dobrinja and Mojmilo, Sarajevo's most devastated districts.
June 19	Renewed bombardment of civilian neighborhoods, particularly Dobrinja.
June 20	U.N. convoy shelled.
June 22	Shelling reportedly kills nineteen civilians, wounding more than one hundred. *The New York Times* reports that Karadžić was shown on Serbian television peering at Sarajevo through field glasses and congratulating the gunners.
June 26	Children's ward of Jezero Hospital reported bombarded by artillery fire and rockets.
June 27	Effort to start relief flights reported stopped by Serbian attacks on the airport.
June 28	President François Mitterand of France visits as shelling continues.
July 1	First U.N. convoy enters Sarajevo with fifteen tons of food.
July 13	On the one hundredth day of siege, four power-transmission lines were dynamited by

	Serbian forces, cutting off electricity and running water to the city.
July 14	Electricity restored to a few buildings. Serbian forces reportedly reinforced with new 155-millimeter howitzers from Serbia.
August 1	A Bosnian military offensive fails to break the siege. Attendants at Koševo Hospital tell *The Washington Post* that an average of ten to fifteen bodies has been received by the morgue there since April. On this day, Serbian forces opened fire on a bus evacuating children from a Sarajevo orphanage, killing two infants.
August 2	The bus carrying the orphans resumed its journey but was halted at a Serbian roadblock where nine of the infants were removed from the bus on the ground that they were Serbs.
August 4	A mortar attack on the funeral for the two children killed on the bus evacuating orphans injured the grandmother of one of the infants.
August 6	Some three hundred women, old men and children driven from their home villages by Serbian militiamen arrived in Sarajevo. They reported to have been required by the Serbian forces to crawl part of the way.
August 18	Five persons were killed and at least two dozen wounded by mortar fire on a hotel sheltering 1,500 displaced. U.N. officials suspended relief flights after a radar unit "locked on" to a British relief plane. A convoy of seventeen buses carrying 1,000 women and children was allowed to leave Sarajevo.

August 20	At least eleven were reported killed in the day's shelling and a U.N soldier from Ukraine was killed by a sniper.
August 22	At least thirty reported killed in shelling and sniper fire.
August 28	At least ten killed in shelling. In a four-day period, Koševo Hospital treated sixty wounded. In London, Radovan Karadžić denied a siege was taking place. "We do not conduct sieges," *The Washington Post* quotes him as saying. "We defend our territory."
August 30	Fifteen reported killed and about one hundred wounded by a shell fired into the middle of a crowded market.
September 14	Heavy bombardment. At least twenty reported killed and sixty wounded in two hours. *The New York Times* reports that some of the shelling took place from Serbian guns monitored by U.N. observers who stood and watched the firing.
September 19	Multi-ethnic suburb of Stup razed by Serbian forces, driving thousands into central Sarajevo.
October 10	A mortar from Serbian artillery was fired indiscriminately into a crowd of children in Sarajevo, killing three and wounding ten. At least two of the wounded had limbs amputated. At Koševo Hospital in Sarajevo, nine dead and seventy seriously wounded civilians had been received by the traumatology unit that day. One victim was a sixteen-year-old girl named Samra Kapetanović, the other two were a five-year-old girl and a ten-year-old boy. A total of forty-three people reported killed and 194 wounded by bombardment in two days.

October 18	Serbian forces attacked the Sarajevo flour mill, leaving only enough flour for bread and pasta supplies for thirty-six hours.[7]
November 11	A cease-fire begins, broken by only sporadic shelling. About one thousand persons are evacuated in two days.
December 6	Town of Oten, six miles from the center of Sarajevo on the approach to the airport, overrun and destroyed by Serbian forces. Heavy shelling reported.
December 7	Muslim counterattack reported with heavy casualties.
December 21	Doctors in Sarajevo's main hospital reported that one patient had died from the cold.[8] By the end of December, nurses at the State Hospital are unable to work because their hands are frostbitten and covered with blisters and patients shiver under layers of blankets. The hospital's generators have only enough fuel to provide enough heat for three hours at night and three during the day.[9]
December 25	After a three-week suspension for security reasons, relief efforts resumed earlier in the week. Shelling reduced on Christmas Day.

---

[7] John F. Burns, "Serbs' Heavy New Artillery Attack Deprives Sarajevo of Its Flour Mill," *The New York Times*, October 19, 1992.

[8] "Six Planes Reach Sarajevo, Ending 3-Week Relief Hiatus," The Associated Press as reported in *The New York Times*, December 22, 1992.

[9] Peter Maass, "Sarajevo Grapples with a New Enemy — Winter," *The Washington Post*, December 29, 1992.

December 26	A *New York Times* reporter visits Serbian gunners and reports: "Anybody who stops and climbs atop the mud walls can see about what the Serbian gunners see, and it is an astonishing sight. Many of the guns are less than one thousand yards from the high-rise buildings in the center of the city, and perhaps 500 to 1,000 feet above them. . . . it is plain, numbingly so, that the men firing the guns can see exactly what they are hitting. What this means is that the Serbian gun crews cannot have any doubt when their shells strike hospitals, schools, hotels and orphanages and cemeteries where families are burying their dead. . . ."

1993

January 8	Hakija Turajlić, deputy prime minister of Bosnia-Hercegovina, shot point-blank by Serbian gunman as he sits in U.N. vehicle.
January 30	Twenty reported killed and thirty wounded in heavy shelling.
February 1	U.N. forces reported to abandon efforts to repair power lines during a cease-fire because of heavy gunfire.
February 7	Two women and a child were reported killed and five were wounded when shells hit a line of people waiting for water.
March 10	Sniper shots injure a man in downtown Sarajevo, as witnessed by a *Washington Post* reporter.
March 18	*The New York Times* reported that Serbian forces launched the heaviest artillery barrage in months against the capital.

March 21 High point of the fighting. Observers around the city counted 2,398 shells, the largest number of shells since U.N. peacekeeping forces arrived, according to *The New York Times*.

March 22 Fifth consecutive day of heavy bombardment by Serbian forces. A U.N. official observes that most of the shells seem aimed at civilian areas of the city.

APPENDIX G

RELEVANT INTERNATIONAL LAW AS IT APPLIES TO SIEGE WARFARE AND ITS AIM IN THE CURRENT CONFLICT

As noted above, Human Rights Watch and its Helsinki Watch division consider that the purpose of the siege of Sarajevo is to drive out its civilian population and to kill those who refuse to go. This is a legally impermissible purpose. Article 147 of the Fourth Geneva Convention of 1949 provides that "willful killing," "unlawful deportation or transfer" and "extensive destruction and appropriation of property, not justified by military necessity and carried out unlawfully and wantonly" are grave breaches of the Convention, or war crimes.

Protocol I contains a number of other provisions that apply to the siege of Sarajevo. Among them are the following:

- The requirement that "the civilian population and individual civilians shall enjoy general protection against dangers arising from military operations." (Art. 51[1])

- The requirement that "the civilian population as such, as well as individual civilians, shall not be the object of attack." (Art. 51[2])

- The requirement that "indiscriminate attacks are prohibited. Indiscriminate attacks are:

    (a) those which are not directed at a specific military objective;

    (b) those which employ a method or means of combat which cannot be directed at a specific military objective. . . ." (Art. 51[3])

- The requirement that "the following types of attack are to be considered as indiscriminate:

(a) an attack by bombardment by any methods or means which treats as a single military objective a number of clearly separated and distinct military objectives located in a city, town, village or other area containing a similar concentration of civilians and civilian objects. . ." (Art. 51[5])

- The requirement that "civilian objects shall not be the object of attack or reprisals. . . . In case of doubt whether an object which is normally dedicated to civilian purposes, such as a place of worship, a house or other dwelling or a school, is being used to make an effective contribution to military action, it shall be presumed not to be so used." (Art. 52)

- The requirement that "starvation of civilians as a method of warfare is prohibited." (Art. 54[1])

- The requirement that "it is prohibited to attack, destroy, remove or render useless objects indispensable to the civilian population, such as foodstuffs, agricultural areas for the production of foodstuffs, crops, livestock, drinking water installations and supplies . . . whether in order to starve out civilians, to cause them to move away, or for any other motive." (Art. 54[2])

- The requirement that "in the conduct of military operations, constant care shall be taken to spare the civilian population, civilians and civilian objects." (Art. 57[1])

- The requirement that "the Parties to the conflict shall allow and facilitate rapid and unimpeded passage of all relief consignments, equipment and personnel" to the civilian population in the territory of a party to the conflict if the supplies in the territory are not adequate." (Art. 70)

- The requirement that relief personnel "shall be respected and protected." (Art. 71)

Protocol I also spells out the definition of grave breaches in a manner that applies specifically to the conduct of the forces besieging Sarajevo, and the commanders of those forces. It provides that the following are grave breaches, or judicially actionable war crimes:

- "Making the civilian population or individual civilians the object of attack." (Art. 85, [3][a])

- "Launching an indiscriminate attack affecting the civilian population or civilian objects in the knowledge that such attack will cause excessive loss of life, injury to civilians or damage to civilian objects. . . ." (Art. 85, [3][b])

In addition, Protocol I provides that "the fact that a breach of the Convention or of this Protocol was committed by a subordinate does not absolve his superiors from penal or disciplinary responsibility, as the case may be, if they knew, or had information which should have enabled them to conclude in the circumstances at the time, that he was committing or was going to commit such a breach and if they did not take all feasible measures within their power to prevent or repress the breach."